John MacEvilly

An Exposition of the Acts of the Apostles

John MacEvilly

An Exposition of the Acts of the Apostles

ISBN/EAN: 9783743388635

Manufactured in Europe, USA, Canada, Australia, Japa

Cover: Foto ©Lupo / pixelio.de

Manufactured and distributed by brebook publishing software (www.brebook.com)

John MacEvilly

An Exposition of the Acts of the Apostles

AN EXPOSITION

OF THE

ACTS OF THE APOSTLES

CONSISTING OF

AN ANALYSIS OF EACH CHAPTER

AND OF A

COMMENTARY,

CRITICAL, EXEGETICAL, DOCTRINAL, AND MORAL.

BY HIS GRACE

THE MOST REV. DR. MacEVILLY,

Archbishop of Tuam.

"Go ye into the whole world and preach the Gospel to every creature. He that believeth and is baptized, shall be saved; but he that believeth not, shall be condemned."—MARK xvi. 15, 16. "And how shall they preach unless they be sent?"—ROM. x. 15.

DUBLIN:

M. H. GILL & SON, 50 UPPER O'CONNELL STREET,

NEW YORK:

BENZIGER BROTHERS, 113 BROADWAY.

1899.

An Exposition of the Epistles,

PAULINE AND CATHOLIC.

In 2 Vols.   Price 18s.; reduced to 10s.

In a form corresponding with the Gospels.   Fourth Edition, enlarged.

An Exposition of the Gospels of Matthew and Mark.

In 1 Vol.   Third Edition, enlarged.   Price 12s. 6d., reduced to 8s.

An Exposition of the Gospel of St. Luke.

Price 4s. 6d.

An Exposition of the Gospel of St. John.

Second Edition.   Price 10s. 6d., reduced to 5s. 6d.

Acts of the Apostles.

Price 5s. 6d.

DUBLIN : PRINTED BY SEALY, BRYERS & WALKER (A.T.&C.,L.), 94, 95 & 96 MIDDLE ABBEY STREET.

INTRODUCTION

TO

THE ACTS OF THE APOSTLES.

TITLE OF.

THE TITLE prefixed to this Treatise on "The Acts," &c., is read differently in different versions and MSS.

In some, it is "Acts of Apostles;" in others, "The Acts of the Apostles;" in others, "The Acts of the Holy Apostles" with the addition, "written by Luke, the Evangelist."

Owing to this diversity, Critics generally maintain, that the title, admittedly of very high antiquity, was not prefixed by the Sacred writer himself.

"Acts of Apostles"—πραξεις Αποστολων—without the definite article is supposed to be the earliest title. It accurately conveys the Subject of this Treatise, which contains a summary of the doings of the Chief among the Apostles, viz.: Peter and Paul.

The Title "The Acts of the Apostles" with the definite article, *the*, might be calculated to mislead, as conveying that this Treatise was a record, or memoir of the doings of the Apostolic body, which would be erroneous, as it alludes only on a very few occasions to the Apostles as a body. After that, they disappear from view.

Besides dwelling on the labours and discourses of Peter and Paul, it briefly refers, in a passing way, to James the Lesser, Bishop of Jerusalem, who, after Peter took the most prominent part in the deliberations of the Council of Jerusalem (c. xv.); to James the Greater, put to death by Herod; to John the Evangelist; to Barnabas, who though not reckoned among "the twelve" was still regarded as an Apostle (c. xiv. 4).

There is an account also of the beautiful discourse of St. Stephen before the Jewish authorities, his martyrdom in consequence (c. vi.), and of some other Evangelical labourers, who though not of the Apostolic body such as Philip the Deacon, &c., were successfully engaged in the propagation of the Gospel.

This Treatise is divided by some eminent Critics (Beelen with others) into two parts. The most prominent figure in the first part, which embraces the twelve first Chapters, is Peter, the head of the Apostolic College, whose eloquent addresses it summarizes, as well as his successful labours in the conversion of Jews and Gentiles, in pursuance of the exalted commission Divinely accorded him, of feeding, ruling and governing the universal Church, "lambs and sheep," Pastors and people.

The second and larger portion is devoted to the discourses, labours, sufferings, perilous journeys of the Apostle of the Gentiles up to the second year of his first imprisonment at Rome which brings the Treatise to a conclusion.

WRITER OF.

We have the most incontrovertible evidence both *extrinsic* and *intrinsic* in proof of the universally received opinion, that the writer of this Treatise on "The Acts," &c., was St. Luke the Evangelist, who wrote the third Gospel. Hence, it seems to me a useless waste of time at this stage to dwell on the proofs of this universally admitted fact, which hardly anyone denies.

The Holy Council of Trent in its Decree on the inspired Scriptures (SS. IV.) speaking of the Acts as one of the Inspired Books, says—"*Actus Apostolorum a Luca Evangelista Conscripti.*"

For a full personal history of St. Luke, see Preface to his Gospel (Commentary on).

WHEN AND WHERE WRITTEN?

These are points hard to be determined with any degree of accuracy.

As it gives the History of St. Paul down to the second year of his first imprisonment at Rome about the year 61 or 62 of our Era, it is certain it was not written before the expiration of that period. Whether written immediately after that or at Rome at all is a subject of controversy. The opinion of St. Jerome on the subject (*de Scriptoribus Eccles.*, c. 17), who maintains that it was written at Rome, is not shared in by the most eminent Critics.

Most likely, it was written before the destruction of Jerusalem by Titus (A.D. 70). If written after, it would not pass over so important an event, especially as it could point to the verification of our Lord's threats and predictions, so graphically recorded in St. Luke's own Gospel (c. xxi.) which we know to have been sadly realised. By some it is held that it was written in the interval between the destruction of Gaza and the siege of Jerusalem, which took place after Gaza had been utterly destroyed. This, however, is controverted, so that nothing definite can be advanced either in regard to time or place in this matter.

LANGUAGE OF.

It is universally admitted that it was written in Greek of which St. Luke was such a perfect master. Hence the style is more polished and the narrative more in accordance with the Greek idiom than that employed by the other sacred writers of the New Testament. The few Hebrew idioms observable in the discourses of which the sacred writer gives a summary are owing to his having given the words as uttered by the several speakers themselves. Some of them spoke in the Hebrew or Aramaic language, and while the substance of their discourses is given in Greek, their peculiarities of idiom are in many instances retained.

CANONICITY AND INSPIRATION OF.

The Canonicity or Divine authority of the Acts has never been questioned in the Church. Hence, it reckoned among the *Proto-Canonical* Books, as Eusebius testifies in his History (Lib. iii., 25). It has been placed in the several Catalogues of inspired Books from time to time sanctioned by the Church, and lastly it has been defined to be the Inspired Word of God by the General Council of Trent in the Decree, *de Canonicis Scripturis*, SS. IV. Only some few heretical sects questioned its Canonical authority, as it contained some teachings opposed to their peculiar Heretical Tenets. The *Ebionites* rejected it, for proclaiming the abolition of the Mosaic Law, which they maintain to be still in vigour—the *Severians*, for abolishing the distinction of food which they still uphold. The *Manichees*, for its teaching regarding the promise of the Holy Ghost, whom they maintained to be no other than the impious founder of their Heretical sect. But the views of these are held in no consideration whatever.

The *inspired* authority of this Book is now defined by the Church. *Inspiration* does not necessarily imply revelation, although, no doubt, God may sometimes be pleased to *reveal* certain things, which the *inspired* writer may not, humanly speaking, have ascertained. It, by no means, excludes the idea of an inspired writer's employing all available human means to acquire beforehand an accurate knowledge of the several subjects he committed to writing. All we need hold, prescinding from verbal inspiration, is that he was moved by the Holy Ghost, to commit to writing what he knew, and that in the act of writing, he was preserved by the superintending influence of the same Holy Spirit from all error, and guided in the selection and arrangement of the several topics, with full liberty, at the same time to employ his own peculiar and natural style of writing. Hence, we find the same idea expressed differently by several sacred writers, and a peculiar style of narrative maintained by each throughout. Thus, we find St. Luke, so well versed in the Greek language, employing a more polished style, as well in his Gospel as in the Acts, than the other Evangelists. St. Paul, whose early education was of a high order, being brought up "at the feet of Gamaliel," displays in his Epistles a lofty style of eloquence which the other inspired writers could not attain to.

SOURCES OF INFORMATION.

Prescinding altogether from revelation and inspiration, and regarding the matter from a human point of view, St. Luke had the best means of acquiring knowledge on the several subjects recorded in the Acts. He was an eye witness of a greater part of them from the time he joined the Apostle at Troas (c. xvi.), whose constant and inseparable companion he was, with some slight interruptions, till the first imprisonment of the latter with which the Treatise concludes. No doubt, the several leading events and circumstances were well known to the early Christians, who zealously recorded and freely spoke of them. With them St. Luke freely conversed and might have learned all from them. Likely, he kept a Diary, and noted day by day the several events that occurred during his attendance on the Apostle which he could consult when writing the history of the Acts. Moreover, he had the best opportunity of learning from the Apostle himself personally the several facts and circumstances recorded in his narrative.

We can hardly doubt, that an account of the several orations of SS. Peter and Paul were committed to writing of which we have a summary left us by St. Luke.

The Apologetic defence of the Apostles by Gamaliel (v. 34, &c.) at the meeting which Paul, a zealous defender of the Law, most likely, attended, was given St. Luke by Paul who eagerly caught up every word that fell from the lips of Gamaliel, the master he revered.

The letter emanating from the Council of Jerusalem (c. xv.) and that addressed by the Tribune Lycias to the Governor Felix were copies which St. Luke translated and recorded.

AFFECTING ELOQUENCE OF THE SEVERAL ORATIONS.

In reading over the several orations contained in this Treatise of "The Acts," &c., whether of St. Peter, of St. Paul, or St. Stephen, one cannot fail to be impressed with their lofty eloquence and truly Apostolic firmness and intrepidity. The judicious selection of topics and arguments so well suited to the circumstances in which they were delivered is truly marvellous, so that they may be proposed as models for imitation at all times. How different the tone and persuasive line of argument employed by St. Paul when, on several occasions addressing his Jewish co-religionists, for whom he had so ardent an affection, whom he was anxious to conciliate, whose prejudices he wished to soften down, from that employed by him in addressing the learned Pagans, for instance, in the Areopagus at Athens (c. xvii.), and in proclaiming as well there as at Lycaonia (c. xiv.) the fundamental truths of natural religion, which alone they could appreciate. How different his Apologetic defence before King Agrippa, and that before the Pagan Governors of the Province. We cannot too earnestly impress on all Christian teachers charged with guiding their people in the way of Salvation by preaching the Word, "in season and out of season," to make the eloquent and affecting discourses of St. Peter, St. Paul, and St. Stephen, the subject of serious meditation, and follow them as models of imitation at all times, as far as possible. Hardly is there any part of the New Testament so interesting on several grounds, as the inspired History of the infant Church contained in this short Treatise on "The Acts of the Apostles."

CHRONOLOGY. very diff. in acts.

Perhaps the greatest difficulty to be encountered in the Exposition of this Treatise on the Acts is the knotty question of *Chronology*. In this connexion, it may be observed that the several eminent Critics who have applied themselves, with such laudable industry, to elucidate the several points connected with the chronological order and dates of events, have managed to differ materially from one another ; so that nothing determinate has come of their labours.

We think it right to say, that however desirable an accurate System of Chronology may be—and what system can escape the carping criticism of the irreconcileable crew of unbelievers with whom the present world is deluged?—the adoption or rejection of any Table of Chronology does not materially affect the chief, or rather the only object we have in view, which is, to give a plain and accurate Exposition of the Sacred Text for the benefit of such as may think proper to peruse it, leaving writers on chronology to adjust their systems and settle their differences as best they can.

✠ JOHN, ARCHBISHOP OF TUAM.

ST. JARLATH'S, TUAM,
  October 1, 1894.

THE

ACTS OF THE APOSTLES.

(complement of S. Luke's gospel — resumes Ascension &c)

CHAPTER I.

1. *The former treatise I made, O Theophilus, of all things which Jesus began to do and to teach,*   *Preface*

2. *Until the day on which, giving commandments by the Holy Ghost to the apostles whom he had chosen, he was taken up.*   *Life of Christ in brief*

3. *To whom also he shewed himself alive after his passion, by many proofs, for forty days appearing to them, and speaking of the kingdom of God.*   *Cures.*

4. *And eating together with them, he commanded them, that they should not depart from Jerusalem, but should wait for the promise of the Father, which you have heard (saith he) by my mouth.*   *precepts.* *Ascension*

5. *For John indeed baptized with water, but you shall be baptized with the Holy Ghost, not many days hence.*

6. *They therefore who were come together, asked him, saying: Lord, wilt thou at this time restore again the kingdom to Israel?*   *in Israel*

7. *But he said to them: It is not for you to know the times or moments, which the Father hath put in his own power :*

8. *But you shall receive the power of the Holy Ghost coming upon you, and you shall be witnesses unto me in Jerusalem, and in all Judea, and Samaria, and even to the uttermost part of the earth.*

9. *And when he had said these things, while they looked on, he was raised up: and a cloud received him out of their sight.*   *ascend. in to*

10. *And while they were beholding him going up to heaven, behold two men stood by them in white garments.*   *angels add*

11. *Who also said: Ye men of Galilee, why stand you looking up to heaven? This Jesus who is taken up from you into heaven, shall so come, as you have seen him going into heaven.*

12. *Then they returned to Jerusalem from the mount that is called Olivet, which is nigh Jerusalem, within a sabbath-day's journey.*   *apos. return from Olivet*

13. *And when they were come in, they went up into an upper room, where abode Peter and John, James and Andrew, Philip and Thomas, Bartholomew and Matthew, James of Alpheus, and Simon Zelotes, and Jude the brother of James.*   *prayer with B*

A

14. *All these were persevering with one mind in prayer with the women, and Mary the mother of Jesus, and with his brethren.*

15. *In those days Peter rising up in the midst of the brethren said: (now the number of persons together was about an hundred and twenty:)*

16. *Men, brethren, the scripture must needs be fulfilled, which the Holy Ghost spoke before by the mouth of David concerning Judas, who was the leader of them that apprehended Jesus:*

17. *Who was numbered with us, and had obtained part of this ministry.*

18. *And he indeed hath possessed a field of the reward of iniquity, and being hanged, burst asunder in the midst: and all his bowels gushed out.*

19. *And it became known to all the inhabitants of Jerusalem: so that the same field was called in their tongue, Haceldama, that is to say, The field of blood.*

20. *For it is written in the book of Psalms: Let their habitation become desolate, and let there be none to dwell therein. And his bishoprick let another take.*

21. *Wherefore of these men who have companied with us all the time that the Lord Jesus came in and went among us.*

22. *Beginning from the baptism of John, until the day wherein he was taken up from us, one of these must be made a witness with us of his resurrection.*

23. *And they appointed two, Joseph, called Barsabas, who was surnamed Justus, and Matthias.*

24. *And praying, they said: Thou, Lord, who knowest the hearts of all men, shew whether of these two thou hast chosen.*

25. *To take the place of this ministry and apostleship, from which Judas hath by transgression fallen, that he might go to his own place.*

26. *And they gave them lots, and the lot fell upon Matthias, and he was numbered with the eleven apostles.*

ANALYSIS.

This first Chapter of the Acts, &c., which may be regarded as the complement of the Gospel of St. Luke—since it resumes the History of our Lord's Ascension, with which his Gospel closes,—opens with a brief Preface addressed to Theophilus, containing a compendious account of the History of the life of our Lord (1–2).

We have, next, a narrative of the several circumstances that preceded our Lord's Ascension, with instructions, mandates, answers given by him immediately before that important event (3–8). We have, then, a brief history of the Ascension (9). The address of the Angels (10–11). The return of the Apostles from Mount Olivet (12–13). Their persevering union in prayer with the Blessed Virgin (13–14). The address of Peter relative to the sad fall of Judas, the great dignity he forfeited, his infamy, the necessity of electing a suitable substitute, the Prophetic quotation from the Psalms on the subject (14–20). He, next, exhorts them to elect a suitable substitute. He describes the qualities he should possess (21–22). The election of Matthias by lot, after fervent prayer addressed to God (23).

Commentary.

1. The words of this *v.* 1 mean: I had composed, O Theophilus, a former Treatise or narrative (πρωτον λογον) embracing the chief and most important actions and teachings of our Lord Jesus Christ, during his life here on Earth. The term, πρωτον, is frequently used in a comparative sense, signifying not, "*first;*" but, *former.*

"Of all things." The term, "all," cannot be taken literally, in its strict meaning, as it would be impossible to furnish a detailed account of all (John xxiii. 25). Moreover, St. Luke omits many things recorded by the other Evangelists. It, therefore, means the principal actions and teachings of our Divine Redeemer.

"Began to do and to teach." A Hebrew Idiom for "*did and taught.*" Of this we have several examples in the Sacred Scriptures. (Genesis ix. 20; Luke iii. 23, xxiv. 47; Mark vi. 7, xiv. 65, &c.)

"Do," denotes His marvellous works, performed to bring about our Salvation.

"Teach" refers to His Sacred doctrines, spoken and recorded for our instruction.

It is deserving of remark on the part of those engaged in Missionary work, that our Lord, for our instruction, first taught by His divine example, what he afterwards inculcated by word of mouth. Teaching by example is always more effectual than mere teaching by word of mouth. The period of our Lord's teaching may be understood of the entire term of His Sacred life, from His Incarnation to His Ascension, or may be said to embrace the interval between His Baptism by John, when he commenced His missionary life, till He gave His final instructions to His Apostles, on Mount Olivet and mounted up to Heaven.

"O Theophilus." This term most likely designates, not the representative of a particular class or church, as is held by some; but a particular man, or individual, probably, one of St. Luke's converts from Paganism, a man of great moral worth, of exalted station. Hence termed "most excellent," as in St. Luke's Gospel (1–3) where this is more fully explained. Though dedicated or addressed to Theophilus, this Treatise was not meant for him alone, but for the entire Christian world to the end of time, of whom Theophilus may be regarded as the representative. Even in our own time, it is by no means unusual to dedicate or address to individuals, writings meant for the general Public. (See Gospel 1–3. Commentary on.)

2. "Until the day," the fortieth after His Resurrection (*v.* 3).

"Taken up," (*v.* 9). Mounted up to Heaven in a cloud (Luke xxiv. 51).

"Giving Commandments." The Greek Aorist—εντειλαμενος—signifying "*after* he had commanded," may denote one Commandment or more. It was *after* having done so, he mounted up to Heaven. Most likely, reference is made here, chiefly to his last and most comprehensive mandate, "to preach the Gospel to every creature" (Mark xvi, 15, 16) which embraced every thing else.

Text.

1. *The former treatise I made, O Theophilus, of all things which Jesus began to do and to teach.*

2. *Until the day on which, giving commandments by the Holy Ghost to the apostles whom he had chosen, he was taken up.*

Text.	Commentary.

Commentary.

"By the Holy Ghost," may be connected with "giving Commandments," thus conveying that His Commandments were not invested with a human, but a divine character, or, with "Apostles," as if to say, that His Apostles were constituted such, and received their commission from the Holy Ghost.

The words may also mean, that He gave His final instructions to His Apostles regarding the Holy Ghost whose coming in a few days He promised, telling them not to leave the city till He descended upon them.

"The Apostles—the eleven—whom he had chosen," at an early period of His missionary life (Matthew x.; Luke vi.).

"Taken up," mounted up to Heaven in a cloud (*v.* 9) by His own innate Power, through the gift of agility which His glorified body possessed; "taken up in glory" (1 Tim. iii. 16) or, "taken up" by His Father, whose Power was identical with His own, just as He rose from the dead by His own power, and was also resuscitated by His Father.

3. To whom also he shewed himself alive after his passion, by many proofs, for forty days appearing to them, and speaking of the kingdom of God.

3. "To whom," Apostles, He exhibited himself as really alive, risen from the dead. The Resurrection of Christ is constantly referred to by the writers of the New Testament, as established by many proofs, being the foundation of Christian faith, the chief proof of our Lord's Divinity, who predicted it with all its circumstances of time, place, &c.

"After his Passion." His Sufferings ended in an ignominious death. "*Many proofs*," confirming by the clearest and most incontestible evidence, the wonderful miracle of His Resurrection, eating with them, appearing to them, exhibiting his wounds, thus removing all fears of deception.

"Forty days," not continually, but occasionally at intervals, did he exhibit proofs during "forty days."

"Speaking of the Kingdom of God"—the church. He taught them all things appertaining to the Government of His church, with instructions to transmit the same to their successors.

4. And eating together with them, he commanded them, that they should not depart from Jerusalem, but should wait for the promise of the Father, which you have heard (saith he) by my mouth.

4. "Eating together with them." The Greek word, συναλιζομενος— is rendered by some, "*assembled together with them*," a signification the word often bears. It also signifies "*eating*," which is conveyed in its root αλς, *Salt*, so common at all repasts; this is the most suitable meaning here. For it thus furnishes a fresh proof of His Resurrection, on which the Apostles themselves lay great stress (x. 51). It also appears from Mark xvi. 14, that our Lord's final apparition to His Apostles was while they were at table in Jerusalem, whence, that very day, he brought them out to Mount Olivet.

"He commanded that they should not depart from Jerusalem." Likely, Jerusalem had but very little attraction for the Apostles, and they were anxious to leave it on account of the cruel death of their Lord there, and the fear of persecution from the Jews, and other reasons besides. Hence, the mandate given here by our Lord. The Apostles had departed from Jerusalem for Galilee eight days after our

Commentary.

Lord's Resurrection. But now they returned immediately before His Ascension. This was Divinely arranged, as it had been foretold that the Law should come forth from Sion and the word of the Lord from Jerusalem. There it was, that King David exercised the functions of Royalty. There, the greatest hatred and revolt against the Lord's anointed were signally displayed. It was, therefore, meet that there the reign of the new David, His Son, the promised Messiah, should be inaugurated, and the Laws of His Kingdom first promulgated.

"Wait for the promise of the Father" (Luke xxiv. 49). "Promise" is by metonymy, put for the gift promised or the object of the promise, viz., the Holy Ghost. Our Lord has in view to inflame their desire to receive the Holy Ghost. God the Father promised Him of old, through the mouth of the Prophets, especially Isaias xliv. 3 ; Joel ii. 26, &c.

"Which you have heard, " &c. Here there is a transition from the indirect to the direct form of address, occasioned by the animated style of His discourse. Our Lord, before his Passion, frequently spoke of the Holy Ghost, whom His Father was to send them, though promised by himself also (John xiv. 16 ; xv. 26 ; xvi. 7). But out of modesty He calls Him the promised of the Father, the Father being the fountain of the Trinity.

5. "John baptized with water." Our Lord here institutes a comparison between the effects of John's Baptism by water, and His own, through the Holy Ghost, which they were soon to receive in its fulness. This He does with a view of conveying to them that this promise of the Father was soon to be fulfilled in their regard.

"Not many days hence," after the lapse of ten days, Pentecost Sunday. He does not specify the day, in order to keep them in a state of expectant vigilance, longing desire, and anxious preparation.

The words of our Lord in this v. are evidently allusive to those of the Baptist (Matthew iii. 14 ; Luke iii. 16 ; John i. 33. See Commentary on Matthew iii.). The preceding words were spoken by our Lord to His disciples, on the occasion of His last appearance to them at table. He, then, took them out to Mount Olivet (Luke xxiv. 50) where the words of following vv. were spoken.

6. "Come together," viz., the Apostles, disciples, and other followers assembled on Mount Olivet, at His Ascension. The Apostles, doubtless, believed Him to be the Messiah. However, their faith being somewhat imperfect before the descent of the Holy Ghost, they shared in the erroneous ideas of their countrymen regarding the restoration by the Messiah, of the temporal rule of Israel, in a style of splendour far exceeding that of Solomon. This Kingdom, long since destroyed, was now in the hands of Herod, a stranger from Idumea. Hence the words, "restore again," to its former splendour. Their

5. For John indeed baptized with water, but you shall be baptized with the Holy Ghost, not many days hence.

6. They therefore who were come together, asked him, saying: Lord, wilt thou at this time restore again the kingdom to Israel?

Text.

Commentary.

minds are turned aside from all thoughts of the promised Spirit and His priceless Spiritual gifts to considerations of earthly grandeur.

"At this time." After having displayed Almighty Power in raising Himself from the dead. "Wilt thou," after the lapse of "not many days," now at hand, when sending the Holy Ghost at the same time, restore to Israel her lost Kingdom? The disciples hoped that he would have redeemed Israel (Luke xxiv. 21) and rescue the people from the odious yoke of the Romans. They seemed to have no doubt of the *fact*—they enquire only regarding the *time.*

7. But he said to them: It is not for you to know the times or moments, which the Father hath put in his own power:

7. Gently rebuking them for their inordinate curiosity, without directly answering them. Our Lord tells them, it was no business of theirs, or of any other creature, to pry into the secrets of the Divine Mind reserved by God in the depths of His own Infinite counsels, in which His Consubstantial Son essentially and fully participated.

8. But you shall receive the power of the Holy Ghost coming upon you, and you shall be witnesses unto me in Jerusalem, and in all Judea and Samaria, and even to the uttermost part of the earth.

8. If they could understand it, our Lord gives the answer. He conveys to them that His would be a Spiritual Kingdom, founded on His death and Resurrection, of which they were destined to be witnesses, commencing with Jerusalem from which the Law was to go forth, and carried by them to the uttermost bounds of the Earth, even to the entire Gentile world, to whom the Gospel was to be preached. He adds this for their consolation, after repressing their undue curiosity. Whence was the extraordinary vigour and energy necessary for them, as founders and propagators of this Spiritual Kingdom, to be derived? Whence the power, on the part of weak, ignorant fishermen, to cope successfully with Kings and tyrants and learned Philosophers, and successfully bring all under subjection to the yoke of Christ? It was from the power of the Holy Ghost, who would soon descend on them, and by His power only they could succeed. "But you shall receive the power of the Holy Ghost coming upon you." The whole Earth was open to them, not even excepting "Samaria," heretofore forbidden to them. Our Lord conveys to His Apostles that His Kingdom should be established far beyond the precincts of Judea, and that they should be instrumental in carrying on and pushing forward the great work.

9. And when he had said these things, while they looked on, he was raised up: and a cloud received him out of their sight.

9. "Raised up." Gradually mounting up by His own power; blessing them as He ascended (Luke xxiv. 51). Then, it was, that, at His Triumphal Ascension, the words were verified, "*adorent cum omnes Angeli Dei*" (Heb. i. 6). "*Quis est iste qui venit de Edom,*" &c. (Isaias lxiii.). "*Attollite portas principes vestras . . . et introibit Rex Gloriæ*" (Ps. lxiii.).

Among the sights St. Augustine longed to see, was a Roman triumph. "*Romam triumphantem.*" How poor must the most gorgeous Roman triumph appear, compared with this Magnificent Procession, when all Heaven was emptied of its countless hosts, to meet their

Commentary.

triumphant Lord with His splendid trophies, the Saints and just of the old Law, whom rescued from the jaws of death, He carried in His train to grace His triumph, throwing open to them the gates of Heaven so long closed. "*Elevamini portæ æternales*" (Ps. xxiii.).

"*And a cloud received Him,*" &c. This "cloud" was produced anew for the purpose. A bright "cloud" is often a symbol of the presence of the Deity (Exod. xi. 34; Numbers ix. 15; Matthew xvii. 5). "*Nubes et caligo in circuitu ejus*" (Ps. xcvi.). In the clouds He shall come again in glory, to judge mankind. Unlike Elias, snatched away in a whirlwind (4 Kings ii. 11), our Lord mounted up gradually by His own innate Divine power, without any external aid, so that His glorified body could be seen vanishing out of sight; thus furnishing an additional proof of the reality of His Resurrection.

10. "Beholding Him." Anxiously looking after Him, with a steadfast, loving gaze, as He was vanishing out of sight.

"Two men." Clearly, angels in human form. Angels are sometimes called men (Luke xxiv. 4).

"White garments." This indicates their heavenly origin, and denotes the glory and triumph of our Lord, whose messengers they were. Angels are sometimes represented as appearing in white apparel (John xx. 12; Matthew xxviii. 3).

"Stood by them," suddenly and supernaturally.

10. And while they were beholding him going up to heaven, behold two men stood by them in white garments.

11. "Ye men of Galilee." Most of the Apostles were Galileans. Our Redeemer's followers were mostly from that obscure and despised Province, God thus selecting the weak and poor, preferably to the powerful and rich (1 Cor. i.).

"Why stand you looking," &c.? Conveying, that henceforth, they must no longer expect to enjoy His visible presence. They must see Him by faith only. They must live by faith, bereft of His corporal presence, until the day when He shall return and visibly appear in Majesty, to judge the world. They should look forward to His second coming.

"This Jesus . . . shall so come as you have seen Him." This self-same Man God shall come in glory one day, seated on a cloud, with all the ensigns of Majesty to judge the world.

11. Who also said: Ye men of Galilee, why stand you looking up to heaven? This Jesus who is taken up from you into heaven, shall so come, as you have seen him going into heaven.

12. "They returned to Jerusalem," in obedience to our Lord's final instructions, commanding them to remain there for some time.

"Olivet," so called from the olive trees that grew there in great abundance. It would seem it was from this Mount our Lord ascended, at the eastern slope of which lay Bethany, whither, as we learn from St. Luke, our Lord brought His disciples before He ascended. (See St. Luke xxiv. 50, Commentary on.) Likely, it was from this eastern slope He ascended.

12. Then they returned to Jerusalem from the mount that is called Olivet, which is nigh Jerusalem, within a sabbath-day's journey.

Text.

Commentary.

Oriental travellers inform us, that our Lord indelibly impressed His foot prints on the spot, which no abrasure could obliterate. St. Helena built a magnificent church there. But no vaulting or covering could stand over the spot; so that it was constantly exposed to view. It was near this place Lazarus and his sisters lived. *Near* it was the scene of our Lord's bloody sweat and agony. Hence, it was meet that it should be the scene of His final glorious triumph.

"A Sabbath-day's journey"—the distance the Jews were allowed to travel on the Sabbath day; something about an English mile. The Law about the Sabbath-day's journey was not a Mosaic ordinance. It was introduced by the Rabbins. For this they fixed the distance that should intervene between the Ark and the people (Josue iii. 4)—or, the distance allowed by law between the centre and farthest boundaries of a Levitical city (Numbers xxxv. 4).

13. And when they were come in, they went up into an upper room, where abode Peter and John, James and Andrew, Philip and Thomas, Bartholomew and Matthew, James of Alpheus, and Simon Zelotes, and Jude the brother of James.

13. "And when they were come in, they went up," &c. The vulgate punctuation, is, "*and when they were come in to the upper room, they went up,*" &c. The Greek punctuation followed by our English version is preferred by several able Commentators, A. Lapide among the rest. This "upper room" was, likely, in some private house. Here, probably, our Lord celebrated the Last Supper. Here, took place two apparitions after the Resurrection (John xx. 19, 26). Here, the Holy Ghost descended on the Apostles. It was not in the Temple, as some would infer from St. Luke (xxiv. 53: See Commentary on).

"Where abode Peter," &c. Here they spent one portion of their time, communing with God in prayer and with each other in pious conversation. They also devoted another portion of their time to the service of the Temple, attending there regularly and at stated hours (Luke xxiv. 53).

It is deserving of remark, that in the several Catalogues of the Apostles given by the sacred writers (Matthew x.; Luke vi.) Peter always is placed at their head, indicating the Primacy conferred on him by our Lord over the entire Church.

14. All these were persevering with one mind in prayer with the women, and Mary the mother of Jesus, and with his brethren.

14. "Persevering with one mind in prayer." Unanimity and concord was a great help towards obtaining their requests, as discord or divisions would be a great obstacle (St. Cyprian, Epis. 8).

"With the women," most likely refers to these pious and holy women headed by Magdalen, who followed our Lord and ministered to Him out of their temporal substance (Luke viii. 2). This shows, the room was not in the Temple, where men and women were kept apart.

"With Mary the mother of Jesus." She is here particularized and specially distinguished, as she had been by the Angel, from all other women. Prayers in which she joins must have infallible efficacy. This is the last notice taken of her in the Sacred Scriptures.

"And His brethren," the near relatives of our Lord (Matthew xii. 46; xiii. 55; John vii. 5). St. Augustine tells us "the relations of the

Commentary.

Blessed Virgin were called, the brethren of our Lord. It was the custom of the Scriptures to call near blood relations and kinsmen, brethren " (Tract xxxiii. 3, in Joannem). Hence the absurdity of the opinion that holds them to be the offspring of Joseph by a former marriage. If they were such, our Lord would have commended His Blessed Mother to them at His death, rather than to St. John.

15. "In those days," in the interval between the Ascension and Pentecost, while they were abiding together before the descent of the Holy Ghost.

" Peter rising up," &c. Already Peter begins to exercise the Primacy conferred on him by our Lord (Matthew xvi., &c.) in proposing to the assembled Apostles the filling up of the vacancy effected in the Apostolic College, by the fall of the Traitor, Judas, and the substitution of another in his place. He thus carries out the mandate, "*confirm thy brethren*" (Luke xxii. 32). Whatever might be his own personal powers in the matter, he prudently remits the whole affair to his colleagues, of which he was head and chief.

"Number of persons." Greek, "*of names*," which signifies *persons.*

16. "Men, brethren." All were united, as members of one family, by the common bonds of faith and charity. This was a solemn form of address.

"The Scripture must needs be fulfilled." The prediction of God cannot be falsified. This, however, by no means implies the absence of liberty in man's actions. If there be question of human actions, God predicts what he foresees man is to do in time, by his own free will. Man does not perform them because God foresees or predicts them. But God foresees them in the manner in which man is to perform them in time, that is, freely. The prevision of God no more interferes with the liberty of man in the performance of a future act, than the actual vision or seeing it performed at the present moment, interferes with the liberty of the agent, who now performs it. The knowledge and foreknowledge are external to the act, in both instances (see John xii. 39 : Commentary on).

" Which the Holy Ghost spoke before by the mouth of David concerning Judas." The quotation is read in *v.* 20. It *primarily* referred to David's traitorous counsellor, Achitophel (2 Kings xv. 23), but *secondarily* and *mystically* to the Traitor, Judas, " who was the leader," &c. This is narrated (John xviii. 3).

17. "Numbered with us." He was of the number of Apostles called and elected by our Lord, and was associated with them, invested with full Apostolic powers.

"And had obtained part," &c. The Greek would convey, and had *been allotted* or obtained by lot a place in "this ministry." This conveys

15. *In those days Peter rising up in the midst of the brethren, said: (now the number of persons together was about an hundred and twenty:)*

16. *Men, brethren, the scripture must needs be fulfilled, which the Holy Ghost spoke before by the mouth of David concerning Judas, who was the leader of them that apprehended Jesus.*

17. *Who was numbered with us, and had obtained part of this ministry.*

| Text. | Commentary. |

Text.

Commentary.

the gratuitousness of his call, which on his part was quite independent of his merits, just as happens in the case of those who having no claim to it, obtain a thing by casting lots. It was, however, wisely and deliberately determined on the part of God. "Men cast lots; but, God determines the choice."

18. And he indeed hath possessed a field of the reward of iniquity, and being hanged, burst asunder in the midst: and all his bowels gushed out.

18. "Purchased a field," or caused it to be purchased, as it was he gave the purchase money, which he flung back to the Priests (Matthew xxvii. 5-8) wherewith, not he, but they purchased it. Hence, said by *Catachresis*, to purchase it himself.

"The reward of iniquity." It was purchased with the blood money which Judas received in payment for the iniquitous betrayal of his Divine Master.

"And being hanged." St. Matthew says he did it himself. "He went and hanged himself with a halter" (xxvii. 5). The apparent discrepancy between the account given here and that given by St. Matthew (xxvii. 5-8), is easily explained. The explanation given fully in St. Matthew (see Commentary on). Both conjointly give a full account of the unhappy event. Similar was the unhappy end of the treacherous Achitophel (2 Kings xvii. 23), a type of Judas, both as to his crime and unhappy death.

19. And it became known to all the inhabitants of Jerusalem: so that the same field was called in their tongue, Haceldama, that is to say, The field of blood.

19. "It became known," &c., viz., the whole history of Judas' treason, his unhappy end, after having returned the blood money with which the field was purchased. Hence, the field was called, in their tongue, viz., the Aramaic or Syro Chaldaic—the language in use after the captivity—"Haceldama," which Luke interprets for Theophilus to mean "the field of blood." For a full account see St. Matthew xxvii. 5, &c. (Commentary on).

Some Commentators of note—among them Beelen—are of opinion that the words recorded, vv. 18, 19, were not spoken by St. Peter on this occasion; but, only inserted parenthetically by St. Luke here in his history, for the information of Theophilus, as nothing was said about it by St. Luke, in his Gospel addressed to Theophilus.

20. For it is written in the book of Psalms: Let their habitation become desolate, and let there be none to dwell therein. And his bishoprick let another take.

20. "For it is written in the Book of Psalms, *let their habitation,*" &c. The *first* member of this quotation is from Psalm (lxviii. 26). It is in the plural, in the original. In almost all Greek copies, it is written in the singular in this place, "*let his habitation,*" &c. in accommodation to the case of Judas, to whom St. Peter, under the guidance of the Holy Ghost, applies it.

The Greek for "habitation," επαυλις, originally denoted a shepherd's hut. It was afterwards generally used to denote a dwelling of any sort.

"Become desolate," given over to desolation and utter ruin.

The *second* member, "*and his bishoprick,*" &c. is taken from Psalm (cviii. 8) *and,* indicates another and a different quotation. It signifies, *also,* as if to say, it is also written. This Psalm was full of

Commentary.   **Text.**

maledictions on the unhappy Judas. St. Augustine informs us, that in this Psalm. David curses Doeg, who betrayed him to Saul, and in him, Judas, of whom Doeg was a type.

"His Bishopric." His office of Apostle. In the original, the word denotes the office of *Inspector* or *Superintendent*, sometimes applied to Roman officials (Cicero, Lib. 7, Ep. ad Attium.) Here, in its application to Judas, it denotes the office of Apostle, conferred on Matthias.

21. He, therefore, proceeds to the election of a successor to Judas, in fulfilment of David's prediction.

21. *Wherefore of these men who have companied with us all the time that the Lord Jesus came in and went out among us,*

22. It is, therefore, fit or necessary that one of those men who have been associated with us during the time that our Lord freely conversing with us, laid open His whole life and lived familiarly with us, commencing with His public life, when John ministering Baptism to him, pointed Him out as the expected Messiah, as the lamb of God ; until the day "He was taken up from us," to heaven, should be appointed or made along with us, an authoritative "witness" of His Resurrection—the crowning mystery of His life—and the great undeniable proof of His Divinity.

22. *Beginning from the baptism of John, until the day wherein he was taken up from us, one of these must be made a witness with us of his resurrection.*

"Came in and went out" is a Hebrew Idiom, denoting the whole course and actions of life.

"One of these," by Hyperbaton, refers to the words, "wherefore of these," &c., *v.* 21.

Special reference is made to our Lord's Resurrection, which was the great fundamental proof of His Divinity—the great truth which was the Summary of the Apostolic preaching, without which our faith would be vain. (1 Cor. xv. 14.) It was the formal cause of man's justification, "*Resurrexit propter justificationem nostram*" (Rom. iv.).

23. "And they appointed two," &c. "Appointed" means proposed, put forward, nominated as candidates. The fact of their confining the declaration of the Divine choice to "two," who were deemed most worthy by the assembled Church, could not be understood of any attempt to restrict the free choice of God. It is not for us to enquire, why it was confined to two, as it was done under the influence of the Holy Ghost.

23. *And they appointed two, Joseph, called Barsabas, who was surnamed Justus, and Matthias.*

"Joseph, called Barsabas," meaning, the Son of Sabas, "who was surnamed Justus." This may be a proper name, given him to distinguish him from others ; or, it may have been given him, as title of honor, on account of his well-known sanctity. St. Chrysostom inclines to this latter opinion (Hom. 3 in Acta.). He was said to be one of the seventy-two (Eusebius i. 12).

Text.

Commentary.

The original, Ιουστος, is a sort of Latinized Greek, expressive of the Latin epithet given to Joseph. At this period of Jewish History, while the Jews were subject to Rome, it sometimes happened that Latin terms were introduced into the Greek, which was in common use. The Evangelist did so occasionally when writing in Greek. Such are the terms, *Prætorium, Legio, Sudarium*, &c. (A. Lapide).

Joseph is said to be the brother of James the lesser and Jude, son of Alpheus and Mary, and thus related to our Lord.

"And Matthias"—a contraction for *Mathathias*, which signifies, *a gift from God.* This name was common amongst the Jews. It is said he was one of the seventy-two disciples.

24. And praying, they said: Thou, Lord, who knowest the hearts of all men, shew whether of these two thou hast chosen.

24. "And praying, they said." They have recourse to prayer in common, that God would be pleased to make known, in some unmistakeable way, the Divine choice.

"Thou, O Lord." This is addressed to our Blessed Saviour, who had now ascended into heaven. To Him omniscience is here attributed. "Lord" is usually addressed to our Divine Redeemer. He is called "Lord" (v. 21), and it is meet that Peter, the head of the Church, should here address Him by whom the other Apostles were chosen.

"Show," declare, which of the two Thou hast chosen. It is remarked by St. Chrysostom that they do not ask Him to choose; but, assuming that the choice had been already determined on, in His Divine omniscience, to make known the choice He had made. God alone could immediately choose an Apostle (John vi. 70).

25. To take the place of this ministry and apostleship, from which Judas hath by transgression fallen, that he might go to his own place.

25. "To take the place," to be substituted in the Apostolic ministry in room of Judas. "Of this ministry and apostleship," are by Hendyades put for "*of this Apostolic Ministry*," "from which Judas hath by transgression fallen," by the commission of the most heinous of all crimes, the betrayal of his Divine Lord and Master, who had raised him to a dignity so exalted.

"That he might go" expresses not the intended design, but the consequence or result of Judas's action. "To his own place"—the place deserved by his crime, and thus made "his own"—the place alone suited for him, his destined place in hell. "Heaven could not receive him. Earth could not bear him on her surface" (St. Bernard in Psalm xciv., viii.). Regarding the words "his own place" there is a diversity of opinion. But, the most common opinion understands it of hell. Our Lord himself calls him "the son of perdition" (John xvii. 12).

26. And they gave them lots, and the lot fell upon Matthias, and he was numbered with the eleven apostles.

26. "And they gave them lots." How this was done cannot be defined for certain. Whether by voting or by inscribing the two names on tablets to be afterwards drawn out of an urn, the first drawn to be possibly the chosen party. The latter is rendered probable by the words, "the lot fell on Matthias."

Commentary.

"Gave them." The Greek αυτων, means "*their*" lots, that is, the lots of those who were to be elected.

We sometimes find the casting of lots for deciding and determining matters of great importance, sanctioned, in several instances, in the Old Testament, which need not be mentioned here in detail.

Here, the merits of both Candidates were unquestionable. Recource, therefore, to lots to determine which of two worthy subjects might be chosen could be safely resorted to. No doubt, the Apostles, acting under Divine influence, felt they could safely do so. It is not, however, to be inferred from particular cases, of a peculiar nature, as here, that it is generally lawful to look for extraordinary manifestations of the Divine Will or expose exalted responsible functions connected with the Salvation of Souls to hazard by the casting of lots, when ordinary safe means of determining matters could be resorted to. This was a special case and could not establish a precedent. The Apostles only did it *once*, and they did so clearly by the order of God, and under Divine influence. So that as the eleven Apostles were chosen by Christ, the choosing of the twelfth would not be left to man, but to God, who signified His choice by the extraordinary procedure of casting lots, after having been invited by the infant Church, through fervent prayers.

"And the lot fell on Matthias," whose merits before men were not so distinguished as were those of "Joseph the *Just*." It may be, possibly, in the judgment of God, that Matthias was possessed of greater prudence for Government. God selects men to high offices of His own free will and choice.

"And He was numbered with," &c. The Greek for "numbered" means, by "common suffrages;" conveying, that all present praised and extolled the Divine choice. God had chosen. Men expressed their full approval of the Divine choice.

CHAPTER II

1. *And when the days of the Pentecost were accomplished, they were all together in one place:*

2. *And suddenly there came a sound from heaven, as of a mighty wind coming, and it filled the whole house where they were sitting.*

3. *And there appeared to them parted tongues as it were of fire, and it sat upon every one of them:*

4. *And they were all filled with the Holy Ghost, and they began to speak with divers tongues, according as the Holy Ghost gave them to speak.*

5. *Now there were dwelling at Jerusalem, Jews, devout men out of every nation under heaven.*

6. *And when this was noised abroad, the multitude came together, and were confounded in mind, because that every man heard them speak in his own tongue.*

7. *And they were all amazed, and wondered, saying: Behold, are not all these, that speak, Gallileans?*

8. *And how have we heard, every man our own tongue wherein we were born?*

9. *Parthians, and Medes, and Elamites, and inhabitants of Mesopotamia, Judea, and Cappadocia, Pontus, and Asia.*

10. *Phrygia, and Pamphilia, Egypt, and the parts of Lybia about Cyrene, and strangers of Rome.*

11. *Jews also, and proselytes, Cretes, and Arabians: we have heard them speak in our own tongues, the wonderful works of God.*

12. *And they were all astonished, and wondered, saying one to another: What meaneth this?*

13. *But others mocking, said: These men are full of new wine.*

14. *But Peter standing up with the eleven, lifted up his voice, and spoke to them: Ye men of Judea, and all you that dwell in Jerusalem, be this known to you, and with your ears receive my words.*

15. *For these are not drunk, as you suppose, seeing it is but the third hour of the day.*

16. *But this is that which was spoken of by the prophet Joel:*

17. *And it shall come to pass, in the last days (saith the Lord.) I will pour out of my Spirit upon all flesh: and your sons and your daughters shall prophesy, and your young men shall see visions, and your old men shall dream dreams.*

18. *And upon my servants indeed, and upon my handmaids will I pour out in those days of my spirit, and they shall prophesy.*

19. *And I will shew wonders in the heaven above, and signs on the earth beneath: blood and fire, and vapour of smoke.*

20. *The sun shall be turned into darkness, and the moon into blood, before the great and manifest day of the Lord come.*

21. *And it shall come to pass, that whosoever shall call upon the name of the Lord, shall be saved.*

22. *Ye men of Israel, hear these words: Jesus of Nazareth, a man approved of God among you, by miracles, and wonders, and signs, which God did by him, in the midst of you, as you also know;*

23. *This same being delivered up, by the determinate counsel and foreknowledge of God, you by the hands of wicked men have crucified and slain.*

24. *Whom God hath raised up, having loosed the sorrows of hell, as it was impossible that he should be holden by it.*

25. *For David saith concerning him: I foresaw the Lord before my face: because he is at my right hand that I may not be moved.*

26. *For this my heart hath been glad, and my tongue hath rejoiced: moreover my flesh also shall rest in hope.*

27. *Because thou wilt not leave my soul in hell, nor suffer thy Holy one to see corruption.*

28. *Thou hast made known to me the ways of life: Thou shalt make me full of joy with thy countenance.*

29. *Ye men, brethren, let me freely speak to you of the patriarch, David; that he died and was buried; and his sepulchre is with us to this present day.*

30. *Whereas therefore, he was a prophet, and knew that God hath sworn to him with an oath, that of the fruit of his loins one should sit upon his throne;*

31. *Foreseeing this, he spoke of the resurrection of Christ. For neither was he left in hell, neither did his flesh see corruption.*

32. *This Jesus hath God raised again, whereof all we are witnesses.*

33. *Being exalted therefore, by the right hand of God, and having received of the Father the promise of the Holy Ghost, he hath poured forth this which you see and hear.*

34. *For David ascended not into heaven; but he himself said · The Lord said to my Lord, sit thou on my right hand,*

35. *Until I make thy enemies thy footstool.*

36. *Therefore let all the house of Israel know most certainly that God hath made both Lord and Christ, this same Jesus, whom you have crucified.*

37. *Now when they had heard these things, they had compunction in their heart, and said to Peter, and to the rest of the apostles: What shall we do, men and brethren?*

38. *But Peter said to them: Do penance, and be baptized every one of you in the name of Jesus Christ, for the remission of your sins: and you shall receive the gift of the Holy Ghost.*

39. *For the promise is to you, and to your children, and to all that are far off, whomsoever the Lord our God shall call.*

40. *And with very many other words did he testify and exhort them, saying · Save yourselves from this perverse generation.*

41. *They therefore that received his word, were baptized: and there were added in that day about three thousand souls.*

42. *And they were persevering in the doctrine of the apostles, and in the communication of the breaking of bread, and in prayers.*

43. *And fear came upon every soul: many wonders also and signs were done by the apostles in Jerusalem, and there was great fear in all.*

44. *And all they that believed, were together, and had all things common.*

45. *Their possessions and goods they sold and divided them to all, according as every one had need.*

46. *And continuing daily with one accord in the temple, and breaking bread from house to house, they took their meat with gladness and simplicity of heart:*

47. *Praising God, and having favour with all the people. And the Lord increased daily together such as should be saved.*

ANALYSIS.

In this chapter is recorded the visible descent of the Holy Ghost, so often promised and so long expected, with some of its attendant circumstances, time, manner, form of parted tongues, result in the action taken by the Apostles (1-4). Effect of this stupendous miracle, on the inhabitants of Jerusalem, viz., confusion and amazement (6-8). Astonishment on the part of strangers from the countries the most remote, who happened to be in Jerusalem at the time (9-12). The sarcastic gibes and mockery on the part of some (13). The apologetic defence by St. Peter and his refutation of the calumny uttered against the Apostles (14-15). His proofs from the Prophet, Joel, that all this had been predicted (16-21). His defence of our Lord's authority and power, as demonstrated by miracles (22-23), by His resurrection predicted by David (24-31), confirmed by the testimony of the Apostles (32), by His Ascension and Power in Heaven. The happy effect of this address in the conversion of his hearers, numbering about 3,000 (36-41). The edifying life and spiritual exercises of their converts (42-47)

Text.

1. *And when the days of the pentecost were accomplished, they were all together in one place:*

Commentary.

1. "And when the days of Pentecost," &c. In the Greek, "days" is in the singular, "the day." The term, according to our Vulgate reading, "the days," refers to the interval between the Pasch, and the Feast of Pentecost. The words, then, would mean; when the fifty days—(*Pentecost* was a term in use among the Hellenistic Jews, meaning *fifty* or *fiftieth*)—that intervened between the Pasch and Pentecost, were accomplished. The *Jewish Pasch* took place on the 15th day of Nisan—formerly called *Abib*, the first month of the sacred year—on whatever day of the week the 15th *Nisan* fell. According to Jewish custom, the celebration commenced on the previous evening, or, the 14th Nisan. The Christian Pasch took place on the Sunday immediately following the 15th *Nisan*. Counting then, from the morrow of the Sabbath (Leviticus xxiii. 15), as had been done by the Jews, who, during the Second Temple, kept Pentecost 50 days after the 16th Nisan, a period of fifty days intervened between that and Pentecost Sunday. Then, Sunday was the fiftieth day, and on it, the Festival was pretty far advanced, as it commenced, according to Jewish rite, on the preceding evening. We find it by no means unusual in the Gospels to say, a thing occurred after a certain period, though that period was not accomplished. This is observable in regard to our Lord's Resurrection, which is said to have occurred *after* the third day, though it occurred *on* the third day. The same remark is true of our Lord's circumcision (Luke ii. 21), which took place on the 8th day; also, in regard to the time of our Lady's purification. Also Genesis xli., 18-20. Here, the fifty days are said to be accomplished, although the event took place on the *fiftieth*.

Commentary.

The same observation applies to the Greek reading, "When the day was accomplished." The event recorded took place early in the day. The Greek reading confines the celebration to one fixed certain Festival day, Pentecost, which took place at a period of the year between Pasch and Tabernacles. Pasch, Pentecost, and Tabernacles were the three great Jewish Festivals. Pasch and Tabernacles had octaves. Not so Pentecost, although it practically had been celebrated for seven days.

As Pentecost took place at the end of 7th week from Pasch, it is called "the Feast of Weeks" (Exodus xxxiv. 23; Leviticus xxv. 15-16; Numbers xxviii. 26).

It is also called "the Feast of Harvest" (Exodus xxiii. 16), as it was celebrated in thanksgiving for the harvest. On it, the Jews presented to the Lord, the first fruits of the harvest in the form of bread baked from the new corn, and also a portion of the new flour (Exodus xxvii. 16; Leviticus xxiii. 17; Numbers xxviii. 16). Hence called "*the day of first fruits*" (Numbers xxviii. 26).

On it was commemorated the giving of the Law on Sinai, which took place on the 50th day after the Hebrews left Egypt.

Our Pentecost commemorates, in a more excellent way, the objects of the Jewish Pentecost. First, the giving of the New Law and its solemn promulgation to the world. Secondly, the plentiful effusion of the *first fruits*, far more precious and far more excellent than the Jewish fruits, as then are bestowed on us in abundance, the first fruits of the Holy Ghost.

"They were all together in one place." "All" is restricted by some to the Apostles. But, the application of the Prophecy of Joel (*vv.* 17-20) to "daughters" and "handmaids" makes it more probable that the term embraced the 120 mentioned (*c.* i. *v.* 14).

"In one place." Most likely, this refers to the "upper room" (*c.* i. 14), a portion of the "*house*" referred to, in following *v.* 2. The Greek adds, ὁμοθυμαδον—*with one accord*, of the same mind, by which it is conveyed that union and charity attracts the Holy Ghost into men's souls.

2. "Suddenly," without their expecting the Holy Ghost to descend on them in this way. By this it was conveyed, First, that the plenitude of the gifts of the Holy Ghost was gratuitous, independent of personal merits. Secondly, that the operations of the Holy Ghost are not tardy, but, active, quick and energetic, "*nescit tarda molimina virtus spiritus sancti.*"—St. Ambrose.

"There came a sound" (ηχος, means any noise), a loud noise, "from heaven," rushing over them, from above, not laterally or horizontally, as the sound of strong wind comes. The word indicates also the source whence the gifts of God come to us, " *omne donum perfectum* . . . *desursum est* (St. James i. 17). This sound was like that produced by a strong rushing wind, sweeping along. It is generally supposed there was no wind, the air being still, which heightens the wonder. The Text,

2. *And suddenly there came a sound from heaven, as of a mighty wind coming, and it filled the whole house where they were sitting.*

B

"as of a mighty wind coming," (ὥσπερ, φερομένης) conveys as much. It was *like* unto the sound of a strong wind, as in next verse, "tongues as it were of fire," not really, "*fire*."

This sound symbolized the sound of the preaching of the Gospel throughout the earth "*in omnem terram exivit sonus eorum*," &c., and also the power of the Holy Ghost as well as the mighty results He would accomplish. It had the effect of stimulating those present to a desire of receiving the Holy Ghost.

The Holy Ghost formerly appeared under several emblems or sensible signs; at one time, in the form of a dove, as at our Lord's Baptism; at another, of a bright cloud, as at the Transfiguration; again, as a gentle-breathing "*insufflans* . . . . *accipite spiritum sanctum*." Here, under the form of fire, so emblematic of his several operations.

"And it (the sound) filled the whole house," a Hebraism for the apartment in this private house, conveying that all there would be replenished with the gifts of the Holy Ghost.

"Sitting" denotes not the posture, but only where they were remaining, some, perhaps, standing; others, on their knees; others, sitting, calmly awaiting the descent of the Holy Spirit.

3. And there appeared to them parted tongues as it were of fire, and it sat upon every one of them:

3. "And there appeared to them parted tongues," &c. The Greek for appeared, ὤφθησαν—means, "*seen by them*." "Parted tongues." By "*parted*" some understand, that each tongue looked as if split, when it sat on the head of each; others, that though entire and not cloven in itself, each was parted and separated from the other, so that a distinct tongue appeared over each of those present.

"And it sat upon every one of them." "It," the flame, in a lambent form, assuming the appearance of a tongue, rested or appeared on the head of each. This denoted the gentle gliding down or descent of the Holy Ghost.

Fire was regarded as an emblem of God's holy presence. Thus, Exodus iii. 2, 3—we have the burning bush; the descent on Sinai in fire (Exodus xix. 16-20). God is said to be a "consuming fire" (Deut. iv. 24; Psalm xviii. 12-14).

Fire was employed to symbolize the presence of the Holy Ghost. Here, it typified in the peculiar form of tongues the gift of tongues conferred on the Apostles, and also the divine eloquence of Apostolic men in preaching with power and effect the Gospel of God.

The natural properties of fire symbolized the gifts of the Holy Ghost, displayed in cleansing, purifying, consuming, enlightening, &c.

The tongues were not real fire. They only had the appearance of fire, "as *it were* of fire."

4. And they were all filled with the Holy Ghost, and they began to

4. "All filled with the Holy Ghost." That is to say, the Holy Ghost, the Third Person of the Adorable Trinity, took possession of them; His Divine influence pervaded all their faculties, making them sharers, as far as their capacity would allow, and to the full extent of their dis-

Commentary.

positions, of the fulness of these heavenly gifts intrinsically possessed, in an infinite degree by Him in common with the Father and the Son. The first external manifestation, and, as it were, the first fruit of these was the gift of tongues, symbolized by the tongues which appeared over each, in the form of fire.

"And they began to speak with divers tongues." In Greek it is, "*other* tongues." They began to speak languages of which they were, no doubt, hitherto ignorant (*vv.* 8-11), different from their own.

"According as the Holy Ghost gave them to speak." According as the faculty of speaking these strange languages, hitherto unknown to them, was given them by the Holy Ghost. The words convey that they were hitherto ignorant of them, and that they spoke them not because they knew them, but as the Holy Ghost empowered them.

Their own language of Galilee was the Syro-Chaldaic. Possibly, some of them may have some knowledge of Greek and Latin, spoken in a way among the Jews. But the words employed by St. Luke clearly convey that they spoke the several tongues (*vv.* 8-11), to them hitherto unknown, under the miraculous influence of the Holy Ghost.

5. "Dwelling at Jerusalem." Jerusalem was the chief seat of the Jewish religion. "*Dwelling*" (κατοικοῦντες) may either mean stopping there for a time, or making it a permanent abode. "Jews." This strictly referred to the descendants of the two tribes, Judah and Benjamin, that remained faithful and formed the kingdom of Judah, unlike the ten other tribes, that fell into schism under Jeroboam. These latter were called Israelites. In course of time, however, the term "Jews" embraced, without distinction, all the descendants of the twelve tribes of Israel.

"Devout men" refers to their spirit of reverence towards God, which inclined them to observe His commandments. Those referred to here are different from the natives of the city.

As Jerusalem was the chief seat of the Jewish religion, many Jews scattered abroad among the Gentile nations, in the several dispersions of the Jewish nation, flocked thither, on the occasion of the great festivals, to satisfy their devotion. Of these, some returned home after the festivals to their permanent place of abode; others remained for some time to study the Jewish Law, and become better acquainted with its principles. The very expectation of the Messiah, at this time, caused some to dwell permanently in Jerusalem.

Like Rome, now, the chief seat of Christianity, Jerusalem had its colleges and public religious institutions. Others may have come and remained there for some time engaged in traffic. The words "devout men," which insinuates the object of their present visit, would make it probable that these dwellers at Jerusalem had only a temporary abode there, having come to attend religious worship, and then, after some time, returned to the several countries, more particularly specified, next verses, where they had their permanent abode.

Text.

speak with divers tongues, according as the Holy Ghost gave them to speak.

5. Now there were dwelling at Jerusalem Jews, devout men out of every nation under heaven.

| Text. | Commentary. |

Commentary.

"Out of every nation under heaven"—an hyperbole, signifying all parts of the earth, every quarter of the globe. In the enumeration (*vv.* 8-11), there are several nations and peoples of the earth besides not referred to at all. "*Every nation*" expresses, therefore, a general, not a universal, proposition. The Providence of God so arranged it that every nation, in a general way, would furnish witnesses of this wonderful prodigy.

6. And when this was noised abroad, the multitude came together, and were confounded in mind, because that every man heard them speak in his own tongue.

6. "And when this was noised abroad." "The Greek is, "*and this voice being spread abroad.*" "*Voice*" is understood by some of the "sound as of a mighty wind" (*v.* 2), which was not confined to the house where the Apostles were assembled, but had been heard throughout the city. By others, of the rumour of this wonderful prodigy of the tongues, which quickly spread throughout the city and reached the ears of all, who quickly came together to witness it. "The multitude," as well natives of the city as strangers, amounting to many thousands, as appears from the number of the converted (*v.* 41).

"Confounded in mind." The Greek συνεχύθη would mean thrown into a state of great excitement, as if they were out of their minds, which was succeeded by feelings of amazement (*v.* 7).

7. And they were all amazed, and wondered, saying: Behold, are not all these, that speak, Galileans?

7. "Amazed." This sensation succeeded the state of mental excitement they were first thrown into.

"Galileans." Proverbially ignorant and uncouth, their dialect, barbarous. They were isolated and unacquainted with other nations and their refined language. Hence the amazement caused by their speaking in the refined language of other nations. The word "Galilean," was a well-known term of reproach among the Jews. This rendered the miracle more striking. Julian the Apostate, it is said, would fain, out of contempt, substitute the term *Galileans* for Christians. Hence, on the point of death, pouring out his life's blood, he defiantly cried out, "*Vicisti Galilee.*" The Galilean was too strong for him. These were known to be the disciples of our Lord, whose followers were chiefly from Galilee. Their accent, also, would show them to be such (Matthew xxvi. 73).

8. And how have we heard, every man our own tongue wherein we were born?

8. "How have we heard," &c. The Greek has the present "*we hear.*" Each of us hears these men speak our *native* tongue, the language of the country wherein we were born.

9. Parthians, and Medes, and Elamites, and inhabitants of Mesopotamia, Judea, and Cap-

9. "Parthians," &c. To render the miracle more marked, St. Luke enumerates the several nationalities there represented. Beginning with the east, he proceeds westward. He speaks of the Jews or Jewish proselytes residing in these countries.

"Parthians." Their country was a portion of Persia, remarkable

Commentary.

among the ancients for fighting on horseback, and in the act of flight discharging their arrows behind them with unfailing precision and effect. Their language was the *Persian.*

"Medes." Living under the same rulers as the Persians. They are often spoken of in the Sacred Scriptures. Their language, *Persian.*

"Elamites." Their country was situated on the Persian Gulf. Probably so called from Elam, the son of Sem, who settled there as well as his posterity (Genesis x. 22). Some understand the word of Persia. The Greeks called the country *Elymais.* Language, *Persian.*

"Mesopotamia." A well-known region, lying between the Tigris on the east, and the Euphrates on the west, extending from the source of these two rivers to Babylon on the south. The language, *Aramaic,* spoken in the Babylonish dialect, while the inhabitants of

"Judea" spoke the same Aramaic language in the Jerusalem dialect. Some critics would have it that there is a mistake here in the Sacred text; that it was meant for *India* or *Indumea,* as the Galileans spoke the language of Judea. Others say the language of Judea was to them, in a great measure, an unknown tongue, their peculiar accent and idiom differing so much from the accent and idiom of the Jews—others, adhering to the accuracy of the Sacred text, say the sacred writer simply meant to convey that they spoke all languages, *known* and *unknown.*

"Cappadocia." Their language, probably, a mixture of Greek and Syriac. Ancient writers describe this country as remarkable for wickedness, like the other places commencing with C—viz., Crete (Titus i. 12) and Cilicia.

"Asia," as distinguished from Pontus and Cappadocia, refers to Proconsular Asia, often called *Ionia,* having for capital, Ephesus.

10. "Phrygia," a province of Asia Minor. "Pamphylia," another province of same. The language of these provinces was *Greek.*

"Egypt." This country is too well known to dwell upon it. A great portion of the people of Alexandria—two fifths—were Jews (Josephus, Philo, &c.).

"Lybia." The ancients called the entire of Africa "Lybia." Here there is question of that part of "Lybia" bordering on Egypt called Cyrenaica from its capital, Cyrene.

"About Cyrene." The district of "Cyrene," with Cyrene for capital, had a great many Jewish inhabitants. Pliny informs us this district had five celebrated cities. Hence, called *Pentapolis.*

"And strangers of Rome." The Greek might be better rendered, " *and Romans sojourning there* " (i.e.), at Jerusalem, Roman Jews, whether Jews by birth or proselytes, citizens of Rome, who took up their residence at Jerusalem either permanently, or came only to attend the Great Festivals and join in religious worship.

11. "Jews also, and proselytes." Whether native born Jews descended from Jewish families ; or, proselytes converted from Paganism to the

Text.

padocia, Pontus and Asia.

10. *Phrygia, and Pamphilia, Egypt, and the parts of Lybia about Cyrene, and strangers of Rome.*

11. *Jews also, and proselytes,*

Text.

Cretes and Arabians; we have heard them speak in our own tongues the wonderful works of God.

Arabic

Jewish religion. This refers to all mentioned in the preceding, including Cretans and Arabians, mentioned immediately after, and not confined, as some would have it, to the Romans only, "strangers of Rome,"

"Cretes" who earned for themselves the unenviable reputation of being liars and deceitful. (Titus i. 12, 13). Their language was the Greek.

"Arabians"—their language, the Arabic. In the above enumeration, there seems to be some confusion. But the sacred writers quote the language of men—who were greatly excited and amazed.

"The wonderful works of God." In Greek. *The great things of God;* the wonderful miracles in regard to every thing connected with His Divine Son, His birth, life, death, Resurrection, Ascension, &c., such as are spoken of in the following discourse of St. Peter.

12. *And they were all astonished, and wondered, saying one to another: What meaneth this?*

12. "They were all astonished," &c., viz.: The foreign Jews referred to, most of those present. The Greek word for "wondered," conveys that they were in a state of hesitancy and perplexity regarding a matter to them inexplicable. "What meaneth all this?" How comes this to pass?

13. *But others mocking, said: These men are full of new wine.*

13. "Others," a different class, probably, the Jews of Jerusalem, who understood none of those foreign languages, enemies of our Lord's disciples, said in a jeering mood, casting ridicule on the entire affair.

"Full of new wine." They are under the influence of drunkenness. The Greek word, γλευκους, "*sweet drink*," is commonly understood of wine. It does not mean, *newly made* wine. Pentecost which occurred in May or June was too early for the vintage of that year, which took place later on, in August. Hence it means unfermented wine, which was more intoxicating than the thinner wines commonly in use. Some say, this is meant as a sneer at the humble condition of the Apostles, as no men of position would use the wine of last year. Strange charge, as if men indulging in sweet wine, could on that account give utterance to foreign tongues.

14. *But Peter standing up with the eleven, lifted up his voice, and spoke to them: Ye men of Judea, and all you that dwell in Jerusalem, be this known to you, and with your ears receive my words.*

14. Peter, the divinely constituted visible head of the church, representing her invisible founder, with characteristic ardour, now comes forward to defend the Apostles and our Lord himself, who commissioned them, from so foul a calumny. He stands up in order to make himself heard, "with the eleven" who also very, likely, stood up with him, in token of their respect, and in order to express their concurrence in what he was divinely inspired to utter. What the idiom or language he employed was, is, a subject of controversy. It is supposed by many eminent Interpreters, that he addressed them in the vernacular of the country—*The Syro-Chaldaic* or *Aramaic* of Palestine, so that almost all understood him. Likely, the foreign Jews retained still, with their knowledge of the language of the countries of their abode, a knowledge of the language of the country of their origin also. It may be too

Commentary.

that the miracle of tongues was continued here, God so disposing it, that his hearers, foreigners as they were, understood his words, though strange to them; or, the words having the *sound* of his native tongue for each, the one language spoken became diversified and transformed in the ears of each into his own native tongue. Of this we have an example in the life of St. Francis Xavier, who speaking one tongue was understood by different peoples as if he were speaking their own language.

This address of St. Peter is composed of two parts. In the first part, taking advantage of the circumstances, to defend the miracle and the Apostles against calumnies and ridicule, he shows from the wonderful event, which was, the subject of scorn—that the times of the Messiah had now arrived. In the second part, he shows from our Lord's miracles, that he was the long-expected Messiah.

" Ye men of Judea." Native born Jews, "and all you that dwell in Jerusalem," all you—besides native born Jews—proselytes or strangers who now dwell in Jerusalem. These comprised the whole assembly.

" Receive my words." Listen attentively to what I am about to say to you.

15. "These," himself and the others.

" The third hour of the day." The Jews divided their days and nights into twelve equal parts, counting from sunrise to sunset. Now subject to Rome, they adopted the Roman system of calculating time. Days and nights they divided into twelve hours at all seasons. Hence, their hours were longer or shorter at several periods of the year. Not only were their civil duties, but also their Sacred and Ecclesiastical duties regulated by this division of time (Mark xv. 25). (See Matthew xxvii. 45; Commentary on.)

They divided the twelve hours of the day into four *greater* hours or principal parts, each comprising three common hours. The first great hour commencing at sunrise, continued three hours, and terminated at 9 o'clock, half the time from sunrise to midday. The next great or principal hour commenced at a time corresponding with 9 o'clock with us, that is three hours after sunrise, and ended at midday. This was the hour referred to here.

" The third hour of the day." This was the earliest of the hours of prayer, at which the morning sacrifice was offered, midway between sunrise and noon. It was customary with the Jews to abstain from meat or drink on their Sabbaths and Festivals till after this hour. Sometimes, even until midday. (Lightfoot, *Horæ Hebraicæ.*) It was very unlikely—there was the strongest presumption to the contrary—that after a night of prayer and preparation for the great Festival of Pentecost, the disciples who made religion their profession, would indulge in intoxicating drinks, which was peculiar to dissolute and abandoned characters only. St. Peter's address was his vindication and defence.

16. This is but the fulfilment, in reality, of the words spoken by the Prophet Joel (ii. 28–32). Hence, far from being a matter for reproachful

was spoken of by the prophet Joel:

17. *And it shall come to pass, in the days (saith the Lord,) I will pour out of my Spirit upon all flesh: and your sons and your daughters shall prophesy, and your young men shall see visions, and your old men shall dream dreams.*

taunts, the whole occurrence should be reverentially treated, as emanating from one of their own divinely inspired Prophets.

17. "*In the last days.*" The Hebrew of Joel has "*after these things.*" In the rendering of St. Peter, "the last days," clearly refer to the Christian Dispensation, the last age of the world, from our Lord's coming to the final consummation of all things. The "*Lord hath said*" are found not in the beginning, as here, but at the end of the Prophecy of Joel (ii. 32). Placed in the beginning, they fix the mind on the source whence it emanates and beget greater feelings of respect.

"*I will pour out of my spirit,*" may mean, portions of "my spirit," a plentiful effusion, denoting great abundance of the gifts of the Holy Ghost, whether, "ministrations" or "operations," all varying, but emanating from one and the same spirit (1 Cor. xii. 4–11). "*Of my spirit,*" this is the reading according to the Septuagint. In the Hebrew it is, "my spirit," "*shall pour out my spirit,*" denoting the Holy Ghost sent by the Son. "Of my spirit" denotes distribution of gifts just as God wills to give in greater or lesser measure. To the Holy Ghost is appropriated the giving of grace which is common to the entire Trinity.

"Upon all flesh," all mankind without distinction of age, sex, profession or condition "will prophesy." This is not necessarily confined to the prediction of future events, though primarily signifying this. It sometimes signifies communicating under Divine influence, the knowledge of the hidden things of God, or explaining, in intelligible language, the inspired utterances of others ; or speaking, in foreign tongues (1 Cor. xiv.), the meaning it bears here.

"Visions," whether in real, visible form, or, in ecstasy interiorly impressing upon them the images of things, conveying real and Divine knowledge, in regard to the supernatural and hidden things of God.

"Visions" are suited to the temperament of youth.

"Dreams" suited to old age. Visions and dreams are often employed, as the medium of communicating the Divine will and heavenly revelations. Whenever a dream comes from God, as in the case of Joseph, it will be ascertained without fail. Visions and dreams were (as in Numbers xii. 6) two particular forms of Divine manifestations. The meaning of the whole passage is ; the marvellous results of this spirit of prophecy poured out on all flesh will be, that your sons and your daughters, your old men, and your young men, every age, and sex, shall participate in the gifts of the Holy Spirit.

18. *And upon my servants indeed, and upon my hand-maids will I pour out in those days of my Spirit, and*

18. "And upon my servants," &c. The words for "and" in the Greek means, *nay even.* In the Hebrew of Joel, the reading is, "and upon *the* servants," &c., conveying that no class is excluded from sharing in the gifts of the Holy Ghost. The most abject, even slaves of both sexes, the castaways of society, shall be sharers. These men and women of servile condition are called *my* servants ; because in their abject con-

Commentary.

dition they serve God and are loved by Him, with whom there is no distinction between slave and free.

The Septuagint and Vulgate reading "*my* servants," would imply that the words refer to the religious worshippers of God of both sexes.

"*And they shall prophesy,*" are not found in the Prophecy of Joel. They are added by St. Peter for greater emphasis' sake.

In order to stimulate his hearers to render themselves worthy of the promises conveyed in the Prophecy of Joel, St. Peter continues to quote from this Prophecy and sets before their eyes the frightful calamities which those alone will escape, "*who shall invoke the name of the Lord.*"

19. Not unlikely, the prodigies mentioned here and quoted from Joel have immediate reference to the unheard of calamities that befel the Jewish nation in the sack of Jerusalem *under Titus*, in punishment of their obstinate infidelity and resistance to grace, shown in their rejection of their long expected Messiah, their crimes culminating in the crucifixion of the Son of God. The interval between our Lord's death and the final end of all things was comparatively very brief, and the woes that befell Jerusalem were only a type of those that are to take place at the end of the world. Hence, it is likely, that here, as in Matthew (c. xxiv.) there is reference to the phenomena, that are to usher in the final end of all things. We are informed by Josephus (De Bello, Jud. vi. 3) and Tacitus (Hist. v. 13) that prodigies took place at the destruction of Jerusalem '*evenerunt prodigia . . . Visæ per cælum concurrere acies, rutilantia arma, et subito, nubium igne conlucere templum; apertæ repente delubri foresæ, et cætera.*"

"*Heaven above and earth beneath,*" "*above and beneath,*" are not in Joel. They are added by St. Luke.

"*Blood*" is understood of a shower of blood, of which Josephus speaks.

"Fire," the fiery phenomena in the sky. "*vapours of smoke.*" In Hebrew, "*pillars of smoke*" columns of vapour like smoke ascending aloft from the bowels of the earth, or from the ruins of burning cities—the veriest picture of desolation.

20. An hyperbolical form of expression not uncommon in Sacred Scripture (Isaias xiii. 10; Jerem. iv. 13; Ezech. xxxii. 7) well suited to the imagination of Eastern peoples.

"*Before the great and manifest day,*" &c. The Hebrew for "manifest" means, *terrible*. It refers, in the first instance, to the siege of Jerusalem, and, in the next, to the day of judgment of whose dreadful precursory Phenomena, those that occurred at the destruction of Jerusalem were a mere figure.

21. "*Whosoever,*" be he Jew or Gentile, "*shall call upon,*" &c., embracing the Christian religion—"shall be saved" from ruin here. If it refers to the siege of Jerusalem, it was literally fulfilled in the case of

they shall prophesy.

19. *And I will shew wonders in the heaven above, and signs on the earth beneath: blood and fire, and vapour of smoke.*

20. *The sun shall be turned into darkness, and the moon into blood, before the great and manifest day of the Lord come.*

21. *And it shall come to pass that whosoever shall call*

Text.	Commentary.

Text.

upon the name of the Lord, shall be saved.

Commentary.

the Christians, who by Divine admonition, fled to Pella, beyond the Jordan before the final destruction of Jerusalem (Eusebius, *Hist. Eccles.* Lib. iii. c. 5).

---

22. Ye men of Israel, hear these words: Jesus of Nazareth, a man approved of God among you, by miracles and wonders and signs, which God did by him, in the midst of you, as you also know:

22. In order to escape these calamities, invoke the name of the Lord, embrace the religion of our Lord Jesus Christ, whom I now mean to make known to you.

"*Men of Israel.*" Their natural, and, therefore, honourable appellation. He had already addressed them, as Jews (v. 14).

"*Jesus of Nazareth.*" The name by which our Lord was commonly known; often applied to Him by the Jews in scorn and reproach.

"*Approved of God.*" Accredited as His envoy. "*Among you*," for your sakes, for your benefit.

"*Miracles, wonders,*" &c. The same stupendous miraculous works performed by our Lord during His life, publicly and privately, among the Jews, are here regarded under a threefold aspect.

"*Miracles,*" in proof of Omnipotent power. *Wonders,* as stupendous portents and departure from the Laws of Nature, calculated to beget astonishment. "*Signs,*" as a means of accrediting an envoy from heaven, or in any way manifesting the Divine Will. It is in this last-mentioned relation they are regarded here by St. Peter, as proofs of the Divine mission of Jesus.

It is remarked here by commentators that it is only as an *envoy from God* St. Peter here regards our Lord, without formally propounding, though by no means questioning, His Divinity, in which light his hearers were as yet unprepared to regard Him.

"*In the midst of you,*" &c. These miracles were incontestible, wrought publicly, so as not to be denied or gainsayed.

---

23. This same being delivered up, by the determinate counsel and foreknowledge of God, you by the hands of wicked men have crucified and slain.

23. St. Peter now following up the chief subject of his discourse, proceeds to treat of the terrible crime of the Jews, in subjecting to the death of the cross Him whose Divine mission was so clearly proved. This delicate subject he treats, however, with wonderful prudence, avoiding, as much as possible, giving offence or creating prejudices. Without extenuating their guilt, he puts forward, in the first instance, the foreknowledge of God and His Eternal Decree, determining on the death of His Son as the means marked out, in His Infinite Wisdom, for accomplishing the salvation of mankind. Hence, foreseeing from Eternity that in abandoning His Son to the fury of the Jews, they would subject Him to the death of the cross, He, therefore, by a *permissive* Decree, determined on doing so, thus securing the ends of Redemption This, however, did not diminish the crime of those wretched Deicides, who acted all along as free agents. "Delivered" does not refer to the treason of Judas. It has the meaning of the words of St. Paul (Romans viii. 32) "sed pro nobis omnibus *tradidit illum,*" delivered over to His enemies, being sent round from one tribunal to another. St. Peter so puts it, that they might be regarded as the agents in carrying out God's

Commentary.

Eternal Decree. Joseph acted similarly, in order to assuage the grief of his afflicted brethren (Genesis xl., 5).

In the Vatican edition of the Vulgate (A.D. 1598) for "crucified" it is "*afflicting*," But the Greek reading προσπηξαντες, "*affixing* Him" to the cross, is the most probable reading.

"*And slain.*" If some of those present had no hand in our Lord's crucifixion—and likely many of them were present—their nation had.

"Hands of wicked men." The Greek ανομων, lawless men, who had no law, is allusive to Pilate and the other Romans, pagans who were not "under the law." Although our Lord was condemned and crucified by the Romans, it was the Jews that handed Him over to them. It was they planned and arranged His condemnation. Although fixed by the Decree of God, it was their own free act. The foreknowledge of God no more interferes with man's free agency than remembrance interferes with a *past* act or vision with the present. God foresees a future act just as it takes place, or as it is performed—viz., by the free will of man (see Gospel, John xii. 39, Commentary).

24. "God raised up." Our Lord, who was God, raised himself up from the dead, as He had repeatedly promised. His resuscitation was the act of the Adorable Trinity. In condescension to the intelligence and feelings of his hearers who were not in a mood to admit his Divinity, St. Peter speaks of Him as a great distinguished Prophet, without denying his Divinity.

24. *Whom God hath raised up, having loosed the sorrows of hell, as it was impossible that he should be holden by it.*

"Having loosed the sorrows of hell." There is a diversity of reading here. In the Greek it is, "*having loosed the sorrows of death.*" There is, however, no great difference as to sense; for by "*hell*" is meant the receptacle of the souls of *men who died* before Christ. The body was consigned to the tomb, the soul to the region called "hell" and kept there, as expressed in the words "*because thou wilt not leave my soul in hell,*" &c. (v. 27). Some understand the Greek word for "sorrows" (ὠδυνας) to mean *cords* or *cables*. This accords well with the word *loosing*, or *having loosed*. The phrase, *loosing cords*, which kept our Lord bound in the embraces and arms of death is more intelligible than "loosing *sorrows*," though this, too, will make sense, if understood, of the great pains our Lord endured, which were put an end to by being raised to a new life in His Resurrection. It would thus be allusive to the pains of parturition conveyed by the word ωδυνας, and our Lord's birth into a new life in His Resurrection (Acts xiii. 33).

The original Hebrew word is sometimes rendered ωδινας in the Septuagint, even when it is meant for *cords*. The meaning of the words in our version is, that in raising Himself up from the dead, God overcame the empire of death and hell, dissolving, destroying, putting an end to all the pains and dolours that usually accompany death and follow it. Hell or death is here personified, as appears from the words "*holden by it.*"

"Because it was impossible," &c. Considering the Divine nature

Text.

Commentary.

of our Lord, "the author of life" (iii. 17 ; John v. 26), and especially the prophecies regarding the Son of God, which argument St. Paul employs (Acts xiii. 33). It is to this prediction of His Resurrection, and all its circumstances, St. Peter here refers. These prophecies could not possibly be frustrated, God made a liar, and the end of His mission frustrated, which would be the result, if he did not fully overcome death and rise to a glorious and immortal life.

---

25. For David saith concerning him: I foresaw the Lord before my face: because he is at my right hand that I may not be moved.

25. "For David saith," in Psalm xv. The first portion of this Psalm literally refers to David himself as a type of Christ. But, in the latter part (*vv.* 8-11) the Psalmist, like one transported beyond himself, literally and primarily refers to Christ. To him only can this latter part of the Psalm literally refer. Of himself, David could not say with truth, that his body would not see corruption.

"*I foresaw the Lord,*" &c. In all the actions, sufferings and incidents of my life, I looked to the Lord, as my protector who would rescue me from every tribulation, and bestow on me a glorious and immortal life.

"*Because He is at my right hand,*" always by me to guard and protect my human nature.

"*That I may not be moved,*" may suffer no injury.

---

26. For this my heart hath been glad, and my tongue hath rejoiced: moreover my flesh also shall rest in hope.

26. "*My heart,*" &c., expresses very great interior joy, which was also exteriorly expressed.

The Hebrew for "my *tongue*" is, *my glory.* It means, *I myself,* the word, *glory,* being an honourable epithet. Thus we say of a man, *your Majesty, your Highness,* meaning *himself.*

"*Shall rest*" securely, in the sepulchre for some time, "*in hope,*" with the certain hope of my near resuscitation and the glory in store for me.

---

27. Because thou wilt not leave my soul in hell, nor suffer thy Holy one to see corruption.

27. "*Leave my soul,*" which after its separation from the body, shall descend to the regions of the dead, it shall not be permitted to remain there. It shall be united to my body, reposing in the tomb, so that both united may enjoy a glorious and immortal life. It is quite certain, that our Lord, after death, descended to the "Limbo of the Fathers," where the just of old were detained until the gates of Heaven, so long closed, were thrown open by the death of Christ, "*Thy holy One,*" our Lord, the author and source of holiness itself, was Himself pre-eminently "*holy.*"

---

28. Thou hast made known to me the ways of life: Thou shalt make me full

28. "*Hast made known.*" A prophetical past, on account of the certainty of accomplishment. The Hebrew has the *future,* "*Thou shalt make known or teach me,* the ways of life," the way of returning to life in my resurrection, so as to point it out to others, viz., the Patriarchs and Saints, who are to rise with me, and all who are to be raised up on

Commentary.

the last day. My resuscitation is to be a model of their Resurrection which is the way to life and glory eternal.

"*Make me full of joy*," &c. In the Hebrew it is, "*the abundance of joy shall be for me before thy countenance.*" My soul in the interval between my death and Resurrection shall see the joy of thy countenance and my body, though the same soul, in its resuscitation, gifted with the qualities of glorification, shall also be filled with *all* joy. Clearly these words are not applicable to David.

29. He here shows that the quotation from Psalm xv. cannot apply to David, who was dead, buried and subject to putrefaction; but, only to our Lord risen, after being three days in the grave.

"Men, brethren." Words of affectionate regard, to avoid all offence in what he was about telling them. Instead of saying at once and directly that the passage regarded Christ and not David, the Apostle adopts a conciliatory form of language; some among them, who held David in the greatest veneration might possibly understand the words of Psalm xv. to refer to him directly. He styles him "a Patriarch"—a term of honor and veneration—being the head of the Royal line, to which the promises regarding the Messiah were made, "was buried; and his sepulchre," where his remains, after being subjected to putrefaction, are enclosed,

"Is with us," may be seen in our midst here in Jerusalem "till the present day." Hence, the words, "shall not see corruption," cannot apply to him.

Josephus testifies (Antiqu., xvi. 7, 1) that David's Mausoleum was an object of veneration in his day. St. Jerome bears witness, that it might be seen in the days of the Emperor Adrian, when it fell to pieces. Ep. xviii.

A. Lapide observes that St. Peter says nothing of David's body or soul, which by this time had mounted on High, ascending glorious with the band of Patriarchs, &c., whom, at his ascension, our Lord had to accompany him, as so many trophies, to grace his glorious triumph.

30. "A prophet" inspired by God's holy spirit (Matthew xxii. 43), he knew from Divine Revelation that by God's unchangeable Decree, sanctioned by a solemn oath, one of his posterity would occupy his throne. The following words found in the Greek, but omitted in the Vulgate, "*according to the flesh he would raise up Christ,*" are omitted in several versions and MSS., and are regarded by most eminent critics, as of dubious authenticity. The passage makes sense without them.

31. Foreseeing this to occur at a future day, he predicted the Resurrection of Christ, in the words, "*thou shalt not leave my soul,*" &c. These words were fulfilled in him, "For neither was he left in Hell," &c.

Text.

of joy with thy countenance.

29. Ye men brethren, let me freely speak to you of the patriarch David; that he died, and was buried; and his sepulchre is with us to this present day.

30. Whereas therefore he was a prophet, and knew that God had sworn to him with an oath, that of the fruit of his loins one should sit upon his throne;

31. Foreseeing this, he spoke of the resurrection of Christ. For neither was he left in hell, neither did his flesh see corruption.

Text.	Commentary.
32. *This Jesus hath God raised again, whereof all we are witnesses.*	**32.** The prophecy regarding Christ's Resurrection has been fulfilled. We, Apostles, who saw Him, and conversed with him are witnesses of His Resurrection as an incontrovertible fact, that cannot be gainsayed or called in question.
33. *Being exalted therefore by the right hand of God, and having received of the Father the promise of the Holy Ghost, he hath poured forth this which you see and hear.*	**33.** The effect or consequence of this resuscitation was, that He was taken up by the power of God into Heaven, and having received from His Father the Holy Spirit whom He promised His Apostles (John xiv. 6, xvi. 7), He abundantly poured forth the manifold and varied gifts, which bring under your sense of hearing in the various tongues spoken, and the sense of seeing in the fiery forms of these tongues, His visible presence amongst you.
34. *For David ascended not into heaven; but he himself said: The Lord said to my Lord, sit thou at my right hand,*	**34-35.** In corroboration of his proof derived from the visible manifestation referred to in preceding verse, that Christ ascending on high sent down the Holy Ghost, the Apostle adduces the words of David (Psalm cix.), predicting the exaltation of Christ. The very Jewish Doctors themselves did not deny that the words of this Psalm (cix.) referred to Christ (Matthew xxii. 42, 46).
35. *Until I make thy enemies thy footstool.*	"David ascended not into Heaven," to send down the Holy Ghost. It was Christ did so.

"Sit on right hand" ("right hand" with the Hebrews meant, *power*), refers to our Lord's humanity. As man, He was the most exalted Being in Heaven, next to God, occupying the highest place next him. As God, he was equal to the Father; as man, the next after Him.

"Footstool" conveys the deepest humiliation (see Matthew xxii. 44, &c. Commentary).

| **36.** *Therefore let all the house of Israel know most certainly, that God hath made both Lord, and Christ, this same Jesus, whom you have crucified.* | **36.** "House," the entire family or descendants of Israel. "Know most assuredly," from the Resurrection of our Lord, from His elevation up to Heaven, from the sending down of the Holy Ghost, shown in the miracles of tongues, &c., from the Prophecies just quoted, let them firmly believe, that God has constituted this same Jesus, viewed according to His human nature. "Lord of all things "—"and Christ." That is to say, the long expected Messiah of the Jewish Nation, whom He anointed in His Incarnation and Union with the Eternal Word, with the oil of gladness beyond his fellows. |

"Whom you have crucified," thus, rendering yourselves guilty of the greatest crime ever perpetrated on this earth. In this peroration and conclusion of his discourse, he meant to excite in them feelings of compunction and to stimulate them to penance, which, with the aid of God's grace, he succeeded in doing.

| **37.** *Now when they had heard* | **37.** "They had compunction," exteriorly produced by the words of Peter, and interiorly, "in their heart," efficaciously produced by the |

Commentary.

grace and unction of the Holy Ghost enlightening and stimulating them. The Greek for "had," κατενυγησαν, means, *transpierced*, as if by some sharp instrument. They were pierced in their hearts with bitter, pungent sorrow—"compunction," on account of the crime of putting our Lord to death, whom they now believed and knew to be their long promised Messiah.

"What shall we do?" in expiation of so dreadful a crime.

38. "Do penance," which implies change of heart, in the first instance, also good works worthy of penance.

"And be baptised every one of you in the name"—by the authority, or in the faith "of Jesus Christ," and the external profession of that faith, by embracing his religion and becoming his followers.

The Greek for "in," επι, *upon*, would imply that their Baptism should be grounded on the profession of the Christian religion. "For the remission of your sins," so that, through this rite as an instrument, you may receive the remission of your sins. "And you shall receive the gift of the Holy Ghost." Shall receive the Holy Ghost with His gifts. This is understood by some of the Sacrament of Confirmation given through the imposition of hands, administered in the early ages of the Church immediately after, or simultaneously with, Baptism.

However, since the giving of the Holy Ghost was not confined to the rite of confirmation, as in the case of the Apostles themselves; nay, He was given in some cases *before* it, as happened Cornelius the Centurion: Hence, it is better to understand it of giving of the Holy Ghost, in due circumstances to the faithful, apart from the rite of imposition of hands.

In this it is not implied that Baptism was given in "the name of Jesus," but only in the form prescribed by our Lord Himself (Matthew xxviii. 19). Likely, St. Peter had fully instructed them on these points.

39. In proof that they will receive the Holy Ghost, he tells them that to the Israelites in general, in whatever place they are, many of them here present from even the most distant nation under heaven ("far off") was made the promise announced by Joel (*v.* 17) regarding the effusion of the Holy Ghost.

"And their children," their sons and daughters referred to by Joel, limited neither to time nor place. It embraced "all flesh."

The terms, "afar off," are frequently employed in the Old Testament to designate the Gentiles, who were to be co-heirs of Abraham's promises (Galatians iii. 29 ; iv. 28), in opposition to those "near," which denotes the Jews. However, it militates against its application here, that St. Peter needed to be informed by a heavenly vision, after this, of the call of the Gentiles (Acts x. 10, &c.) Moreover, it was of the Jews, Joel spoke. "Whomsoever the Lord our God shall call." Besides being of the race of Abraham, they needed a Divine call to be partakers of the promised blessings.

Text.

these things, they had compunction in their heart, and said to Peter, and to the rest of the apostles: What shall we do, men and brethren?

38. But Peter said to them. Do penance, and be baptized every one of you in the name of Jesus Christ, for the remission of your sins: and you shall receive the gift of the Holy Ghost.

39. For the promise is to you, and to your children, and to all that are far off, whomsoever the Lord our God shall call.

Text.	Commentary.

Text.

40. *And with very many other words did he testify and exhort them, saying: Save yourselves from this perverse generation.*

41. *They therefore that received his word were baptised: and there were added in that day about three thousand souls.*

42. *And they were persevering in the doctrine of the apostles, and in the communication of the breaking of bread, and in prayers.*

43. *And fear came upon every soul: many wonders also and signs were done by the apostles in Jerusalem, and there was great fear in all*

Commentary.

40. The entire of St. Peter's discourse is not given here. The same may be said of his other discourses, as well as those of St. Paul and of others recorded in this narrative of the Acts.

"Did he testify," by adducing the testimony of Scripture, the Prophecies regarding our Lord, the sanctity of his life, his miracles in life and death, the testimony of the Apostles, who were so many eye-witnesses, that his teachings and sayings regarding Christ were true.

"This perverse," unbelieving, unrepenting "generation." Similar are the words (Matthew xii. 39). They should strive not to be involved in the common ruin in store for the wicked unbelievers. This is the practical summary of St. Peter's exhortation.

41. "Received his word," voluntarily and believed. In the words, "whom the Lord shall call," is asserted the necessity of Divine grace; here, is vindicated human liberty, as a principle of free action.

"Added," joined the Church or congregation of the faithful already formed.

42. "Doctrines," &c., continually assisting at the teachings and instructions of the Apostles.

"And in the communication of the breaking," &c. "By communication" is meant their mutual charitable intercourse with each other in their ordinary union, especially on the occasion of their meeting at the Agapes or feasts of love and charity, usually celebrated, after the example of the Apostles and of our Lord himself, before approaching the Holy Eucharist.

"And in the breaking of bread" is commonly understood of the Blessed Eucharist, which is termed "bread" by St. Paul (1 Cor. x. 15). That it could not refer to any common or profane partaking of food, seems most likely, independently of the fact, that the ordinary partaking of bread is spoken of, *v.* 46. From the whole context, there is clearly question of a religious act.

The article is placed before "bread and prayers, "*the bread, the prayers.*" The Syriac has, *the breaking of the Eucharist.* Some commentators on this passage remark, that here allusion is evidently made to the unbloody sacrifice of the mass. "*Breaking of the bread,*" no common bread. "*The prayers,*" fixed prayers usually said on occasion of this celebration.

43. A feeling of reverential awe, created by the wonders witnessed on Pentecost Sunday, succeeded the derision first manifested (*v.* 13).

"Many wonders," &c. The Apostles confirmed their teaching, and especially their testimony regarding our Lord's Resurrection and Ascension into Heaven, whence, He sent down the Holy Ghost, by performing marvellous wonders in accordance with the powers promised them (Luke xvi., &c.).

Commentary.

"In Jerusalem." These words are rejected by some commentators, as they are wanting in several MSS. They are, however, found in several MSS. and versions, Coptic, Italic, Vulgate, and several old Greek MSS. Patrizzi regards them as genuine, and as meant to convey, that these marvellous occurrences were confined to Jerusalem.

"And there was great fear," &c., are wanting in several MSS., and are regarded by some as not of the text; since, they would seem to be only a repetition of the idea conveyed in the preceding words, "and fear came," &c.

44. Having spoken of the Apostles, he now describes the relations of the faithful with one another.

"Were together." Not that they had the same lodging—a thing quite impossible, considering their numbers, even after the foreign Jews had left for their own homes.

It simply means that being entirely united, having but one heart and one soul, they exhibited great fraternal union and concord and frequently met, as members of one united family, especially in the Temple and place of Divine worship. Likely, in their social relations and gatherings, they formed a society distinct, as far as possible, from the unbelieving Jews, intercourse with whom might prove a source of danger to the newly converted.

"And had all things common," so far as the relief of distress was concerned. In this respect, there was no such thing as *mine and thine.* The rich among them, voluntarily and of their own free accord sold their property, at least in part, in order to have at hand the means of relieving their indigent brethren; so that so far as the relief of distress was concerned, voluntary charity handed to the indigent the goods their richer neighbours possessed.

It does not appear that those blessed with earthly goods among the early Christians sold off *all* their property, and divested themselves of *all* right and title to them. The contrary may be inferred from c. iv. 32-34. They sold off *all that was necessary* to relieve the destitute.

45. "Possessions," immovable property, lands, houses. "Goods," moveable personal property. These they sold, and divided to all as each one needed.

The infant Church of Jerusalem was modeled on the life of our Lord and His Apostles. The same mode of life is still continued in religious communities whose members, for greater perfection sake, have everything in common, without any private property. This economy was confined to the Church of Jerusalem. The Apostles in preaching the Gospel did not think fit to establish it generally. Indeed the exhortations of St. Paul to have collections made for relieving the poor (2 Cor. ix., &c.) would show there was no such condition of things among the churches he founded. The condition of the Church of Jerusalem was peculiar. Owing to the confiscation of property, it was

44. *And all they that believed, were together, and had all things common.*

45. *Their possessions and goods they sold, and divided them to all, according as every one had need.*

c

Text.	Commentary.

very poor (Heb. x. 34, xiii. 2-3, 16). St. John had property (John xix. 27). Neither did our Lord nor His Apostles *command* the faithful to throw all their property into a common fund.

The condition of things among the first Christians of Jerusalem gives no sanction whatever to the wicked principles of modern communism, which are simply impracticable and absurd. Unlike the wicked principles or practice advocated by these disturbers of public order, the community of goods referred to here was:—1, perfectly *free* and *spontaneous* (Acts v. 4); 2, *local* and special, confined to the Church of Jerusalem, as appears from the collections set on foot by St. Paul in other churches, in which he supposed they retained their possessions, to relieve the necessities of the saints (1 Cor. xvi. ; 2 Cor. ix.); 3, *transitory*, even in the Church of Jerusalem itself ; (this economy the Apostles did not think fit to establish in other churches) ; 4, not *essential to the existence* or well-being of the church or salvation of men; (St. Peter, on being asked what was necessary for salvation, only inculcated Baptism and Penance) ; 5, neither did our Lord or His Apostles insist upon it. On the contrary, St. Paul in several of his Epistles inculcates alms deeds, and speaks of them as free—by no means compulsory.

46. And continuing daily with one accord in the temple, and breaking bread from house to house, they took their meat with gladness and simplicity of heart:

46. He describes the life observed by the first Christians. "Continuing daily," with persevering assiduity, they attended daily with one accord, at the usual hours of prayer, the public services in the Temple. *At this time,* "in order to bury the Synagogue with honor," it was allowed the first Christians to join in Jewish rites and ceremonies. Most likely they celebrated their own Christian Liturgy and offered up the Christian sacrifice.

"Breaking bread." Here we have not the article "*the*" prefixed— "*the bread*," as in v. 42, where it is commonly understood of the Eucharist. "From house to house," privately partaking of food in their own houses.

"They took their meat with gladness" is a fuller explanation of "breaking bread," and shows that here there is not question, as in v. 42, of the Blessed Sacrament, but only of social intercourse. It refers to their ordinary meals, of which they partook in common, now in one house, now in another. Some say there is allusion to the Agapes.

"With gladness." Overjoyed at the blessings of Christianity bestowed on them, ever rejoicing in the ordinary circumstances of life.

"Simplicity of heart." With moderation ; generous to all who needed it.

47. Praising God and having favour with all the people. And the Lord increased daily together such

47. Constantly engaged in the Divine praises. "Having favour with the great body of the people, who admired their edifying, inoffensive manner of life, their benignity and accommodating charity. "And the Lord increased daily together." The number of those who were associated with the Church assembled on Pentecost day at Jerusalem, and were thus placed in the way of salvation.

Commentary.

In the Greek we have for "increased daily together"—the usual rendering of *in idipsum* of the Vulgate—"added daily to the Church such as should be saved," a paraphrase for "Christian believers."

"Together" is the introduction to next chapter (iii.). In some ancient codices, "Peter and John went up together," &c. (*c.* iii., *v.* 1).

Most likely the Vulgate is the correct reading, and the words mean the Lord added to the church and increased daily "together," so as to live in each other's company, and form a compact, united community, such as, listening to the words of Peter (*v.* 40), seceded from the Synagogue, and entered into the church, where they were placed in the way of salvation.

Text.

as should be saved.

CHAPTER III.

1. *Now Peter and John went up into the temple at the ninth hour of prayer.*

2. *And a certain man who was lame from his mother's womb, was carried; whom they laid every day at the gate of the temple, which is called Beautiful, that he might ask alms of them that went into the temple.*

I cured

3. *He, when he had seen Peter and John about to go into the temple, asked to receive an alms.*

by

4. *But Peter with John fastening his eyes upon him, said: Look upon us.*

5. *But he looked earnestly upon them, hoping that he should receive something of them*

Peter

6. *But Peter said: Silver and gold I have none; but what I have, I give thee: In the name of Jesus Christ of Nazareth, arise, and walk.*

7. *And taking him by the right hand, he lifted him up, and forthwith his feet and soles received strength.*

8. *And he leaping up, stood, and walked, and went in with them into the temple, walking, and leaping, and praising God.*

9. *And all the people saw him walking and praising God.*

10. *And they knew him, that it was he who sat begging alms at the beautiful gate of the temple: and they were filled with wonder and amazement at that which had happened to him.*

11. *And as he held Peter and John, all the people ran to them to the porch which is called Solomon's, greatly wondering.*

address.

12. *But Peter seeing, made answer to the people: Ye men of Israel, why wonder you at this? or why look you upon us, as if by our strength or power we had made this man to walk.*

13. *The God of Abraham, and the God of Isaac, and the God of Jacob, the God of our fathers, hath glorified his Son Jesus, whom you indeed delivered up and denied before the face of Pilate, when he judged he should be released.*

Pure done
not man

14. *But you denied the Holy one and the Just, and desired a murderer to be granted unto you.*

faith)

15. *But the author of life you killed, whom God hath raised from the dead, of which we are witnesses.*

16. *And in the faith of his name, this man, whom you have seen and known, hath his name strengthened; and the faith which is by him, hath given this perfect soundness in the sight of you all.*

17. *And now, brethren, I know that you did it through ignorance, as did also your rulers.*

18. *But those things which God before had shewed by the mouth of all the prophets, that his Christ should suffer, he hath so fulfilled.*

In ". do penance".

19. *Be penitent, therefore, and be converted, that your sins may be blotted out.*

20. *That when the times of refreshment shall come from the presence of the Lord, and he shall send him who hath been preached unto you, Jesus Christ.*

21. *Whom heaven indeed must receive, until the times of the restitution of all things, which God hath spoken by the mouth of his holy prophets, from the beginning of the world.*

22. *For Moses said: A prophet shall the Lord your God raise up unto you of your brethren, like unto me: him you shall hear according to all things whatsoever he shall speak to you.*

23. *And it shall be, that every soul which will not hear that prophet, shall be destroyed from among the people.*

24. *And all the prophets, from Samuel and afterwards, who have spoken, have told of these days.*

25. *You are the children of the prophets, and of the testament which God made to our fathers, saying to Abraham: And in thy seed shall all the kindreds of the earth be blessed.*

26. *To you first God, raising up his Son hath sent him to bless you; that every one may convert himself from his wickedness.*

ANALYSIS.

In this chapter we have an account of the miraculous cure, by St. Peter, of a lame man, with several accompanying circumstances, which placed the reality of the miracle beyond all cavil or dispute, and elicited the wonder and amazement of the people (1-12). The address of Peter, showing that this miracle was brought about, not by human agency, but by the power of Christ and by faith in Him (12-17). His exhortation to penance recommended on several grounds (19-26).

Commentary.

1. " Now," immediately after the occurrences recorded in preceding chap. ii., St. Luke here specifies, in particular, one of the miraculous wonders wrought by the Apostles recorded in a general way, c. ii., v. 43.

" Peter and John went up into the temple." The Greek places here the words commonly found in the last verse of preceding chapter. " Together." " Went up." The Zorobabelic Temple rebuilt by Herod was situated on an elevated part of the city, Mount Moria, the site of the ancient Temple of Solomon. " At the ninth hour of prayer." This was about 3 o'clock in the afternoon. The followers of our Lord made it a practice to resort to the Temple for devotional exercises. The ninth hour was the time fixed for evening sacrifice. The fixed hours for public prayer in the Temple among the Jews were the *third*, our 9 o'clock (ii. 15), *sixth* (our 12 o'clock), *ninth* (3 o'clock with us). Daniel "adored three times a-day" (Daniel vi. 10). David, *evening*, *morning*, and *mid-day* (Ps. 54, 18).

2. "A man lame from his mother's womb," and well known as such. Hence, no fear of collusion or deception as to his ailment or subsequent miraculous cure.

"The gate of the temple called Beautiful." It is not agreed upon among commentators what "the gate," here termed, "beautiful" referred to. No gate of this name is spoken of by Josephus or other Jewish authors. It refers, according to some, to the gate of Nicanor, leading from the court of the Gentiles to that of the women. It was so

Text.

1. *Now Peter and John went up into the temple at the ninth hour of prayer.*

2. *And a certain man who was lame from his mother's womb, was carried: whom they laid every day at the gate of the temple, which is called Beau-*

tiful, that he might ask alms of them that went into the temple.

called, because, according to a Jewish tradition, the hand of that furious enemy of God's people was attached to it by Judus Machabæus, as a trophy of the glorious victory he achieved in a battle wherein Nicanor was slain.   Josephus tells us (Bell. Ind., c. v. 5, 3), that it was made of Corinthian brass, or overlaid with it, equal in value to gold, and exquisitely wrought.   It surpassed all the others in magnificence. Hence, called " *Beautiful*," Others say, there is question of the gate called _Susan_, the principal gate on the east side.   On it was sculptured in relief a representation of the city of Susa, the chief city of Persia, as expressive, from the days of Zorobabel, of the loyalty of the Jews to the Persian Powers. This was contiguous to the Portico of Solomon, whither the Apostles repaired after the miracle. Owing to the great concourse of people there it was a place advantageous for asking alms. Hence, some commentators say it was the gate here spoken of.

3. *He, when he had seen Peter and John about to go into the temple, asked to receive an alms.*

" That he might ask alms," &c.   From the earliest times it was quite a common practice with mendicants to plant themselves at the gates of churches.

4. *But Peter with John fastening his eyes upon him, said: Look upon us.*

4. " Look upon us " in order to fix his attention on the subsequent miracle, and make him see that the miracle was performed by the Apostles.

5. *But he looked earnestly upon them, hoping that he should receive something of them.*

6. *But Peter said : Silver and Gold I have none; but what I have I give thee: In the name of Jesus Christ of Nazareth, arise, and walk.*

6. " I have none."   No private funds of his own for dispensing in charity. The common fund was not at his disposal for such purposes.

" What I have," given me for the benefit of others.   It was not from himself, but owing to the power promised by our Lord (Mark xvi. 17, 18) and given him, he performed the miracle.

" In the name," by the power and authority " of Jesus Christ," &c., whose instrument I simply am, " of Nazareth," the title commonly given him, the name under which this man may have heard of him, as a crucified malefactor and seducer.

" Arise and walk."   The command conveyed the power of working the miracle by the Apostle.

7. *And taking him by the right hand, he lifted him up, and forthwith his feet and soles received strength.*

7. " Forthwith," instantly.   " His feet and soles."   " _Soles_" in the Greek means "_ankle bones_" owing to the weakness of which he could not support his body, "received strength." All the circumstances point to an undoubted miracle. Commentators remark that in the use of terms connected with the human frame, the technical accuracy of Luke, the Physician, is observable.

8. *And he leaping up*

8. " Leaping up " expresses the joy he felt. It may be also expressive of his first essay at walking.   He next " stood," then

Commentary.

"walked," regularly, like the rest. The fact of his walking, which he was not used to, having been a cripple from a child, is a clear proof of the miracle.

"Praising God," to whom he knew he was indebted for his cure. For St. Peter did not even pretend that it came from himself. Here, we have a literal fulfilment of the Prophecy of Isaias (xxxv. 6) "then, shall the lame man leap, as a hart."

9. "All the people." The very crucifiers of our Lord saw the miracle and its suddenness. There could be no collusion or fraud. The Apostles were strangers to the man that was cured. Some of them carried him to the place where he was daily placed to solicit alms from the passers by.

10. "Filled with wonder," &c. The effect of the miracle on their feelings.

11. "Held Peter and John." Closely clinging to them in token of gratitude as they were leaving the Temple after prayer.

"All the people" moved by curiosity at what occurred assembled in this place of public resort at the hour of prayer, which furnished St. Peter with a suitable opportunity of preaching the truth of the Christian faith. "Porch," a covered passage on the east side of the Temple, "of Solomon." This was a part of the great Temple of Solomon, which escaped demolition at the destruction of Solomon's Temple by Nabuchodonozor (4 Kings xxv. 15). It was to the East of the Temple. Hence, called by Josephus the *Oriental Portico* (Antiq. xx. 9, 7).

12. "Made answer," does not always mean a reply to a question. Frequently it is used, as here, to signify making a statement or entering on a discourse with or without a previous question.

"Strength or power." The Greek word for "power" means piety or *religious merit*. This is preferred by some, as the Vulgate reading would seem to be a mere tautology. The Vulgate, however, is preferred by many eminent commentators, as more emphatically describing the feelings of the people who regarded not the piety or personal merits of the Apostles, but their power only.

stood, and walked, and went in with them into the temple, walking, and leaping, and praising God.

9. *And all the people saw him walking and praising God.*

10. *And they knew him, that it was he who sat begging alms at the Beautiful gate of the temple: and they were filled with wonder and amazement at that which had happened to him.*

11. *And as he held Peter and John, all the people ran to them to the porch which is called Solomon's, greatly wondering.*

12. *But Peter seeing, made answer to the people: Ye men of Israel, why wonder you at this? or why look you upon us, as if by our strength or power we had made this man to walk?*

Text.

13. *The God of Abraham, and the God of Isaac, and the God of Jacob, the God of our fathers, hath glorified his Son Jesus, whom you indeed delivered up and denied before the face of Pilate, when he judged he should be released.*

14. *But you denied the Holy one and the Just, and desired a murderer to be granted unto you.*

15. *But the author of life you killed, whom God hath raised from the dead, of which we are witnesses.*

16. *And in the faith of his name, this man, whom you have seen and known, hath his name strengthened: and the faith which is by him, hath given this perfect soundness in the sight of you all.*

17. *And now, brethren, I know that you did it through*

Commentary.

13. "The God of Abraham," &c. The friend, the protector and bountiful rewarder of Abraham, &c. Speaking to Moses (Exod. iii. 6, &c.) God first called Himself by that epithet.

"The God of our Fathers." He it is that performed this wonder (v. 16).

"Hath glorified," honoured His Son, Jesus. "Whom you delivered up" to the Romans to be crucified, "and denied" to be your Messiah, your promised deliverer, "before the face of Pilate," who, convinced of His innocence, "for he could find no cause in Him," judged that He should be released. Against the deliberate judgment of a Pagan judge, who through fear afterwards consented to condemn Him, they insisted on His death, thus displaying the intensity of their malice and deliberate hate.

14. "The Holy One." An epithet frequently applied to our Lord (Mark i. 24; Luke iv. 34). The article prefixed in the Greek designates Him as "Holy" of His own essence and Divine nature. Infinite sanctity itself.

"A murderer," Barabbas. Here their conduct is powerfully contrasted with that of Pilate, a pagan, not favoured with the lights vouchsafed to them.

15. "Author of life." Our Lord is the source of all life, physical and spiritual. A powerful contrast here between Barabbas, the destroyer of life, and Jesus, the source of it in all.

"God raised from the dead." The Resurrection of Christ, the foundation of all Christian faith, is frequently insisted on in several passages of the New Testament.

"We are witnesses." The Apostles, disciples, and several followers of our Lord, amounting to a vast number, saw our Lord after His Resurrection, and conversed with Him. God Himself confirmed their testimony regarding this fundamental truth, with miracles.

16. "In the faith," &c. The faith of Peter and John. It don't appear the man cured had any faith or knowledge of Him previously.

"Hath his name," that is, himself, "strengthened," by our power and strength, "whom you have seen and known" to be a cripple from his birth.

"Faith which is in Him." In our Lord Jesus Christ, as author and finisher of our faith.

"Perfect soundness." The Greek conveys complete restoration to the use of his limbs.

"In the sight of you all." It is incontestible, and will stand the test of investigation.

17. After having proved, by a freedom of speech truly Apostolic, that they were guilty of the hideous crime of Deicide, and uttered hard truths, He now wishes to extenuate their guilt, addressing them "as

Commentary.

brethren," and by kindness He wishes to inspire them with hope of pardon. He puts forward the same excuse, "ignorance," which our Lord Himself advanced in their behalf—"they know not what they do." He by no means insinuates that they were innocent. He had stated the contrary (*v.* 14). But, with a view of moving them to repentance by the hope of pardon, He says, their crime, in itself enormous, was extenuated by the fact of their not knowing Him to be their long-expected Messiah.

"As did also your rulers." The chief men among the Jews were more guilty than the masses of the people. From the evidences placed before them, they could have known that He was their long expected Messiah. Blinded by passion, they, in their fury, proceeded to compass the death of a just man, whom a pagan judge pronounced innocent. Had they known Him to be the long expected Deliverer of their nation, they would not have treated Him as they had done. Still, they were not innocent or free from guilt.

18. Anticipating an objection that might suggest itself—viz., if Christ were the Messiah, why suffer Himself to be thus treated? St. Peter shows, if He did not, He could not be regarded as the Messiah at all, since, all the prophets concurred in predicting his death and sufferings. All these occurrences were predicted beforehand, and God caused them to be fulfilled in the manner predicted. Without altogether excusing them or pronouncing them innocent—for they were afterwards called upon to *repent* for their wickedness—St. Peter prudently mitigates the hard sentence passed upon them, and wishes to excite them to sorrow and the hope of pardon, from the consideration that, although sinning, they were the instruments in carrying out the merciful design of God in the way in which it occurred—viz., through Jewish malice, the redemption of all mankind, themselves included. The foreknowledge of God did not diminish their guilt. For God foresaw it in the way it was to happen—viz., freely, through their deliberate guilt and malice. The Apostle mentions it to inspire them with the hope of pardon. How all the prophets foretold is not so clear. It is understood of the prophets in a *general* way, or taken on the *whole*, without stating that *each individual* prophet foretold it. However, it may be said that they all either literally or mystically, explicitly or implicitly, foretold it. Hence, of our Lord on His way to Emmaus, it is said that "beginning at Moses and *all the Prophets*, He expounded the things said concerning Him" (Luke xxiv. 27).

19. "Therefore," as your sin so heinous, though extenuated by ignorance, resulted in the redemption of mankind, "repent and be converted" to the Lord, who mercifully ransomed you, in order that, with the hope of pardon in your hearts, "your sins may be blotted out" and cleansed away by a full remission. The idea, according to some, is borrowing from the practice among the ancients of effacing with the blunt end of

Text.

Commentary.

the stylus, characters impressed on soft wax by the sharp point of same. It also is allusion to the act of creditors blotting out debts due (Coll. ii. 14). According to others, the idea is borrowed from the practice of washing parchment and effacing the characters impressed. This would very appropriately apply to the remission of sins in the waters of Baptism.

20. *That when the times of refreshment shall come from the presence of the Lord, and he shall send him who hath been preached unto you, Jesus Christ,*

20. "When the times," &c. The Greek for " when " is ὅπως—*that*, or, *in order that*, signifying the *final* cause. The passage, which is not free from difficulties in its construction, would mean—in order that the times of refreshment would be accelerated when, after the toils and warfare of this life, they shall be admitted to that everlasting rest, that sabbatism which God enjoys and shares with His servants (Heb. iv. 3-7) ; a refreshment which " shall come from the presence of the Lord." " Presence of the Lord," by a Hebrew idiom means the *Lord Himself*, who is to confer it.

"And He shall send Him," His eternal Son, "Jesus Christ," who hath been preached to you." The Greek word for " preached " means *pre-ordained*, or marked out by God, at the end of time, at his second coming to judgment, to confirm the promises made your Fathers (Rom. xv. 8). The final end of all things is not to arrive, till after the conversion of the Jews (Rom. xi. 26-29). The passage would then seem to convey, that the conversion of the Jewish people would have the effect of bringing on the final end of all things sooner, than would otherwise occur, in the designs of God's Providence.

21. *Whom heaven indeed must receive, until the times of the restitution of all things, which God hath spoken by the mouth of his holy prophets, from the beginning of the world.*

21. "Whom heaven, indeed, must receive." It was a common belief among the Jews, that the Messiah would reign on earth for ever (John xii. 34). St. Peter meets this prejudice by declaring he ascended into Heaven, as seen by the Apostles and others.

"Until the time of the restoration of all things," the full restoration of all things had already commenced with our Lord's coming, to be completed on the day of judgment (2 Peter iii. 13). It would be a " restoration " of mankind to the condition destined for them, if man had not fallen.

The visible creation has been deteriorated by sin. It now groans and yearns for its emancipation from the slavery of corruption, to the full enjoyment of the liberty suited to the Sons of God (Rom. viii. ; 2 Peter iii. 10-13). The Apostle in this passage wishes to convey, that if the Jewish nation became repentant and turned to God, the end of all things would soon come, and the human race put in the enjoyment of peace and rest, after being restored to the condition they would have been in, had man originally not fallen, and continued faithful to God.

22. *For Moses said: A prophet shall the Lord your God raise*

22. "For, Moses," &c. Among the other Prophets who prophesied regarding our Lord as their Messiah, was Moses whose authority, as their Lawgiver, was of the greatest weight with the Jews. St. Peter shows here

Commentary.

that far from opposing or giving up the Law of Moses—in preaching our Lord, they are only carrying out the express commands of Moses, who himself uttered a prediction regarding Him and inculcated obedience to Him.

" *A Prophet shall the Lord your God*," &c., " raise up," commission, authorize to come to you.

Looking to the context of Deut., whence these words are taken (xviii. 15-17) several commentators include under the word " Prophet " a series of authorized teachers, whom God would, from time to time, send to withhold the Jewish people from the false teachers, Diviners, &c., of the neighbouring Idolotrous Gentiles. Whatever may be the truth of that opinion, the word admittedly, refers to our Lord, who was *by excellence* the greatest among these teachers. The Jews themselves would seem to understand it so. "Art thou the Prophet?" (John i.) Moses commands them to *obey* Him, which they can still do, since He lives and exercises supreme authority in Heaven. They should, therefore, attend to the injunctions of Moses in reference to Him.

" Of your own brethren," your own race and nation, " like unto me." There are several points of *similarity*, not *equality*. They were not, however, similar in all things, but only in some points, especially as to making known the will of God to the people, both being "raised up," or commissioned by God to do this. The comparison can be urged no further, nor in other respects. The difference between both being infinite (Heb. iii. 3, 7).

23. " *It shall be.*" It will surely, and, of necessity, take place, St. Peter quotes from Deuteronomy not literally, but only the meaning.

" *Which will not hear*," or obey, that Prophet commissioned with authority to declare the will of God.

" *Shall be destroyed*." For which it is in Hebrew. " *I shall require it of him*," that is, make him answer for it. In the Septuagint, it is, " *I shall be present, as an avenger*," shall punish him. The usual way for punishing grievous sinners among the Jews was, by *exterminating* them from among the people, subjecting them to all the penalties of excommunication ; thus depriving them of all the privileges of the Jewish people and cutting them off, which was the greatest punishment inflicted by Jewish law. From this, those present could see that by continuing to disobey our Lord, they would be subjected to the heaviest punishment here and hereafter. *Here*, in the utter destruction of their city and the attendant horrors, which the Christians being forewarned, escaped by flying to Pella. But as he speaks of the punishment at the final restoration of all things, most likely, there is question of their punishment *hereafter*, in the day of judgment and the Eternal tortures of Hell. As they could now have recourse to him, although in Heaven, they should do so and repent of their sins.

24. " *And*." In Greek means, *nay even*. Not only Moses, who *holds the* highest place, but, " all the Prophets," denoting many of them, in

Text.

up unto you of your brethren, like unto me: him you shall hear according to all things whatsoever he shall speak to you.

23. *And it shall be, that every soul which will not hear that prophet, shall be destroyed from among the people.*

24. *And all the prophets,*

Text.

from Samuel and afterwards, who have spoken, have told of these days.

Commentary.

general, without specifying them individually, " from Samuel," who with all the Prophets that succeeded him, " have told, of those days." Have distinctly foretold the several occurrences that took place in connection with Jesus of Nazareth, all the events of His life from His birth, from the commencement of His reign on earth, till the final consummation of all things. To these predictions the Jews should pay heed. Likely, from Moses to Samuel no Prophet arose, God was consulted in the *interim* and gave His responses through Urim and Thummim (Exod. xxviii. 30; Numbers xxvii. 21).

We have hardly any Prophecy of Samuel relating to our Lord, unless it be the famous Prophecy of Nathan, recorded (2 Kings vii. 13, 14), which the Jews called 2nd Samuel, (as they considered 1st and 2nd Kings, was written by Samuel, at least in part); and, hence, as recorded by him, this is called Samuel's prediction. Or, it may be St. Peter refers to some Prophecy of Samuel relating to our Lord, not written, but, known to the Jews.

25. You are the children of the prophets, and of the testament which God made to our fathers, saying to Abraham: And in thy seed shall all the kindreds of the earth be blessed.

25. "The children " (in Greek, *sons*) " of the Prophets," not that they were the lineal descendants of the prophets. The Hebrew words often mean, as here, those to whom any thing belongs, whether by inheritance or otherwise. The meaning, then, is, they, it is, to whom the oracles of the Prophets appertain, also the Covenant made by God with their Fathers, Abraham (Genesis xii. 3 ; xxvi. 4), Isaac and Jacob.

"Saying to Abraham." To him were the promises first made. He was the Father of the faithful. " Thy seed," posterity. This is applied by St. Paul (Galatians iii. 15) to our Lord, as it is here by St. Peter.

Kindreds. The Greek (πατριαι) those deriving their origin from one common parent, Jews as well as Gentiles. These latter were the spiritual sons of Abraham, no less than the Jews, "blessed," rendered happy. They should, therefore, by embracing their Messiah, avail themselves of the promises made, which promises, strictly speaking, could not be a *Covenant* as between God and His creatures. The solemn promises made by God were, however, called a *Covenant*, to show their *firmness* and solemnity.

26. To you first God, raising up his Son, hath sent him to bless you; that every one may convert himself from his wickedness.

26. To you first," &c. In the order of God's Providence, the Gospel was to be first preached to the Jews, beginning at Jerusalem (Luke xxiv. 47).

" Raising up " does not refer to our Lord's Resurrection ; it only signifies commissioning him, sending him, with authority, as in *v.* 22.

" That everyone may convert himself," &c. Here, the prospect of pardon and forgiveness is held out to them, which they may obtain by penance and conversion to God. The Apostle wishes to convey to them, that now, the Messiah having come, they, as well as all the other " *kindreds*" of the earth, by being converted to Him, may look for happiness, and the pardon of all their sins.

CHAPTER IV.

1. *And as they were speaking to the people, the priests, and the officer of the temple, and the Sadducees, came upon them.*

2. *Being grieved that they taught the people, and preached in Jesus the resurrection from the dead.*

3. *And they laid hands upon them, and put them in hold till the next day; for it was now evening.*

4. *But many of them who had heard the word, believed; and the number of the men was made five thousand.*

5. *And it came to pass on the morrow that their princes, and ancients, and scribes, were gathered together in Jerusalem.*

6. *And Annas the high-priest, and Caiphas, and John, and Alexander, and as many as were of the kindred of the high-priest.*

7. *And setting them in the midst, they asked: By what power, or by what name, have you done this?*

8. *Then Peter, filled with the Holy Ghost, said to them: Ye princes of the people, and ancients, hear.*

9. *If we this day are examined concerning the good deed done to the infirm man, by what means he hath been made whole;*

10. *Be it known to you all, and to all the people of Israel, that by the name of our Lord Jesus Christ of Nazareth, whom you crucified, whom God hath raised from the dead, even by him this man standeth here before you whole.*

11. *This is the stone which was rejected by you the builders, which is become the head of the corner.*

12. *Neither is there salvation in any other. For there is no other name under heaven given to men, whereby we must be saved.*

13. *Now seeing the constancy of Peter and of John, understanding that they were illiterate and ignorant men, they wondered; and they knew them that they had been with Jesus.*

14. *Seeing the man also who had been healed standing with them, they could say nothing against it.*

15. *But they commanded them to go aside out of the council; and they conferred among themselves.*

16. *Saying: What shall we do to these men? for indeed a known miracle hath been done by them, to all the inhabitants of Jerusalem it is manifest, and we cannot deny it.*

17. *But that it may be no farther spread among the people, let us threaten them that they speak no more in this name to any man.*

18. *And calling them, they charged them not to speak at all, nor teach in the name of Jesus.*

19. *But Peter and John answering, said to them: If it be just in the sight of God, to hear you rather than God, judge ye.*

20. *For we cannot but speak the things which we have seen and heard.*

(marginal notes: "people", "miracle", "assembled", "7")

21. *But they threatening, sent them away, not finding how they might punish them, because of the people; for all men glorified what had been done, in that which had come to pass.*

22. *For the man was above forty years old, in whom that miraculous cure had been wrought.*

23. *And being let go, they came to their own company, and related all that the chief priests and ancients had said to them.*

24. *Who having heard it, with one accord lifted up their voice to God, and said: Lord, thou art he that didst make heaven and earth, the sea, and all things that are in them.*

25. *Who, by the Holy Ghost, by the mouth of our father David, thy servant, hast said: Why did the gentiles rage, and the people meditate vain things?*

26. *The kings of the earth stood up, and the princes assembled together against the Lord, and against his Christ.*

27. *For of a truth there assembled together in this city against thy holy child Jesus, whom thou hast anointed, Herod, and Pontius Pilate, with the gentiles and the people of Israel.*

28. *To do what thy hand and thy counsel decreed to be done.*

29. *And now, Lord, behold their threatenings, and grant unto thy servants, that with all confidence they may speak thy word,*

30. *By stretching forth thy hand to cures, and signs, and wonders to be done by the name of thy holy Son Jesus.*

(marginal note: "of Prayer")

31. *And when they had prayed, the place was moved wherein they were assembled, and they were all filled with the Holy Ghost, and they spoke the word of God with confidence.*

(marginal notes: "life of Christians")

32. *And the multitude of believers had but one heart and one soul: neither did any one say that aught of the things which he possessed, was his own; but all things were common unto them.*

33. *And with great power did the apostles give testimony of the resurrection of Jesus Christ our Lord; and great grace was in them all.*

34. *For neither was there any one needy among them. For as many as were owners of lands or houses, sold them, and brought the price of the things they sold.*

35. *And laid it down before the feet of the apostles. And distribution was made to every one, according as he had need.*

36. *And Joseph, who, by the apostles, was surnamed Barnabas (which is by interpretation, the son of consolation), a Levite, a Cyprian born,*

37. *Having land, sold it, and brought the price, and laid it at the feet of the apostles.*

ANALYSIS.

In this chapter is recorded the violence offered the Apostles by the Jewish authorities for preaching to the people (1-3). The conversion of large numbers (4). The questioning of the Apostles by the leading men of the Jewish priesthood (5-8). Peter's address, his vindication of his conduct, and exposition of doctrine (8-13). Consultation among the assembled authorities as to how the Apostles were to be treated (13-20). The liberation of the Apostles out of fear of the people, and on account of the incontestable evidence of the miracle (21-22). The solemn, united prayer to God on the part of the assembled faithful (24-30). The effect of this solemn prayer fully manifested (31). The edifying manner of life pursued by the first Christians, their charitable disinterestedness (32-37).

Commentary.

1. "**Priests.**" These likely belonged to the Sanhedrim. They seemed to possess some authority to prevent the Apostles from preaching in the Temple.

"The officer of the Temple" very likely, denotes the captain of the guard stationed in the Tower, Antonia, for the purpose of preserving order and preventing tumults in the Temple, especially on the occasion of Great Festivities. The assembling of the people round the Apostles, after the miraculous cure of the lame man, might lead to a riot.

"The Sadducees" (See Matthew iii. 7, xxii. 23, Commentary). They were a kind of freethinking malcontents among the Jews. They denied the existence of spirits, and the spirituality, as also the immortality of the soul. They were particularly opposed to the doctrine of the Resurrection. Although generally at variance with the Pharisees and the heads of the Jewish church, they still joined them against our Lord and his Apostles (See Matthew iii. 7).

"Came upon them," by surprise and unexpectedly, while speaking to the people.

2. "**Grieved,**" in Greek, means, *vexed, annoyed ;* "taught," &c., thus causing their own influence and prestige to be lessened.

"The resurrection of the dead," the general resurrection of all men, of which the Resurrection of Jesus, which they constantly proclaimed, was the model, the exemplary and efficient cause. This was very mortifying to the Sadducees, who saw that the preaching of the Apostles on this point, so opposed to their cherished tenets, was making head among the people. They, therefore, united with the priests in endeavouring to arrest the progress of the Gospel.

3. Forcibly seizing on them, they put them in safe keeping, either in prison or in charge of some guard "till next day," when they were to be brought before the Council. It was now too late in the day to convene a Council.

4. The effect of this persecution was to increase the number of believers among the Jews. "Was made five thousand." This form of expression would seem to signify, not that this number were just now converted and assembled in Solomon's porch ; but, that by the accession of the "many" now converted, to the number of converts already existing, the entire Church now amounted to this number, which shows the wonderful power of God's grace in so short a time after Pentecost. The interval, though not stated, must be very short.

5. The assembly of the Sanhedrim, or great council of the nation, which wielded such authority, probably, the first time, since they condemned our Lord, shows the alarm caused the heads of the Jewish Church by the successes of the Apostles. Hence, they leave **nothing** undone to stop

Text.

1. And as they were speaking to the people, the priests, and the officer of the temple, and the Sadducees, came upon them.

2. Being grieved that they taught the people, and preached in Jesus the resurrection from the dead :

3. And they laid hands upon them, and put them in hold till the next day ; for it was now evening.

4. But many of them who had heard the word, believed ; and the number of the men was made five thousand.

5. And it came to pass on the morrow, that their princes, and

| **Text.** | **Commentary.** |

Text.

ancients, and scribes, were gathered together in Jerusalem:

Commentary.

them. For a full account of the Synedrium, or, as the Talmudists termed it, the *Sanhedrin* (See Matthew xxvi. 57, Commentary). Seventy-one (72) judges constituted the Sanhedrim, the High Priest being always President. It was composed of the High Priests, that is, such as enjoyed the dignity of High Priests, together with the heads of the twenty-four (24) classes into which the Priests were divided—"the ancients or elders, the chiefs of the Tribes and heads of families; the *Scribes*" (See Matthew xxvi. 3). There is no mention of the High Priests here. Hence, the description of the *Sanhedrim* here is incomplete, though, of course, the High Priests formed no inconsiderable portion of the assembly. It was before these same men our Blessed Lord was arraigned; it was they handed him over to Pilate (Matthew xxvi. 50). It was before the same that Peter denied our Lord (Matthew xxii. 70. &c.).

"In Jerusalem"—in Greek, "*into* Jerusalem," conveying that such members of the *Sanhedrim* as were not actually at the time in Jerusalem, repaired thither for the trial of the Apostles.

6. And Annas the high-priest, and Caiphas, and John, and Alexander, and as many as were of the kindred of the high-priest.

6. Having referred, in a general way, to the *Sanhedrim*, he now mentions some of its most prominent members, "Annas, Caiphas," &c (See Luke iii.). "John and Alexander," men clearly of eminence among the body, "and as many," &c., may denote members of the family of Annas and Caiphas, or those nearly related to them.

7. And setting them in the midst, they asked: By what power, or by what name, have you done this?

7. "And setting," &c., assigning them as culprits a place where all the judges or assembled members of the *Sanhedrim* might easily see them.

"What power," from God, or any other source? "Name." What name did you invoke in order to perform this work? Although they knew it was by the power and invocation of the name of Jesus, still they hoped the Apostles might say it was by the Divine power, without specially referring to the name of Jesus; and thus, some confusion as to the distinct name of Jesus might arise (St. Chrysostom, Hom. x. in Acts).

"You," is derisive. You, who are of no consideration.

"This" cure. They would not express what it was.

8. Then Peter, filled with the Holy Ghost, said to them: Ye princes of the people, and ancients, hear:

8. "Filled with the Holy Ghost" denotes a particular actual grace given him on this occasion, strongly influencing him; different or distinct from the habitual graces given him on Pentecost Sunday. Ordinary and habitual grace would not suffice for heroic deeds. A new actual grace is required. Thus, it is said of Sampson, on occasion of his wonderful displays of strength, "the spirit of the Lord came strongly upon him" (Judges xv. 14).

How different is Peter's conduct from what it had been on a former occasion. Then, trembling at the empty chidings of a silly maid, he

Commentary.

denied his Lord. Now, as head of the Apostolic College, boldly confronting the united authority of the Jews, he makes reparation for his former crime by loudly proclaiming his Divine Messiahship, preaching the glorious Resurrection of the Crucified, whose power they were after witnessing in the miraculous cure of the lame man. Showing the deference due to their office, he respectfully addresses them as representatives of *the* supreme authority among the Jews, "Princes of the people," &c. Before the *same* Council, the *same* men, in the *same* place and city, he repaires the scandal he gave in denying his Divine Master.

9. "If we this day," &c. If notwithstanding the evidence of the fact, we are to be treated as criminals, brought to trial and subjected to judicial examination for the good deed of having bestowed the blessing of a perfect cure on the infirm man—which should be rather a subject of praise—and called to render an account of how "he has been made whole." "*If*" conveys surprise at such an extraordinary proceeding, a matter scarcely credible.

10. As you ask by what *name* we did this, be it known to you and all the world, it was by invoking the name and exercising the power "of our Lord Jesus Christ of Nazareth." The term of Nazareth was the epithet by which our Lord was known and scornfully referred to by the Jews. "Crucified," "raised from the dead." The contrast is so striking. *They* put him to death. *God raised* him up from the dead. The accusers now become the accused. With singular intrepidity and courage, St. Peter heretofore so timid, charges them with the greatest crime that could be perpetrated, the murder of their own long-expected Messiah and deliverer, putting to death the author of life.

"Standeth here," &c. It may be that the cured man was imprisoned or guarded with the Apostles, and, very likely, brought forward at the trial to confront them.

11. He shows that the ignominious death and Resurrection of our Lord was predicted by the Prophets. He thus strengthens his argument, especially with the Jews, who valued so much the oracles of their inspired Prophets. The first part of Psalm cxvii., from which the quotation is taken, literally refers to David himself. The second part, also quoted, could refer to our Lord only, in its literal sense, and is quoted by our Lord as applying to Himself (Matthew xxi. 42). Here is a metaphorical allusion to architecture; skilful architects place in the corners of a building the largest and most binding stone, in order to unite and sustain the two walls of the building. It thus gets the most important place. St. Peter applies this prediction to our Lord, who was scornfully rejected by the Jewish rulers, the Priests, and Scribes, the builders of the Synagogue, who should labour for the construction of God's spiritual house, and should, therefore, be the first to

9. *If we this day are examined concerning the good deed done to the infirm man, by what means he hath been made whole;*

10. *Be it known to you all, and to all the people of Israel, that by the name of our Lord Jesus Christ of Nazareth, whom you crucified, whom God hath raised from the dead, even by him this man standeth here before you whole.*

11. *This is the stone which was rejected by you the builders, which is become the head of the corner.*

Text.

Commentary.

receive our Lord. But while they rejected Him, God placed Him as the head "corner stone," sustaining, upholding, and fusing into one the two peoples, Jews and Gentiles, who were to form the Church. He united the old and new dispensations. In Him all the elect of old were justified, no less than the children of the New Law. To this our Lord alludes (Matthew xxi. 42. See Commentary on).

Isaias had predicted it (xxviii. 16). See also 1 Peter 2-4.

12. Neither is there salvation in any other. For there is no other name under heaven given to men, whereby we must be saved.

12. Having assured them in figurative terms, that Christ was the Messiah, St. Peter now, in language devoid of all figure, adds, as a consequence, that in him only can man find eternal Salvation.

"*Name*" often signifies person or being. No one else can save us from the consequences of sin, viz., hell and damnation ; and bestow on us eternal joy and peace in Heaven—the chief object of our Lord's Mission. The Apostle avails himself of this corporal cure to place before the assembled *Sanhedrim* the greater cure and salvation from Hell which our Lord came to bring about.

Our Lord is frequently marked out, "*given*" as the source of this greater and universal Salvation. (John iii. 16), (1 Cor. iii. 5), (1 Tim. ii. 6), &c.

"Must be saved" in the present order of Divine Providence, whereby our Lord is constituted the only source of eternal life and salvation.

13. Now seeing the constancy of Peter and of John, understanding that they were illiterate and ignorant men, they wondered; and they knew them that they had been with Jesus.

13. "*Constancy*," in Greek, *boldness of speech*. implying also intrepidity and courage in circumstances of danger.

"And of John." We have no evidence here that John spoke. Likely he showed by his countenance that he assented to what Peter spoke, and endorsed it. Possibly he may have spoken, though not recorded here.

"Illiterate," without the benefit of education.

"Ignorant," Greek, ἰδιῶται, men leading a private life, not used to speak in public, displaying the character of rudeness, peculiar to the Galileans (Matthew xxvi. 73). Hence, their surprise, "they wondered."

"They knew that they had been with Jesus." Some of the Assessors of the *Sanhedrim* could not but have seen Peter and John on more than one occasion present with the other Apostles when our Lord taught in public. St. John was known to the High Priest (John xviii. 15). Knowing, then, these ignorant, timid Galileans to have been disciples of our Lord, they could not understand the extraordinary change wrought in them, so as to become so eloquent and courageous. This added to their confusion and astonishment.

14. Seeing the man also who had been healed standing with them, they could say nothing against it.

14. The presence of the man, whose cure could not be gainsayed, added to their perplexity as to what course to pursue.

Commentary.

15. "Outside the council," the place where the council was held.

16. "A known,' incontrovertible, miracle. All Jerusalem knows it. We cannot deny it.

17, 18. Fancying these timid Galileans would not dare to violate an order coming from so powerful a body "they charged them," commanded them, not "to speak at all," in Greek, μη φθεγγεσθαι, "*open their lips.*" Little did they take into account the change wrought in them, and the spirit of fortitude that descended on them.

19. The Apostles intrepidly, but modestly, reply, by appealing to themselves if it "was just in the sight of God," who judges all things *truly,* to hear and *obey* them "rather than God," whose will and mandate they were carrying out, to "preach the Gospel to every creature."

20. For knowing for certain that Christ is the Messiah, who commanded them to preach the Gospel, they declare they could not be silent, thereby conveying they could not obey the *Sanhedrim* in this matter.

21. "Threatening them," in a still more stern way, "Not finding how they might punish them." They could not punish them without causing a tumult among the people and losing their own influence.

"Glorified what had been done." In Greek, "glorified *God* for what had been done" on account of the miracle.

Text.

15. But they commanded them to go aside out of the council; and they conferred among themselves,

16. Saying: What shall we do to these men? for indeed a known miracle hath been done by them, to all the inhabitants of Jerusalem: it is manifest, and we cannot deny it.

17. But that it may be no further spread among the people, let us threaten them, that they speak no more in this name to any man.

18. And calling them, they charged them not to speak at all, nor teach in the name of Jesus.

19. But Peter and John answering, said to them: If it be just in the sight of God, to hear you rather than God, judge ye.

20. For we cannot but speak the things which we have seen and heard.

21. But they threatening, sent them away, not finding how they might punish them, because of the people; for all men glorified what had been done, in that which had come to pass.

Text.

22. *For the man was above forty years old, in whom that miraculous cure had been wrought.*

23. *And being let go, they came to their company, and related all that the chief priests and ancients had said to them.*

24. *Who having heard it, with one accord lifted up their voice to God, and said: Lord, thou art he that didst make heaven and earth, the sea, and all things that are in them.*

25. *Who, by the Holy Ghost, by the mouth of our father David, thy servant, hath said: Why did the Gentiles rage, and the people meditate vain things?*

26. *The kings of the earth stood up, and the princes assembled to-*

Commentary.

22. The age of the man, a cripple from his birth, well known to the people, placed the miracle beyond doubt.

23. "Their own company." Their fellow Apostles and possibly others who might have joined them in prayer while Peter and John were under trial.

"Chief Priests and Ancients." They alone gave judgment, not the Scribes, who are passed over here.

24. "Lifted up their voice," that is in prayer, "to God," with one accord, heartily and fervently joining in the prayer, which some one among them, very likely Peter, recited aloud, with the cordial assent of the company there present. Possibly the form of prayer may have been in common use before this, chiefly found in Psalm cxlv. 6. This is the second public prayer addressed by the primitive Church to God— (the first is in *c.* i. 24). They invoke His Omnipotence as one of the chief grounds of hope against their persecutors. They refer to His omniscience (next verse) predicting all their persecutions and trials. The Greek for "Lord," δεσποτα, not κυριος, denotes God's *absolute, ruling* power. κυριος, possessor or master, having propriety right in a thing.

25. They now appeal to God for knowledge, who predicted these things. "By the Holy Ghost" is not found in the Greek. The passage shows that David to whom this Psalm (ii. 1, &c.), (though its author is not mentioned in the Psalm), is here attributed, spoke under the influence of Divine Inspiration. Now, they say, the events predicted have taken place. The Messiah is come; and they appeal to God, who predicted it, for protection.

"*Why have the Gentiles,*" &c. This is supposed to have reference directly and immediately to our Lord. It is, however, held by some that it is only in a *mystical sense*—often the principal sense intended by the Holy Ghost—it refers to Him. At all events, it must be admitted from this passage that it refers to Him chiefly.

"*Gentiles raged.*" Romans and Idumeans. The words of next verse "*against the Lord and His Christ*" expressed in next *v.* 26, are understood here, "and the people," Jewish people, "vain things" combined in foolish and abortive designs, that came to nought. "The Lord," *Jehovah*, and His anointed Son. Our Lord Himself seems to allude to this (Luke xviii. 31, 32).

26. "*The Kings,*" &c. Herod the Idumean, Pontius Pilate, who represented Cæsarism, "*stood up*" to oppose, "*and the Princes assembled*" entered into consultation. This regards, in the first place, the members of the *Sanhedrim*, though the prophecy is not confined to

Commentary.

them exclusively. In some copies, these words are read interrogatively thus, " *Why have the Princes assembled,*" &c.

27. "Of a truth" as an undoubted fact, the above prophecy has been fulfilled in regard to our Lord. "Anointed" as king, as is expressed in the very Psalm ii. 6, "But I am appointed king." In the Hebrew, "I myself appointed my king" "*my king*" because he reigned by my command.

28. "To do" against thy Son Jesus, not whatever they pleased, but "what thy hand," thy power, "and thy counsel," thy will, "decreed to be done" by others (see 11-23). God did not Himself do it. But, by His decree, permitted it *to be done.* The Greek word for "to do" denotes man's guilt; "to be done," γενεσθαι, denotes God's unalterable decree. St. Leo says : *præsciendo quod faciendum esset, Deus non coegit ut fieret . . . . Dominus Jesus Christus in nullo, auctor eorum criminum fuit, sed usus est obcæcatæ plebis insania quomodo et perfidiæ Traditoris, quem ab immanitate concepti sceleris revocare dignatus est* (Sermo 16, de Passione).

29. They pray not to be released from persecutions, but for courage and constancy to enable them not to be deterred from intrepidly preaching and advancing the cause of the Gospel.

30. They also pray for a continuance *of* miraculous powers in the name of Jesus, as evidences of His Divinity, and a means of advancing His glory.

31. "The place was moved." This denotes a violent agitation of the earth, which seems miraculous. It was regarded as a proof that their prayer was heard. Among Jews and Gentiles the quaking of the earth was looked upon as undoubted evidence of the presence of God. As regards the Jews (see Isaias xxix. 6; Ps. xviii. 6; Habacuc iii. 6-11). As regards the Gentiles (see Virgil, *Æneid*, iii. 90).

" *They* were all filled," &c., received a new strengthening impulse to preach with courage the word of God. For this they prayed. They also obtained the second object of their petition, viz., a continuance of the power to work miracles (*v.* 33).

Text.

gether against the Lord, and against his Christ.

27. For of a truth there assembled together in this city against thy holy child, Jesus, whom thou hast anointed, Herod, and Pontius Pilate, with the gentiles and the people of Israel.

28. To do what thy hand and thy counsel decreed to be done.

29. And now, Lord, behold their threatenings, and grant unto thy servants, that with all confidence, they may speak thy word,

30. By stretching forth thy hand to cures, and signs, and wonders to be done by the name of thy holy Son Jesus.

31. And when they had prayed, the place was moved wherein they were assembled, and they were all filled with the Holy Ghost, and they spoke the word of God with confidence.

COMMENTARY ON

Text.

32. *And the multitude of believers had but one heart and one soul: neither did any one say that aught of the things which he possessed, was his own ; but all things were common unto them.*

33. *And with great power did the apostles give testimony of the resurrection of Jesus Christ our Lord ; and great grace was in them all.*

34. *For neither was there any one needy among them. For as many as were owners of lands or houses, sold them, and brought the price of the things they sold,*

Commentary.

32. "The multitude of believers," five thousand (c. iv. 4) "one heart and one soul," indicating the closest and tenderest union. Plutarch, in his life of Cato, quotes a saying, "two friends, *one* soul." This tender union was evidenced in their relations with one another. They showed this in act, in the distribution of their property and their unselfishly giving up what they possessed to relieve the distressed members of their body.

33. Their prayer in regard to the power of working miracles having been heard, they accordingly perform miracles in corroboration of their zealous preaching of the Gospel, especially the Resurrection of Christ, the foundation of all Christian faith. Some interpret "great power" to mean the zealous preaching of the Gospel, as in the case of St. Paul (1 Cor. ii. 4).

"Great grace," &c. By this some understand grace properly so called, which, undoubtedly, was accorded them in an extraordinary degree, and was manifested among the faithful, as shown by their disinterestedness, as in next verse. Others understand it of favour with the people, a sense in which the Greek word, χαρις, is sometimes taken (c. ii. 47). It was very important for them that it should be so, considering what occurred at the meeting of the *Sanhedrim*. Their union and charity towards the poor caused them to be held in great esteem among the people.

Some commentators hold that this *v.* 33 is misplaced owing to the negligence of copyists, that *v.* 34 should immediately follow *v.* 32, or that *v.* 33 should be read parenthetically.

34. The account of the demeanour and qualities of the faithful commencing at *v.* 32 was interrupted in *v.* 33, and is here resumed again.

"For." The corresponding Greek word is understood by Beelen to signify "therefore," expressing a conclusion from *v.* 32. "No one needy" allowed to suffer want. The reason of this is given in a general way in *v.* 32, "all things common," &c. It is explained here more particularly how this was done.

"For as many," &c. The words here used indefinitely by no means convey that all the Christian converts sold their entire property and possessions, giving up their title to them ; but only parted with whatever portion was *necessary* to relieve the pressing wants of their indigent brethren with whom all things were common as to use, so far as was necessary. This, however, was not obligatory, but rather quite voluntary, as appears from the case of Ananias (c. v. 4) ; and the singling out of Joseph (*v.* 36) as a singular instance of generosity would indicate the same. Doubtless, he had many imitators who sold so much of their property as was necessary for the relief of the poor.

This edifying economy practised in the early Christian Church of

Commentary.

Jerusalem was neither general nor permanent. The Apostles, in their intercourse with their Gentile converts, did not deem it wise to establish it. Hence, their appeals to the churches they founded on behalf of the poor. It is not likely that even in the Church of Jerusalem men sold all they possessed—St. John had retained some property (John xix. 27), nor is there any evidence that in Jerusalem they sold all their property, save as far as was necessary to relieve their distressed brethren.

35. "And laid it down," conveys that it was left for disposal "before the feet," &c., in token of respect and reverence. The Apostles finding the duty of distributing their alms becoming too burdensome and distracting, as it interfered with prayer and preaching the word (c. vi. 1, 2), appointed others for this special duty (c. vi. 1, 2).

36. "Joseph," which is sometimes read with a Greek termination, *Joses*. However, the vulgate reading is the more probable. He is different from the Joseph mentioned (i. 23), "by the Apostles *was* surnamed Barnabas." St. Luke explains the meaning of *Barnabas* to be "the son of *consolation*" The strict etymology of the Hebrew word means "son of *Prophecy*." But, St. Luke interprets "son of *consolation*," or *exhortation*, because one of the chief ends of prophecy was to exhort, console; and it would seem that Barnabas afterwards displayed this gift in an eminent degree. Barnabas is most probably singled out because of his exemplary liberality, and of his being afterwards distinguished as a zealous preacher of the Gospel. He is frequently referred to in the Acts as the companion of St. Paul, xi. 22-30; xii. 25; xiii. 1-50.

St. Luke interprets it "the son of consolation," or rather *exhortation*. παρακλησεως. Barnabas was most probably surnamed the son of *exhortation* on account of his talent and success in preaching, and the gift of prophecy with which Barnabas was favoured was given in the Church for instruction unto edification.

"A Levite" descended from Levi. The Levites were employed in the lower services of the temple and assisting the priests in the discharge of their office.

"A Cyprian born." After the captivity the Jewish race were dispersed all over the earth. There were many Jews in the Island of Cyprus (Dion. Lib. 68, 69).

37. "Having land, sold it." By Divine arrangement (Numbers xviii. 20 23) the Levites, as a tribe, were prohibited from holding lands in Judea, except pasture lands in the immediate vicinity of their cities (Numbers xxx. 3, 4). This prohibition did not comprise individuals even in Judea nor the countries outside Judea. This prohibitory law in regard to the Levites had fallen into disuse (Jeremiah xxxii. 7). Moreover, the property of Barnabas may have been in Cyprus. Levites could purchase land and have a title to it in right of their wives.

35. And laid it down before the feet of the apostles. And distribution was made to every one, according as he had need.

36. And Joseph, who, by the apostles, was surnamed Barnabas (which is by interpretation, the son of consolation), a Levite, a Cyprian born,

37. Having land, sold it, and brought the price, and laid it at the feet of the apostles.

CHAPTER V.

1. *But a certain man named Ananias, with Saphira his wife, sold a piece of land.*

2. *And by fraud kept back part of the price of the land, his wife being privy thereunto: and bringing a certain part of it, laid it at the feet of the apostles.*

3. *But Peter said: Ananias, why hath satan tempted thy heart, that thou shouldst lie to the Holy Ghost, and by fraud keep part of the price of the land?*

4. *Whilst it remained, did it not remain to thee? and after it was sold, was it not in thy power? Why hast thou conceived this thing in thy heart? Thou hast not lied to men, but to God.*

5. *And Ananias hearing these words, fell down, and gave up the ghost. And there came great fear upon all that heard it.*

6. *And the young men rising up, removed him, and carrying him out buried him.*

7. *And it was about the space of three hours after, when his wife, not knowing what had happened came in.*

8. *And Peter said to her: Tell me, woman, whether you sold the land for so much? And she said: Yea, for so much.*

9. *And Peter said unto her: Why have you agreed together to tempt the Spirit of the Lord? Behold the feet of them who have buried thy husband are at the door, and they shall carry thee out.*

10. *Immediately she fell down before his feet, and gave up the ghost. And the young men coming in, found her dead: and carried her out, and buried her by her husband.*

11. *And there came great fear upon the whole church, and upon all that heard these things.*

12. *And by the hands of the apostles were many signs and wonders wrought among the people. And they were all with one accord in Solomon's porch.*

13. *But of the rest no man durst join himself unto them; but the people magnified them.*

14. *And the multitude of men and women who believed in the Lord was more increased:*

15. *Insomuch that they brought forth the sick into the streets, and laid them on beds and couches, that when Peter came, his shadow at the least might overshadow any of them, and they might be delivered from their infirmities.*

16. *And there came also together to Jerusalem a multitude out of the neighbouring cities, bringing sick persons, and such as were troubled with unclean spirits; who were all healed.*

17. *Then the high-priest rising up, and all they that were with him (which is the heresy of the Sadducees), were filled with envy.*

18. *And they laid hands on the apostles, and put them in the common prison.*

19. *But an Angel of the Lord by night opening the doors of the prison, and leading them out, said:*

20. *Go, and standing speak in the temple to the people all the words of this life.*

21. *Who having heard this, early in the morning entered into the temple, and taught. And the high-priest coming, and they that were with him, called together the council, and all the ancients of the children of Israel; and they sent to the prison to have them brought.*

22. *But when the ministers came, and opening the prison, found them not there, they returned and told,*

23. *Saying: The prison indeed we found shut with all diligence, and the keepers standing before the doors : but, opening it, we found no man within.*

24. *Now when the officer of the temple, and the chief priests heard these words, they were in doubt concerning them, what would come to pass.*

25. *But one came and told them : Behold the men whom you put in prison, are in the temple standing, and teaching the people.*

26. *Then went the officer with the ministers, and brought them without violence : for they feared the people, lest they should be stoned.*

27. *And when they had brought them, they set them before the council. And the highpriest asked them,*

28. *Saying: Commanding we commanded you that you should not teach in this name : and behold you have filled Jerusalem with your doctrine, and you have a mind to bring the blood of this man upon us.*

29. *But Peter and the apostles answering, said: We ought to obey God rather than men.*

30. *The God of our fathers hath raised up Jesus, whom you put to death, hanging Him upon a tree.*

31. *Him hath God exalted with his right hand, to be prince and saviour, to give repentance to Israel, and remission of sins.*

32. *And we are witnesses of these things, and the Holy Ghost, whom God hath given to all that obey Him.*

33. *When they had heard these things, they were cut to the heart, and they thought to put them to death.*

34. *But one in the council rising up, a Pharisee, named Gamaliel, a doctor of the law respected by all people, commanded the men to be put forth a little while.*

35. *And he said to them : Ye men of Israel, take heed to yourselves what you intend to do, as touching these men.*

36. *For before these days rose up Theodas, affirming himself to be somebody, to whom a number of men, about four hundred, joined themselves: who was slain : and all that believed him were scattered and brought to nothing.*

37. *After this man rose up Judas of Galilee in the days of the enrolling, and drew away the people after him : he also perished : and all, even as many as consented to him, were dispersed.*

38. *And now therefore I say to you, refrain from these men, and let them alone : for if this counsel or this work be of men, it will come to nought.*

39. *But if it be of God, you cannot overthrow it : lest perhaps you be found even to fight against God. And they consented to him.*

40. *And calling in the apostles, after they had scourged them, they charged them that they should not speak at all in the name of Jesus, and they dismissed them.*

41. *And they indeed went from the presence of the council rejoicing that they were accounted worthy to suffer reproach for the name of Jesus.*

42. *And every day they ceased not, in the temple, and from house to house, to teach and preach Christ Jesus.*

ANALYSIS.

In this Chapter, we have an account of the terrible Judgment of God upon Ananias and Sapphira his wife, for having conspired to act a deceitful part in regard to the Apostles (1–10). The terror consequent in the publication of this judgment (11). The miraculous cures wrought by the Apostles circulated far and near (12–16) The violence offered the Apostles who were thrust into prison (12–18). Their liberation by the hand of an Angel, who commanded them to preach to the people (19–21). The confusion and embarrassment of the authorities, who, sending for the Apostles, rebuked them (22–28). The spirited reply and defence of Peter (29–32). The apologetic vindication of the Apostles by Gameliel (33–39). Notwithstanding the unmerited scourging inflicted on them, they still zealously continued to preach (40–42).

Text.	Commentary.
1. *But a certain man named Ananias, with Saphira his wife, sold a piece of land.*	1. "But." marks the contrast which St. Luke institutes between the single minded and open hearted generosity of Barnabas, as described in the foregoing chapter, and the parsimonious avarice of Ananias, which he is now about to describe. "Sold a piece of land." The Greek man properly means, a possession. From *v.* 3, it appears to be property in land.
2. *And by fraud kept back part of the price of the land, his wife being privy thereunto: and bringing a certain part of it, laid it at the feet of the apostles.*	2. "And by fraud kept back." The Greek means, *to set apart for private use,* to *purloin* a portion of what was common or belonged to another. Now, Ananias while professing, in a religious way, to transfer it to the Apostles for common use, secreted, *purloined* a part of it; and was thus guilty of lying hypocrisy and vain glory. Some of the Fathers, among whom St Jerome (Ep. viii., ad. Demetriam), say that he vowed it. His wife, Sapphira, was privy to it, and willingly became a partner in his guilt. For this, they were visited with signal and awful punishment. "Part of the price of the land." "Land" is not in Greek. It is however in the Vulgate. "Laid it at the feet," &c., clearly professing to devote it all to God.
3. *But Peter said: Ananias, why hath satan tempted thy heart, that thou shouldst lie to the Holy Ghost, and by fraud keep part of the price of the land?*	3. Peter, as head of the Church, exercises authority, having received a revelation from above as to Ananias' hypocrisy; similar was the case of Eliseus and Giezi (4 Kings v. 25). "Satan tempted." Why did you consent to Satan's temptation? It was in yielding to the temptation, that the sin consisted. The Greek for "tempted" is "*filled thy heart,*" that is, made you so presumptuous or daring, so strongly incited you, as to "tell a lie," &c. The Greek word for "tell a lie," would signify *to deceive* the Holy Ghost, thus tempting God, as if he could not detect the fraud. It was the Holy Ghost that inspired the Apostles. Hence, the lie was committed against the inspirer of the Apostles (St. Cyril of Jerusalem, Catech. xvi., 8). Others understand it of a vow to devote all to God. By violating it, he lied to God.

Commentary.

4. "Whilst it remained" unsold, "did it not remain," &c., as thine own possession, with full power and title to it, to dispose of it at will.

"And after it was sold," the price was your own. This shows the cession of the goods by the people was quite free and voluntary. No Law to constrain them.

"Why hast thou conceived?" &c. made up thy mind to do such a thing. This shows his liberty of action in the matter.

"Not lied to men," &c., chiefly, not so much to men, "but to God." He lied to men, but it was principally to God, whom they represented. So that the offence against them almost vanished, in presence of the offence to God. It is said above he lied "to the Holy Ghost;" here "lied unto God." Hence, the Holy Ghost is God, and a Divine Person; since it is only to a person, one can tell a lie. A peculiar sin against the Holy Ghost is here specified; just as, by appropriation, certain sins are said to be against God the Father; others, against the Son; so here against the Holy Ghost. This is said by appropriation. For every sin is against each of the Three Persons of the Adorable Trinity. Sins committed against each of the Three Persons, say, the Father, indicate that He is a distinct Person. The same holds in regard to the Son, so does it also, in regard to the Holy Ghost.

5. Seeing his sin, in attempting to deceive God, supernaturally disclosed, Ananias felt the sudden stroke of Divine vengeance would follow; so falling down, he expired. All the circumstances show this was not the result of any natural sudden stroke, but rather the effect of Divine vengeance, and of God's Judgment. The repetition of the same result, a few hours afterwards, in regard to his wife, shows that this double death was a chastisement from God, who followed up the severe rebuke of His representative by a most signal punishment. He wished to terrify others, by placing before the infant Church a striking example of His justice.

"All that heard it," either at the meeting of the faithful, or throughout the city, as the news of this terrible event, very likely, soon spread through the city.

6. "The young men." The article "the" would seem to point to the young men who attended the assembly of the faithful in some official capacity, preparing the place, arranging seats, looking after the books, probably also charged with burying the dead. This will account for their promptitude, on this occasion, to perform spontaneously the office of burying the dead man.

"Removed him," in Greek, "wound him up," in several folds of linen in winding sheets, which, according to Jewish custom, was an immediate preparation for "removing him." Save in case of embalming, the Jews always, for sanitary reasons, owing to the heat of the climate, and to avoid legal defilement arising from contact with a corpse (Numbers xix. 11, &c.), had their dead buried at once.

Text.

4. Whilst it remained, did it not remain to thee? and after it was sold, was it not in thy power? Why hast thou conceived this thing in thy heart? Thou hast not lied to men, but to God.

5. And Ananias hearing these words, fell down and gave up the ghost. And there came great fear upon all that heard it.

6. And the young men rising up, removed him, and carrying him out, buried him.

Text.

7. *And it was about the space of three hours after, when his wife, not knowing what had happened came in.*

8. *And Peter said to her: Tell me, woman, whether you sold the land for so much? And she said: Yea, for so much.*

9. *And Peter said unto her: Why have you agreed together to tempt the Spirit of the Lord? Behold the feet of them who have buried thy husband are at the door, and they shall carry thee out.*

10. *Immediately she fell down before his feet and gave up the ghost. And the young men coming in, found her dead: and carried her out, and buried her by her husband.*

11. *And there came great fear upon the whole church, and upon all that heard these things.*

12. *And by the hands of the apostles were many signs and wonders wrought among the people. And they were all with one accord in Solomon's porch.*

Commentary.

7. Sapphira, who was a sharer in Ananias' guilt, was visited with a like punishment.

8. "For so much." The precise sum specified by Ananias.

9. "Agreed together." Conspired "to tempt the Spirit of the Lord." One is said to tempt God when he unnecessarily, tests or puts to trial, any of God's attributes, power, wisdom, &c. Here, it was testing his omniscience, as he spoke through the Apostles, whether he knew of the fraud committed in secret.

10. "Behold the feet," &c. The footsteps of the young men just returning, were heard. Peter, with a clear Prophetic insight, commands beforehand, that the same sad function should be performed in her case, as well as in that of her husband. Clearly, it was the result of Divine interposition, which Peter announces beforehand. How awfully sudden is God's Judgment sometimes?

11. "The whole church," "the brethren" (i. 15), "all the believers" (ii. 44), who gradually increased so as to form the mystical body of Christ.

12. By the hands," &c., by the Apostles themselves. "Many signs," &c., numerous miracles "in Solomon's porch." This was covered, adjoining the Temple to the East, called "Solomon's porch," either because originally built by Solomon—it was left undestroyed by the Chaldeans, and preserved amidst the ruins of the Temple—or, because it was built anew on the site of the porch built by Solomon, on the Eastern side of the hill (Josephus, de Bello, c. vi.) ; (iii. 11. See Notes).
"With one accord." They, doubtless, were there for the purposes of public worship.

Commentary.

13, 14. "But of the rest." There is a great diversity of opinion, who are referred to here. Some say "the rest" mean, those in good circumstances, such as Ananias. For they are contrasted with the "people" in general who "magnified" the Apostles. Others understand by them, the unbelieving portion of the inhabitants of Jerusalem, who had no wish to become converted. These kept aloof; while the faithful and such as had any desire to embrace the faith, joined familiarly with them. While the influential portion kept aloof, as well as those who had no desire to become converted, the mass of "the people magnified them," on account of their miracles and teaching. The result was, that they joined the Church, every day, from both sexes, men and women.

15. "Insomuch that they brought," &c. Owing to the immediate connexion of this verse with what is recorded, *v.* 12, Commentators generally hold that *vv.* 13, 14 are to be read parenthetically, connecting the words of this *v.* immediately with *v.* 12. This seems a very natural connexion. Many miracles were wrought by the Apostles (*v.* 12). "Insomuch that they brought," &c., "they brought forth," that is, the friends of the sick did so.

"His shadow might overshadow them." This shows the popular belief in the power of St. Peter to work miracles. He is specially noted, because it was he cured the lame man in the temple (*c.* iii. 4), and moreover, he had been most prominent in his discourses, and, possibly, it might have been known that he was divinely constituted the head of the Apostolic College, the rock of the Church. Something similar to this is recorded (Acts xix. 12), where it is said contact with the aprons and handkerchiefs brought from the body of St. Paul effected cures, also, Matthew ix. 21, 22, in which the exercise of our Lord's power in this respect is spoken of.

16. "Out of the neighbouring cities," attracted by the rumours that were bruited abroad regarding Peter's miraculous powers.

"Sick, and such as were troubled with unclean spirits." Those troubled with unclean spirits are put down as different from "the sick." For a full explanation of this possession by devils (See Commentary, St. Mark *c.* i. 23-26). "Unclean spirits," because they incited men to acts of impurity.

"Who were all healed," of the infirmities which demoniac possession entailed.

17. "The High Priest." Probably Caiphas, a determined enemy of our Lord. "Rising up" refers to mental excitement, which roused him to action. This also applies to the assessors of the Sadducean sect, who shared in his views. "They that were with him." The Sadducees were specially hostile to our Lord and His doctrines. It would seem they held high offices among the Jews, and, at this time, their party was pre-

Text.

13. But of the rest no man durst join himself unto them; but the people magnified them.

14. And the multitude of men and women who believed in the Lord was more increased:

15. Insomuch that they brought forth the sick into the the streets, and laid them on beds and couches, that when Peter came, his shadow at the least might overshadow any of them, and they might be delivered from their infirmities.

16. And there came also together to Jerusalem a multitude out of the neighbouring cities, bringing sick persons, and such as were troubled with unclean spirits; who were all healed.

17. Then the high-priest rising up, and they that were with him (which is the heresy of the

Text.	**Commentary.**

Sadducees,) were filled with envy.

dominant in the *Sanhedrim*. One of their chief tenets was the denial of the resurrection of the body, which the Apostles preached with such success. This chiefly excited them and stung them with envy.

18. And they laid hands on the apostles, and put them in the common prison.

18. "Common prison," as if manifestly guilty, not a *private* prison, for examining into their conduct. Here, they are supposed to be guilty, without further inquiry.

19. But an Angel of the Lord by night opening the doors of the prison, and leading them out, said:

20. Go, and standing speak in the temple to the people all the words of this life.

19, 20. "An angel," &c. Here, God miraculously interposed, when all seemed to be lost. This happened during the night, and doubtless was known the following day throughout the city.

"In the Temple"—the most conspicuous place, where their miraculous liberation could be known to all.

"All the words." All the doctrines, "of this life," spiritual and eternal life, of which Christ's Resurrection was a pledge; on account of teaching this, they were cast into prison.

21. Who having heard this, early in the morning entered the temple, and taught. And the high-priest coming, and they that were with him, called together

21. "Early in the morning." Greek, *day break.*

"All the ancients of the children of Israel." Who these were, as contra-distinguished from the members of the Council or *Sanhedrim* is not agreed upon. They are supposed by many to be men of great repute and experience among the Jews, and although not members of the *Sanhedrim*, they were, on some important occasions, invited to attend as assessors and advisers of the Council. This was considered the best course to be adopted in certain critical cases of emergency.

the council, and all the ancients of the children of Israel: and they sent to the prison to have them brought.

22. But when the ministers came, and opening the prison, found them not there; they returned and told,

23. Saying: The prison indeed we found shut with all diligence, and the keepers standing before the doors; but opening it, we found no man within.

24. Now when the officer of the temple, and the chief priests heard these words, they

24. "Officers of the Temple" (see c. iv. 1). "They were in doubt," a state of *perplexity*, not knowing what to think of the whole affair,—as they did not seem to recognise the hand of God miraculously stretched forth—or what would it all result in.

were in doubt concerning them, what would come to pass.

25. But one came and told them: Behold the men whom you put in prison, are in the temple standing, and teaching the people.

26. Then went the officer with the ministers, and brought them without violence; for they feared the people, lest they should be stoned.

27. And when they had brought them, they set them before the council. And the high-priest asked them,

28. Saying: Commanding we commanded you that you

28. "Commanding, commanded," *most strictly* commanded you. This is read interrogatively in some Greek copies. Did we *not strictly* command you?

Commentary.

" In this name," the name of Jesus, or proclaim His doctrines.

" To bring the blood," &c. Make us guilty of the crime of having murdered him. make us responsible for his death.

29. Peter answering in his own name, and that of his fellow Apostles, who were of the same mind with him.

" Ought to obey God," &c. In a conflict of injunctions, God is to be obeyed first, and man's commands if opposed to His, utterly disregarded. The Apostles thus inform the *Sanhedrim* of their Divine commission to preach the Gospel.

30. " The God of our Fathers," conveys an allusion to the several prophecies regarding Jesus. " Hath raised up Jesus " from the dead (c. iii. 15 ; iv. 10). " Hanging Him on a tree," the tree of the Cross. The antithesis is striking. They put Him to death. God raised Him up from the dead.

31. " Exalted " in his glorious Ascension. " To be Prince and Saviour." These two words are supposed by some eminent Commentators (Beelen, &c.) to convey one idea, " the Prince of Salvation," the author of our salvation, as expressed by the Apostle (Hebrews ii. 10). As " Prince," He exercises His power and dominion now seated at the right hand of His Father, in giving the means of salvation, in tendering the grace of repentance, and bestowing on men the remission of their sins. St. Peter having fearlessly charged them, without in the slightest degree, extenuating the grossest guilt in crucifying their Messiah, here holds out hopes of pardon. From motives of prudence, however, he confines the great blessings of salvation to " Israel." It might not be prudent for him at *present* to extend these blessings to the *Gentiles*. He does so, however, later on (c. xi. 18).

32. " We are witnesses of these things," viz.: Our Lord's Resurrection and Ascension, and the other wonderful events of His sacred life (i. 8-22 ; ii. 32).

" And the Holy Ghost." So is also the Holy Ghost, who could testify only to truth. To these things he bore testimony by descending on those miraculously with His several gifts of tongues, &c., " who obey Him," and embrace the faith preached by the Apostles, whom He guided and inspired.

33. " Cut to the heart." The Greek word means *cut with a saw*, conveying the idea of violent agitation and rage. " They thought," &c. They deliberately resolved to put them to death.

Text.

should not teach in this name : and behold you have filled Jerusalem with your doctrine, and you have a mind to bring the blood of this man upon us.

29. But Peter and the apostles answering, said: We ought to obey God rather than men.

30. The God of our fathers hath raised up Jesus, whom you put to death, hanging him upon a tree.

31. Him hath God exalted with his right hand, to be prince and saviour, to give repentance to Israel, and remission of sins.

32. And we are witnesses of these things, and the Holy Ghost, whom God hath given to all that obey him.

33. When they had heard these things, they were cut to the heart, and they thought to put them to death

34. *But one in the council rising up, a Pharisee, named Gamaliel, a doctor of the law, respected by all the people, commanded the men to be put forth a little while.*

35. *And he said to them: Ye men of Israel, take heed to yourselves what you intend to do, as touching these men.*

36. *For before these days rose up Theodas, affirming himself to be somebody, to whom a number of men, about four hundred, joined themselves: who was slain: and all that believed him were scattered and brought to nothing.*

37. *After this man rose up Judas of Galilee in the days of the enrolling, and drew away the people after him: he also perished; and all, even as many as consented to him, were dispersed.*

34. " Rising up " from the seat which he occupied in the Council, in order to address his colleagues of the *Sanhedrim* "a Pharisee." The High Priest and many members of the Council were Sadducees, determined enemies of our Lord, and violently opposed to the doctrine of the Resurrection. The Pharisees actively differed with them on the doctrine of the resurrection of the dead, so zealously preached by the Apostles. "Gamaliel," only once more is there mention of him in the Scriptures (xxii. 3) when he is said to have been the teacher of St. Paul, "a Doctor of the Law," an expounder and interpreter of the law of Moses, "respected by all the people." His advice and opinion, therefore, carried great weight. He is supposed by some to have been in secret a follower of our Lord, or at least favourably disposed towards the believers—"a little while," quite usual in regard to men on their trial (iv. 15).

36. " Before these days," how long cannot be accurately ascertained. Gamaliel prefaces his prudent counsel by quoting a two-fold precedent to enforce what he was going to advise.

"Theodas." This was a common name among the Jews. But who he was or when he raised the standard of revolution is not known. The fact of the case being mentioned before that of Judas of Galilee would show that he rendered himself remarkable before Judas appeared.

The event here referred to must be different from the insane attempt at revolution by one Theodas recorded by Josephus (Anal. xx. 5-1). The dates are quite different. The occurrence recorded by Josephus took place after this, while Fadus was Procurator of Judea, in the reign of the Emperor Claudius, whereas this referred to by Gamaliel occurred in the reign of Tiberius. There may have been several such attempts at revolution under different men, called Theodas, of whom there were, doubtless, several in Judea which Josephus may have passed over as not deserving of notice. There is, therefore, no necessity for reconciling the account given by Josephus as to chronology with the account given here by St. Luke, as they likely referred to different events brought about by different men altogether. At all events, even if they referred to the same event, St. Luke, apart from inspiration, is as respectable an authority any day as Josephus.

37. "Judas of Galilee." Josephus (Antiq. xvii., chap. x.) speaks of him as a Galilean from the place where he resided, and (Antiq. xviii. 1) as a *Gaulonite* from the place of his birth, as he was originally from *Gamala.*

"In the days of the enrolling." There is reference not to the *first* census ordered by Augustus (Luke ii. 2) when Our Lord was born (see Luke ii. 2, Commentary), but of a census later on under Cyrinus, then ordinary Governor of Syria, to which Judea was annexed after the banishment of Archelaus. Cyrinus himself came into Judea to take an account of the property of the inhabitants and to dispose of Archelaus' property. He now acted as *ordinary* Governor; whereas, at the *first* census, he acted in capacity of *extraordinary* commissioner to assist

Commentarp.   **Tert.**

Sentius Saturninus, who at the time of this first enrolling was ordinary Governor of Syria. It was on the occasion of this second census that Judas, taking with him as associate, *Saddouak*, a Pharisee, raised the standard of revolt, and perished with a multitude of his followers. His was the beginning of a series of revolts that ended in the final destruction of Jerusalem and utter ruin of the nation, under Titus.

38. "And now," and as regards the present case, "refrain from these men," from any threats, violence or punishment in regard to them. "Let them alone," unharmed. "This counsel or this work," this plan, or work which the Apostles propose carrying out, "be from men," a mere human device, like the cases just quoted, "it will come to nought" of itself, without any interference on the part of the *Sanhedrim*.

39. "Cannot overthrow it." God is too powerful and unchangeable to allow his design to be frustrated by weakness and malice.

"They consented to him." Allowed themselves to be persuaded by him. This they did in part, so far as putting them to death was concerned; but not altogether, as they treated them badly; they "scourged them." Likely they did so to uphold their own authority with the people who knew they had issued several mandates which the Apostles justly undervalued.

40. "Scourged them." Inflicted the number of stripes allowed by law (2 Cor. xi. 24). Thus was verified Our Lord's prediction in their regard (Mat. x. 17). It was meant to subject them to humiliation and cast a stigma on the Christian profession.

The counsel and reasoning of Gamaliel in this famous dilemma were excellent in regard to this *present particular* case. But, taken in the *general* application, by no means admissible, liable to be abused by heretics, as well as by the enemies of religion and social order, to claim full unrestrained liberty for the propagation, and unrestricted practice of immoral teachings and practices, which those charged with authority in Church and State have a perfect right, nay, are bound, in virtue of their office, to prevent and check by every legitimate means.

41. "Accounted worthy." Deserving of the high Christian privilege of being assimilated to their Lord, who suffered ignominy and reproaches in the cause of justice.

42. Far from being deterred from preaching Jesus, as the *Sanhedrim* expected, as the result of their humiliation, they, on the contrary, persevered in preaching both publicly and privately.

38. *And now therefore I say to you, refrain from these men, and let them alone: for if this counsel or this work be of men, it will come to nought.*

39. *But if it be of God, you cannot overthrow it; lest perhaps you be found even to fight against God. And they consented to him.*

40. *And calling in the apostles, after they had scourged them, they charged them that they should not speak at all in the name of Jesus, and they dismissed them.*

41. *And they indeed went from the presence of the council rejoicing, that they were accounted worthy to suffer reproach for the name of Jesus.*

42. *And every day they ceased not, in the temple, and from house to house, to teach and preach Christ Jesus.*

E

1. *And in those days, the number of the disciples increasing, there arose a murmuring of the Grecians against the Hebrews, for that their widows were neglected in the daily ministration.*

2. *Then the twelve, calling together the multitude of the disciples, said: It is not fit that we should leave the word of God, and serve tables.*

3. *Therefore, brethren, look ye out among you seven men of good reputation, full of the Holy Ghost and wisdom, whom we may appoint over this business.*

4. *But we will give ourselves continually to prayer, and to the ministry of the word.*

5. *And the discourse pleased all the multitude. And they chose Stephen, a man full of faith and the Holy Ghost, and Philip, and Prochorus, and Nicanor, and Timon, and Parmenas, and Nicolas, a proselyte of Antioch.*

6. *These they placed in the presence of the apostles: and they, praying, imposed hands upon them.*

7. *And the word of the Lord increased; and the number of the disciples was multi- plied very much in Jerusalem: a great multitude also of the priests obeyed the faith.*

8. *Now, Stephen, full of grace and fortitude, did great wonders and miracles among the people.*

9. *But certain men of the synagogue, that is called of the Libertines, and of the Cyre- neans, and of the Alexandrians, and of those that were of Cilicia and Asia, rose up disputing with Stephen:*

10. *And they were not able to resist the wisdom and the spirit with which he spoke.*

11. *Then they suborned men to say, that they had heard him speaking words of blasphemy against Moses and against God.*

12. *They stirred up, therefore, the people, and the ancients, and the Scribes; and running together, they took him, and brought him before the council.*

13. *And they set up false witnesses, who said: This man ceaseth not to speak words against the holy place and the law:*

14. *For we have heard him say, that this Jesus of Nazareth shall destroy this place, and shall change the traditions which Moses delivered to us.*

15. *And all they who sat in the council, looking earnestly upon him, saw his face as it were the face of an Angel.*

ANALYSIS.

In this chapter we have an account of the election and ordination of the seven first Deacons to discharge certain functions specially assigned to them (1-6). The large number of conversions (7). The triumph of Stephen over his adversaries in disputa- tion (8-10). The false accusations brought against him by false witnesses suborned for the purpose (11-15).

Commentary.

1. "And in these days." When the Apostles, after having been liber-ated from prison, were intrepidly preaching the Gospel of Jesus Christ (c. v. 42), whereby the number of the faithful was increased.

"There arose a murmur." The Greek word, γογγυσμος—means *secret* or *whispering complaints*. "Of the Greeks against the Hebrews," by "the Greeks," or *Hellenists* are meant, as opposed to "the Hebrews," not Christian proselytes from among the Gentiles—there is no evidence that the Gentiles were as yet admitted into the Church—but converted Jews born and living outside Palestine, using the Greek language in their daily social intercourse with one another, and employing the Septuagint in their synagogues and public worship. These came up to Jerusalem for the Great Festivals.

"Hebrews," natives of Palestine, who, in the ordinary concerns of life and public worship, used the Aramaic dialect of Palestine, termed in Scripture, the Hebrew language.

"For that their widows," destitute widows were, specially marked out among the poor, in the infant Church, for special care and consider-ation.

"Were neglected," overlooked, not treated impartially, or, as liberally as the Hebrew widows.

"In the daily ministration," distribution of alms, contributed in com-mon, according to the usage of the time, to provide the indigent with food, clothing and other necessaries of life.

2. "The twelve" Apostles. Matthias had been associated with the eleven.

"The multitude," of the murmurers.

"It is not reason," *fitting* or *becoming*. "Leave the word of God," give up the preaching of the Gospel, which might be interrupted by their having charge of temporal affairs.

"And serve tables," occupied with temporalities, money, food, clothing, &c.

3. "Wherefore," to put an end to complaints, "look ye out among you," select from among yourselves, from your own body, as to leave no ground for suspicion or complaint.

"Seven, men," &c., who bear a well-known character for integrity.

"Full of the Holy Ghost," as far as can be seen from external con-duct men distinguished for piety emanating from the Holy Ghost.

"Wisdom," prudence in the management of the duties appertaining to the office to be assigned to them.

"Whom we may appoint over this business," of impartially distri-buting the alms destined for the relief of the poor—The people select or recommend ; but, the Apostles retain the right of appointing.

4. "Continually." The Greek word means, persevering assiduity, "to prayer." The article, prefixed in the Greek, would show there is

Text.

1. And in those days, the number of the disciples in-creasing, there arose a mur-muring of the Grecians against the Hebrews, for that their wi-dows were neglected in the daily minis-tration.

2. Then the twelve calling together the multitude of the disciples, said: It is not fit that we should leave the word of God, and serve tables.

3. Therefore, brethren, look ye out among your seven men of good reputa-tion, full of the Holy Ghost and wisdom, whom we may appoint over this business.

4. But we will give our-

*selves continu-
ally to prayer,
and to the
ministry of the
word.*

question of public liturgical prayer, of which the chief part was, the Holy and Eucharistic sacrifice. Prayer is a very necessary part of a Pastor's duty, in order to secure for his labours the blessing of God, from whom must come the success and fruit of his labours. *Manent itaque* (says St. Bernard, Ep. cc. i.) *verbum, exemplum, oratio, major autem his est oratio nam et operi and voci gratiam et efficaciam promeretur.*

*5. And the
discourse
pleased all the
multitude.
And they chose
Stephen, a man
full of faith
and of the Holy
Ghost, and
Philip, and
Prochorus, and
Nicanor, and
Timon, and
Parmenas,
and Nicolas, a
proselyte of
Antioch.*

5. "The saying," advice or injunction. "Stephen," who proved himself in every way fitted for this office. He was the first afterwards to seal with his blood, his testimony of Jesus Christ. Hence, regarded, as the first martyr, and deservedly placed first on the list. "Nicolas" is said by some, to have been the founder of the sect of Nicolaites, referred to in terms of condemnation (Revel. ii. 6, 15.) This however, is denied by others.

"A proselyte of Antioch," born of Gentile parents, he embraced Judaism, thus becoming a Jewish Proselyte. He afterwards became a Christian. The names are all Greek. But, as the Hebrews at this time, assumed Greek names, likely, some of the seven selected were from among the Hebrew Christians.

*6. These they
placed in the
presence of the
apostles: and
they, praying,
imposed hands
upon them.*

6. "And they praying," &c. By prayer and imposition of hands, the Apostles conferred on them the Sacred Order of Deaconship Although not *de fide*, it is theologically certain, that Deacons receive the Sacrament of Orders. The Council of Trent defines (ss. xxiii can. vi.) that besides Bishops and Priests, Ministers also (surely, these mean *Deacons*), belong to the divinely instituted Hierarchy of the Catholic Church. The qualities required in Deacons by the Apostles, "full of the Holy Ghost, wisdom," &c., would show that their destination was something higher than mere secular ministrations. The same ceremonies are employed in their regard, as in the ordination of Bishops and Priests, viz.: imposition of hands and prayer. Deacons exercised spiritual functions, Stephen preached, Philip baptized, *c.* viii. Whenever St. Paul speaks of Deacons, he does so, in connexion with Bishops.

St. Luke, no doubt, does not distinctly state, that Deaconship was a Sacred Institution. He only makes the exercise of the ministry of relieving widows, the *occasion* of describing the institution of Deacons. However, he does not confine their functions to this exclusively, though, indeed, it was a great exercise of Christian charity.

*7. And the
word of the
Lord increased;
and the number
of the disciples
was multiplied
very much in
Jerusalem: a
great multi-
tude also of the
priests obeyed
the faith.*

7. "The word of God," &c. The preaching of the Gospel was attended with great success, of which St. Luke gives a signal example in the conversion of a "great multitude of Priests," doubtless, the most determined opponents of the Gospel. These joined the Church, "obeyed the faith," which requires obedience of the haughty intellect and stubborn will of men. (2 Cors. x. 5, &c.)

Commentary.

8. By a sudden transition, St. Luke gives the history of Stephen, first on the list of those selected for Deaconship, and describes the events which led to his death, "full of grace," the gifts of the Holy Ghost, and especially the gift of "fortitude."

9. "Now there arose," stood up to resist him.

"Synagogues of the Libertines. (For the meaning of "synagogue." See Matthew iv. 23, Commentary.)

"Wherever a sufficient number of Jews could be found in the several Provinces to form a congregation they had their synagogue, and sometimes more than one in towns. Jerusalem alone, in the time of our Lord, is said to have 480 synagogues. The foreign Jews resorting to Jerusalem either for doctrine or business purposes, or for studying the Sacred and religious ordinances, had, each nation, their synagogues, to which they resorted for religious purposes.

"Of Libertines." By these are commonly understood manumitted slaves, or freedmen who were brought to Rome as prisoners of war, and thus reduced to a condition of slavery, particularly in the time of Pompey. Some of these slaves, on becoming freedmen and receiving their liberty, returned to their own country and formed a synagogue of their own, called of the *Libertini* or Freedmen, which their descendants frequented afterwards.

"And of the Cyrenians." Jews from Cyrene in Africa, who had a synagogue of their own.

"And of the Alexandrians." Jews from Alexandria.

"Cilicia," its capital Tharsus, was the native city of St. Paul. Hence, it is by no means unlikely, that this distinguished disciple of Gamaliel was among the disputants here referred to.

"Asia." Pro-Consular Asia. Cicero pro Flacco says. "*Asia vertra, ut opinor, Constat ex Phrygia, Myria, Caria, et Lydia.*"

10. "Not able to resist," or advance any solid reply in refutation of his reasoning.

"The wisdom and the spirit," the wisdom of the spirit, that spoke through him, as his organ. Hundreds.

For "spirit that spoke," the Greek is, *the spirit by which he spoke*, under whose influence he spoke "*non vos estis qui loquimini*," &c. (Matthew x. 20).

11. "Then they suborned," &c. Unable to reply to the arguments of Stephen, they become enraged, and determine on his destruction by having recourse to violent measures. In their fury, they put forward wicked men for this purpose to make false charges against him. "against Moses," their divinely commissioned Legislator, "and against God," by whom Moses was commissioned. Blasphemy against Moses was chiefly levelled against God Himself.

Text.

8. *Now Stephen, full of grace and fortitude, did great wonders and miracles among the people.*

9. *But certain men of the synagogue, that is called of the Libertines, and of the Cyreneans, and of the Alexandrians, and of those that were of Cilicia and Asia, rose up, disputing with Stephen:*

10. *And they were not able to resist the wisdom and the spirit with which he spoke.*

11. *Then they suborned men to say, that they had heard him speaking words of blasphemy against Moses and against God.*

Text.

12. *They stirred up, therefore, the people, and the ancients, and the Scribes; and running together, they took him, and brought him before the council.*

13. *And they set up false witnesses, who said: This man ceaseth not to speak words against the holy place and the law:*

14. *For we have heard him say, that this Jesus of Nazareth shall destroy this place, and shall change the traditions which Moses delivered to us.*

15. *And all they who sat in the council, looking earnestly upon him, saw his face as it were the face of an Angel.*

Commentary.

12. "The ancients," the members of the *Sanhedrim*. The more easily to accomplish their object, and gratify jealous revenge, the enemies of Stephen created a popular movement against him.

"Brought him to the Council," the *Sanhedrim*, the great Council of the nation, supreme in matters of religion (Matthew xxvi. 3-57). Probably, an extraordinary meeting was summoned for the occasion.

"Running together, they took him." Suddenly coming on him, probably when engaged through the city in the duties of his office.

13. False witnesses," who not only quoted whatever Stephen might have said relative to the cessation of Jewish rites and ceremonies, which was, surely to take place; but, perverted them to a false meaning, never intended by St. Stephen, thus acting the part of "false witnesses."

14. St. Stephen only gave expression to the utterances of our Lord Himself. Our Lord never said He would destroy the temple. He only predicted its destruction by the Gentiles, on account of the crimes of the Jews.

"And shall change." Utterly abolish the Jewish ritual observances in regard to festivals and sacrifices. Our Lord predicted these would cease: Stephen went no farther. A similar false charge was alleged against our Lord Himself, at His Passion by suborned witnesses (Matthew xxvi. 61).

The Jews were particularly sensitive in regard to everything that affected the Law of Moses.

15. "Looking on him" steadfastly, curious to see what reply he would make to charges so grave.

"As if it had been the face of an angel." His face reflected a majestic beauty truly heavenly. "*Abundantia Cordis*" (says St. Hilary, Hom. in Steph.) "*transierat in decus corporis et in facie pulchistudinis candor, splendorque animi ejus exundabat.*" His countenance was such as angels present when they appear in human form. It was radiant with glory and heavenly splendour, displaying candour and a calm reliance on God's Providence. The obstinate hearts of his furious persecutors were but little affected or moved by it.

CHAPTER VII.

*Paternal dealings of,
with Jews.*

1. *Then the high-priest said: Are these things so?*
2. *And he said: Ye men, brethren, and fathers, give ear.　The God of glory appeared to our father Abraham, when he was in Mesopotamia, before he dwelt in Charan:*

Cal

3. *And he said to him: Go forth out of thy country and from thy kindred, and come into the land which I will show thee.*

Abra

4. *Then he went out of the land of the Chaldeans, and dwelt in Charan: and from thence, after his father was dead, he removed him into this land, in which you now dwell.*
5. *And he gave him no inheritance in it, no not the pace of a foot: but he promised to give it him in possession, and to his seed after him, when he had not a son.*
6. *And God said to him: That his seed should sojourn in a strange country, and that they should bring them under bondage, and treat them ill for four hundred years:*
7. *And the nation which they shall serve I will judge, said the Lord: and after these things they shall go out, and shall serve me in this place.*
8. *And he gave him the covenant of circumcision: and so he begot Isaac, and circumcised him the eighth day; and Isaac Jacob; and Jacob the twelve patriarchs.*
9. *And the patriarchs, moved with envy, sold Joseph into Egypt: and God was with him.*
10. *And he delivered him out of all his tribulations, and gave him favour and wisdom in the sight of Pharao king of Egypt; and he appointed him governor over Egypt, and over all his house.*
11. *Now there came a famine over all Egypt and Chanaan, and great tribulation: and our fathers found no food.*
12. *But when Jacob had heard that there was corn in Egypt, he sent our fathers the first time:*
13. *And at the second time Joseph was known by his brethren; and his kindred was made known to Pharao.*
14. *And Joseph, sending, called thither Jacob his father, and all his kindred, seventy-five souls.*
15. *So Jacob went down into Egypt: and he died, and our fathers.*
16. *And they were translated to Sichem, and were laid in the sepulchre which Abraham bought for a sum of money of the son of Hemor, the father of Sichem.*
17. *And when the time of the promise drew near, which God had promised to Abraham, the people increased and were multiplied in Egypt.*
18. *Till another king arose in Egypt, who knew not Joseph.*

Persecution

19. *This same, dealing deceitful with our race, afflicted our fathers, that they should expose their children, to the end they might not be kept alive.*

Joseph's

20. *At the same time was Moses born, and he was acceptable to God; and he was nourished three months in his father's house.*
21. *But he being exposed, Pharao's daughter took him up, and nourished him for her own son.*

Host

22. *And Moses was instructed in all the wisdom of the Egyptians; and he was powerful in his words and in his aceas.*

me

23. *And when he was full forty years old, it came into his heart to visit his brethren the children of Israel.*

*o
pa.*

24. *And having seen a certain man suffer an injury, he defended him; and striking the Egyptian, he avenged him who suffered the injury.*

25. *And he thought that his brethren understood that God by his hand would save them ; but they understood it not.*

26. *And the next day he showed himself to them that were at strife, and would have reconciled them in peace, saying : Men, ye are brethren ; why hurt ye one another ?*

27. *But he that did the injury to his neighbour thrust him away, saying : Who hath appointed thee prince and judge over us ?*

28. *Wilt thou kill me, as thou didst yesterday kill the Egyptian ?*

29. *And Moses fled upon this word, and became a stranger in the land of Madian, where he begat two sons.*

30. *And when forty years were expired, there appeared to him, in the desert of Mount Sina, an Angel in a flame of fire in a bush.*

31. *And Moses, seeing it, wondered at the sight : and as he drew near to view it, the voice of the Lord came to him, saying :*

32. *I am the God of thy fathers, the God of Abraham, the God of Isaac, and the God of Jacob. And Moses, being terrified, durst not behold.*

33. *And the Lord said to him : Loose thy shoes from off thy feet ; for the place wherein thou standest is holy ground.*

34. *Seeing I have seen the affliction of my people, which is in Egypt, and I have heard their groaning, and am come down to deliver them : and now come, and I will send thee into Egypt.*

35. *This Moses whom they refused, saying : Who hath appointed thee prince and judge ? him God sent a prince and redeemer, by the hand of the Angel who appeared to him in the bush.*

36. *He brought them out, doing wonders and signs in the land of Egypt, and in the Red Sea, and in the desert for forty years.*

37. *This is that Moses who said to the children of Israel : A Prophet will God raise up to you out of your own brethren, as myself : him shall you hear.*

38. *This is he who was in the church in the wilderness, with the Angel who spoke to him on Mount Sina, and with our fathers : who received the words of life to give us ;*

39. *To whom our fathers would not be obedient, but repulsed him, and in their hearts returned back into Egypt.*

40. *Saying to Aaron : Make us gods to go before us : for as to this Moses, who brought us out of the land of Egypt, we know not what has become of him.*

41. *And they made a calf in those days, and offered sacrifice to this idol, and rejoicing in the works of their own hands.*

42. *And God turned, and gave them up to serve the host of heaven ; as it is written in the book of the prophets : Did you offer victims and sacrifices to me for forty years in the desert, O house of Israel ?*

43. *And you took unto you the tabernacle of Moloch, and the star of your god Rempham, figures which you made to adore them : and I will carry you away beyond Babylon.*

44. *The tabernacle of the testimony was with our fathers in the desert, as God ordained for them, speaking to Moses that he should make it according to the form which he had seen :*

45. *Which also our fathers, receiving, brought in with Jesus into the possession of the gentiles, whom God expelled from the face of our fathers, until the days of David :*

46. *Who found grace in the sight of God, and desired that he might find a tabernacle for the God of Jacob.*

47. *But Solomon built him a house.*

48. *But the Most High dwelleth not in houses made by hands, as the prophet saith :*

49. *Heaven is my throne, and the earth is my footstool.   What house will you build for me? saith the Lord; or what is the place of my rest?*

50. *Hath not my hands made all these things?*

51. *With a stiff neck and uncircumcised heart and ears you always resist the Holy Ghost: as your fathers did, so do you also.*

52. *Which of the prophets have not your fathers persecuted? And they have slain those who foretold of the coming of the Just One; of whom you have been now the betrayers and Murderers:*

53. *Who have received the law by the disposition of Angels, and have not kept it.*

54. *Now, hearing these things, they were cut to the heart, and they gnashed with their teeth at him.*

55. *But he, being full of the Holy Ghost, looking up steadfastly to heaven, saw the glory of God, and Jesus standing at the right hand of God. And he said: Behold, I see the heavens opened, and the Son of man standing at the right hand of God.*

56. *And they, crying out with a loud voice, stopped their ears, and with one accord rushed in violently upon him.*

57. *And having cast him out of the city, they stoned him: and the witnesses laid down their garments at the feet of a young man whose name was Saul.*

58. *And they stoned Stephen, invoking, and saying: Lord Jesus, receive my spirit.*

59. *And kneeling down, he cried out with a loud voice, saying: Lord, lay not this sin to their charge. And when he had said this, he fell asleep in the Lord. And Saul was consenting to his death.*

ANALYSIS.

In this chapter, we have an account of Stephen's lengthy address to the assembled council. In it he gives an interesting history of the Paternal dealings of God with the Jewish people. It commences with the call of Abraham, the father of the faithful. He also adduces some leading incidents of his life (1-8). After a brief allusion to Isaac and Jacob, and to the merciful dealings of Joseph in regard to his brethren in Egypt, the persecutions of God's people after the death of Joseph (8-19), he dwells at some length on the history of Moses, the giving of the law—the ingratitude and stubborn stiffneckedness of the people—their miraculous deliverance and egress from Egypt (20-46). The building of the Temple (46-50). He next inveighs against the Jews as incredulous, stubborn, imitators of their Fathers who persecuted the Prophets (51-54). The rage of the Jews at the well-merited charges made against them by Stephen, his martyrdom (54-59).

Commentary.

1, 2. "Brethren," the younger members, his own coevals. "Fathers," the elder members of the *Sanhedrim*, the pontiffs and judges, before whom he was to plead his cause. His opening address, so respectful and courteous, was calculated to gain their good will. The assessors of the *Sanhedrim*, pontiffs and judges, he calls "fathers"; the others present he calls "brethren."

"The God of glory," the fountain and source of all glory: entitled, therefore to the greatest reverence. He was therefore calumniously charged with *blaspheming* Him.

"Appeared to our father, Abraham," in whom the Jews gloried as their spiritual father. How he appeared is not said. In Genesis (xii. 1) it is said "God spoke to Abraham." Perhaps the words "God of glory" might point to some glorious apparition vouchsafed to Abraham.

Text.

1. *Then the high-priest said: Are these things so?*

2. *And he said: Ye men, brethren, and fathers, give ear. The God of glory appeared to our father Abraham, when he was in Mesopotamia, before he dwelt in Charan:*

| Text. | Commentary. |

"When he was in Mesopotamia," &c.   In Genesis (xi. 31) we are told Abraham with his father and all his kinsfolk dwelt in Haran, whither his father Thare brought them. *After* that (*c.* xii. 1) God spoke to Abraham, and commanded him to go forth out of his country, &c. (*v.* 3). Hence, it was not "*before*" he dwelt in Charan. The reply commonly given is that God gave the command, "Go forth," &c., on two different occasions. First, when he was in Ur of the Chaldeans in Mesopotamia (Genesis xv. 7). There he received the mandate to go forth to *Charan* (the Greek for *Haran*), which was nearer Canaan, his ultimate destination. And God's providence so arranged it that Thare migrated there with his whole family, Abraham included, who thus obeyed the Divine mandate when accompanying his father. The same mandate was repeated when Abraham was in Charan.

1

2

Others maintain that there is question only of one apparition or mandate given to Abraham in Ur of the Chaldeans, which mandate was conveyed in the language here quoted from Genesis (xii. 1); that in compliance with this mandate, Abraham, with his father's family, repaired to *Charan* or *Haran*. It is to this call reference is made (Genesis xii. 1): "And the Lord said to Abraham," which means the Lord *had heretofore* said to Abraham, while in Ur of the Chaldeans, and in compliance with this mandate formerly given, Abraham moved once more from Charan to Canaan.

When it is said "he was in Mesopotamia," the term is taken in a wide sense, so as to embrace not only the country placed between the two rivers Tigris and Euphrates—whence the Greek name, Mesopotamia, *between the two rivers*—but also the neighbouring country of the Chaldeans. Hence it is said (*v.* 4) "he went out of the country of the Chaldeans" while in Mesopotamia.

3. *And he said to him: Go forth out of thy country and from thy kindred, and come into the land which I will show thee.*

3. "*Go forth*," &c.   These words are mostly quoted from the Septuagint, with some trifling points of difference.

4. *Then he went out of the land of the Chaldeans, and dwelt in Charan: and from thence, after his father was dead, he removed him into this land, in which you now dwell.*

4. "Land of the Chaldeans."   *Ur* of the Chaldeans. "And from thence, after his father was dead," &c.   Here an objection is raised by the enemies of Revelation, who charge Stephen with stating what is not true. They say it is impossible to reconcile Stephen's statement here with what is said in Genesis (xi. 32), viz., that Thare was 205 years old at his death; that Abraham was born to him when he was 70 years old (xi. 25); and that Abraham was 75 years when he left Charan for Canaan (Genesis xii. 4).   Thus Thare would be only 145 years at his death.

The reply commonly adopted is that the words of Genesis would not prove that Abraham was born to Thare when he was 75 years old. All

Commentary.

they would prove is that Thare was 75 years *before* any children were born to him; but how long after that, they were born is not stated. Abraham might have been born several years after that; and although Abraham was placed first, this might have been done out of respect to him as head and father of all believers; but it would by no means prove he was the first born. We find in several places of Scripture that members of families are not set down according to the dates of their birth. In Paralip (*c.* i. 28) Ismahel is placed after Isaac. On the list of the descendants of the sons of Jacob, those of Juda are placed first, though he was only the fourth son of Jacob (1 Paralip iv. 1, &c.). Several similar instances might be adduced. The objection, then, goes for nothing, unless it be proved that Abraham was born when Thare was 70 years of age, which the words of Genesis (xi. 32) will not establish; and that Abraham was the first born, which is by no means clear, although mentioned first, for the reason already assigned, viz., out of respect for the father of the faithful. He may have been the youngest, and born when Thare was 130 years old, as stated in the Samaritan Pentateuch. There is no evidence to the contrary. This disposes of the objection.

5. "No inheritance," no permanent, fixed possession. Abraham himself *purchased* a field for burial from the children of Heth (Genesis xxiii. 15, 16). "No, not the pace," &c., a kind of proverbial expression, signifying no land at all, be it ever so small.

"And to his seed," &c. "And" is taken, not in a conjunctive, but in an expletive sense, signifying, *namely.* For in the first and third promise it is made to his seed (Genesis xii. 7, xv. 18). In the promise made to him on the *second* occasion, it is said, "*Tibi* dabo *et semini* tuo (xiii. 15); *et* has the force of, *namely.*

"No child," nor, humanly speaking, any prospect of it. This shows the great heroic faith of Abraham (Rom. iv. 18, 19; Heb. xi. 11). In the same sense, that is, referring to their posterity, was the promise renewed to Isaac and Jacob (Genesis xxvi. 3, xxviii. 13).

6. "Sojourn in a strange land," Egypt, "four hundred years" (Genesis xv. 13). In Exodus (xii. 40) it is said, "they sojourned four hundred and thirty years." In Genesis Moses and St. Stephen here speak of four hundred years in *round* numbers, which, in a general customary way, would embrace 430 years.

As a general reply to other chronological difficulties, it is also likely the 430 years are to be computed from the calling of Abraham and the promise made to him, to the exit of the Jews from Egypt. An accurate or demonstrative solution can hardly be expected in matters concerning ancient records, or in regard to difficulties and perplexities of a chronological character.

7. "*The nation,*" Egypt particularly, "judge," practically, by inflicting signal punishment.

Text.	Commentary.

Text.

they shall serve I will judge, said the Lord : and after these things they shall go out, and shall serve me in this place.

Commentary.

"Serve me," worship me. I shall be their God; and they, my people.

8. And he gave him the covenant of circumcision: and so he begot Isaac, and circumcised him the eighth day: and Isaac Jacob; and Jacob the twelve patriarchs.

8. He established with him a covenant of which "circumcision" was the seal as well as a part, Abraham and his posterity binding themselves, on their part, by an obligation to submit to it. It was a sign of the special promises on the part of God, to the children of Abraham. Between *God* and man there could not be, strictly speaking, a covenant; on the part of God, it is a gratuitous promise.

" And so," in virtue of God's promise, or covenant (xvii. 2, 21), " he begot Isaac " (Genesis xvii. 17).

9. And the patriarchs,

9, 10. (Genesis xxvii., xli.)

moved with envy, sold Joseph into Egypt: and God was with him.

10. And he delivered him out of all his tribulations, and gave him favour and wisdom in the sight of Pharao king of Egypt; and he appointed him governor over Egypt, and over all his house.

11. Now there came a famine over all

11, 12. "Our Fathers," his ten sons, Benjamin and Joseph were not with them.

Egypt and Chanaan, and great tribulation : and our fathers found no food.

12. But when Jacob had heard that there was corn in Egypt, he sent our fathers the first time:

13. And at the second time Joseph was known by his brethren; and his kindred was made known to Pharao.

14. And Joseph, sending, called thither Jacob his father, and all kindred seventy-five souls.

13, 14. Genesis xlv. 4-16. "In seventy-five souls." In Genesis (xlvi. 27; Exod. i. 5; Deut. x. 22), the number is said to be seventy (70). The Septuagint has seventy-five which Stephen clearly followed. The Septuagint included in the number, five descendants of Joseph, two, the sons of Manasses, three of Ephraim, begotten in Egypt. Why the Septuagint did so is not so easily seen. Likely, it was because they were of the same stock with the original settlers. But, as Joseph and his two sons are reckoned among the seventy that entered Egypt, although already there, so, the Septuagint acted similarly in regard to Joseph's descendants, who were born in Egypt and did not come down with the Israelites. These chronological questions, at so remote a period, are not easy of explanation.

15. So Jacob went down into Egypt ; and he died, and our fathers.

15. "And he died, and our Fathers." The sons of Jacob died in Egypt during the 215 years that the Israelites sojourned there, before they entered Canaan.

16. And they were translated to Sichem, and were laid in the sepulchre

16. "Translated." This refers to the twelve sons of Jacob only, but not to Jacob himself, who was buried in Hebron (Genesis xlix. 31, xxiii. 19).

The bodies of the sons of Jacob were translated from Egypt to

Commentary.

Sichem. This is stated regarding the bones of Joseph (xxiv. 32). Although the Scripture says nothing of it; doubtless, the bodies of the other sons of Jacob were carried from Egypt to Sichem. This Stephen must have learned from tradition. St. Jerome (Ep. 86) says: their tombs were seen in his day in Sichem. Josephus, however (Antiq. 2, 8, 2), following a different tradition, says they were buried in Hebron.

"That Abraham bought," &c. This passage is a source of embarrassment to Commentators when striving to reconcile it with the narrative in Genesis. It would seem to attribute to Abraham a purchase which, so far as the Scripture account goes, he never made. The words here can hardly be understood of the purchase made by Abraham for sepulchral purposes from the children of Heth (Genesis xxiii. 16-20), as may be seen on reading over the passage referred to. Hence, some Expositors understand Stephen to refer to the purchase made by Jacob (Genesis xxxiii. 19). These would substitute *Jacob* for *Abraham* here, as if the mistake arose in course of time on the part of copyists—a supposition or principal of solution which, besides being gratuitous, is quite dangerous and inconvenient (*Beelen*). The purchase spoken of here is quite different in all its circumstances (viz., the vendors, the price, the land bought, &c.), from that made by Jacob (Genesis xxxiii. 19). Hence, as there is no mention made in Scripture of the purchase here spoken of, which was different from the purchase of ground for the sepulchre made from the children of Heth (Genesis xxiii. 16-20), St. Stephen must have learned it from tradition, from which source he knew of the translation of the bodies of the Patriarchs from Egypt to Sichem.

But, here another difficulty arises. It is said here "Hemor was the son of Sichem," whereas in (Genesis xxxiii. 19) he is said to be the "*Father* of Sichem" (Josue xxiv. 23). But "the sons of Hemor" are the sons of a *Hemor*, different from the *Hemor* here spoken of. Whether there be any error in the utterance attributed to St. Stephen here, whose inspiration we are not bound to defend, St. Luke's inspiration is by no means affected by it ; since, as an inspired historian, he only records what was spoken by another.

17. "Promise," to bring the Hebrews out of Egypt after 400 years (verses 6, 7).

18. "Knew not," ignored. Did not gratefully recognise the well-known, priceless benefits conferred by Joseph on the land of Egypt.

Text.

which Abraham bought for a sum of money of the son of Hemor, the father of Sichem.

17. *And when the time of the promise drew near, which God had promised to Abraham, the people increased and were multiplied in Egypt,*

18. *Till another king arose in Egypt, who knew not Joseph.*

possible Errors.

1. *Abraham's pu*

{ *prob. tradition; not mentioned*

2. *Hemor pa Sic*

Text.

19. *This same dealing deceitful with our race, afflicted our fathers, that they should expose their children, to the end they might not be kept alive.*

20. *At the same time was Moses born, and he was acceptable to God; and he was nourished three months in his father's house.*

21. *But he being exposed, Pharao's daughter took him up, and nourished him for her own son.*

22. *And Moses was instructed in all the wisdom of the Egyptians; and he was powerful in his words and in his deeds.*

23. *And when he was full forty years old, it came into his heart to visit his brethren the children of Israel.*

24. *And having seen a certain man suffer an injury, he defended him; and striking the Egyptian, he avenged him who suffered the injury.*

25. *And he thought that*

Commentary.

19. " Dealing craftily," employing cunning, deceitful devices to bring about the utter destruction of our "race," nation, ancestors.

"Afflicted," acted with injustice and cruelty. "Expose," &c. (Exod. i. 16-22).

20. "At the same time." During this cruel period (Exod. ii. 2, &c.). "Acceptable to God." " To God," by a Hebrew idiom, conveys that he was exceedingly handsome or comely (Exod. ii. 2, &c.).

21. "Exposed." Placed in a basket on the banks of the Nile (Exod. ii. &c.).

22. "Instructed," taught, educated in "all the wisdom," &c. As the adopted son of Pharaoh's daughter (Exod. ii. 10).

"Mighty," while in Pharaoh's court. Josephus records that while there, he gained a signal victory over the Ethiopians (Antiq., lib. ii. c. 10).

"In words." Gifted with great popular eloquence (Josephus, Antiq., lib. iii. 1-4).

His humble self-depreciation (Exod. iv. 10) had reference only to some organic defect. Hence, God told him (v. 12), "I shall be in thy mouth."

23. "Forty years old." This Stephen learned from tradition. "It came into his heart," he conceived the idea, formed the resolve.

"To visit," bring aid, "to his brethren," &c. Having relinquished Pharaoh's Court with all its pleasures and enjoyments (Hebrews xi. 24).

24. "Suffer wrong," maltreated, struck by an Egyptian. This Stephen omits, as being well known to his hearers.

"Striking the Egyptian." He slew him and buried him in the sand (Exodus ii. 12). Most likely, under Divine impulse, he felt, that he acted justly in doing so.

25. The Hebrews were well aware, that they were to be liberated from the Egyptian bondage. From all the circumstances of his visit,

Commentary.

his readiness to expose his life in defending them, and taking vengeance on one of their oppressors, Moses supposed they would regard him as the instrument in the hand of God for bringing them salvation, that their deliverance from the oppressive yoke of the Egyptions was near at hand. But, they did not regard him in that light.

26. "Showed himself," came unexpectedly on them. There were only two Hebrews quarrelling. The whole incident was known to his hearers. Hence, Stephen only gives it substantially, without describing it circumstantially.

"And would have remedied," &c., by employing moral persuasion.

27, 28. "Did the injury," the aggressor in the case (Exodus ii. 14).
that did the injury to his neighbour thrust him away, saying: Who hath appointed thee prince and judge over us?

28. Wilt thou kill me, as thou didst yesterday kill the Egyptian?

29. Moses finding that his act, which he supposed to be secret, was publicly known, and fearing the vengeance which Pharaoh would execute on hearing it, "fled" for his life. "Upon this word" of reproach being addressed to him, "a stranger," a sojourner, with the intention of dwelling there for a time.

30. "Forty years," from the time he fled from Egypt. During that time, he sojourned in Madian. He was then 80 years old. All this St. Stephen ascertained, as he did several other matters, from tradition. "There appeared," &c., "in the desert of Mount Sina." The desert in which Mount Sina was situated, Exodus iii. 1 has "Horeb." But there is no discrepancy, as Sina and Horeb are two distinct summits, springing from one and the same mountain, and having the same base.

"An Angel," in next v. 31 called "the Lord." Likewise Exodus iii. 2-11, He is called "the Lord." "God," &c. It is disputed among Expositors whether the "Angel" here spoken of was not God Himself, the word "Angel" signifying messenger, *Created* or *Increated*. Our Lord Himself is called the Angel of the Great Council.

By many it is held that here, as well as in several other passages, there is question of a created angelic spirit, who represented God, spoke by the authority of God, and, by Divine permission, assumed certain functions appertaining to God alone. But this he did, speaking on the part of God, as His representative and organ.

By others it is maintained that there is question directly of God Himself, the Second Person of the adorable Trinity, who on the occasions referred to in the Old Testament, assumed a human form, used a human voice, perfectly similar to that which He afterwards exhibited when He "became flesh," becoming personally and hypostatically united to the Divine Person of the Eternal Word.

Text.

his brethren understood that God by his hand would save them; but they understood it not.

26. And the next day he showed himself to them that were at strife, and would have reconciled them in peace, saying: Men, ye are brethren; why hurt ye one another?

27. But he

29. And Moses fled upon this word, and became a stranger in the land of Madian, where he begat two sons.

30. And when forty years were expired, there appeared to him, in the desert of Mount Sina, an Angel in a flame of fire in a bush.

Text.

Commentary.

"In a flame of fire," *real* fire, otherwise, it could cause no wonder that it did not consume the bush.

31. *And Moses, seeing it, wondered at the sight: and as he drew near to view it, the voice of the Lord came to him, saying:*

31. He wondered at seeing the bush on fire, without being consumed.

32. *I am the God of thy fathers, the God of Abraham, the God of Isaac, and the God of Jacob. And Moses, being terrified, durst not behold.*

32. "*The God of thy Fathers,*" their protector and wonderful rewarder.

33. *And the Lord said to him: Loose thy shoes from off thy feet; for the place wherein thou standest is holy ground.*

33. The order of narrative is somewhat different from that given in Exodus iii. 5. "Loose the shoes," &c. In the east, to put off the shoes, was a mark of reverence. It was quite usual among the Jews, as uncovering the head is with us.

"*Holy ground,*" sanctified by the presence of God.

34. *Seeing I have seen the affliction of my people, which is in Egypt, and I have heard their groaning, and come down to deliver them: and now come, and I will send thee into Egypt.*

34. "*Seeing I have seen,*" &c., an emphatic form of expression according to Hebrew usage.

"*I will send thee.*" Exodus iii. 7-10.

35. *This Moses whom they refused, saying: Who hath appointed thee prince and judge? him God sent a prince and redeemer, by the hand of the Angel who appeared to him in the bush.*

35. "Refused," to listen to on a former occasion, although it was the act of only one man; still, he seems to have represented the feelings of all.

"Redeemer." The Greek word would signify redeeming another from bondage by paying his ransom (λυτρον), which is expressive of the Redemption through Christ, of whom Moses was a type.

St. Stephen, who was charged with blasphemy against Moses, reminds his hearers of the ingratitude shown by their Fathers, whose character they inherited, towards their deliverer. He covertly charges the Jews of the present day, with similar ingratitude; and this naturally served as a preparation for his charges made explicitly against them (*vv.* 51, 52).

The whole style is very emphatic, as shown in the prominence given to the article, "this Moses," him, &c.

Commentary.

"*By the hand of the Angel.*" *Cum manu Angeli*, armed with the protecting power of the Angel.

36. " He brought them," &c. (Exodus vii., xiii., xiv.)

37. "*A prophet*," &c., taken from Deuteronomy (xviii. 15-18, see c. iii. 22). In introducing this quotation, St. Stephen wished to call to mind, that a Messiah was promised them, whom they were obliged to hear and obey. Stephen, who was charged with being opposed to Moses, here shows he was well aware of and acknowledged the Divine authority of Moses. Hence, he was not opposed to him ; nay, even, by pointing to a new Legislator, he by no means detracted from the authority of Moses, since Moses himself announced this.

38. " The Church," the assembly of the Children of Israel rescued from Egypt and placed under the guidance of Moses.
" In the wilderness," of Sina. He it was, that was with the assembly of the people, whom he called together.
" With the Angel, who spoke to him . . . and with our Fathers," between whom and the Angel that announced the law, he acted as mediator.
" Words of life," life-giving commandments.

39. (Exodus xxxiii. 1-23 ; Numbers xiv. 4.) " In their hearts," having a wish or desire to return to Egypt (Numbers xi. 5). It may mean, to imitate the depraved morals of the Egyptians. Not likely, after all they suffered in Egypt, they had any desire to return there.

40. " *Make us Gods*." The plural for the singular—a thing by no means unusual—as there was question of only one false god. Possibly, they asked for idols, one or more, as might suit.
" To go before us," guide and conduct us in the desert, in place of Moses.

41. (Exodus xxxii. 2-4). St. Stephen shows how prone their ancestors were to the worship of idols and to desert the true God.

Text.

36. He brought them out, doing wonders and signs in the land of Egypt, and in the Red Sea, and in the desert for forty years.

37. This is that Moses who said to the children of Israel: A Prophet will God raise up to you out of your brethren, as myself: him shall you hear.

38. This is he who was in the church in the wilderness, with the Angel who spoke to him on Mount Sina, and with our fathers: who received the words of life to give to us ;

39. To whom our fathers would not be obedient, but repulsed him, and in their hearts returned back into Egypt,

40. Saying to Aaron: Make us Gods to go before us: for as to this Moses, who brought us out of the land of Egypt, we know not what has become of him.

41. And they made a calf in those days, and offered sacrifice to this idol, and rejoicing in the works of their own hands.

F

Text.

42. *And God turned, and gave them up to serve the host of heaven; as it is written in the book of the prophets: Did you offer victims and sacrifices to me for forty years in the desert, O house of Israel?*

Commentary.

42. "God turned" away from them by the subtraction of His special graces.

"And gave them up." This He did *negatively*, by abandoning them; by merely tolerating them; by the subtraction of His graces, absolutely necessary to save them from sin.

"God," says St. Thomas (Ep. ad. Rom. *c.* i. 24), "hands men over to sin, not directly, but indirectly, by withdrawing His grace necessary to save them from sinning, in the same way, as by taking away a prop or support from one, you would be said to cause his fall. In this way, the *first* sin is the cause of the *second*, the *second*, the punishment of the first."

God may be said to be the *negative*, but, by no means, the *positive* cause of sin.

"The host of heaven," sometimes denotes the angels (Luke ii. 13; 3 Kings xxii. 19); sometimes, the stars (Deuteronomy iv. 19; Isaias xxxiv. 4). The latter is clearly the meaning here. This is shown from the words of Amos, quoted here by Stephen.

"In the Book of the Prophets" (Amos v. 25-27). Although there is reference here to the Prophet Amos, the word is used in the plural, the twelve minor Prophets being bound up by the Hebrews in one book or volume. St. Stephen quotes Amos from memory in proof that the Israelites were addicted to the worship of false gods in the desert.

"*Did you offer?*" &c. This interrogative form is equivalent to a *negative*. "You did *not offer*," &c. Some understand the Greek interrogative not to imply a negative, but an affirmative answer, "*yes*, you did;" and still your perversity was such that conjointly with my worship you took unto you "the Tabernacle of Moloch." St. Stephen could not in truth universally or *absolutely* deny that the Israelites offered up sacrifices to the true God. It would be contrary to fact to say so. Although on stated occasions they clung to the worship of the true God, still they abandoned the true God and worshipped idols; and their offerings to God were comparatively so few as to be counted almost for nothing, particularly if their idolatrous acts were borne in mind.

Circumcision was interrupted during their forty years sojourn. So was also the Paschal celebration. And although the daily sacrifices had not completely ceased, still, in the eyes of God, this official celebration, considering their idolatrous dispositions, were but of little value.

It was not so much for their neglect to offer sacrifices that God reproaches the people, as for their turning from Him to the worship of false gods. It would seem that after leaving Egypt the people had always a longing for the worship of the idols of Egypt, and privately practised it, more or less unknown to Moses or Aaron, who would not tolerate it for a moment. In the Mosaic *Legislation* there are several ordinances meant to combat this tendency to worship on the part of the people, which it seems Moses suspected (Leviticus xvii. 9). He manfully condemns Moloch worship (Leviticus xviii. 21).

Moses, in his history. only once, apart from their worship of the

Commentary.

golden calf, expressly makes mention of the idolatry of which they were guilty shortly before his death (Numbers xxv. 1). While dwelling in Settim, in the country of the Moabites, the people committed fornication with the daughters of Moab, adored their gods and were initiated to Beelphegor. Hence, although there is no denying the tendency of the people to idolatry during the forty years' sojourn in the desert, still here, most likely, there is no question of idolatrous acts during that period, but only of the particular act of idolatry committed in Settim just referred to.

43. " *You took unto you,*" &c. Instead of honouring Me, you rather took up and carried about from place to place, for pompous ceremonial purposes, in the act of practising idolatrous worship.

"The Tabernacle," &c. The portable tent or little cases in which were incased the image of the false god, Moloch. These images being small were easily carried about. They were in some manner like the silver shrines of Diana manufactured at Ephesus (xix. 24) and the small statues concealed by Rachel (Genesis xxxi. 34).

In the Hebrew for "*Moloch*" we have "*your king*" in allusion to the royal dignity with which the Gentiles invested their gods. *Moloch* seems to be derived from, or rather to be a modification of the Hebrew word, *Malak, which signifies king*. Moloch was the god of the Ammonites and Moabites, in whose honour children were burned alive (Levit. xvii. 17; xx. 2). In the valley of Hinnon, outside Jerusalem, these abominable cruelties were sometimes practised by the Israelites in imitation of the Chanaanites in honour of this false god (see Mathew v. 22, Commentary on).

This *Moloch*, said to represent the planet *Saturn*, or the sun, or Mercury, is identified by many with the false god *Baal*, which signifies *Lord*, *Moloch* (king) and Baal (*Lord*), would seem to be interchangeable terms (Jeremiah xxxii. 15, xix. 5). Human sacrifices were offered to both.

"And the star of your god, Rempham," which would seem to represent some god whom they worshipped. The Hebrew for Rempham is *chiun*. This was rendered so by the Septuagint translators, who made the translation in Egypt. *Raiphan* easily made *Rempham*. This they probably did, because, in the Coptic language in use in Egypt, *Rempham* is the same as the Hebrew *chiun*. It is thought by many to represent the planet *Saturn*, *chiun* signifying *just*, and the reign of *Saturn* was regarded by the poets as remarkable for justice.

"*Figures which you made*" put in apposition to the preceding.

" And," in consequence, owing to your idolatry.

" *Beyond Babylon*," in punishment of their abondoning Him.

In Amos, it is "*beyond Damascus*." St. Stephen gives the sense. They were transported through Syria, and therefore "*beyond Damascus*" to Babylon. St. Stephen points out more explicitly than does Amos the place of their captivity or deportation in punishment of their idolatry.

43. *And you took unto you the tabernacle of Moloch, and the star of your god Rempham, figures which you made to adore them: and I will carry you away beyond Babylon.*

Text.	Commentary.
	Some of them were carried not only beyond Damascus to Babylon, but even to Persia beyond Babylon (2 Machab. 1–19).

44. *The tabernacle of the testimony was with our fathers in the desert, as God ordained for them, speaking to Moses that he should make it according to the form which he had seen:*

44. St. Stephen having refuted one of the charges alleged against him (c. vi. 13, 14), viz., of having undervalued Moses and his law, now proceeds to the refutation of the other, viz., that he spoke disrespectfully of the temple. This charge he refutes, by professing his belief in the Divine institution of the tabernacle which preceded the temple, and of the temple itself (v. 47). He opposes their tabernacle or tent to the tents of *Moloch*, &c.

"Of the testimony." It was a testimony or proof of God's presence among them and of His protection visibly extended to them.

The word "testimony" refers to the Tables of the Law placed in the ark which the Tabernacle contained. The law was the testimony of God's will.

"According to the form," &c. The fact of God's showing a form or pattern, a plan of details, on the Mount shows the Divine sanction which Stephen did not mean to deny or depreciate. The sanctuary, with its contents, though fabricated by human hands, was a Divine work (Exod. xxv. 8–10).

45. *Which also our fathers, receiving, brought in with Jesus into the possession of the gentiles, whom God expelled from the face of our fathers, until the days of David:*

45. "Receiving" as a sacred heritage. The generation that came out of Egypt were all excluded from Canaan, except Caleb and Josue in punishment of their infidelity. Hence, it was the next generation that "*received*" it.

"Brought in with Jesus." Josue, "into the possession of the Gentiles," the land then occupied by the Chanaanites, "whom God drove out," &c. He continued to drive them out until the days of David, when the subjugation commenced by Josue was completed.

"Unto the days of David." These words in connexion with the preceding more probably convey that the tabernacle introduced by Josue continued to be the place of worship, the centre of God's manifestations until the time of *David*, who wished to build a temple, a *more suitable* dwelling place for His glory and permanent residence. This seems to be the true interpretation.

For Stephen seems to describe the duration of Divine worship in the Tabernacle, while in the Land of Promise, up to the time for building the temple.

46. *Who found grace in the sight of God, and desired that he might find a tabernacle for the God of Jacob.*

46. "Found grace," &c. Very dear to God, prospered in all his ways.

"And desired." This is allusive to his vow (Ps. cxxxii. 1, &c.), "a Tabernacle," a fixed place of abode for the ark, which was hitherto carried about in a moveable Tabernacle. The Greek word (σκηνωμα), would convey the idea of a fixed place of abode, compared with σκηνη, the term for Tabernacle or *tent* in which the ark hitherto reposed.

Commentary.

47. This great privilege denied to David, was reserved for his son Solomon.

48. Having fully replied to the false charges brought against himself, as having blasphemed against Moses and his law, as well as against the temple, St. Stephen wishes now to remove the erroneous ideas the Jews had formed in regard to their possession of the temple to which they fancied God was in some measure confined, and in regard to the great feeling of false security, with which the possession of the temple inspired them. On the possession of the temple, and their having it amongst them, they placed even a superstitious reliance, as if this was all sufficent for their safety (Jeremias vii. 4). St. Stephen wishes to combat the exaggerated importance the Jews attached to their temple, as if all religion depended on it, and as if God's presence, worship and manifestations were confined to it. He would also seem to insinuate that, possibly, one day, the temple might be destroyed, God's special presence withdrawn, His worship not confined to it. Since by his omnipresence, he fills all creation.

" Houses made by hand." The original has only " made by hands :" but, it denotes "houses." "As the Prophet saith " (Isaias lxvi. 1, 2).

49. The words of this verse are taken from Isaias (lxvi. 1, 2), not strictly ; but, as to sense.

"Heaven," is His royal seat, more worthy than the wings of the cherubim in the ark. "The earth, His footstool," far above the propitiatory of the ark.

"What house will you build Me," sufficient to contain My immensity ? He does not exclude external worship ; but, only when accompanied with the interior feelings of piety, is it acceptable.

50. " Hath not My hand," &c. Conveying that He can build nothing He does not already possess. In the original, this is read, not interrogatively, but affirmatively. The sense, however, is still the same.

51. This sudden transition from the calm language of historical recital, and from an apologetic tone to the language of vehement and bitter reproach, which has no connexion with the preceding, would seem to indicate, that the hearers, including the judges, members of the Sanhedrim, seeing the force and tendency of his remarks, showed their displeasure in gestures and clamorous excitement. Seeing this, St. Stephen at once reproaches them with their hereditary stubborness and resistance to the interior motions and promptings of Divine grace.

"Stiffnecked." a term found in several parts of Scripture applied to the Jews (Exod. xxxii. 9.; xxxiii. 3-5 ; Deut. ix., &c.)

The idea is a figurative one, having reference to oxen that kick against being yoked. In its application to man, it conveys the idea of stubborness and opposition to restraint.

Text.

47. But Solomon built him a house.

48. But the Most High dwelleth not in houses made by hands, as the prophet saith :

49. Heaven is my throne, and the earth is my footstool. What house will you build for me? saith the Lord: or what is the place of my rest?

50. Hath not my hand made all these things?

51. With a stiff neck and uncircumcised heart and ears you always resist the Holy Ghost: as your fathers did, so do you also.

Text.	Commentary.

"Uncircumcised in heart." Unwilling to submit to the restraints of the Law of Moses, circumcision being the peculiar mark of a Jew. Their hearts were full of Pagan passions and desires to "resist the Holy Ghost," by resisting the interior grace, which always accompanies the preaching of the miracles of Christ and of his Apostles.

52. *Which of the prophets have not your fathers persecuted? And they have slain these who foretold of the coming of the Just One; of whom you have been now the betrayers and murderers:*

52. This interrogative is equivalent to an emphatic assertion, conveying a general truth in regard to their well-known national trait, relative to the persecution of Prophets (Matthew xxiii. 29-35).

"Who foretold," &c. The chief announcement made by the Prophets, regarded the future Messiah. It greatly aggravated their guilt to slay those who foretold the greatest of blessings. The cruel treatment of the Prophets of old arose not only from their predictions regarding our Redeemer: they were persecuted for other reasons also, viz.: for correcting the people and reproaching them with their vices, it being the duty of the Prophets, not only to predict future events, but to teach, admonish, reprehend, &c.

"And they had slain." "And," *nay even*, signifies that besides persecuting the Prophets for general reasons, they persecuted them specially "who foretold," &c., for this *particular reason* also.

"The betrayers." By having handed Him over to the Gentiles, through the treason of Judas, who was a mere instrument in their hands.

53. *Who have received the law by the disposition of Angels, and have not kept it.*

53. The Law of which you boast so much, and charge me with undervaluing, forbids murder, and this Law you have not observed or guarded.

"By the disposition of Angels." (εις διαταγας αγγελων) is rendered by Kenrick; after Martini (an Italian), and Allioli (a German) "*through the instrumentality of Angels.*" Patrizzi thinks the words may mean "*at the dispositions or ministrations of Angels.*"

Others understand the words to mean "*in the presence of the Angels arranged in their different ranks and divisions,*" who were witnesses of the giving of the Law; thus adding to its solemnity. All these circumstances aggravated the guilt of those who violated a law so solemnly promulgated.

54. *Now, hearing these things, they were cut to the heart, and they gnashed with their teeth at him.*

54. "Cut to the heart." Roused to the highest pitch of anger, which they could no longer restrain. This they gave expression to by "gnashing their teeth," an indication of intense rage.

55. *But he, being full of the Holy Ghost, looking up steadfastly to heaven, saw the glory of God,*

55. "Full of the Holy Ghost." Imbued with the spirit of fortitude, which made him despise their sanguinary threatenings. Turning to prayer, he raised up his eyes, gazing intently on heaven. Elevated beyond himself, "he saw," in a fit of ecstasy, "the glory of God," the Majesty and Almighty Power of the Father, surrounded with heavenly

Commentary.

glory, circumfused with fiery splendour. "And Jesus standing," &c. He is generally represented as *sitting*. But while the word *sitting* indicates His posture as Judge, "standing" indicates the posture of one prepared to come to the relief of his struggling valiant soldier, and receive him on entering Heaven. This is conveyed by St. Gregory (Hom. in Evang. xxix. 7). "*Sedere, judicantis est. Stare, vero pugnantis vel adjuvantis. Stephanus in labore certaminis, stantem vidit quem adjutorem habuit.*"

"Behold I see the Heavens opened" The Empyreal Heavens, the dwelling-place of the blessed. Stephen saw this Heaven flung open; his eye elevated by God's supernatural concursus or power penetrated these patent Heavens as far as the Empyreal Heaven to behold God's glory and Jesus standing at His right hand.

"And the Son of Man." A designation often applied by our Lord to Himself, first used in Daniel (vii. 13, 14) and but rarely applied by others to Him in the New Testament as here, and Apocalypse (i. 13, xiv. 14). A similar phrase used by our Lord (Matthew xxvi. 64) was considered, as here, to be blasphemous. St. Stephen, full of the Holy Ghost, with the spirit of intrepidity, fearlessly tells the Jews that He whom they persecuted and put to death was now in power and majesty, enjoying Heavenly glory.

56. They affecting to be shocked at the blasphemy uttered by Stephen "stopped their ears" so as not to hear further blasphemies and thus show their horror of what they heard. This is, probably, said of the people.

"With one accord" rushing tumultuously in a body.

57. "Casting him out," &c. In Leviticus (xxiv. 14-23) it was prescribed that the blasphemer should be stoned outside the camp, and afterwards it was enacted he should be stoned outside the cities (Deut. xxii. 16).

"They stoned him," the punishment allotted for blasphemy (Levit. xxiv. 16).

"Witnesses." The false witness, who bore testimony against him (vi. 13). The Law of Moses ordained, with a view of preventing false accusations, that the witnesses (Deut. xvii. 7) should be the first to execute the sentence. Then all the people joined, "laid their garments," outer garments—a thing usually done in any laborious enterprise—in order to have their hands free, as the stones used on such occasions were rather large and heavy.

"At the feet . . . Saul," the future Apostle of the Gentiles. He abetted and assented to the cruel act of murder (*c.* xvii. 20).

"A young man," about thirty years at the time. When in prison in Rome, addressing Philemon, he calls himself "an old man" (Philemon 9).

Text.

and Jesus standing at the right hand of God. And he said: Behold, I see the heavens opened, and the Son of man standing at the right hand of God.

56. And they, crying out with a loud voice, stopped their ears, and with one accord rushed in violently upon him.

57. And having cast him out of the city, they stoned him: and the witnesses laid down their garments at the feet of a young man whose name was Saul.

Text.	Commentary.

Text.

58. *And they stoned Stephen, invoking, and saying: Lord Jesus, receive my spirit.*

59. *And kneeling down, he cried out with a loud voice, saying: Lord, lay not this sin to their charge. And when he had said this, he fell asleep in the Lord. And Saul was consenting to his death.*

Commentary.

58. " Receive my spirit." Admit my soul into Thy kingdom of eternal bliss.

59. " Falling on his knees," which he did voluntarily in the attitude of prayer, wishing also to die in the same posture.

" Lay not this sin," &c. So like the dying prayer of his Heavenly Master (Luke xxiii. 34).

The Greek word would convey the idea of not weighing their sins in the scales of Divine retribution.

" He fell asleep," which gives an idea of the calm composure of the death of the just so peaceful and so happy. It also conveys that their death is only a short slumber from which they were soon to be awakened in the glory of the Resurrection.

From this came the usage of calling the burying places of the faithful *cemeteries* or *sleeping places* where their bodies repose for a time awaiting the General Resurrection, when they shall be aroused from their long slumbers.

" And Saul was consenting," &c. Approved of it as indicated by his conduct (*v.* 17). St. Luke here wishes to convey that though Paul took no part in the act of *stoning* still he fully approved, and as such was guilty, conformably to the teaching of the Apostle (Rom. i. 32). These latter words are placed in some versions at the beginning of next chapter. But the division, according to the Vulgate arrangement, is clearly the more judicious one, as these words are connected with the preceding ; and a new subject is introduced in the opening words of next chapter, " and at that time," &c. This division, according to the Vulgate, is justly preferred by many among the most judicious critics.

CHAPTER VIII.

1. *And at that time there was raised a great persecution against the church which was at Jerusalem ; and they were all dispersed through the countries of Judea, and Samaria, except the apostles.*

2. *And devout men took order for Stephen's funeral, and made great mourning over him.*

3. *But Saul made havoc of the church, entering in from house to house, and dragging away men and women, committed them to prison.*

4. *They therefore that were dispersed, went about preaching the word of God.*

5. *And Philip going down to the city of Samaria, preached Christ unto them.*

6. *And the people with one accord were attentive to those things which were said by Philip, hearing, and seeing the miracles which he did.*

7. *For many of them who had unclean spirits crying with a loud voice, went out.*

8. *And many, taken with the palsy, and that were lame, were healed.*

9. *There was therefore great joy in that city. Now there was a certain man named Simon, who before had been a magician in that city, seducing the people of Samaria, giving out that he was some great one :*

10. *To whom they all gave ear, from the least to the greatest, saying : This man is the power of God, which is called great.*

11. *And they were attentive to him, because, for a long time, he had bewitched them with his magical practices.*

12. *But when they had believed Philip preaching of the kingdom of God, in the name of Jesus Christ, they were baptized, both men and women.*

13. *Then Simon himself believed also ; and being baptized, he stuck close to Philip. And being astonished, wondered to see the signs and exceeding great miracles which were done.*

14. *Now when the apostles, who were in Jerusalem, had heard that Samaria had received the word of God, they sent unto them Peter and John.*

15. *Who, when they were come, prayed for them, that they might receive the Holy Ghost.*

16. *For he was not as yet come upon any of them ; but they were only baptized in the name of the Lord Jesus.*

17. *Then they laid their hands upon them, and they received the Holy Ghost.*

18. *And when Simon saw, that by the imposition of the hands of the apostles, the Holy Ghost was given, he offered them money,*

19. *Saying : Give me also this power, that on whomsoever I shall lay my hands, he may receive the Holy Ghost. But Peter said to him :*

20. *Keep thy money to thyself, to perish with thee, because thou hast thought that the gift of God may be purchased with money.*

21. *Thou hast no part nor lot in this matter. For thy heart is not right in the sight of God.*

22. *Do penance therefore, from this thy wickedness ; and pray to God, if perhaps this thought of thy heart may be forgiven thee.*

23. *For I see thou art in the gall of bitterness, and in the bonds of iniquity.*

24. *Then Simon answering, said: Pray you for me to the Lord, that none of these things which you have spoken may come upon me.*

25. *And they indeed having testified and preached the word of the Lord, returned to Jerusalem, and preached the gospel to many countries of the Samaritans.*

26. *Now an Angel of the Lord spoke to Philip, saying: Arise, go towards the south, to the way that goeth down from Jerusalem into Gaza: this is desert.*

27. *And rising up, he went. And behold a man of Ethiopia, an eunuch, of great authority under Candace, the queen of the Ethiopians, who had charge over all her treasures, had come to Jerusalem to adore.*

28. *And he was returning, sitting in his chariot, and reading Isaias the prophet;*

29. *And the Spirit said to Philip: Go near, and join thyself to this chariot.*

30. *And Philip running thither, heard him reading the prophet Isaias. And he said: Thinkest thou that thou understandesth what thou readest?*

31. *Who said: And how can I, unless some man shew me? And he desired Philip that he would come up and sit with him.*

32. *And the place of the scripture which he was reading was this: He was led as a sheep to the slaughter; and like a lamb without voice before his shearer, so openeth he not his mouth.*

33. *In humility his judgment was taken away. His generation who shall declare, for his life shall be taken from the earth?*

34. *And the eunuch answering Philip said: I beseech thee, of whom doth the prophet speak this? of himself, or of some other man?*

35. *Then Philip, opening his mouth, and beginning at this scripture, preached unto him Jesus.*

36. *And as they went on their way, they came to a certain water; and the eunuch said: See, here is water: what doth hinder me from being baptized?*

37. *And Philip, said: If thou believest with all thy heart, thou mayest. And he answering, said: I believe that Jesus Christ is the Son of God.*

38. *And he commanded the chariot to stand still; and they went down into the water, both Philip and the eunuch: and he baptized him.*

39. *And when they were come up out of the water, the Spirit of the Lord took away Philip; and the eunuch saw him no more. And he went on his way rejoicing.*

40. *But Philip was found in Azotus; and passing through he preached the gospel to all the cities, till he came to Cesarea.*

ANALYSIS.

We have an account of the extension of the Church occasioned by the dispersion and persecution consequent on the martyrdom of Stephen, of which Saul was the most active agent (1-4). The success of Philip's preaching in Samaria—the miracles wrought by him (5-9)—the numerous conversions effected by him. Among others, Simon Magus, embraced, or pretended to embrace, the faith (9-13). The mission of Peter and John to administer confirmation and bestow the gifts of the Holy Ghost (14-17). The impious offer by Simon Magus, whom Peter exposes and rebukes with merited severity (18-24). The interviews, suggested by Divine inspiration, of Philip with the eunuch of Queen Candace. The conversion of the latter, after due instruction and Baptism (27-40).

Commentary.

1. "And at that time," in Greek, "*that day*," refers to the period immediately succeeding the death of Stephen.

"A great persecution." St. Paul himself testifies that many of the early Christians were put to death.

"Against the Church at Jerusalem"—the first founded.

"All dispersed." All, taken in a morally universal sense, denotes a large number. Some remained, who required the ministration and pastoral care of the Apostles. A large number consulted for their safety by flight, following the counsel of our Lord (Matthew x. 23). This was providentially arranged, for the greater spread of the Gospel, which they failed not to make known in Samaria, Judea, &c. (c. i. 8). Some of them went to Phenice, Cyprus, and Antioch, and preached the Gospel there (c. xi. 19).

"Except the Apostles," who remained in face of the storm; probably, in order to attend those of the faithful, who lay hid; and to give an example of courage and constancy.

2. "Devout men." This, according to some, may refer to religious men, still of the Jewish persuasion, who, unlike Saul, utterly disapproved of the murder of Stephen. As for *devout* Christians they were dispersed; and if they were Christians St. Luke would have said so. Joseph of Arimathea and Nicodemus acted similarly in regard to our Lord (John xix. 3-8). Patrizzi, however, thinks there is reference made to " devout men " among the believers.

"Took order." The Greek signifies taking charge of everything appertaining to his burial, washing, embalming, &c.

"Great mourning," in the way usual among the Jews. This expressed their strong disapproval of the crime of his murderers.

3. " But Saul," &c. Some expositors (Beelen, &c.) are of opinion that *vv.* 2, 3 should be enclosed in a parenthesis, and that *v.* 4 should be connected immediately with *v.* 1. The words, "they, therefore," would seem to warrant this.

"Made havoc." The original ἐλυμαίνετο conveys the idea of wild beasts, devastating a country. So Saul acted the wild beast in his fury against the Christians. In the next words is shown how he acted the part of infuriated persecutor, "entering in from house," &c., wherever any suspected Christian might be. Persecution only served to spread the Gospel. "*Sanguis martyrum ; semen Christianorum.*" (Tertullian.) "Committed them to prison." The *Sanhedrim*, whose agent he was, had this power; but not the power of life and death.

4. "They, therefore," &c. "Therefore" is resumptive of the subject of dispersion referred to in *v.* 1.

"Preaching," in Greek, *Evangelizing*, announcing the glad tidings of redemption through Christ, each in his own way; some, with authority in public discourses; others, privately in conversation with their neighbours, and in their edifying conduct.

Text.

1. And at that time there was raised a great persecution against the church which was at Jerusalem ; and they were all dispersed through the countries of Judea, and Samaria, except the apostles.

2. And devout men took order for Stephen's funeral, and made great mourning over him.

3. But Saul made havoc of the church, entering in from house to house, and dragging away men and women, committed them to prison.

4. They therefore that were dispersed, went about preaching the word of God.

Text.

5. *And Philip going down to the city of Samaria, preached Christ unto them.*

6. *And the people with one accord were attentive to those things which were said by Philip, hearing and seeing the miracles which he did.*

7. *For many of them who had unclean spirits, crying with a loud voice, went out.* 8. *And many, taken with the palsy, and that were lame, were healed.*

9. *There was therefore great joy in that city. Now there was a certain man named Simon, who before had been a magician in that city, seducing the people of Samaria, giving out that he was some great one:*

10. *To whom they all gave*

Commentary.

5. " Philip," the Deacon (*c.* vi. 6) called "an Evangelist, one of the seven" (xxi. 8). If Philip, the Apostle, were meant, he would have imposed hands on them (*v.* 14, &c).

"Samaria," Not the *country* but *city* of Samaria, which retained its ancient name, though at the time changed by Herod into *Sebaste* or *Augusta*.

" Preached Christ." This he did in virtue of a special commission.

6. "With one accord, were attentive," &c. Unanimously, in great numbers, embraced the teaching on witnessing the miracles he wrought.

7. "For many," our construction is rather complicated. In the Greek, for πολλοι we have πολλων which accurately conveys the meaning thus : "Out of many of them who had unclean spirits, these (spirits) departed or were expelled, crying out with a loud voice."

9. " Great joy," arising from the miraculous cures and restoration to health, as well as from the wonderful conversions.

"A certain man, ... Simon, who," &c. In this construction, according to the Vulgate, "who" has no meaning. It is omitted in the Greek. " A certain man had been before "—the arrival of Philip—"a magician." &c.

The study and practice of magic generally prevailed among the ancients. Those who practised it, designated *magi*, or wise men, were held in the highest estimation among the Eastern Nations, especially the Chaldeans and Persians. Their chief occupation was the study of Philosophy, Astronomy, Medicine, &c. (see Matthew. xi). In course of time they fell into disrepute. They used enchantments, had re course to Astrological predictions and jugglery of all sorts (Isaias ii. 6 ; Daniel i. 20 ; ii. 2).

The Jews were prohibited under the severest penalties from having recourse to them (Leviticus xx. 6).

"Seducing the people," &c. The Greek word means, *astonishing* the people, causing amazement among them.

"Giving out," boasting that he was "some great one," some superior personage, which he endeavoured to prove by his incanta. tions practised on the credulity of every description of people.

10. "The power of God," &c. The organ or instrument employed by the supreme power of God for displaying His Divine wonders. It

Commentary.

may be meant to be regarded as some kind of Divinity, some Divine Legate or the expected Messiah (St. Jerome in *c.* 24 ; Matthew ; St. Augustine de Heres. *c.* 1). We are informed by St. Justin, Tertullian, &c., that a statue was erected in his honour in the Isle of the Tiber by order of Claudius and the Roman Senate, with the inscription, *Simoni, Deo Sancto*, though this is denied by others, but without reason. The testimony of St. Justin, who says he saw it, is decisive on the point.

for a long time, he had bewitched them with his magical practices.

12. *But when they had believed Philip preaching of the kingdom of God, in the name of Jesus Christ, they were baptized, both men and women.*

13. "Simon himself believed also." Whether he really believed or only acted the hypocrite is disputed. Even those who hold that his faith was real say it was not a living faith accompanied by charity, only a sort of intellectual faith, not unlike that of the demons who, compelled by the evidence of facts, "believe and tremble" (St. James ii. 19). Indeed, the severe reproof given him by St. Peter for his impious conduct furnishes a strong presumption in favour of this opinion. "*Desideravit* (says St. Augustin in Psalm xxx.) *non gratiam sed potentiam, non unde liberaretur ; sed unde extolleretur.*"

"He stuck close to Philip." It was usual with converts at the time to cling to their masters.

14, 15. "Sent unto them Peter," &c. Not by the exercise of any authority, especially when Peter, the head of the Church, was concerned. They only, as a community, urged and persuaded them to go ; so that Peter would be the first to admit the Samaritans, as he was the first afterwards to receive the Gentiles, into the Church.

The object the Apostles had in view in going to Samaria in compliance with the wishes of the Apostolic body was to communicate the gifts of the Holy Ghost in an increase of grace and sanctity, and by external miraculous manifestations (*v.* 18).

16. "Not yet come upon them" in any special visible manner. "Only baptized in the name of Jesus," that is, by the authority and in the manner instituted by the Lord Jesus when he commanded to Baptize "in the name of the Father and of the Son," &c. The phrase is meant to distinguish the *Baptism instituted by our Lord* from the *Baptism of John.* "In the name" may also mean *into* the name of the Lord Jesus so as to become His followers and be aggregated with those who embraced His sacred teaching and religion.

17. "They laid their hands," &c. Besides the increase of sanctifying and interior grace given them through the Apostles, in addition to that received in Baptism, there can be no doubt that this descent of the Holy Ghost was also attended by certain visible effects seen by Simon

Text.

ear, from the least to the greatest, saying: This man is the power of God, which is called great.

11. And they were attentive to him, because,

13. Then Simon himself believed also ; and being baptized, he stuck close to Philip. And being astonished, wondered to see the signs and exceeding great miracles which were done.

14. Now when the apostles, who were in Jerusalem, had heard that Samaria had received the word of God, they sent unto them Peter and John.

15. Who, when they were come, prayed for them, that they might receive the Holy Ghost.

16. For he was not as yet come upon any of them ; but they were only baptized in the name of the Lord Jesus.

17. Then they laid their hands upon them, and they

Text.

Commentary.

Magus (*v.* 18.) It was this power of miracles and not the graces given that he wished to purchase. This power of speaking strange tongues, of working miracles, &c., it was that Simon saw and offered money for. It is certain that *unction* accompanied the *imposition of hands*. But, St. Luke only mentions here, for brevity sake, one of the sensible elements. As at the Baptism of the eunuch (*v.* 27) he is described as only professing his faith in the Divinity of our Lord, though other points were required. Both always went together. Hence, the Holy Fathers said at one time, that the Holy Ghost was given by the imposition of hands; at other times, by the Holy Unction. As they regarded both, as only one, they designated at times only one of the two things that were inseparably united. Thus, Tertullian, uniting both (de Resurrectione Carnis. cap. viii.) says, "*caro ungitur, ut anima consecretur; caro signatur ut anima muniatur; caro manus impositione obumbratur, ut anima spiritu illuminatur,*" though, in his treatise against Marcion, he only speaks of the Unction.

Catholic writers are unanimous in asserting, that in this action of the Apostles, in which Philip the Deacon had no part,—the Apostles being deputed to perform it,—there is question of the holy Sacrament of Confirmation, instituted by our Lord Jesus Christ as one of the seven Sacraments of the New Law. We have here all the conditions of a Sacrament. 1, minister, viz.: the Apostles; 2, the sensible-sign, viz.: imposition of hands, accompanied, no doubt, with *unction;* 3, the effect, viz., a new and special communication of *Sacramental* grace through the descent of the Holy Ghost.

18. *And when Simon saw, that by the imposition of the hands of the apostles, the Holy Ghost was given, he offered them money,*

18. Clearly, the presence of the Holy Ghost in those confirmed was manifested by sensible signs, gift of tongues, prophecies, miracles, added to interior grace (as in *c.* xix. 6). For these Simon offered "money," in order to perpetuate his infamous delusions practised on the Samaritans. Hence, the odious term, *Simony,* expressive of the enormous crime of purchasing for money sacred and spiritual things.

19. *Saying: Give me also this power, that on whomsoever I shall lay my hands, he may receive the Holy Ghost. But Peter said to him:*

19. "That on whomsoever I shall lay," &c. Simon wished to have the power of imparting these gifts to others.

20. *Keep thy money to thyself, to perish with thee, because thou hast thought that the gift of God may be purchased with money.*

20. The words of this passage, though in the form of an imprecation, hardly consistent with Peter's exhortation to repentance (*v.* 22) are generally regarded as an expression of the heinousness of Simon's crime; and prophetic of the fate that awaited him, as a deterrent to others, unless he did penance. Similar forms are found in the Psalms of David apparently imprecatory.

"The Simoniacal Heresy—the first to assail the Church—was nipped

Commentary.

in the bud by the sword of Apostolical vengeance "—(St. Gregory, Ep. 114).

"Thou hast thought," &c., conveys the utter inequality between worthless pelf and the exalted and priceless gifts of God, which could not be matter for such impious traffic.

21. "*Part, lot*," express the same thing with greater emphasis and force. They mean that Simon is utterly unfit to share in the exalted gifts of imposing hands on the baptized and giving the Holy Ghost, as "his heart was not right in the sight of God," the searcher of hearts, being filled with ambitious pride, avarice, and love of evanescent popularity. "In this matter." The Greek is, *this word*. "Word" is used by the Hebrews for the thing it signifies.

22. Peter, who by Divine light, got an insight into Simon's sinfulness (23) invites him to do penance, and under the influence of this change of heart and penitential spirit (for a contrite and humbled heart God never despises, Ps. l.), to approach God in prayer.

"If perhaps this thought"—wicked device and purpose—"of thy heart may be forgiven thee." The doubt as to his forgiveness does not regard God's power or beneficence; but Simon's sincere dispositions, whom Peter saw to be still in permanent obduracy.

23. "For I see," from your impious offer and Divine revelation.

"Gall of bitterness." A Hebrew form for *bitter gall*, expressive of black malice, injurious to others; perverse malignant dispositions, hostile to Christianity.

"Bonds of iniquity." Sunk in wickedness of the worst kind, bound in the chains of sin. The Greek for "in" is, εις, *into*, which, though joined to a verb of repose, conveys the idea of motion, and of rushing headlong into a thing.

24. These words can hardly be regarded as expressive of a sincere desire of amendment. Simon very likely regarded the menaces of Peter, as pointing to the result of some enchantment to be removed by him who practised it. It was not the malice of his sin he felt concerned for, but only the punishment, like Pharaoh and Antiochus. He was not sincerely repentant. Far from reforming his wicked life, it is said he continued his evil practices (St. Ireneus, *lib.* 1, *cap.* 20-23), and acquired great fame afterwards at Rome from the practice of magic and sorcery. His end is not known for certain.

25. "Testified." Given convincing proofs of the truths of the Gospel. They were not idle during their stay in the city of Samaria.

"Many countries." Samaria itself was only *one country* or province.

Κωμας – villages.

Text.

21. Thou hast no part nor lot in this matter. For thy heart is not right in the sight of God.

22. Do penance therefore, from this thy wickedness; and pray to God, if perhaps this thought of thy heart may be forgiven thee.

23. For I see thou art in the gall of bitterness, and in the bonds of iniquity.

24. Then Simon answering, said: Pray you for me to the Lord, that none of those things which you have spoken may come upon me.

25. And they indeed having testified and preached the

word of the Lord, returned to Jerusalem, and preached the gospel to many countries of the Samaritans.

Commentary.

Hence, the Greek reading *"villages"* is the genuine one. They preached in *several villages* on their way to Jerusalem.

κωμας - villages.

26. Now an Angel of the Lord spoke to Philip, saying: Arise, go towards the south, to the way that goeth down from Jerusalem into Gaza: this is desert.

26. The word *"angel"* designates the office of messenger, "the Lord." It may be the Spirit of God Himself (29-39). As it occurred in day time, most likely he appeared in a visible form. From the word "arise," some infer that Philip was in bed, and the occurrence, a dream. But, looking to Hebrew usage, the word "arise" does not necessarily mean this. It means to prepare for some course of action. "South" of Samaria, where he had been preaching.

"This is desert." According to some, this means a place mostly uninhabited. Others understand it to refer to "the way" that passed through desolate places, and is distinguished from other ways. This was the road that would bring him to the place where he would meet the eunuch.

27. And rising up, he went. And behold a man of Ethiopia, a eunuch, of great authority under Candace, the queen of the Ethiopians, who had charge over all her treasures, had come to Jerusalem to adore.

27. "An eunuch," men of this description being usually employed in discharging offices in the palace. The term is often applied to officers of court, without reference to their bodily condition. Here, most likely, the man was not, strictly speaking, an eunuch. He was a great officer of State, the Queen's treasurer. (*ευνη. led — εχω. have care of*)

"Candace." Some expositors hold that this was a family name, assumed by the Queens of Ethiopia; like Pharaoh among the Egyptians. *cf. "chamberlain" in Eng. & U.S. (N.J.)*

"Had come to Jerusalem," &c. Most likely he was a Jew or Jewish proselyte. In the latter case, he could not be an eunuch, strictly speaking, as such were not admitted as Jewish proselytes.

"To adore." It was not unusual with foreign Jews to attend the great Jewish Festivals, Pasch, Pentecost, &c., at Jerusalem, and religiously assist at the leading functions of public worship—sacrifices and all religious ceremonies—in the Temple. At Jerusalem only was it allowed to offer sacrifices (Deut. xiv. 23). The word "adore" frequently bears the meaning of sacrificing (Genesis xxii. 5, John iv. 20, xii. 20, &c.). If these were questions merely of praying, that he might do any where, as well as at Jerusalem.

28. And he was returning, sitting in his chariot, and reading Isaias the prophet;

28. "Reading" aloud, "Isaias the prophet." The Prophecy of Isaias, which is often termed an anticipated Gospel, owing to the vivid account it gives by anticipation, of the several circumstances connected with the life and death of our Lord, was the portion of Scripture the eunuch was reading and directly meditating upon. The events, which recently took place in Jerusalem, in connection with our Lord's death and Resurrection, and the discourses to which they gave rise, added

Commentary.

special interest to the Prophecy of Isaias, where they were described beforehand.

29. "And the Spirit" of God, the angel or messenger referred to (v. 26). "Go near," &c. Join company with the man in the chariot.

30. Philip was inspired to put this question, which the eunuch took in good part.

31. The answer, according to the Greek construction, implies a *negative*. It runs thus: "For how can I," &c., as if to say, *I do not.* "For how can I," &c. Unless some man, more learned and better versed in Scripture—"show me." The Greek is *guide* or direct me.

Grotius remarks on this passage. "This eunuch did not find the Scriptures so perspicuous as they are now made, not only by handicraft men, but by shoemakers, tailors, and even by women." The Scriptures contain many things in themselves hard to be understood, difficult for all and very injurious to *some*. (2 Peter iii. and 32.)

32. And the place "passage" of the Scripture (Isaias liii. 7, 8). "*He was led as a sheep,*" &c. This is according to the Septuagint version, differing but little from the Hebrew. He, was, therefore, reading from the Septuagint. This passage, as was universally admitted, referred to the Messiah; and Philip applied it to him. Isaias adopting the Prophetic style, speaks of the future event, as past or present, owing to the certainty of its accomplishments.

33. This is also according to the Septuagint; but very different from the Hebrew, which runs thus: "From prison was He taken,"—which is expressed here "in humility," or in the humiliation he was subjected to. "Humility" here has the same sense as in Psalm ix. "Vide *humilitatem meam*, that is, *humiliationem meam.*"

"*His judgment was taken away.*" Which means that He was in humiliation, bereft of friends to stand by Him, His just sentence was denied to Him and he was condemned to an unjust, ignominious death. He was oppressed by an unjust judgment.

"*His generation who shall declare.*" Generally understood of His

Text.

29. And the Spirit said to Philip: Go near, and join thyself to this chariot.

30. And Philip running thither, heard him reading the prophet Isaias. And he said: Thinkest thou that thou understandest what thou readest?

31. Who said: And how can I, unless some man shew me? And he desired Philip that he would come up and sit with him.

32. And the place of the scripture which he was reading was this: He was led as a sheep to the slaughter; and like a lamb without voice before his shearer, so openeth he not his mouth.

33. In humility his judgment was taken away. His generation who shall declare, for his life shall be taken from the earth?

G

Text.	Commentary.

Divine origin, of His eternal generation begotten of his father. The depth of his humiliation and the injustice perpetrated on Him will be seen in having *His life taken away from the earth*. Others understand it of the wicked generation or class of men among whom he lived, who in return for the manifold benefits conferred on them during His mortal life, ungratefully repaid all by taking away His life and subjecting Him to an ignominious death. Who, then, can sufficiently describe the crimes of the guilty generation of men of His own day, by whom He was thus treated?

34. *And the eunuch answering Philip, said: I beseech thee, of whom doth the prophet speak this? of himself, or of some other man?*

34. "Answering" is frequently used in Scripture, to speak to one whether addressed before or not. "Of himself." There was hardly anything in the text to determine to whom it referred. Possibly this text was urged to prove that Jesus of Nazareth whose claim to Messiahship was put forward within the few preceding days in Jerusalem, and whose death was compassed by the Jews, was their long-expected Messiah; and the eunuch, on his journey, was profoundly meditating on the sense of the passage, as to whether it could apply to the Messiah. It seemed self-contradictory, that he would be a great prince, and at the same time subjected to such humiliations. It was this made the eunuch inquire whether the passage might not be understood of Isaias himself.

35. *Then Philip, opening his mouth, and beginning at this scripture, preached unto him Jesus.*

35. "Opening his mouth," a form of expression, conveying that he commenced to debate fully and solemnly on an important subject (see Matthew v. 1). "And beginning at this scripture." Taking up this very passage of Isaias, from which the eunuch was reading, he dilated fully on its meaning and applicability to our Lord, stating that the prophet referred to Jesus, and that Jesus was the eternal Son of God. "And preached unto him Jesus," His Gospel, His Divinity, Incarnation for the love and salvation of mankind, the necessity of being ingrafted in Him by baptism and other practical points of Christian doctrine.

36. *And as they went on their way, they came to a certain water; and the eunuch said: See, here is water: what doth hinder me from being baptized?*

36. "A certain water." A pool or rivulet containing water enough for the rite of baptism, "what doth hinder," &c.? Clearly, Philip had, previously, among other points, instructed him as to the necessity of baptism to be introduced into the church and ingrafted on the body of Christ.

37. *And Philip said: If thou believest with all thy heart, thou mayest. And he answering, said: I believe that Jesus Christ is the Son of God.*

37. "If thou believest," &c. Faith is the first and most essential condition for baptism. It must not only be a mere act of intellect. It must come from the "heart," from the will and affections also. These words imply a full belief in all the truths of the Gospel, of which Philip no doubt, placed before him a summary, all founded on the leading truth of the Divinity of Jesus Christ; from the answer of the eunuch, "I believe that Jesus Christ is the Son," &c., it is quite clear, this was the first truth insisted upon.

Commentary.

The authenticity of the words " thou believest," &c., is questioned by some distinguished critics. They are wanting in some MSS. " I believe that Jesus Christ," &c. This conveys a full belief in all that Jesus Christ, the Eternal Son of God, the infallible truth has revealed with a belief in the leading articles of the Apostles' Creed, which, no doubt, Philip briefly taught the eunuch. St. Luke only mentions this fundamental article of the Divinity of our Lord. It must be that Philip also taught the eunuch the necessity of contrition for the remission of sin.

38. " Went down into the water." This would look like baptism, by *immersion*. However, that would not necessarily follow. He might go down into the water, and receive a baptism different from *immersion*. The mode of conferring it is a matter of discipline, which may vary at different times. There is no decretorial proof here as the mode in which this baptism was administered, whether by *immersion* or otherwise. It might be done by pouring out, or infusion while *in* the water as well.

39. " Up out of the water." The Greek particle may mean *from* as well as, *out of*. " Took away Philip." How, it is not stated here, whether miraculously or supernaturally carried through the air, as is recorded in some cases in the Old Testament (3 Kings xviii. 12; 4 Kings ii. 11; St. Paul, 2 Cor. xii., 2, 4), thus confirming the faith of the eunuch. Others understand it of strong suggestions imperatively urging Philip to depart at once from the society he would fain enjoy much longer.

40. " Was found." According to those, who assign a supernatural complexion to the preceding narrative, it means; carried through the air. He found himself suddenly in Azotus. According to others it simply means, he came to Azotus; was not heard of till he came to Azotus. The former interpretation seems the more natural, if we consider the angelic influences at work all through. Azotus on the Mediterranean was over thirty miles from Gaza.

" And passing through," &c. He preached the Gospel in all cities that lay between Azotus and Cæsarea, viz., Joppa, Lydda, Askelon, Arimathea, &c., situated on the sea coast.

Cæsarea formerly called *Strato's Tower*, was over sixty miles north of Azotus. It was rebuilt by Herod and called " Cæsarea," in honour of Augustus Cæsar, to whom a temple was built by Herod; a statue of the Emperor was also erected by him, at the mouth of the harbour. The seaport was called *Sebaste*, the Greek term for Augustus.

This city of Cæsarea adorned by sculptures, buildings and porticoes, was the seat of government. There the Roman governor of Judea resided.

38. And he commanded the chariot to stand still; and they went down into the water, both Philip and the eunuch: and he baptized him.

39. And when they were come up out of the water, the Spirit of the Lord took away Philip; and the eunuch saw him no more. And he went on his way rejoicing.

40. But Philip was found in Azotus; and passing through, he preached the gospel to all the cities, till he came to Cæsarea.

CHAPTER IX.

1. *And Saul as yet breathing out threatenings and slaughter against the disciples of the Lord, went to the high-priest,*

2. *And asked of him letters to Damascus, to the synagogues : that if he found any men and women of this way, he might bring them bound to Jerusalem.*

3. *And as he went on his journey, it came to pass that he drew nigh to Damascus. and suddenly a light from heaven shined round about him.*

4. *And falling on the ground, he heard a voice saying to him : Saul, Saul, why persecutest thou me ?*

5. *Who said : Who art thou, Lord ? And he : I am Jesus whom thou persecutest. It is hard for thee to kick against the goad.*

6. *And he trembling and astonished, said : Lord, what wilt thou have me to do ?*

7. *And the Lord said to him : Arise, and go into the city, and there it shall be told thee what thou must do. Now the men who went in company with him stood amazed, hearing indeed a voice, but seeing no man.*

8. *And Saul arose from the ground, and when his eyes were opened, he saw nothing. But they leading him by the hands, brought him to Damascus.*

9. *And he was there three days without sight, and he did neither eat nor drink.*

10. *Now there was a certain disciple at Damascus, named Ananias : and the Lord said to him in a vision : Ananias. And he said : Behold I am hear, Lord.*

11. *And the Lord said to him : Arise, and go into the street that is called Strait, and seek in the house of Judas, one named Saul of Tarsus. For behold he prayeth.*

12. *(And he saw a man named Ananias, coming in and putting his hands upon him, that he might receive his sight.)*

13. *But Ananias answered : Lord, I have heard by many of this man, how much evil he hath done to thy saints in Jerusalem :*

14. *And here he hath authority from the chief priest to bind all that invoke thy name.*

15. *And the Lord said to him : Go thy way, for this man is to me a vessel of election, to carry my name before the gentiles, and kings, and the children of Israel.*

16. *For I will shew him how great things he must suffer for my name's sake.*

17. *And Ananias went his way, and he entered into the house : and laying his hands upon him, he said : Brother Saul, the Lord Jesus hath sent me, he that appeared to thee in the way as thou camest : that thou mayest receive thy sight, and be filled with the Holy Ghost.*

18. *And immediately there fell from his eyes as it were scales, and he received his sight, and rising up he was baptized.*

19. *And when he had taken meat, he was strengthened. And he was with the disciples that were at Damascus, for some days.*

20. *And immediately he preached Jesus in the synagogues, that he is the Son of God.*

21. *And all that heard him were astonished, and said : Is not this he who persecuted in Jerusalem those that called upon this name ; and came hither for that intent, that he might carry them bound to the chief priests ?*

22. *But Saul increased much more in strength, and confounded the Jews who dwelt at Damascus, affirming that this is the Christ.*

23. *And when many days were passed, the Jews consulted together to kill him.*

24. *But their laying in wait was made known to Saul. And they watched the gates also day and night, that they might kill him.*

25. *But the disciples taking him in the night, conveyed him away by the wall, letting him down in a basket.*

26. *And when he was come into Jerusalem, he essayed to join himself to the disciples, and they all were afraid of him, not believing that he was a disciple.*

27. *But Barnabas took him and brought him to the apostles, and told them how he had seen the Lord, and that he had spoken to him, and how in Damascus he had dealt confidently in the name of Jesus.*

28. *And he was with them coming in and going out in Jerusalem, and dealing confidently in the name of the Lord.*

29. *He spoke also to the gentiles, and disputed with the Greeks: but they sought to kill him.*

30. *Which when the brethren had known, they brought him down to Cesarea, and sent him away to Tarsus.*

31. *Now the church had peace throughout all Judea and Galilee and Samaria, and was edified walking in the fear of the Lord, and was filled with the consolation of the Holy Ghost.*

32. *And it came to pass, that Peter, as he passed through visiting all, came to the saints who dwelt in Lydda.* (*s.e. Joppa - n.w. of Jerus.*)

33. *And he found there a certain man named Eneas, who had kept his bed for eight years, who was ill of the palsy.* da-

34. *And Peter said to him: Eneas, the Lord Jesus Christ healeth thee: arise, and make thy bed. And immediately he arose.*

35. *And all that dwelt at Lydda and Saron saw him: who were converted to the Lord.*

36. *And in Joppe there was a certain disciple named Tabitha, which by interpretation is called Dorcas. This woman was full of good works and alms-deeds which she did.*

37. *And it came to pass in those days, that she was sick and died. Whom when they had washed, they laid her in an upper chamber.*

38. *And forasmuch as Lydda was nigh to Joppe, the disciples hearing that Peter was there, sent unto him two men, desiring him that he would not be slack to come unto them.*

39. *And Peter rising up went with them. And when he was come, they brought him into the upper chamber: and all the widows stood about him weeping, and shewing him the coats and garments which Dorcas made them.*

40. *And they all being put forth: Peter kneeling down prayed, and turning to the body, he said: Tabitha, arise. And she opened her eyes: and seeing Peter, she sat up.*

41. *And giving her his hand, he lifted her up. And when he had called the saints and the widows he presented her alive.*

42. *And it was made known throughout all Joppe; and many believed in the Lord.*

43. *And it came to pass that he abode many days in Joppe, with one Simon a tanner.*

ANALYSIS.

The Chapter commences with the wonderful and miraculous conversion of Saul on his way to persecute the Christians of Damascus, which was perfected by the instructions of Ananias, whose fears occasioned by the persecuting character of Saul were dissipated by Divine assurances on the subject (1-18). The zeal of Saul in preaching the Gospel, the conspiracy on the part of the Jews to kill him (19-25), His escape (25). The distrust of the faithful of Jerusalem regarding him on account of his repute, as Persecutor, quieted by the intervention of Barnabas, who introduced him to the Apostles (26, 27). The machinations of the Gentiles to kill him. Hence his escape to Tharsus (29, 30). The miracles wrought by Peter in the restoration to health of Eneas (32-35). The wonderful miracle wrought by him in raising Tabitha or Dorcas from the dead, which caused the conversion of many (36-43).

Text.

1. *And Saul as yet breathing out threatenings and slaughter against the disciples of the Lord, went to the high-priest,*

Commentary.

1. "And Saul," who had already rendered himself prominently conspicuous in the persecution of the Christians, was now "as yet," in the interval between the present time and the death of Stephen, indulging still, his passion for persecution, shown in the murder of Stephen.

"Breathing out." Furiously agitated, displaying a violent thirst for vengeance. "Threatenings," all kinds of threatening and denunciatory language. "And slaughter," designs of wholesale murder "against the disciples of our Lord," the converted believers. He had a hand in putting to death a great number of Christians (Acts xxvi. 10, 11).

"Went to the High Priest,"

2. *And asked of him letters to Damascus to the synagogues: that if he found any men and women of this way, he might bring them bound to Jerusalem.*

2. "And asked of him letters," &c. The letters were written by the authority of the *Sanhedrim* and signed by the High Priest, as President of the Council. Some say the conversion of St. Paul took place in the thirty-fifth year of our era, three years after our Lord's death. In that case the High Priest was Caiphas, who was deposed by Tertullus.

If it occurred later, the High Priest was Theophilus. To the *Sanhedrim*, belonged to take cognizance of offences against religion. The Romans connived at their doing this beyond the precincts of Judea, wherever synagogues were found, dependent on the *Sanhedrim*.

"Asked." He himself volunteered to act as persecutor ; "Letters," credentials conveying a commission or *authorization.* "To Damascus " a celebrated well-known city of Asia, mentioned in Scripture 1: a city, in the days of Abraham (Genisis xv. 2). After various vicissitudes, it was ultimately taken by Selim, A.D. 1517. Ever since, it has been subject to the Saracens.

It was well-known to Saul, that a large number of Christians had been at Damascus, and the credential letters gave him the power vested in the *Sanhedrim* to punish all offences against religion. The policy of the Romans was to leave the exercise of such power to the *Sanhedrim*, reserving for themselves the confirmation of the sentence of death.

"To the Synagogues." Over whom the *Sanhedrim* exercised authority.

"Men and women," even "women," were not spared, which shows intense hatred.

"Of this way," of thinking and believing ; of this sect.

"Bring them bound," for trial before the *Sanhedrim*, whose powers in matters pertaining to religion, the Romans sanctioned or connived at, save in the supreme case of death, specially reserved for themselves.

3. *And as he went on his journey, it came to pass that he drew nigh to Damascus : and suddenly a light*

3. "While travelling along the road, and when he was near Damascus—how near, no one can tell—the important event here mentioned, took place.

"Suddenly." With the suddenness of a flash of lightning. It was not, however, a flash of lightning. It was the transcendent, overwhelming, dazzling glory, surrounding our Lord Himself, as at his Transfigura-

Commentary.

tion (John xvii. 5). It was our Lord Himself, personally appearing to St. Paul in His glory, which Paul recognized, calling Him "Lord" (*v.* 5). For Barnabas declared "*how* he had seen the Lord in the way (*v.* 27). He himself says (1 Cor. ix. 1, xv. 8),that he saw our Lord. Similar is the language (1 Cor. ix. 1). He now sees resuscitated, living, glorious, our Lord, whom he supposed to be dead.

"A light from heaven," from the sky, "above the brightness of the sun (xxvi. 13).

"About him," and his companions also (xxvi. 13).

4. Overpowered by the dazzling light, he fell to the ground, and so did those who were with him, overawed by the majesty of what they saw (xxvi. 14). It is not opposed to this, that "they stood amazed" (*v.* 7), for they might have soon risen to their feet.

"He heard a voice, Saul, Saul." The word is repeated for emphasis sake.

"Why,"—for what reason, on account of *what* provocation? "persecutest thou me," viz., in his chosen members. He was head of the body whose members Saul was engaged in furiously and relentlessly persecuting.

5. "Lord" does not imply Divinity. It is only a term of courteous reverence elicited by the terror he was in. Up to this, Saul did not for certain acknowledge Jesus Christ to be God. Similar is the meaning of Magdalen's words, when she thought she was addressing the gardener (John xx. 15).

"I am Jesus," &c. In chap. xxii. 8, it is "I am Jesus of Nazareth," in which is conveyed that the humble Nazarene, whom Paul despised, as if nothing good could come out of Nazareth, is now Lord of all. He now appears to him in glory.

"It is hard for thee to kick," &c. A proverbial expression with the Greeks and Romans, conveying that obstinate and stubborn resistance to lawful authority and rebellion against those who have a right to command is injurious to the man who resists. The idea is borrowed from stubborn oxen kicking against the "goad," or sharp piece of iron used to urge them on. By kicking, they injure themselves. This according to the conjecture of some, denotes the resistance Paul had been giving before our Lord appeared to him, to the interior emotions of grace urging him to desist from the persecution he was practising. The example and admonition of his former teacher, Gamaliel (xxii. 3) who embraced the faith, may have served to disquiet him and cause some remorse of conscience.

6. What he saw and heard created a feeling of terror and alarm on reflecting on the wicked course he had been pursuing.

"Lord." The term here denotes the supreme reverence due to Him as God and Saviour. "What wilt thou," &c., shows his thorough

from heaven shined round about him.

4. And falling on the ground, he heard a voice saying to him: Saul, Saul, why persecutest thou me?

5. Who said: Who art thou, Lord? And he I am Jesus whom thou persecutest. It is hard for thee to kick against the goad.

6. And he trembling and astonished, said: Lord, what wilt thou have me to do?

Text.	Commentary.

conversion and prompt change of heart. Giving up his own wicked will and feeling of opposition to God, he now professes at once his willingness to embrace in all things God's Adorable Will.

7. *And the Lord said to him: Arise, and go into the city, and there it shall be told thee what thou must do. Now, the men who went in company with him stood amazed, hearing indeed a voice, but seeing no man.*

7. "The Lord"—our God and Saviour—"arise." He was still prostrate (*v.* 8, xxvi. 16).

"Go into the city"—Damascus close by (*v.* 3). The whole narrative is more circumstantially detailed by St. Paul himself (c. xxvi. 16-18) in his address to King Agrippa.

"And there it shall be told thee," &c. In this we see the wonderful and mysterious ways of God's Providence in carrying out his designs. He might himself have instructed him on the spot. But, no; it pleased Him to employ the ministry of an humble disciple at Damascus for perfecting His beneficent designs. In this He had also in view to test Paul's humility, obedience and self abnegation.

"The men . . . . stood amazed." The Greek word for amazed (ϵννϵοι) means *struck dumb*, unable to speak. They were struck *mute* with terror. It may be, when the first feeling of alarm which prostrated them (xxvi. 14) subsided, they *stood* up *immediately*, while Paul, who was chiefly concerned in the matter, continued prostrate. In *c.* xxvi. 14, it is said they were "all fallen on the ground." This occurred, as the *immediate* effect of the light, *before* they heard the voice. Here we have an account of what took place *after* the first feeling of panic and alarm was over. They stood up immediately. It may be, the word, "*stood*," has no particular meaning; that it merely denotes the feeling of alarm they felt, without reference to what position they were in, whether *standing* or *prostrate*.

"Hearing, indeed, a voice," probably means hearing a sound, but not understanding the articulate utterance and meaning as it was understood by Saul.

8. *And Saul arose from the ground, and when his eyes were opened, he saw nothing. But they leading him by the hands, brought him to Damascus.*

8. "And when his eyes were opened." The Greek would be more properly rendered, and *although* his eyes opened, "or with eyes opened." For while prostrate, his eyes were opened, looking at our Lord in His glorious appearance. But, when he rose up, on account of the dazzling, intense brightness of the light emanating from the glorified body of Jesus, his eyes though opened, were bereft of the faculty of seeing "for three days," *v.* 9.

9. *And he was there three days without sight, and he did neither eat nor drink.*

9. "And he did neither eat," &c. Terror and remorse, suspense and perplexity, as he received no intimation as to what he was to do, joined with fervent and absorbing prayer for pardon of his sins, for heavenly light to remove his state of perplexity, made him indifferent and unconcerned about all corporal sustenance.

Commentary.

10. " A certain disciple," a Christian, who had already heard of Saul's violent persecution of his fellow-believers (*v.* 13). "Ananias," the term would indicate a Jew by birth converted to the faith.

11. "For he prayeth." Fear him no longer, as a fanatical persecutor of the Christians. He is now a different man, completely changed, engaged in fervent prayer for light, guidance and forgiveness. This would point to the manner Paul spent the three days in question.

12. Very likely, the words of this verse are parenthetical, inserted by St. Luke, to inform us that while our Lord was addressing Ananias in a vision, Saul was favoured with another vision, assuring him that Ananias, whose name he gives, was no impostor, and would soon show him, on the part of God, what he was to do. "*Quid Te oporteat facere*" (*v.* 7).

13. In this Ananias expresses his fears and surprise. Probably, Ananias, informed by letters from the faithful of Jerusalem, or by public rumour, or by some Christians who fled on account of the persecution from Jerusalem to Damascus, heard all about Paul's fanaticism and persecuting violence.
"Thy saints." The term always applied by the Apostle, in his Epistles, to Christians.

14. " And here " in this very city. Likely, the companions of Saul published all about him, and so it reached Ananias.

15. " Go thy way." A brief form of expressing that God will do what is just and reasonable. Here, it is a repetition of God's instructions to Ananias regarding Saul.
"A vessel of Election." "Vessel," according to Hebrew usage, signifies an organ or instrument. "Election," chosen, like the other Apostles, to carry out My designs of mercy. "Carry My name." Proclaim My attributes as God and Man, Creator and Redeemer of mankind.

Text.

10. *Now there was a certain disciple at Damascus named Ananias: and the Lord said to him in a vision: Ananias. And he said: Behold, I am here, Lord.*

11. *And the Lord said to him: Arise, and go into the street that is called Strait, and seek in the house of Judas, one named Saul of Tarsus. For behold he prayeth.*

12. *(And he saw a man named Ananias, coming in and putting his hands upon him, that he might receive his sight.)*

13. *But Ananias answered: Lord, I have heard by many of this man, how much evil he hath done to thy saints in Jerusalem:*

14. *And here he hath authority from the chief priests to bind all that invoke thy name.*

15. *And the Lord said to him: Go thy way, for this man is to me a vessel of election to carry my name before the gentiles, and kings, and the children of Israel.*

Text.

Commentary.

"Before the Gentiles." The different nations of the earth. Paul was in a special manner constituted the Apostle of the Gentiles (Rom. xi. 13, xv. 16 ; Gal. ii. 8).

"And kings." This he did (Acts xxv. 23, xxvi. 1).

"And children of Israel." This he did at once (20, 21).

16. *For I will show him how great things he must suffer for my name's sake.*

16. "I will show him," &c. As a proof that he will be a distinguished instrument to be employed by Me, I will have him suffer much on My account, and hence he will be distinguished in My service. His success will be proportioned to his fortitude and constancy in enduring evils. That he did suffer this is shown from the picture he draws for us (2 Cor. xi.) and his subsequent History in these Acts of the Apostles.

17. *And Ananias went his way, and he entered into the house : and laying his hands upon him, he said: Brother Saul, the Lord Jesus hath sent me, he that appeared to thee in the way as thou camest: that thou mayst receive thy sight, and be filled with the Holy Ghost.*

17. In obedience to our Lord's command, Ananias, proceeded to his destination, "and laying his hands upon him." It was not for the purpose of giving the Sacrament of Confirmation. There is no evidence that Ananias was in a position to do so—moreover, Saul was still unbaptized, and Ananias himself states the object : "that thou mayst receive thy sight," which he did on the spot, "and be filled with the Holy Ghost," through the baptism, he was immediately to receive. The imposition of hands restored his sight. Baptism gave him the Holy Ghost." It may be, that with the effect of baptism, Paul received in an extraordinary way the grace of Confirmation without the eternal rite, as did the Apostles on Pentecost Sunday.

18. *And immediately there fell from his eyes as it were scales, and he received his sight ; and rising up he was baptized.*

18. The teguments that fell from his eyes and impeded his sight were like "scales." They fell, as if "scales" had fallen, with which fishes and serpents are covered. The cure being so sudden, and, so far as human agency was concerned, without any human adequate cause, shows that it was manifestly miraculous.

"He was baptized." As there is no mention of having received the necessary previous instruction in the truths of faith, it is most likely our Lord Himself fully instructed him during the three days preceding his baptism. Hence, he says (Gal. i,) he received the Gospel, not from man, but from Jesus Christ.

19. *And when he had taken meat, he was strengthened. And he was with the disciples that were at Damascus, for some days.*

19. He recovered his natural strength, weakened by previous fasting.

After his communion he proceeded to Arabia, and then again came back to Damascus. St. Luke makes no mention of his journey to Arabia.

20. *And immediately he preached Jesus in the synagogues, that he is the Son of God.*

20. This shows the genuine sincerity of his conversion.

Commentary.

21. " Persecuted." The Greek word would convey, *ravaged*, deprived of life.

ished, *and said: Is not this he who persecuted in Jerusalem those that called upon this name; and came hither for that intent, that he might carry them bound to the chief priests?*

22. "Increased," &c. Animated and armed with greater energy and zeal in preaching the Gospel. "Confounded," *creating* confusion among them; *confuting* them by argument.

"Affirming" by undeniable proofs "that this" our Lord "is the Christ," the long-expected anointed Messiah.

23. Very likely the "many days" embrace the term within which he had been in Arabia; probably, a term of about three years. This is omitted by St. Luke. St. Paul himself tells us (Gal. i. 17) he went to Arabia after his conversion, and returned to Damascus, and after three years he went up to Jerusalem, not straightway from Arabia, but from Damascus, whither he had returned, and encountered the murderous designs of the Jews, who "consulted together to kill him."

24. "Watched the gates" (2 Cor. xi. 32) which were the only avenues for escape as the cities were surrounded with high walls. St. Paul says (2 Cor. xi. 32) it was the governor under Aretas who did so, no doubt, at the instigation of the Jews, he himself being, probably, a Jew, and sharing in the feelings of his co-religionists. Up to the death of Tiberius (A.D. 37) Damascus was under the Romans. Probably Aretas got it from the Romans under Caligula, Tiberius' successor.

"Watched the gates." It was the Jews that got the city authorities to do so.

night, *conveyed him away by the wall, letting him down in a basket.*

26. "And when he was come" for the first time, three years after his conversion, "to Jerusalem," whither he had fled from Damascus; "and they were all afraid of him." Likely owing to civil disturbances or the war between King Aretas and Herod, not to speak of the difficulty of communication at the time, the news of his conversion had not reached the Christians of Jerusalem, and the Jews would have concealed it had they known it.

"Not believing he was a disciple" or a sincere believer.

Although, they might have heard something of his conversion and its circumstances; still, they seemed inclined to regard the whole affair as a feint to deceive them, and persecute them still more.

27. "Barnabas," between whom and Paul there may have been heretofore friendly relations, receiving him benevolently and hospitably, while others stood aloof and shunned him, as a suspect, took him and introduced him to the Apostles, Peter and James, the only Apostles who, it *seems*, were then at Jerusalem (Gal. i. 18).

Lord, *and that he had spoken to him and how in Damascus he had dealt confidently in the name of Jesus.*

Text.

21. *And all that heard him were aston-*

22. *But Saul increased much more in strength, and confounded the Jews who dwelt at Damascus, affirming that this is the Christ.*

23. *And when many days were passed, the Jews consulted together to kill him.*

24. *But their laying in wait was made known to Saul. And they watched the gates also day and night, that they might kill him.*

25. *But the disciples taking him in the*

26. *And when he was come into Jerusalem, he essayed to join himself to the disciples, and they all were afraid of him, not believing that he was a disciple.*

27. *But Barnabas took him and brought him to the apostles, and told them how he had seen the*

Text.

28. *And he was with them coming in and going out in Jerusalem, and dealing confidently in the name of the Lord.*

29. *He spoke also to the gentiles, and disputed with the Greeks; but they sought to kill him.*

30. *Which when the brethren had known, they brought him down to Cæsarea, and sent him away to Tarsus.*

31. *Now the Church had peace throughout all Judea and Galilee and Samaria, and was edified, walking in the fear of the Lord, and was filled with the consolation of the Holy Ghost.*

Commentary.

28. "He was with them," &c., lived on terms of friendly intercourse, as Apostle and convert to the faith. He abode with them only about a fortnight (Gal. i. 8).

"Dealing confidently," &c.   He courageously proclaimed our Lord to be God.

"In the name."   By the authority of the Lord Jesus.

29. "To the Gentiles," &c.   "Gentiles," though found in the Vulgate, is found in no Greek Codex, nor in any ancient version save the Ethiopic.   It is wanting in several old Latin copies.   Hence, generally regarded as spurious, and supposed to be introduced by some copyist.   Indeed the time for preaching to the Gentiles had not yet arrived   It might, however, be said with Bellarmine (Rom. Pont. 22) that St. Paul did not yet preach to the Gentiles, but was only preparing the way for it by refuting the objections of the Gentiles.

"Disputed with the Greeks."   The Greek *Hellenists* denoted those Jews who scattered all over the world, spoke the Greek language, as their national language.   St. Paul himself was a Hellenist Jew.   These are contrasted with the "Hebrews," Jews, who spoke the Hebrew, or Aramaic of Palestine; called in the Scriptures of the New Testament, *Hebrew*.

30. On being made aware of the wicked designs of the Hellenists against St. Paul the Christians of Jerusalem took measures for his safety.   "Cæsarea," of Palestine, "Tharsus," his native city.   Likely, St. Paul preached the Gospel in Cilicia (Gal. i. 21).

31. The Church had peace.   (In Greek, *churches*); freed from the persecution which commenced with the death of Stephen.

"All Judea," &c.   The three provinces into which Palestine was divided, and to which the preaching of the Gospel was in a great measure hitherto confined.   In other places, too, there were several converted Jews.   But St. Luke speaks only of these three districts as it was in them persecution was so rife.

This cessation from persecution was probably owing to the conversion of the chief agent of persecution. Saul now became the most ardent and most zealous propagator of the faith.   It may also be in some measure owing to the persecution the Jews themselves were suffering from Caligula who ordered his statue to be set up in the Temple, and instructed his lieutenant, Petronius, to extinguish in blood any attempt at opposition (Josephus, Antiq. xviii.; viii. 2–9; de Bello xi. c. 10).   They had, therefore, themselves something else to mind besides persecuting the Christians.

"Edified."   A metaphorical expression, allusive to raising a material building.   In a spiritual sense, it denotes an increase in grace and sanctity; in a physical sense, an increase of numbers.   The former is

Commentary.   **Text.**

chiefly meant as in following words : "walking," living, regulating their lives "in the fear of the Lord," walking in the way of his commandments and practising his true worship.

"Filled with the consolations." Interior peace and abundant graces "of the Holy Ghost."

32. Peter, who had up to this remained at Jerusalem to guard his flock against the effects of persecution, now availing himself of the temporary lull and calm, sets about discharging his office of Supreme Pastor of the entire fold, and visiting them in their several settlements.

"Lydda," afterwards called Diospolis, or city of Jupiter, situated near the Mediterranean, about thirty miles north of Jerusalem, fifteen, to the east of Joppe. It belonged to the tribe of Ephraim.

32. And it came to pass, that Peter, as he passed through visiting all, came to the saints who dwelt at Lydda.

33. "Æneas." Judging from his Greek name he would seem to be a Gentile or Hellenist Jew, whether a Christian does not appear. If he were, likely St. Luke would have said so, as he does regarding "Tabitha" "a certain disciple." He only speaks of "Eneas" as "a certain man."

33. And he found there a certain man named Æneas, who had kept his bed for eight years, who was ill of the palsy.

34. And Peter said to him: Eneas, the Lord Jesus Christ healeth thee: arise, and make thy bed. And immediately he arose.

35. "All." Taken in a morally universal sense. "Saron," a large, fertile plain extending along the Mediterranean coast from Carmel to Joppe, having Carmel to the north.

35. And all that dwelt at Lydda and Saron saw him: who were converted to the Lord.

36. "And in Joppe." The Greek for "and" is "but" (δε), putting the following still greater miracle in opposition to the preceding. "Joppe," now Jaffa, a seaport on the Mediterranean (Jonas i. 3) in the tribe of Dan, having Cæsarea, thirty miles to the north; it was forty-five miles north-west of Jerusalem.

"Tabitha." A Syro-Chaldaic word, the same as "Dorcas" in the Greek, signifying a kind of goat, which the Italians term Gazella—antelope. The name is expressed in Syriac and Greek. She was known by both names.

"Good works and alms-deeds." "Alms-deeds" are specially mentioned among "good works," as it was in this she was specially distinguished; and it was to this kind of good works the miracle may be ascribed.

36. And in Joppe there was a certain disciple named Tabitha, which by interpretation it called Dorcas. This woman was full of good works and alms-deeds which she did.

37. "An upper chamber." A retired apartment in the upper part of the house. They had gone through the usual preparation for interment.

37. And it came to pass in those days, that she was sick and died. Whom when they had washed, they laid her in an upper chamber.

Text.

38. *And forasmuch as Lydda was nigh to Joppe, the disciples hearing that Peter was there, sent unto him two men, desiring him that he would not be slack to come unto them.*

39. *And Peter rising up went with them. And when he was come, they brought him into the upper chamber: and all the widows stood about him weeping, and shewing him the coats and garments which Dorcas made them.*

40. *And they all being put forth: Peter kneeling down prayed, and turning to the body, he said: Tabitha, arise. And she opened her eyes: and seeing Peter, she sat up.*

41. *And giving her his hand, he lifted her up. And when he had called the saints and the widows, he presented her alive.*

42. *And it was made known throughout all Joppe; and many believed in the Lord.*

43. *And it came to pass that he abode many days in Joppe, with one Simon a tanner.*

Commentary.

38. " Nigh to Joppe," about *six* miles distant.

"To come to them," to console them. There is no evidence that they expected the miracle of her resuscitation, especially as the *Apostles* had not yet raised anyone to life.

40. "All put out," lest they might interrupt his fervent prayer. In this was followed the example left us by our Blessed Lord on the occasion of raising the daughter of Jairus (Matthew ix. 24; Mark v. 40).

43. " Many days." A considerable time. Patrizzi holds it embraced only some months, but not an entire year.

"Simon the tanner." On account of contact with the dead bodies of animals, the trade of tanner was regarded by the Jews as impure. However, in his humility, St. Peter paid no heed to this Rabbinical opinion.

CHAPTER X

1. *Now there was a certain man in Cesarea, named Cornelius, a centurion of the band which is called the Italian,*

2. *A religious man, and one that feared God with all his house, who gave much alms to the people, and prayed to God always.*

3. *He saw in a vision manifestly, about the ninth hour of the day, an Angel of God coming in to him, and saying to him: Cornelius.*

4. *And he, beholding him, being seized with fear, said: What is it Lord? And he said to him: Thy prayers and thy alms have ascended for a memorial in the sight of God.*

5. *And now send men to Joppe, and call hither one Simon, who is surnamed Peter:*

6. *He lodgeth with one Simon a tanner, whose house is by the sea-side: he shall tell thee what thou must do.*

7. *And when the Angel who spoke to him was departed, he called two of his household servants, and a soldier that feared the Lord, of those who were under him:*

8. *To whom when he had related all, he sent them to Joppe.*

9. *And on the next day, whilst they were going on their journey, and drawing near to the city, Peter went up to the higher parts of the house to pray, about the sixth hour.*

10. *And, being hungry, he was desirous to taste somewhat. And as they were preparing, there came upon him an ecstasy of mind;*

11. *And he saw heaven opened, and a certain vessel descending, as it were a great sheet, let down by the four corners from heaven to the earth.*

12. *In which were all manner of four-footed beasts, and creeping things of the earth, and fowls of the air.*

13. *And there came a voice to him: Arise, Peter; kill and eat.*

14. *But Peter said: Far be it from me, Lord; for I have never eaten any common and unclean thing.*

15. *And the voice spoke to him again the second time: That which God hath purified, do not thou call common.*

16. *And this was done thrice: and presently the vessel was taken up again into heaven.*

17. *Now, whilst Peter was doubting within himself what the vision which he had seen should mean, behold, the men who were sent by Cornelius, inquiring for Simon's house, stood at the gate.*

18. *And when they had called, they asked if Simon who is surnamed Peter lodged there?*

19. *And as Peter was thinking on the vision, the Spirit said to him: Behold, three men seek thee.*

20. *Arise, therefore, go down, and go with them, doubting nothing; for I have sent them.*

21. *Then Peter, going down to the men, said: Behold, I am he whom you seek: what of the cause for which you are come?*

22. *And they said, Cornelius, a centurion, a just man, and one that feareth God, and that hath good testimony from all the nation of the Jews, received an answer of a holy Angel, to send for thee into his house, and to hear words from thee.*

23. *Then bringing them in, he lodged them. And the day following he arose, and went with them: and some of the brethren from Joppe accompanied him.*

24. *And the day after he entered into Cesarea. Now Cornelius was waiting for them, having called together his kinsmen and special friends.*

25. *And it came to pass when Peter was come in, Cornelius met him, and falling down at his feet, worshipped.*

26. *But Peter raised him up, saying: Rise, I myself also am a man.*

27. *And talking with him, he went in, and found many that were come together.*

28. *And he said to them: You know how abominable a thing it is for a man that is a Jew to keep company or to come to one of another nation; but God hath showed to me not to call any man common or unclean.*

29. *Wherefore, making no doubt, I came when I was sent for: I ask, therefore, for what cause you have sent for me?*

30. *And Cornelius said: Four days ago, until this hour, I was praying in my house at the ninth hour, and, behold, a man stood before me in white apparel, and said:*

31. *Cornelius, thy prayer is heard, and thy alms are remembered in the sight of God.*

32. *Send, therefore, to Joppe, and call hither Simon, who is surnamed Peter: he lodgeth in the house of Simon a tanner, by the sea-side.*

33. *Immediately, therefore, I sent to thee; and thou hast done well in coming. Now, therefore, all we are present in thy sight, to hear all things whatsoever are commanded thee by the Lord.*

34. *Then Peter, opening his mouth, said: In truth I perceive that God is no respecter of persons:*

35. *But in every nation he that feareth him, and worketh justice, is acceptable to him.*

36. *God sent the word to the children of Israel, preaching peace through Jesus Christ: (he is Lord of all).*

37. *You know the word which hath been published through all Judea: for it began from Galilee, after the baptism which John preached,*

38. *Jesus of Nazareth: how God anointed with the Holy Ghost, and with power; who went about doing good, and healing all that were oppressed by the devil: for God was with him.*

39. *And we are witnesses of all things which he did in the land of the Jews, and in Jerusalem: whom they killed, hanging him upon a tree.*

40. *Him God raised up the third day, and gave him to be made manifest,*

41. *Not to all the people, but to witnesses preordained of God, even to us, who ate and drank with him after he rose again from the dead.*

42. *And he commanded us to preach to the people, and to testify that it is he who hath been appointed by God to be the judge of the living and of the dead.*

43. *To him all the prophets give testimony, that through his name all receive remission of sins who believe in him.*

44. *While Peter was yet speaking these words, the Holy Ghost fell upon all them that were hearing the word.*

45. *And the faithful of the circumcision, who had come with Peter, were astonished because the grace of the Holy Ghost was also poured out upon the gentiles.*

46. *For they heard them speaking with tongues, and magnifying God.*

47. *Then Peter answered: Can any man forbid water, that these should not be baptized, who have received the Holy Ghost as well as we?*

48. *And he commanded them to be baptized in the name of the Lord Jesus Christ. Then they entreated him to stay with them some days.*

ANALYSIS.

In this Chapter, is recorded the conversion of Cornelius the centurion, who instructed by an Angel, sent for Peter to Joppe (1-8). Peter's ecstatic vision (9-17). Explained by the arrival of the messenger sent by Cornelius, who explains the purport of the message sent him (24-34). Peter's discourse on the Divinity of our Lord and his heavenly mission to earth to redeem mankind (34-43). The miraculous effusion of the Holy Ghost, and numerous conversions followed by the Baptism of the converts (44-48).

Commentary.

1. "Cæsarea," of Palestine. *Cæsarea Philippi* was a great way off from Joppe.

"Cornelius." The name is Roman. Generally supposed to be a Gentile (x. 28, xi. 1). Allusion is clearly made to him and those who were with him as Gentiles.

"A centurion," commander of one hundred men.

"Italian band," as contradistinguished from the divisions in which men from remote quarters and provinces of the empire were enrolled. The men of this band, "Italians," probably, claimed superiority over others.

2. "A religious man." A pious worshipper, "fearing God," according to the lights of the Natural Law, and, consequently, observant of the Divine Commandments through a reverential fear of God. It may be, that his residence among the Jews gave Cornelius a more definite idea of the true God, whom he served according to his lights, following the dictates of the Natural Law.

"Giving much alms to the people," in which he is contrasted with the Roman officials, who made it a point to fleece and rob the subject people.

"And always praying to God." Likely, while his mind was constantly raised up to God, he fervently prayed for light to be directed in the paths of salvation, by embracing the form of religion most pleasing to God.

3. "Manifestly," conveys that it was for certain a real vision, while he was at prayer (*v.* 30) about the "ninth hour of the day," or three o'clock. 3 p.m.

"An angel," assuming a visible body, deputed from God, stood before him. His prayers and almsdeeds (*v.* 4) rendered him pleasing to God, who sent His angel. The occasion was a very important one; the calling of the Gentile world in the person of this devout *Centurion*.

4. "Seized with fear." The usual effect supernatural visions and appearances have on men, as we find everywhere recorded in the SS. Scriptures.

Text.

1. *Now there was a certain man in Cæsarea named Cornelius, a centurion of the band which is called the Italian.*

2. *A religious man, and one that feared God with all his house, who gave much alms to the people, and prayed to God always.*

3. *He saw in a vision manifestly, about the ninth hour of the day, an Angel of God coming in to him, and saying to him: Cornelius.*

4. *And he, beholding him, being seized with fear, said.*

H

Text.	Commentary.
What is it, Lord? And he said to him: Thy prayers and thy alms have ascended for a memorial in the sight of God.	"Lord," here a term of courtesy, equivalent to "*Sir*," as it was not likely Cornelius regarded Him as God. "For a memorial." These good works have been wafted up before God to serve as a reminder of what you did, and cause Him to remember you in mercy and with complacency.
5. And now send men to Joppe, and call hither one Simon, who is surnamed Peter:	5. "And now." Now, then. "One Simon," &c. It was congruous that the head of the Church should be the first to introduce the Gentiles within its saving fold.
6. He lodgeth with one Simon a tanner, whose house is by the sea-side: he shall tell thee what thou must do.	6. "Lodges as a guest with one Simon," &c. "He will tell thee." These words are not found in some Greek MSS. They seem, however, to be necessary in order that Cornelius should know why he was to send for Peter to Joppe. St. Peter himself says Cornelius spoke to him in these or similar words (xi. 14).
7. And when the Angel who spoke to him was departed, he called two of his household servants, and a soldier that feared the Lord, of those who were under him:	7. This God-fearing soldier was, no doubt, influenced by the example of Cornelius on whom he was in constant attendance.
8. To whom, when he had related all, he sent them to Joppe.	8. He told the servants and the soldier all that occurred and why he sent them to Joppe (*v.* 22).
9. And on the next day, whilst they were going on their journey, and drawing near to the city, Peter went up to the higher parts of the house to pray, about the sixth hour.	9. "Higher parts of the house." The flat roof, the place usually resorted to for prayer. "Sixth hour." 12 o'clock. The more religious among the Jews had recourse to the exercise of prayer, not only when people in general did so, viz., morning and evening, but also at mid-day (Psalm iv. 17; Daniel vi. 10-19).
10. And, being hungry, he was desirous to taste somewhat. And as they were preparing, there came upon him an ecstacy of mind:	10. "Preparing." Cooking the repast. Probably, it was dinner hour. "Ecstasy of mind." This sudden condition of mind would show its supernatural character, as sent from above. "Ecstasy" means that state in which the soul of a man is, as if alienated supernaturally from the body, to the contemplation of intelligible objects presented to the mind.

Commentary.

11, 12. A linen vessel or great sheet tied above at the four extremities thus preventing the contents from falling off, so as to present the form of a vessel, containing all kinds of animals tame and wild, clean and unclean, without distinction, "was let down from heaven." No doubt, among the others might be counted these animals—swine, &c.—whose flesh the Jews were not allowed to eat. Whether he saw all this in reality or merely in mental contemplation is not determined.

12. In which were all manner of four-footed beasts, and creeping things of the earth, and fowls of the air.

13. "A voice." Some (among whom Beelen) say, mentally, he seemed to hear it. Others (Patrizzi, &c.) a real voice.

"Arise," proceed, . . . "and eat," without any distinction of food, clean or unclean.

14. "Common and unclean." Considering the Jewish distinctions of food. They called "unclean," food commonly used by the Gentiles. But it was only unclean food as such, but not, strictly speaking, common food; that was prohibited. Hence, here "common" and "unclean" food should be joined, viz., *common* food, that is also *unclean*.

15. "God has cleansed," or declared pure, do not regard as common or impure.

16. "Thrice," to impress the whole occurrence more deeply on Peter's mind. "And was taken up to heaven." A symbolical history of God's dealing with His Church. She was established and came down from Heaven and returned thither.

17. Now, whilst Peter was doubting within himself what the vision which he had seen should mean, behold, the men who were sent by Cornelius, inquiring for Simon's house, stood at the gate.

18. "Called," to enquire about Peter.

19. "The Spirit" of the Lord by whose influence he was guided and directed, "said to him" by an interior inspiration.

20. "Doubting nothing." These men were Gentiles, between

Text.

11. *And he saw heaven opened, and a certain vessel descending, as it were a great sheet, let down by the four corners from heaven to the earth.*

13. *And there came a voice to him: Arise, Peter; kill, and eat.*

14. *But Peter said: Far be it from me, Lord; for I have never eaten any common and unclean thing.*

15. *And the voice spoke to him again the second time. That which God hath purified, do not thou call common.*

16. *And this was done thrice: and presently the vessel was taken up again into heaven.*

18. *And when they had called, they asked if Simon, who is surnamed Peter, lodged there?*

19. *And as Peter was thinking on the vision, the Spirit said to him: Behold, three men seek thee.*

20. *Arise,*

Text.

therefore, go down, and go with them, doubting nothing; for I have sent them.

21. *Then Peter, going down to the men, said: Behold, I am he whom you seek: what the cause for which you are come?*

22. *And they said, Cornelius, a centurion, a just man, and one that feareth God, and that hath good testimony from all the nation of the Jews, received an answer of a holy Angel, to send for thee into his house, and to hear words from thee.*

23. *Then bringing them in, he lodged them. And the day following he arose, and went with them: and some of the brethren from Joppe accompanied him.*

24. *And the day after he entered into Cæsarea. Now Cornelius was waiting for them, having called together his kinsmen and special friends.*

25. *And it came to pass when Peter was come in, Cornelius met him, and falling down at his feet, worshipped.*

26. *But Peter raised him up, saying: Rise, I myself also am a man.*

27. *And talking with him, he went in, and found many that were come together.*

28. *And he said to them: You know how abominable a*

Commentary.

whom and the Jews there was still a wall of separation debarring almost all intercourse. Hence, the Spirit assures Peter.

"I have sent them." Though directly sent by Cornelius, it is under my guidance and inspiration he did so.

21. "Going down to the men," In the Greek it is added "*who were sent to him by Cornelius.*" But these words are wanting in many MSS. and versions, and are generally rejected as spurious. Bloomfield asserts "They have been with reason cancelled by every editor of note."

23. "Some of the brethren." Six converts to Christianity (xi. 12) as witnesses of the course of events. This would have the effect of mollifying Jewish prejudices then so rife.

24. "The morrow after;" the day they set out on their journey; the fourth day after the vision of Cornelius (*v.* 30).

25. "Adored." Cornelius, as a pious, God-fearing man, could not intend this as an act of supreme worship, which he knew could be paid to God alone. But, knowing Peter to be a friend of God vested with supernatural powers, he paid him great reverence, exhibited in his prostration.

26. Peter's humility, however, shrunk from such honours. Besides, he knew it was not conformable to Roman custom to pay such save to Divinity, and the Romans present might regard it as an act of supreme worship paid to a God. When St. John prostrated himself before the angel, though from a man so enlightened, it could not mean divine worship, but only an act of civil homage, the angel, out of humility, declined it (Apoc. xix. 10).

28. "How abominable." In Greek, *illicit.* There was no express enactment in the Pentateuch prohibiting intercourse with the Gentiles. But it was implied and practically acted on by the Jews, who following

Commentary.

the Mosaic institutions and customs, kept aloof from the Gentiles, St. Peter mildly and considerately uses the words "of another nation." It is observed by Salmeron that St. Peter wisely employs this preface, to avoid scandalizing the Jews present, who saw him, a Jew, consort with pagans, and in order that the Gentiles seeing that God was propitious to them would be animated with the desire of embracing the faith. He thus satisfied Jews and Gentiles.

29. "I ask, therefore," &c. He knew it already, but it was right that the statement should be made before all present by Cornelius himself, whose words carried great weight with all. "For what cause?" intent, or purpose.

30. *And Cornelius said: Four days ago, until this hour, I was praying in my house at the ninth hour, and, behold, a man stood before me in white apparel, and said:*

31. *Cornelius, thy prayer is heard, and thy alms are remembered in the sight of God.*

32. *Send, therefore, to Joppe, and call hither Simon, who is surnamed Peter: he lodgeth in the house of Simon a tanner, by the sea-side.*

33. "Done well in coming," expressing grateful thanks. "To hear," ready to carry out whatever thou art instructed by God to communicate to us.
done well in coming. Now, therefore, all we are present in thy sight, to hear all things whatsoever are commanded thee by the Lord.

34. "Opening his mouth," beginning to speak. "In very deed," undoubtedly. "I perceive," from all that is occurring around me, and especially in connection with the call of Cornelius, and the various visions accorded to him and me.

"God is not a respecter of persons" (see James ii-1). "Respect or exception of persons" takes place when an unjust preference is shown to one party beyond another, as in the case of a judge who would pronounce sentence on account of the external appearance or circumstance of a person, such as friendship, or rank, or influence, without regard to the merits of the case. The Jews thought God peculiarly favoured them, because they were Jews, and all others excluded from Salvation because they were not. St. Peter now says he perceives how erroneous this is. No one is favoured by God simply because he is a Jew, externally professing Judaism, and carnally descended from Abraham. Nor is any-one excluded from the Divine favour because he is not a Jew (see Romans ix, &c).

35. "But in every nation," and people, without distinction of Jew or Gentile, or without reference to external advantages of any sort, "he that feareth Him," who, under the influence of Divine grace from reverential fear of God, repairs from evil, "and worketh Justice," does good works, aided by God's grace. This is evidently allusive to Cornelius and his . . . . "is acceptable to him" and a sharer in the Divine favour,

Text.

thing it is for a man that is a Jew to keep company or to come to one of another nation; but God hath showed to me not to call any man common or unclean.

29. *Wherefore, making no doubt, I came when I was sent for: I ask, therefore, for what cause you have sent for me?*

33. *Immediately, therefore, I sent to thee; and thou hast*

34. *Then Peter, opening his mouth, said: In truth I perceive that God is no respecter of persons:*

35. *But in every nation he that feareth him, and worketh justice, is acceptable to him.*

Text.

Commentary.

so as to be disposed to be called to the faith and embrace the true religion.

This is a brief epitome of the teaching of St. Paul in his Epistle to Romans, in which he fully explains the doctrine of justification, and God's gracious and gratuitous dealings with man, without distinction of Jew or Gentile. In all this, the preventing and co-operating grace of God is supposed. Since, without God's grace, no one can perform any good work conducive to Salvation. This affords no ground for advocating indifference as regards religion. For, if indifferentism were allowable, might not Cornelius remain as he was, and why should St. Peter go to such trouble to preach to him and his the necessity of embracing the Faith of Jesus Christ, as being for all men the only true means of Salvation, and the only means established by God for obtaining the remission of sin?

The indifference put forward here is not indifference of Faith; but indifference of nations and peoples in regard to God's supernatural favours and gratuitous calls to His Church.

36. *God sent the word to the children of Israel, preaching peace through Jesus Christ: (he is Lord of all).*

37. *You know the word which hath been published through all Judea: for it began from Galilee, after the baptism which John preached,*

38. *Jesus of Nazareth: how God anointed him with the Holy Ghost, and with power; who went about doing good, and healing all that were oppressed by the devil: for God was with him.*

39. *And we are witnesses of all things which he did in the land of the Jews and in Jerusalem: whom they killed, hanging him upon a tree.*

36-38. "God sent the word," &c. Commentators are perplexed about the construction of this and the following verses, chiefly on account of the Greek Text, wherein, after "the word" λογον, we have ("ον") "which," λογον ον απεστειλε, &c. In this construction "word" is in the accusative case, and would seem to have no verb on which to depend. Some commentators (among them Bloomfield) say τον λογον is governed by οιδατε. "You know" (v. 37) and put it in apposition with its equivalent term, ρημα in v. 37, which they say, is repeated thus: "*the word*, ρημα, *I say*." The construction in the Greek should run thus: "*You know that He* (viz., God) *proclaiming peace through Jesus Christ (He is the Lord of all*) sent (or caused to be announced) *to the children of Israel, the word of* the Gospel *which had been announced through all Judea commencing with Galilee, after the Baptism, which John preached. You know.* I say, that the word was sent by God, viz., *Jesus of Nazareth anointed with the Holy Ghost and with power* (with the power of the Holy Ghost) *who went about doing good, healing all that were oppressed by the devil, for God was with him.*" (Steenkiste.)

36. Commencing to catechize Cornelius and those present, St. Peter says "God sent the word," that is, the message of pardon and reconciliation, conveyed in His Gospel. The term, "God" is not in the Greek, but is understood from the context.

"Children of Israel," in the first instance.

"Preaching peace." Pointing out the way of reconciliation with God, and union among themselves.

("For He is Lord of all.") All men are the work of His hands, Jew and Gentile, and he wishes all without distinction, to be saved.

37. "You know the word," the whole Gospel economy, the series of events, connected with the preaching of the Gospel.

Commentary.

"Published," &c. "Galilee" was not far from Cæsarea, so that Cornelius, a religious man, alive to all religious teachings, doubtless had heard of the fame of the Gospel teaching and miracles, which must have spread throughout Palestine and the neighbouring countries. Cornelius and his friends, though not fully instructed in the doctrine of Christ, must have heard of it.

38. "Jesus of Nazareth" depends on "You know."

"How God," the entire Trinity, to whom is common every act, *ad extra*, "anointed," poured out upon him the fulness of the graces of the Holy Spirit at his incarnation, when he was conceived of the Holy Ghost.

Jesus Christ, the man God, was, according to His human nature anointed by the whole Trinity with the plenitude of the graces of the Holy Ghost, in the Hypostatic union.

St. Cyril, of Alexandria, teaches regarding *opera ad extra* "*Quæ omnia sunt a Patre per Filium in Spiritu Sancto.*" St. Peter represents our Lord as "going about doing good," and also as the conqueror of the devil, who held the Gentiles subject to his power.

"Anointed him." A ceremony employed in the inauguration of Kings, Prophets, &c. It points to our Lord as the "Christ," or *anointed*, the expected Messiah.

The operation, whereby the Son of God assumed to himself human nature, though, in reality, common to the Three Persons of the Blessed Trinity, was, however, by appropriation, attributed to the Holy Ghost, who on account of his procession from the Father and Son, is goodness and love itself.

"Holy Ghost, and with power," that is, *the power of the Holy Ghost*, whereby he worked miracles of every degree.

"For God was with him," which more clearly and emphatically expresses what is conveyed in the words "anointed with the Holy Ghost, and with power," viz., that it was in virtue of the *Divine* power our Lord performed the great prodigies.

40. "Made manifest," leaving no grounds for doubting it.

41. "Not to all the people," which, besides being almost impracticable, was unnecessary to establish the truth of His Resurrection.

"Pre-ordained," "elected beforehand, such as Peter himself and the other Apostles, "who did eat and drink," &c., thus showing the reality of his Resurrection. Though our Lord is said (Luke xxiv. 43) to have *eaten* with the Apostles. Nowhere is it said he *drank*. However, it is implied in the repast (John xxi. 13).

42. "To be judge of the living," &c. The Greeks hold a peculiar opinion on this point. They maintain that such of the just as shall be alive at the approach of the day of judgment shall not die, but shall be

Text.

40. *Him God raised up the third day, and gave him to be made manifest.*

41. *Not to all the people, but to witnesses pre-ordained of God, even to us, who ate and drank with him after he rose again from the dead.*

42. *And he commanded us to preach to the people, and to*

Text.	Commentary.

Text.

testify that it is he who hath been appointed by God to be the judge of the living and of the dead.

Commentary.

changed without death. The common doctrine which is in accordance with the SS. Scriptures and the faith of the church at all times is that, all shall die. Hence the word "living" denotes those who shall be alive, immediately before the coming of the Judge, and shall be destroyed by the fire of conflagration which immediately precedes the judge (2 Peter iii. 10). "*Dead,*" such as have been already in their graves. He refers to the Judicial power of the Judge, to inspire them with salutary fear.

43. To him all the prophets give testimony, that through his name all receive remission of sins who believe in him.

43. "All the Prophets," very many, such as Jeremiah, (xxxi, 14)—or all the Prophets, more or less, testify of Christ, directly or indirectly. Peter's discourse, likely, intended to be of longer duration (xi. 15), was interrupted by the descent of the Holy Ghost.

44. While Peter was yet speaking these words, the Holy Ghost fell upon all them that were hearing the word.

45. And the faithful of the circumcision, who had come with Peter, were astonished because the grace of the Holy Ghost was also poured out upon the gentiles.

46. For they heard them speaking with tongues, and magnifying God.

44. "Holy Ghost fell on," &c. Probably, not in a sensible form as on the Apostles on Pentecost Sunday; but, in visible effects, such as speaking and praising God in strange tongues (v. 46), and other marks of his presence.

It is remarked by commentators, that this is a wonderful and singular instance of the giving of the Holy Ghost. He anticipated the ministry of Peter, in order to show that the vocation of the Gentiles was altogether God's own work ; and the converts from Judaism would see that they owed their call and the gifts of the Holy Ghost not to circumcision or to the Law, but to faith in Jesus Christ. Whereas Cornelius received the gifts of the Holy Ghost without Baptism or circumcision, it was a peremptory proof that the Gentiles, in order to receive Baptism and be incorporated with the Church need not be incorporated with the Jewish Church by circumcision or subjection to the Law of Moses.

47. Then Peter answered: Can any man forbid water, that these should not be baptized, who have received the Holy Ghost as well as we?

47. "Answered," often in SS. Scriptures signifies, to begin to speak without reference to any question, or it may imply *answering* some latent question in the mind of the speaker.

"Forbid water." Though they had received the Baptism of the Holy Ghost and all His gifts, still in accordance with the ordinance of our Lord (John iii.) they should receive the Baptism of water, in order to be externally incorporated with the Church, and made one with the body of the faithful.

"Forbid water," clearly shows the necessity of Baptism, when those who were replenished with the gifts of the Holy Ghost should necessarily be subjected to it. "Forbid water," shows it was carried, and that Baptism was administered by *infusion.*

"As well as we" Jews, when He descended on us at Pentecost.

Commentary.

48. "He commanded," &c. Probably, using the ministry of the six who accompanied him. It may be that Peter himself did so. The words may mean, he gave orders to them to prepare at once for Baptism which possibly he himself may have conferred. The words do not necessarily convey that he did not.

It may be asked, what need had Peter of a vision to know that the Gentiles were to be admitted into the Church, after our Lord's express mandate "*docete omnes gentes?*" In reply, it is said, the Apostles did not understand our Lord's injunctions in detail or practice.

"In the name" by the authority, and with the Baptism, in the usual form, "of Jesus Christ."

CHAPTER XI

1. *And the apostles and brethren who were in Judea heard that the Gentiles also had received the word of God.*

2. *And when Peter was come up to Jerusalem, they who were of the circumcision disputed against him,*

3. *Saying: Why didst thou go in to men uncircumcised, and didst eat with them?*

4. *But Peter began and declared to them the matter in order, saying:*

5. *I was in the city of Joppe praying; and I saw in an ecstasy of mind a vision, a certain vessel descending, as it were a great sheet, let down from heaven by four corners; and it came even to me:*

6. *Into which looking I considered, and saw four-footed creatures of the earth, and beasts, and creeping things, and fowls of the air:*

7. *And I heard also a voice saying to me: Arise, Peter; kill, and eat.*

8. *And I said: By no means, Lord; for nothing common or unclean hath ever entered into my mouth.*

9. *And the voice answered the second time from heaven: What God hath made clean call not thou common.*

10. *And this was done three times: and all were taken up again into heaven.*

11. *And, behold, immediately there were three men come to the house wherein I was, sent to me from Cesarea.*

12. *And the Spirit said to me that I should go with them, nothing doubting. And these six brethren went with me also, and we entered into the man's house.*

13. *And he told us how he had seen an Angel in his house, standing and saying to him: Send to Joppe, and call hither Simon, who is surnamed Peter;*

14. *Who shall speak to thee words, whereby thou and all thy house shall be saved.*

15. *And when I had begun to speak, the Holy Ghost fell upon them, as upon us also in the beginning.*

16. *And I remembered the word of the Lord, as he said: John indeed baptized with water; but you shall be baptized with the Holy Ghost.*

17. *If then God gave to them the same grace as to us also who have believed in the Lord Jesus Christ, who was I, that I could oppose God?*

18. *When they had heard these things, they held their peace, and glorified God, saying: God then hath also to the Gentiles given repentance unto life.*

19. *And they indeed who had been dispersed by the persecutions that arose on occasion of Stephen went about as far as Phenice, and Cyprus, and Antioch, speaking the word to none but to the Jews only.*

20. *But some of them were men of Cyprus and Cyrene, who, when they had entered into Antioch, spoke also to the Greeks, preaching the Lord Jesus.*

21. *And the hand of the Lord was with them: and a great number believing was converted to the Lord.*

22. *And the report of these things came to the ears of the Church that was at Jerusalem, and they sent Barnabas as far as Antioch :*

23. *Who when he was come, and had seen the grace of God, rejoiced, and exhorted them all with purpose of heart to continue in the Lord.*

24. *For he was a good man, and full of the Holy Ghost, and of faith. And a great multitude was added to the Lord.*

25. *And Barnabas went to Tarsus to seek Saul : whom when he had found he brought to Antioch.*

26. *And they conversed there in the church a whole year : and they taught a great multitude, so that at Antioch the disciples were first named Christains.*

27. *And in these days there came prophets from Jerusalem to Antioch.*

28. *And one of them, named Agabus, rising up, signified by the Spirit that there should be a great famine over the whole world, which came to pass under Claudius.*

29. *And the disciples, every man according to his ability, resolved to send relief to the brethren who dwelt in Judea :*

30. *Which also they did, sending it to the ancients by the hands of Barnabas and Saul.*

ANALYSIS.

Peter's arrival at Jerusalem (1-2). His defence of his conduct in admitting Gentiles into the Church, which he grounds on the vision vouchsafed to him at Joppe, which he describes (3-14). The external effusion of the gifts of the Holy Ghost. After which all held their peace and acquiesced (14-19). The spread of religion consequent on the preaching and miracles of the disciples (19-21). The prediction of a great famine by Agabus. The charitable resolve to send relief, which was actually forwarded through Barnabas and Saul, to the distressed Christians of Judea (19-30).

Commentary.

1. The rumour regarding the admission of Cornelius and his household into the church was circulated far and wide throughout Judæa. Likely, the Apostles were at this time scattered throughout the different parts of the country.

2. "They that were of the circumcision." Such among them as were over zealous about the Mosaic rite of circumcision and its necessity "contended," disputed with him, as to the propriety of his conduct, and reproached him,

3. "Saying : why didst thou?" &c. In the Greek it is in the assertive, not interrogative form. They held it to be unlawful to hold converse and take food with uncircumcised Gentiles, erroneously fancying the Law of Moses, as they understood it, on these points to be still in vigour. The gifts of the Holy Ghost abundantly poured out on them,

Text.

1. *And the apostles and brethren who were in Judea heard that the Gentiles also had received the word of God.*

2. *And when Peter was come up to Jerusalem, they who were of the circumcision disputed against him,*

3. *Saying : Why didst thou go in to men uncircumcised, and didst eat with them?*

Text.	Commentary.

put the propriety of receiving the Gentiles into the Church beyond dispute. This they don't explicitly upbraid him with; they do so implicitly.

4. But Peter began and declared to them the matter in order, saying:

4. Peter justifies the admission of the Gentiles into the Church, and explains in detail each occurrence in connexion with it so far as he himself was concerned. "In order," in the order in which it took place.

5. I was in the city of Joppe praying; and I saw in an ecstacy of mind a vision, a certain vessel descending, as it were a great sheet, let down from heaven by four corners; and it came even to me:

6. Into which looking I considered, and saw four-footed creatures of the earth, and beasts, and creeping things, and fowls of the air:

7. And I heard also a voice saying to me: Arise, Peter; kill, and eat.

8. And I said: By no means, Lord; for nothing common or unclean hath ever entered into my mouth.

9. And the voice answered the second time from heaven: What God hath made clean call not thou common.

10. And this was done three times: and all were taken up again into heaven.

11. And, behold, immediately there were three men come to the house wherein I was, sent to me from Cæsarea.

12. And the Spirit said to me that I should go with them, nothing doubting. And these six brethren went with me also, and we entered into the man's house.

13. And he told us how he had seen an Angel in his house, standing and saying to him: Send to Joppe, and call hither Simon, who is surnamed Peter;

14. Who shall speak to thee words, whereby thou and all thy house shall be saved.

15. And when I had begun to speak, the Holy Ghost fell upon them, as upon us also in the beginning.

16. And I remembered the word of the Lord, as he said: John indeed baptized with water; but you shall be baptized with the Holy Ghost.

5-16. See preceding chapter.

16. The descent of the Holy Ghost on the Gentiles as well as on the Jews "in the beginning" (*v.* 15) at his visible manifestation on Pentecost Sunday brought to Peter's mind the words spoken by our Lord on the eve of His Ascension (i. 5). "*John, indeed baptizeth,*" &c., which he saw clearly verified in the case of Cornelius and others.

17. If then God gave to them the same grace as to us also who have believed in the Lord Jesus Christ, who was I that I could oppose God?

17. If, then, God bestowed the same spirit on the uncircumcised believing Gentiles, as on us, requiring no other condition save to believe, thus establishing a perfect equality, "Who was I, to withstand God," by refusing to baptize them, to obstruct His gracious designs and holy will clearly manifested in their regard, and refuse to admit into His Church by Baptism those on whom He Himself conferred the exalted Baptism of the Spirit?

18. When they had heard these things, they held their peace, and glorified God, saying: God then hath also to the Gentiles given repentance unto life.

18. "They held their peace." They had no more to say, on seeing the clear manifestations of God's will, but humbly acquiesced in, and conformed, to His holy will.

"Unto life" so as to attain salvation.

Commentary.

19. "Now" is resumptive of the narrative interrupted (c. viii. 4) by the description of the conversion of Saul (ix. 32), the visitation of the churches of Palestine by Peter (33–45), the wonderful events connected with Cornelius, &c. Now, St. Luke resumes the history and doings of those *disciples* who were scattered abroad on the occasion of the martyrdom of St. Stephen, and enters on a new phase of the history of the Acts, chiefly in regard to the preaching of the Gospel to the Gentiles in several prominent places, and especially in regard to the history of St. Paul, the principal events of his life, his Apostolic labours and heroic sufferings in the cause of the Gospel.

"They that had been dispersed by," or owing to, the persecution, on the occasion of the death of Stephen, "went about as far as Phenice." Some of these dispersed disciples, not Apostles, made their way preaching the Gospel as far as Phenice—that tract of country on the shores of the Mediterranean between Judæa and Syria; others, as far as Cyprus, the island over against Phœnicia, others, as far as Antioch, the capital of Syria. All these exiles preached the Gospel to the Jews only.

20. "But some of them" who were dispersed (c. viii. 4), "Cyrene," the capital city of Lybia, these were converted Jews.

"Greeks." Gentiles. The opposition between these and "the Jews only," among whom, doubtless, were found *Hellenistic Jews*, would seem to require that the word "Greeks" would refer to those who were in no sense "Jews" but Pagans. Very likely these men heard at Antioch of Cornelius' conversion, and doubtless this example would influence them to preach to the Gentiles, and admit them into the Church.

21. "The hand of the Lord" was with those teachers, empowering them to perform miracles in corroboration of their teaching which, therefore, was successful in effecting conversions.

The occurrences referred to (19–21) would seem to have taken place during an interval of some years, between the death of Stephen and the mission of Barnabas to Antioch.

22. The rumour concerning the successful labours of the disciples among these Cyprians and Cyreneans at Antioch reached the faithful of Jerusalem and the Apostles themselves who may have been there. Peter and James were there. Hence, the deputation by them of Barnabas to Antioch to confirm by Apostolic authority the successful work of the Cyprian and Cyrenean disciples. They send Barnabas alone as being a Cyprian and Hellenist; he was best fitted for the work, and would give less offence in his communication with the successful preaching of the word.

23. Had seen the grace of God manifest in the conversion and edifying lives of the Gentiles. "The grace of God" was the chief agent in the work of conversion. Free will is also upheld when He

Text.

19. And they indeed who had been dispersed by the persecution that arose on occasion of Stephen went about as far as Phenice, and Cyprus, and Antioch, speaking the word to none but to the Jews only.

20. But some of them were men of Cyprus and Cyrene, who, when they had entered into Antioch, spoke also to the Greeks, preaching the Lord Jesus.

21. And the hand of the Lord was with them: and a great number believing was converted to the Lord.

22. And the report of these things came to the ears of the Church that was at Jerusalem, and they sent Barnabas as far as Antioch:

23. Who when he was come, and had seen the grace of

Text.	Commentary.

Text.

God, rejoiced, and exhorted them all with purpose of heart to continue in the Lord.

24. For he was a good man, and full of the Holy Ghost, and of faith. And a great multitude was added to the Lord.

25. And Barnabas went to Tarsus to seek Saul: whom when he had found he brought to Antioch.

26. And they conversed there in the Church a whole year; and they taught a great multitude, so that at Antioch the disciples were first named Christians.

27. And in these days there came prophets from Jerusalem to Antioch.

28. And one of them, named Agabus, rising up, signified by the Spirit that there should be a great famine over the whole world, which came to pass

Commentary.

exhorts them "with purpose of heart," with firm and determined purposes, "to continue," &c

24. "A good man," &c. "Good," benign, kind; loving God and solicitous for the salvation of his brethren; distinguished for the abundant gifts of the Holy Ghost, especially faith and confidence in God. To these qualities was added his success in the work of the Gospel.

25. Paul went from Jerusalem to Tharsus, his native city. Likely while there he was engaged in his trade of tent-making. Possibly, the Apostles at Jerusalem may have instructed Barnabas to call on him knowing what an effective labourer he would be in preaching the Gospel.

26. "Conversed there." Held sacred meetings for the purposes of worship "for a whole year," and instructed great multitudes in the faith of Christ.

"First named Christians," which shows the wonderful progress the Gospel made at Antioch.

"Christians," the most honourable of all appellations, suggestive of the gratitude we owe our Blessed Saviour, and of our obligation to walk in His footsteps if we wish to share in His glory.

By whom they were so called, whether by Paul or Barnabas, or the Pagans, among whom they lived by way of distinction cannot be ascertained. Likely, it was not meant as a term of reproach. Agrippa uses it in a complimentary sense (Acts xxvi. 28 also 1. Peter iv. 16). Galileans or Nazareans was employed scornfully and reproachfully (ii. 7., xxiv. 5) to designate our Lord's followers.

27. "Prophets," strictly speaking, those who predict future events. In SS. Scriptures, the term is applied to those endowed with the faculty of explaining the SS. Scriptures or mysteries of faith, in an extraordinary way, as the result of sudden enlightenment or inspiration for the moment, without any reference to the prediction of the future. Here, it seems, some of them, had the faculty of foretelling future events.

28. "Rising up" likely he had been in a sitting posture before at one of their meetings. He uttered a prediction regarding St. Paul, (Acts xxi. 10 11). "Signified," conveyed in rather an obscure way (xii. 33). Here, it means to foretell, "by the Spirit," by the interior revelation of the Holy Ghost, or under the influence of inspiration.

"Over the whole world," all over the habitable portions of the globe. The Greek (οἰκουμένην) means inhabited or habitable. Or, as there is

Commentary.

reference to "Claudius" throughout the extent of the Roman Empire, which comprised most of the habitable or civilized portions of the earth (xxiv. 5, Luke ii.). Sometimes, it is employed to denote the *entire* land of Judæa, as contradistinguished from parts only of it.

"Which came to pass." Famine had visited almost all the provinces of the Roman Empire, especially Syria and Palestine, in the fourth year of the reign of Claudius (Josephus, Antiq. xx. 2-6; Eusebius, ii. 2-11; Hist. Eccles.).

We are informed by historians, that three or four famines took place in the reign of Claudius, between the years A.D. 41 and 54. One in particular, referred to here was more general and more severely felt than the rest.

29. The Church of Jerusalem was regarded at that day, as the mother Church. It was very poor. To it the other Churches were, in a great measure, indebted for the spiritual blessings they enjoyed. Hence, it was meet, that out of their temporal wealth, they should relieve her necessities. This was in accordance with the teachings of St. Paul (1 Cor. ix. 11).

The Greek word for "relief," εἰς διακονιαν, means a "*subsidy.*"

29. And the disciples, every man according to his ability, resolved to send relief to the brethren who dwelt in Judæa:

30. "Ancients," πρεσβυτερους—though literally expressing age, was, however, employed among the Jews, to designate the members of the Sanhedrim, who with the High Priest constituted the supreme council of the Jews, whether their age corresponded or not, just as among the Romans, the Senators, whether aged or not, were, on account of their office termed "*Patres.*"

30. Which also they did, sending it to the ancients by the hands of Barnabas and Saul.

After the example of Moses the Apostles, in their Church organizations, called in or appointed sacred ministers, to aid in such ministration as they themselves could not reach or attend to.

The word *Presbyteri*, is here used for the first time in the New Testament to designate Christian ministers. Although used, at first, to designate Christian ministers in general, without distinction of classes or orders; it was, however, in course of time applied to the second order of the clergy. It is *de fide*, that *Bishops* are superior to *Priests* in the twofold power of order and jurisdiction (Council of Trent, SS. 23. Can. vii.).

Likely, here, there is question of perhaps the Apostles themselves, or Bishops or Deacons intrusted with the proper and judicious distribution of the alms among the most *necessitous* objects for relief.

CHAPTER XII.

1. *And at the same time Herod the king stretched forth his hands, to afflict some of the church.*

2. *And he killed James the brother of John with the sword.*

3. *And seeing that it pleased the Jews, he proceeded to take up Peter also. Now it was in the days of the azymes.*

4. *And when he had apprehended him, he cast him into prison, delivering him to four files of soldiers to be kept, intending after the pasch to bring him forth to the people.*

5. *Peter therefore was kept in prison. But prayer was made without ceasing by the church unto God for him.*

6. *And when Herod would have brought him forth, the same night Peter was sleeping between two soldiers, bound with two chains: and the keepers before the door kept the prison.*

7. *And behold an Angel of the Lord stood by him: and a light shined in the room: and he striking Peter on the side raised him up, saying: Arise quickly. And the chains fell off from his hands.*

8. *And the Angel said to him: Gird thyself, and put on thy sandals. And he did so. And he said to him: Cast thy garment about thee, and follow me.*

9. *And going out he followed him, and he knew not that it was true which was done by the Angel: but thought he saw a vision.*

10. *And passing throught the first and the second ward, they came to the iron gate that leadeth to the city, which of itself opened to them. And going out, they passed on through one street: and immediately the Angel departed from him.*

11. *And Peter coming to himself, said: Now I know in very deed that the Lord hath sent his Angel, and hath delivered me out of the hand of Herod, and from all the expectation of the people of the Jews.*

12. *And considering, he came to the house of Mary the mother of John, who was surnamed Mark, where many were gathered together and praying.*

13. *And when he knocked at the door of the gate, a damsel came to hearken, whose name was Rhode.*

14. *And as soon as she knew Peter's voice, she opened not the gate for joy, but running in she told that Peter stood before the gate.*

15. *But they said to her: Thou art mad. But she affirmed that it was so. Then said they: It is his Angel.*

16. *But Peter continued knocking. And when they had opened, they saw him, and were astonished.*

17. *But he beckoning to them with his hand to hold their peace, told how the Lord had brought him out of prison, and he said: Tell these things to James and to the brethren. And going out he went into another place.*

18. *Now when day was come, there was no small stir among the soldiers, what was become of Peter.*

19. *And when Herod had sought for him, and found him not; having examined the keepers, he commanded they should be put to death: and going down from Judea to Cesarea, he abode there.*

20. *And he was angry with the Tyrians and the Sidonians. But they with one accord came to him, and having gained Blastus who was the king's chamberlain, they desired peace, because their countries were nourished by him.*

21. *And upon a day appointed, Herod being arrayed in kingly apparel, sat in the judgment-seat, and made an oration to them.*

22. *And the people made acclamation saying : It is the voice of a god, and not of a man.*

23. *And forthwith an Angel of the Lord struck him, because he had not given the honour to God: and being eaten up by worms, he gave up the ghost.*

24. *But the word of the Lord increased and multiplied.*

25. *And Barnabas and Saul returned from Jerusalem, having fulfilled their ministry, taking with them John, who was surnamed Mark.*

ANALYSIS.

The cruel persecution raised by Herod (1-2). The incarceration of Peter, who was closely guarded (3-6). His liberation by the hand of an Angel (7-11). The confusion consequent thereon, and the death of the guards who were on duty (18). The fearful judgment exercised on Herod, who was eaten up by worms (20-23).

Commentary.

1. "And at the same time." While Paul and Barnabas were ministering at Antioch. The narrative relative to their charitable ministrations is interrupted here by the intervening events recorded as far as *v.* 24 of this chapter, and is resumed at *v.* 25. These intervening events are : Peter is liberated ; Herod dies a shocking death, these two Apostles had reached Jerusalem.

"Herod the king." Agrippa, the son of Aristobulus, and grandson of Herod the Great, the murderer of the Holy Innocents. Agrippa obtained from Caligula and Claudius territories co-extensive with those of his grandfather, Herod the Great.

"Stretched forth his hand" indicates the violent exercise of power.

"To afflict some"—the leading members—"of the Church," as is stated immediately after.

2. "With a sword." By being beheaded or pierced through. This is said by some to be among the most ignominious kinds of capital punishment among the Jews. It seems King Agrippa had the power of life and death. In the time of the Roman government, only the Roman Procurator had it. The Jews had not. "James," the *Greater*, in contradistinction to James, the son of Alpheus, called "the lesser," or "the brother of John," both sons of Zebedee, in whom were fulfilled the predictions of our Lord (Matthew xx. 22). "You shall drink of my cup," &c.

3. "Seeing it pleased the Jews," &c. Agrippa's besetting sin was an inordinate excessive love of popularity. It was from this feeling he meant to put Peter to death. Likely, too, he wished to conciliate the Jews, to whom his dynasty was odious ; and thus prevent them from

Text.

1. *And at the same time Herod the king stretched forth his hands, to afflict some of the church.*

2. *And he killed James the brother of John with the sword.*

3. *And seeing that it pleased the Jews, he proceeded to take*

I

Text.

up Peter also. Now it was in the days of the azymes.

Commentary.

preferring accusations against him with the Roman Emperors, whose creature he was.

"Peter also." One of the most conspicuous men in the Church, who had, moreover, made himself obnoxious by his pungent discourses, and success in effecting conversions.

"Now, it was in the days of the Azymes," that is, within the seven days succeeding the Passover, during which they were not allowed to partake of leavened bread (Exod. xii. 15-18 ; Deut. xvi. 3).

Herod may have apprehended Peter at this particular time to show his attachment to Judaism, and his determination to crush out every other form of religion.

4. And when he had apprehended him, he cast him into prison, delivering him to four files of soldiers to be kept, intending after the pasch to bring him forth to the people.

4. "Apprehended." Arrested him. "Cast him into prison." During the Paschal solemnity no trials of criminals took place, in order that the people might exclusively devote themselves to their religious duties and the ceremonies of the Festival.

"Four files," &c. The Greek is "four *quaternions* of soldiers," each *quaternion* was made up of *four*, so he had sixteen soldiers to guard him. Each *quaternion*, or *four*, were to relieve one another on guard during the watches of the night. Two of them were to remain in the prison with Peter (*v.* 6) who was chained to these two, and the other two were to keep guard at the door of the prison for three hours—the term of night watch—until they were relieved. Agrippa, who was educated at Rome, adhered to the Roman system of having four night watches, of three hours each, during the night. No precaution for securing Peter was omitted.

"To bring him forth," &c. Evidently with the view of having him publicly put to death in presence of the people.

5. Peter therefore was kept in prison. But prayer was made without ceasing by the church unto God for him.

5. "Without ceasing," fervent, persevering prayer. Humanly speaking, there was no hope of his deliverance. God was the only resource who did not fail to respond to the prayers of His Church.

6. And when Herod would have brought him forth, the same night Peter was sleeping between two soldiers, bound with two chains: and the keepers before the door kept the prison.

6. "Brought him forth," to be publicly put to death.

"Same night," immediately preceding the day intended for his execution.

"Bound with two chains." His right hand chained to the left of one soldier, and his left to the right hand of the other, which is said to be usual with the Romans for securing their prisoners.

"The keepers," &c. Besides the two soldiers to whom Peter was bound in prison, two others watched before the door. It was death for a Roman soldier to be caught sleeping at his post. The four on guard were relieved, after three hours, by four others in succession.

Commentary.

7. "An angel of the Lord," no particular angel mentioned, "stood by him," suddenly and unexpectedly.

"A light shone," &c. Such light, reflected from the glorious body assumed by the angel, generally accompanies angels when they appear on earth (Matthew xxviii. 5; Luke ii. 9; xxiv. 4), &c. Possibly, Peter only saw it; or, if it filled the prison, the guards sunk in deep sleep did not see it.

8. "Gird thyself" with thy inner vest.   "Garment," the outer garment, laid aside when he lay down to sleep.   Dress thyself as usual when preparing for a journey.

9. "True"—a reality—"a vision," such as presented itself to him before (x. 11, 12).

10. "First and second ward."   Passed by the soldiers that guarded each ward.   They were Providentially sunk in heavy sleep.

"Iron gate."   The outer gate, secured for greater strength with iron bars.   It opened on the town.

"The angel departed."   Left him, as he was beyond the reach of danger.

11. "Came to himself."   Recovering from the amazement he felt at the entire scene and became capable of reflexion.

"Expectation," &c.   The Jews were anxiously expecting to witness his execution.

Text.

7. And behold an Angel of the Lord stood by him: and a light shined in the room: and he striking Peter on the side raised him up, saying: Arise quickly. And the chains fell off from his hands.

8. And the Angel said to him: Gird thyself, and put on thy sandals. And he did so. And he said to him: Cast thy garment about thee, and follow me.

9. And going out he followed him, and he knew not that it was true which was done by the Angel: but thought he saw a vision.

10. And passing through the first and the second ward, they came to the iron gate that leadeth to the city, which of itself opened to them. And going out, they passed on through one street: and immediately the Angel departed from him.

11. And Peter coming to himself, said: Now I know in very deed that the Lord hath sent his Angel, and hath delivered me out of the hand of Herod, and from all the expectation of the people of the Jews.

Text.

12. *And considering, he came the house of Mary the mother of John, who was surnamed Mark, where many were gathered together and praying.*

13. *And when he knocked at the door of the gate, a damsel came to hearken, whose name was Rhode.*

14. *And as soon as she knew Peter's voice, she opened not the gate for joy, but running in she told that Peter stood before the gate.*

15. *But they said to her: Thou art mad. But she affirmed that it was so. Then said they: It is his Angel.*

16. *But Peter continued knocking. And when they had opened, they saw him, and were astonished.*

17. *But he beckoning to them with his hand to hold their peace, told how the Lord had brought him out of prison, and he said: Tell these things to James and to the brethren. And going out he went into another place.*

Commentary.

12. "Considering" what he should do in the circumstances.

"House of Mary," &c. Probably, the nearest Christian dwelling for affording refuge and protection. The faithful were assembled, and among other objects of petition, jointly praying for Peter's deliverance.

13. "Gate," the vestibule or outer portion of the house.
"To hearken." To hear on enquiry who was there.

14. Overwhelmed with joy, before opening, she ran into the interior of the house to communicate the good news.

15. So unhoped for was his liberation, as happens persons who are anxious about an event, they seem incredulous about it, lest it might not be true. "She affirmed." In Greek, *strongly affirmed.*

"His angel," not *messenger*, as some affirm. Peter *could* have no special *messenger*. Besides, the girl recognised "the voice of Peter." Most likely, they meant his *tutelary* or *Guardian* Angel. The common traditional belief among the Jews was, that each one had a Guardian Angel assigned by God to guard and protect him through life. In the Catholic Church, it is held, not as a *defined* point of faith, but as a truth of *Christian Doctrine*, so that it could not be denied by any sound Catholic that every just man, every man in the state of grace has an *Angel Guardian* specially appointed by God to guard him during life. It seems the more probable opinion, that *every human being*, not excluding infidels, has such a protector assigned him (*See* Matthew xviii. 10, Commentary on).

17. "To hold their peace." Any commotion or excitement might expose them to the fury of their enemies.

"James," the "lesser," Bishop of Jerusalem, son of Alpheus. "Brethren," especially the Apostles, that they might render thanks to God, for having heard their joint prayer.

"Another place." Some safer retreat, till the danger was over. Some say, Cæsarea; others, Antioch; others, Rome.

Commentary.

18. Owing to apprehension of the result, and destined punishment of death in store for their supposed neglect of duty.

19. "Examined the keepers." Probably, the *Quaternion* on guard at the time of Peter's escape, and receiving no satisfactory explanation--any miraculous interposition he would scorn.

"Put to death," in Greek, *led forth* for execution.

."Going down," &c. Full of shame and disappointment at not being able to gratify the Jews and promote his own popularity in putting to death the chief of the religion they detested, quitting Jerusalem, "he went down to Cæsarea," the second capital of his dominions.

20. "Angry." In Greek, harbouring feelings of hostility in his mind. "Tyrians and Sidonians." They may have angered him on account of commercial speculations of some sort, and on account of the admirable port formed by Herod at Cæsarea, which they might fancy to be injurious to their commerce. Tyre and Sidon, situated to the North of Cæsarea, were under the power of the Romans, and in alliance with them. They might have given Herod offence relative to his commercial speculations.

"One accord" in a joint deputation composed of Tyrians and Sidonians.

"Gained Blastus," a Roman name. They prevailed on him to assist them, in their overtures for reconciliation and peace.

"Chamberlain," had charge of Herod's bed chamber, and enjoyed great influence with him. Likely, he was a Roman, and treasurer to the King, who, it is thought, kept his treasures for greater security locked in his bedchamber and secret closets.

"They desired peace." By the re-establishment of friendly relations, they wished to ward off any menaced hostilities that might result from the anger of Herod.

"Their countries were nourished by him." Their chief wealth was gained from commerce, which they did not wish to interrupt with Palestine; and they neglected agriculture. Moreover, the small strip of land, belonging to them, on the coast of the Mediterranean, would not supply provisions for their population, not to speak of the irreparable loss resulting from the cessation of commercial speculations with Palestine. For this, they were, in a great measure, dependent on the adjoining territories of Herod.

21. "A day appointed" to receive the ambassadors of the Tyrians, &c. This was the second day of the games and sports which Herod celebrated in Cæsarea in honour of Claudius Cæsar. Josephus (Antiq. B. xix., c. viii.) gives a full and circumstantial account of it.

Text.

18. *Now when day was come, there was no small stir among the soldiers, what was become of Peter.*

19. *And when Herod had sought for him, and found him not; having examined the keepers, he commanded they should be put to death: and going down from Judæa to Cæsarea, he abode there.*

20. *And he was angry with the Tyrians and the Sidonians. But they with one accord came to him, and having gained Blastus, who was the king's chamberlain, they desired peace, because their countries were nourished by him.*

21. *And upon a day appointed, Herod being arrayed in kingly ap-*

Text.

parel, sat in the judgment seat, and made an oration to them.

Commentary.

" Arrayed in kingly apparel." Josephus (*Ibidem*) tells us "he put on a garment made altogether of silver, of wonderful contexture ; and having come into the theatre of Cæsarea (the place of the games) the reflection of the early sun's rays on his silver garment produced a wonderful effect on the spectators."

"Sat in the Judgment Seat."   Not a throne properly so-called, but an elevated seat or platform, from which he could see all the games and shows and conveniently deliver his oration publicly, in presence of the people, to the ambassadors of the Tyrians and Sidonians.

" And made an oration to them."   Clearly, the Tyrian and Sidonian Ambassadors.

22. And the people made acclamation saying: It is the voice of a god, and not of a man.

22. "Made acclamation," cheered, uttered a loud shout of applause when they heard him speak.   Josephus says it was occasioned by their seeing his splendid apparel.   But, most likely, it was caused by his oration.   For, they said, " it was the *voice* of a god."

"It is the voice of a god," &c.   "The people," viz., the Idolaters, heathen section of the population, urged on by Herod's courtiers.   Not likely that the Jews joined in it.   Josephus says the Jews were incensed with Agrippa for receiving such impious adulation.   Josephus (Lib. Antiq., xix., viii.) says of him, "he neither rebuked the people, nor rejected their impious flattery."   From the sequel and the prompt judgment from heaven on his impiety, in consequence of arrogating to himself the honour due to God, it would seem he was pleased and acquiesced in it.

23. And forthwith an Angel of the Lord struck him, because he had not given the honour to God : and being eaten up by worms, he gave up the ghost.

23. "And forthwith, an Angel," &c.   This shows it was a Divine judgment on his impiety.

"Because he had not given," &c.   By tacitly assenting to, and not rejecting their impious adulation, he impiously arrogated to himself the honour due to God alone.   "I am the Lord and my glory I shall not give to another " (Isaias xlii.).   Herod's guilt was the greater, because, brought up in the Jewish religion, he knew, or ought to have known, how jealous God is in regard to His glory.

"And being eaten up by worms."   Similar was the judgment on Antiochus Epiphanes in punishment of his impiety (2 Machab, ix. 5). Agrippa's grandfather, Herod the Great, died of the same disease. (Josephus, Antiq., c. xvii. 8).   So did Maximin, the persecutor of the Christians (Eusebius, viii. 16) and others.

Josephus, out of motives of delicacy, does not state precisely the loathsome disease of which Herod died. He says it was *Dysentery*. But that too, might be caused by worms in the intestines.   So, there is no contradiction.   St. Luke, himself a physician, is very precise in describing it.

24. But the

24. " The word of the Lord."   The Church founded on God's word

Commentary.

"increased" in the multitudes that joined it. The death, by Divine judgment, of the chief persecutor, Herod, gave the preachers of the Gospel breathing time, of which they availed themselves. The liberation of Peter had a wonderful effect.

25. "After having deposited the alms in the hands of those to whom they were to distribute them, they returned from Jerusalem to Antioch.

Text.

word of the Lord increased and multiplied.

25. And Barnabas and Saul returned from Jerusalem, having fulfilled their ministry, taking with them John, who was surnamed Mark.

CHAPTER XIII.

1. *Now there were in the church which was at Antioch, prophets and doctors, among whom was Barnabas, and Simon, who was called Niger, and Lucius of Cyrene, and Manahen, who was the foster-brother of Herod the tetrarch, and Saul.*

2. *And as they were ministering to the Lord, and fasting, the Holy Ghost said to them: Separate me Saul and Barnabas, for the work whereunto I have taken them.*

3. *Then they, fasting and praying, and imposing their hands upon them, sent them away.*

4. *So they being sent by the Holy Ghost, went to Seleucia: and from thence they sailed to Cyprus.*

5. *And when they were come to Salamina, they preached the word of God in the synagogues of the Jews. And they had John also in the ministry.*

6. *And when they had gone through the whole island, as far as Paphos, they found a certain man, a magician, a false prophet, a Jew, whose name was Bar-jesu.*

7. *Who was with the proconsul Sergius Paulus, a prudent man. He sending for Barnabas and Saul, desired to hear the word of God.*

8. *But Elymas the magician (for so his name is interpreted) withstood them, seeking to turn away the proconsul from the faith.*

9. *Then Saul, otherwise Paul, filled with the Holy Ghost, looking upon him,*

10. *Said: O full of all guile, and of all deceit, child of the devil, enemy of all justice, thou ceasest not to pervert the right ways of the Lord.*

11. *And now behold, the hand of the Lord is upon thee, and thou shall be blind, not seeing the sun for a time. And immediately there fell a mist and darkness upon him, and going about, he sought some one to lead him by the hand,*

12. *Then the proconsul, when he had seen what was done, believed, admiring at the doctrine of the Lord.*

13. *Now when Paul and they that were with him had sailed from Paphos, they came to Perge in Pamphylia. And John departing from them, returned to Jerusalem.*

14. *But they passing through Perge, came to Antioch in Pisidia: and entering into the synagogue on the sabbath-day, they sat down.*

15. *And after the reading of the law and the prophets, the rulers of the synagogue sent to them, saying: Ye men, brethren, if you have any word of exhortation to make to the people, speak.*

16. *Then Paul rising up, and with his hand bespeaking silence, said: Ye men of Israel, and you that fear God, give ear.*

17. *The God of the people of Israel chose our fathers, and exalted the people when they were sojourners in the land of Egypt, and with an high arm brought them out from thence.*

18. *And for the space of forty years endured their manners in the desert.*

19. *And destroying seven nations in the land of Chanaan, divided their land among them, by lot.*

20. *As it were, after four hundred and fifty years: and after these things, he gave unto them judges, until Samuel the prophet.*

21. *And after that they desired a king: and God gave them Saul the son of Cis, a man of the tribe of Benjamin, forty years.*

22. And when he had removed him, he raised them up David, to be king · to whom giving testimony, he said: I have found David, the son of Jesse, a man according to my own heart, who shall do all my wills.

23. Of this man's seed God according to his promise, hath raised up to Israel a Saviour, Jesus,

24. John first preaching, before his coming, the baptism of penance to all the people of Israel.

25. And when John was fulfilling his course, he said: I am not he, whom you think me to be: but behold, there cometh one after me, whose shoes of his feet I am not worthy to loose.

26. Men, brethren, children of the stock of Abraham, and whosoever among you fear God, to you the word of this salvation is sent.

27. For they that inhabited Jerusalem, and the rulers thereof, not knowing him, nor the voices of the prophets, which are read every sabbath, judging him have fulfilled them.

28. And finding no cause of death in him, they desired of Pilate, that they might kill him.

29. And when they had fulfilled all things that were written of him, taking him down from the tree, they laid him in a sepulchre.

30. But God raised him up from the dead the third day:

31. Who was seen for many days, by them who came up with him from Galilee to Jerusalem, who to this present are witnesses to the people.

32. And we declare unto you, that the promise which was made to our fathers,

33. This same God hath fulfilled to our children, raising up Jesus, as in the second Psalm also is written: Thou art my Son, this day have I begotten thee.

34. And to shew that he raised him up from the dead, not to return now any more to corruption, he said thus: I will give you the holy things of David faithful.

35. And therefore, in another place also, he saith: Thou shalt not suffer thy holy one to see corruption.

36. For David, when he had served in his generation, according to the will of God, slept: and was laid unto his fathers, and saw corruption.

37. But he whom God hath raised from the dead, saw no corruption.

38. Be it known therefore to you, men, brethren, that through him forgiveness of sins is preached to you: and from all the things, from which you could not be justified by the law of Moses.

39. In him every one that believeth, is justified.

40. Beware, therefore, lest that come upon you which is spoken in the prophets:

41. Behold, ye despisers, and wonder, and perish: for I work a work in your days, a work which you will not believe, if any man shall tell it you.

42. And as they went out, they desired them, that on the next sabbath, they would speak unto them these words.

43. And when the synagogue was broken up, many of the Jews, and of the strangers who served God, followed Paul and Barnabas: who speaking to them, persuaded them to continue in the grace of God.

44. But the next sabbath-day, the whole city almost came together, to hear the word of God.

45. And the Jews seeing the multitudes, were filled with envy, and contradicted those things which were said by Paul, blaspheming.

46. Then Paul and Barnabas said boldly: To you it behoved us first to speak the word of God: but because you reject it, and judge yourselves unworthy of eternal life, behold we turn to the gentiles.

47. *For so the Lord hath commanded us: I have set thee to be the light of the gentiles; that thou mayest be for salvation unto the utmost part of the earth.*

48. *And the gentiles hearing it, were glad, and glorified the word of the Lord: and as many as were ordained to life everlasting, believed.*

49. *And the word of the Lord was published throughout the whole country.*

50. *But the Jews stirred up religious and honourable women, and the chief men of the city, and raised persecution against Paul and Barnabas: and cast them out of their coasts.*

51. *But they, shaking off the dust of their feet against them, came to Iconium.*

52. *And the disciples were filled with joy and with the Holy Ghost.*

ANALYSIS.

In this Chapter, we have an account of the ordination of Saul and Barnabas in accordance with Divine instructions (1-3). Their mission in Cyprus (4, 5). The signal punishment of the magician, Bar-jesu, who sought to oust them and prevent the conversion of Sergius Paulus (5-11). The conversion of Sergius Paulus (12). The eloquent address of Saul in the synagogue at Perge, in which, after summing up the benefits conferred by God on the Jews, he comes to the death of our Lord and His resurrection, in accordance with the predictions of the Prophets (16-37). The necessity for faith in Him for justification (39-41). The invitation to the Apostles to continue the same subject on the next Sabbath day (42-44). The joy of the Gentiles—envy and opposition on the part or the Jews (45-52).

Text.

1. *Now there were in the church which was at Antioch, prophets and doctors, among whom was Barnabas, and Simon, who was called Niger, and Lucius of Cyrene, and Manahen, who was the foster-brother Herod the tetrarch, and Saul.*

Commentary.

1. Prophets" (*c.* xi. 27).

"Doctors." These wise men endowed with the spiritual gift of teaching the truths of faith in a plain intelligible manner. In the catalogue of spiritual gifts enumerated by St. Paul (1. Cor. xii. 28), "Doctors" are placed third in order. As the "Prophets" explained the truths of faith under the influence of sudden inspiration for the moment; "So did Doctors" do, in a calm, intelligible manner.

"Lucius of Cyrene." Whether it is to him St. Paul alludes (Rom. xvi. 21) is uncertain.

"Niger," so called, probably, from his complexion.

"Foster-brother." The word, probably, here means, the associate, playmate. It was usual with Princes to select children of the same age, as associates or playmates for their children. This was regarded as a high honour.

"Herod" (Antipas). The same who beheaded the Baptist; mocked our Lord. He was, at this time, after being deposed by Claudius, exiled at Lyons. "Tetrarch," called by his former name, though no longer such.

2. *And as they were ministering to the Lord, and fasting, the Holy Ghost said to them: Separate me Saul and Barnabas, for the work*

2. "Ministering." The Greek—λειτουργούντων—literally means engaged in a public work, which the words, "unto the Lord," would point to a work in the service of God, or Divine worship. The words refer to the engagement in public Divine worship, and not merely in prayer or instruction. It would thus, by implication, if not directly, indicate the Sacrifice of the New Law, the chief part of the *Liturgy*, or of Divine worship. If reference were made merely to prayers, a different

Commentary.

form would be used, thus, "*while they were praying*." Nor could it refer to preaching, which is addressed to the *people* and not "to *the Lord*."

"Fasting," is also significant. For the ancient Fathers, Augustine, Basil, &c., tell us, *fasting* always preceded the offering of sacrifice ; but, *fasting* was not necessarily connected with prayer in general (Beelen). Erasmus renders the Greek word, *sacrificantibus*. Kenrick prefers rendering it, *officiating*. Whatever may be the probability of this opinion, no Catholic could think of recurring to a text so dubious, in proof of the sacrifice of the New Law, when there are clear texts, plenty and to spare, from which the existence of the holy sacrifice is proved decretorially and satisfactorily.

"The Holy Ghost said to them," either by internal inspiration, or possibly in an audible tone, to some of them, which they communicated to the others.

"Separate." Set apart by some solemn act, as in next verse indicated by the imposition of hands. What this latter ceremony means is disputed. Some say as Saul was undoubtedly an Apostle called by our Lord Himself before this (Gal. i. 1-15; Acts ix. 20, &c.) the ceremony here could not mean conferring the Episcopal office; that it was only meant to show the communion of pastors and the unity of ministry in the Church. Thus it was ratified by some external ceremony ; the mission was already divinely confided to them.

Others (and this is more generally held) say that there is questions of Episcopal consecration. They may have been already priests. They had already exercised the functions of priests, and are numbered with those, who discharged sacred functions ; or, it may be that Priesthood and Episcopacy were conferred at the same time, which Bellarmine holds to be possible (De Sac. Ord. *c*. 5) and Petavius (Dissert. Eccles., Lib. i., *c.* 2) says it was done at that age of the Church. The words of next verse regarding some imposition of hands, fasting, praying, would seem to be confirmatory of this view, although the difficulties and objections against are very great and hard to be answered.

"Saul and Barnabas." The order is inverted in the Greek. However, the Vulgate reading is well sustained by versions ; and especially the Syriac.

"For the work." The conversion of the Gentile world "taken," chosen them.

3. The Greek means "*after having fasted and prayed*," &c. This solemn mode of proceeding points to the great work before them, of deputing two men, to begin on an organized scale, the conversion of the heathen.

"Sent them away," on their mission, guided and influenced by the Holy Ghost.

4. "By the Holy Ghost." Under whose direction the preparatory

Text.	Commentary.

Text.

being sent by the Holy Ghost, went to Seleucia: and from thence they sailed to Cyprus.

Commentary.

ceremony was carried out. It was He who ordered them to be set apart, and, as some understand it, ordained or consecrated for the purpose.

"Seleucia" on the Mediterranean, situated at the mouth of the Orontes. It was about sixteen miles from Antioch, situated inland, higher up the Orontes.

"Cyprus." The well-known island on the Mediterranean not far from Seleucia. It was the birth-place of Barnabas. The Gospel had been preached there already by others (xi. 19).

Text.

5. And when they were come to Salamina, they preached the word of God in the synagogues of the Jews. And they had John also in the ministry.

5. "Salamina." The chief city of Cyprus, on its eastern shore, destroyed by an earthquake. It was rebuilt by Constantine. Hence, called *Constantia*.

"Synagogue of the Jews." To the Jews they preached the word of God, in the *first* instance. "John" surnamed Mark (*c.* xii. 12). He did not claim to be their equal, who were specially designated by the Holy Ghost to the high office of preaching the Gospel. He held an inferior position. He acted as their travelling companion; probably, making provision for their temporal necessities, so that they might attend uninterruptedly to the preaching of the Word. He may also have assisted them in their spiritual ministry, acting as catechist, &c.

Text.

6. And when they had gone through the whole island, as far as Paphos, they found a certain man, a magician, a false prophet, a Jew, whose name was Bar-jesu.

6. "Paphos," on the western coast, the residence of the Proconsul. Hence, they traversed the entire Island from east to west; no doubt, preaching the Gospel as they went along.

"Magician." For meaning of (see viii.; Matthew ii.)

"False Prophet." Pretending to the gift of foretelling future events, and of being inspired with a knowledge of the Divine will. "A Jew," who pretended to be a Divine Legate of some sort.

"Bar-Jesu." The son of Jesu or Joshue, a name in common use among the Jews.

Text.

7. Who was with the proconsul Sergius Paulus, a prudent man. He sending for Barnabas and Saul, desired to hear the word of God.

7. "With." In the suite, or in attendance on.

"Proconsul." Governor of Cyprus himself. In the days of the Republic, the governors of provinces were appointed directly by the Consuls. Hence, termed Proconsuls, which title they held even in the days of the Empire. Among the provinces given over by Augustus to the Senate and people of Rome was Cyprus. To other provinces, he claimed to appoint governors directly himself.

"Prudent." Intelligent, anxious to arrive at a knowledge of the truth.

"Sending for Barnabas and Saul." The rumour of whose preaching something novel reached this intelligent, liberal-minded governor, anxious for information.

"The Word of God." This was what they announced, though likely, at first, the governor only regarded it as a subject of speculative knowledge.

Commentary.

8. "Elymas." The name by which the imposter was commonly known. Signifying, *wise*, corresponding with the Persian term, *Magus*.

"Withstood them." No doubt, he was present at Saul's, &c., exposition of the Christian faith, and seeing the impression made on the governor, he, probably, by attempting to show the falsity of the reasons advanced, and in the exercise of his pretended science, endeavoured to dissuade the governor from embracing the faith and showing favour to the Christians.

(¹)   (²)

9. Some say he had both names from his infancy. Others, considering that this was the first time that St. Luke uses the term, "Paul," in connection with the conversion of Sergius Paulus say it was assumed to mark the great spiritual triumph of the Apostle, who took the name of his distinguished convert, just as Scipio took the name of *Africanus*, Metellus, *Creticus*, &c. (St. Jerome in Ep. ad Philem). This is the last time St. Luke calls him "*Saul*." Henceforward, as he was about to devote his labours to the conversion of the Gentile world, he calls him exclusively "*Paul*," a Roman name familiar to the Gentiles.

"Filled with the Holy Ghost" indicates the habitual state of his soul, filled with the inspirations of the Holy Ghost which stimulated him to administer to this wretched man and inflict on him, on the part of God, well merited punishment. The words here denote active impulse for the moment and for the occasion. Hence, "looking on him," sternly and steadfastly.

10. He said, "full of all guile." Knowingly practising all kinds of delusion, " and of all deceit." The Greek word conveys the idea of all kinds *of sleight of hand*, sly acts, calculated to impose on simple, ignorant people. The word "*all*" is very emphatic.

"Child of the devil," faithful imitator of him who is the father of lies, and of all deceit (John viii. 44); "enemy of all justice," actively opposed to and hating every thing just and upright. Wicked men hate in others the virtues opposed to their own vices. Hence, it is said in Scripture "*opprimamus justum, contrarius est operibus nostris*."

"To pervert," &c. To make men turn aside from walking in the ways of the Lord, which are always straight, to turn them away from embracing the Gospel, and enter on a course of life crooked and perverse, only suited to imposters and hypocrites.

11. "Now behold." Mind you, the just punishment from God is soon to overtake you.

"Thou shalt be blind." Blindness was an appropriate punishment indicating the dark perversity of his conduct.

"Not seeing the sun." Which clearly indicates his total blindness.

"A mist and darkness." Show the gradual privation of sight, first a film came on his eyes—St. Luke, a physician, uses a term of art—then,

Text.

8. *But Elymas the magician (for so his name is interpreted) withstood them, seeking to turn away the pro-consul from the faith.*

9. *Then Saul, otherwise Paul, filled with the Holy Ghost, looking upon him,*

10. *Said: O full of all guile, and of all deceit, child of the devil, enemy of all justice, thou ceasest not to pervert the right ways of the Lord.*

11. *And now behold, the hand of the Lord is upon thee, and thou shalt be blind, not seeing the sun for a time. And immediately there fell*

Text.	Commentary.
a mist and darkness upon him, and going about, he sought some one to lead him by the hand.	"darkness," until it ended in total privation, "and going about," &c., groping in the dark, for a guide to conduct him (as in Genesis xix. 11).
12. Then the proconsul, when he had seen what was done, believed, admiring at the doctrine of the Lord.	12. "Believed." Embraced the faith, confirmed by such a remarkable miracle. This also showed him that Elymas was an impostor.
13. Now when Paul and they that were with him had sailed from Paphos, they came to Perge in Pamphylia. And John departing from them, returned to Jerusalem.	13. "Paul," &c., and his colleagues. "Perge," the capital of Pamphylia, distinguished for the famous temple of Diana. Whatever John's reasons were for not accompanying them beyond Perge, they did not satisfy Paul, who refused afterwards to have him associated with them. This gave rise to the difference between the Apostle and Barnabas, the latter was kinsman of John Mark. This difference ended in their separation. John, it seems, was afterwards taken into the Apostle's friendship (2 Tim. iv. 11 ; Col. iv. 10.)
14. But they passing through Perge, came to Antioch in Pisidia: and entering into the synagogue on the Sabbath - day, they sat down.	14. They made no stay this time, at Perge. Not so, however, on their return (xiv. 25.) "Antioch of Pisidia." Different from the well-known Antioch of Syria (xi. 19). "Entering into the Synagogue." There must have been a good many Jews there. "Sat down." Assuming the position of Doctors, and conveying that they would be glad to address the congregation. Although specially marked out by the Holy Ghost himself for the conversion of the Gentile world, they deemed it right to attend to the Divine mandate of preaching to the Jews, *first*, "*Judæo primum.*"
15. And after the reading of the law and the prophets, the rulers of the synagogue sent to them, saying: Ye men, brethren, if you have any word of exhortation to make to the people, speak.	15. "And after the reading," &c. A portion of the Pentateuch— "the Law"—was marked off to be read for the assembly, each Sabbath day, in the synagogue. To this was added an appropriate passage from "the Prophets," bearing in sense on the passage read from the Law, or Pentateuch. "The rulers of the Synagogue." The officers, whose duty it was to see that all things were conducted decorously at the meeting. To them it belonged to call on whom they pleased to address the people. "If ye have any word," &c. Their position and intelligent appearance gave grounds for assuming this. "Men, brethren." Showed they have regarded them as fellow-countrymen and of the same religion
16. Then Paul rising up, and	16. "And you that fear God." By those are most probably meant the class termed, *Proselytes of the gate*, who had not been as yet incor-

Commentary.

porated with the Jews, by circumcision ; but, having renounced the worship of idols, adored Jehovah, and were admitted to the Synagogues. There was another class of Proselytes, viz., *Proselytes of justice.* This latter class were incorporated with the Jews by circumcision. They were bound to the observance of the entire Mosaic Law. Not so, the *Proselytes of the gate*, who were bound only by the precepts given to Noah.

17. This is the first discourse recorded by St. Luke in the Acts, as uttered by St. Paul. Every word of it is thoroughly in harmony with his writings in his Epistles. Between it and the discourses of St. Peter and St. Stephen addressed to the Jews, who had not at the time, embraced the Faith, the greatest analogy is clearly discernible. St. Paul seems to adopt the same course that they followed in order to bring around their conversion. In this disourse, instead of proclaiming at once the Divinity of our Lord and the necessity of believing in Him, which might occasion a cry of opposition against Him, he gives a brief account of the History of the Jews, their special election by God, till he comes down to the time of King David, from whose seed our Saviour had sprung. Then briefly alluding to His Death and Resurrection—all in accordance with the ancient prophecies—he points out what he intended to be the main object of his discourse, viz. : the necessity of believing in Him, in order to obtain Salvation (38, 39). He also warns them against the disastrous consequences of unbelief *(vv.* 40, 41).

" The God," &c. This exordium was calculated to secure him an attentive hearing.

" Exalted the people." By multiplying them, asserting them into liberty from a state of degrading bondage, working great prodigies of power in their behalf, humbling their enemies

" And with a high arm," &c. All this is fully detailed in the Book of Exodus.

18. " Endured their manners," &c. Patiently bearing with their perversity and frequent rebellions against him (Psalm xciv. 10).

The above is the reading commonly adopted. Others—and they are neither few nor inconsiderable—adopt a different reading. They maintain that instead of ετροποφορησεν "*Endured,*" it should be ετροφοφορησεν *nourished, fed,* as a nurse feeds her young. This latter reading is found in several excellent MSS. and versions. There is only the difference of one letter φ and π in both. If we consult history it is against the former reading, as it testifies that God did not patiently endure their perversity ; but, rather frequently reproached, threatened, and punished them severely. Moreover, does it not seem unlikely that St. Paul in recounting the benefits bestowed on their fathers, would mention their perversity, which God had patiently to bear with ? More likely, he would refer to their having been miraculously

Text.

with his hand bespeaking silence, said : Ye men of Israel : and you that fear God, give ear.

17. The God of the people of Israel chose our fathers, and exalted the people when they were sojourners in the land of Egypt, and with an high arm brought them out from thence.

18. And for the space of forty years endured their manners in the desert.

Text.	Commentary.

nourished by God, with Manna in their passage, for forty years, through the wilderness.

19. *And des-troying seven nations in the land of Cha-naan, divided their land among them, by lot.*

19. "Destroying" them, as *nations* (Deut. vii. 1), extirpating them as such, several individuals survived.

"Land of Chanaan." The whole country went by the name of the principal nation. This is the land promised their fathers.

"By lot," a process frequently resorted to among the Jews, for deter-mining the most important affairs.

20. *As it were, after four hundred and fifty years: and after these things, he gave unto them judges, until Samuel the prophet.*

20. "As it were," &c. We have great chronological difficulties con-nected with this verse. There are two readings of it, both well supported by MSS. and versions. One, the ordinary Greek reading, according to which "the four hundred and fifty years" are to be connected with what follows, and determine the period or duration of the government of the people by judges.

"After these things," or after the sortition of the lands, some time subsequent to the entrance into the Land of Promise, He gave them judges who ruled for "four hundred and fifty years until Samuel the Prophet," Samuel's own administration included. This is not easily reconciled with 3 Kings, c. vi. 1, where it is stated four hundred and eighty years (480) elapsed between the Exodus and the fourth (4th) year of the reign of Solomon, the date of the building of the Temple.

The other reading followed by the Vulgate, and supported by some of the chief MSS. and versions connects the "four hundred and fifty (450) years" not with what follows, but with the preceding, and computes them from the call and special election of the Jewish people, which began at the birth of Isaac, the heir of the promises, to the sortition of the lands in Chanaan. In this reading there is no need for reconciling this passage with 3 Kings vi. 6, which speaks of a period commencing with the Exodus.

The passage will, then, mean that God gave the children of Israel the land of Chanaan *four hundred and fifty* (450) years after He had chosen our fathers and their posterity to be His peculiar people.

In this computation, the forty (40) years wandering in the desert, and seven (7) years before the distribution of the land are added to the *four hundred* (400) from the time of the promise till the Exodus or end of their bondage.

Commentators generally remark in connection with this and such like passages that Chronological details regarding facts, long since past, are very perplexing. They, moreover, remark that the Chronology here mentioned was commonly held at the time; and that St. Paul, without entering into any disputes about Chronological accuracy or attempting to settle every point regarding it, gave expression to the opinion on the subject usually adopted by the Jews at the time.

Commentary.

21. "Forty years." In Book. of Kings, there is no mention of the duration of Saul's reign.

The Apostle must have learned it from *Tradition*. This number perfectly accords with the narrative of Josephus (Antiq. vii. 11) who says Saul reigned eighteen (18) years before the death of Samuel, and *twenty-two* after it.

22. "Removed." Deprived him of the Royal dignity (1 Kings xxxi. 1-6).

"Giving testimony"—"*according to my own heart*," very pleasing to me, such a man as my heart desires and wishes for. "*My wills* execute my mandates." This testimony is found substantially in (1 Kings xiii. 14, xvi. 1 ; Psl. xxxviii.). David may have deflected from the right path betimes ; but, his public kingly life was uniformly good ; and, after he fell, his repentance was remarkable. His reign, as king, was good, obedient to God's will, unlike Saul, who proved to be perverse.

David is commended for having promoted the worship of God among the people (3 Kings xiv. 8, 9 ; xv. 3-5) and contrasted with Jeroboam and Abias.

23. "Seed," posterity. Our Lord is everywhere known by the designation, "Son of David."

"God, according to His promise," viz., the promises generally made to Abraham and David, that the Messiah would be born of their seed (Gal. iii. 15) which he confirms in *v.* 32.

"Hath raised up to Israel, a Saviour, Jesus." Instead of "raised up," the reading best supported by a preponderance of MSS., and generally preferred, has, "*brought forth* to Israel." It refers not to our Lord's Incarnation ; but, to his having been publicly declared by God, at the commencement of his ministry, at his Baptism, by John, to be the Saviour of all Israel. Hence, aptly called Jesus. The reference here made to the precursory ministry and testimony of John shows there is question of our Lord's coming forth to exercise His ministry.

24. "John preaching," or, as the Greek has it, "*having previously preached*," "before his coming," or His public appearance to exercise His ministry.

In *v.* 23, the Apostle introduces the chief point of his discourse, that Jesus was the promised Messiah, who was to redeem the world. The mention of the word Jesus, so odious to the Jews, and calculated to beget a prejudice, is introduced with great judgment, the promises regarding which, already laid before them, the Jews could not gainsay. With great tact he avails himself of the allusion to David to introduce the mention of the Messiah, who was to be of the seed of David.

The meaning of *vv.* 23, 24, then, is : God, conformably to His promise has declared, pointed out unto Israel Jesus as Saviour, the descendant of King David, after John had prepared the ways for His entry

21. *And after that they desired a king : and God gave them Saul the son of Cis, a man of the tribe of Benjamin, forty years.*

22. *And when he had removed him, he raised them up David, to be king : to whom giving testimony, he said : I have found David, the son of Jesse, a man according to my own heart, who shall do all my wills.*

23. *Of this man's seed God according to his promise, hath raised up to Israel a Saviour, Jesus.*

24. *John first preaching, before his coming, the baptism of penance to all the people of Israel.*

K

Text.

Commentary.

into the functions of His ministry, by preaching the Baptism of Penance unto all the people.

25. *And when John was fulfilling his course, he said: I am not he, whom you think me to be: but behold, there cometh one after me, whose shoes of his feet I am not worthy to loose.*

25. "Fulfilling his course." When in the act of discharging his duties as precursor, he said "I am not he," (see Gospels Matthew iii.; Luke iii. 15 ; John i. 27).

26. *Men, brethren, children of the stock of Abraham, and whosoever among you fear God, to you the word of this salvation is sent.*

26. "Stock of Abraham," native born Jews, his natural descendants through Isaac.

"Fear God." Proselytes. The Apostle earnestly exhorts his countrymen, whether Jews or Proselytes, to accept the message of Salvation, which is the fulfilment of the promises made to their fathers.

" *To you*," is emphatic: To them was the Saviour first sent. "This salvation" indicated in *v.* 23.

27. *For they that inhabited Jerusalem, and the rulers thereof, not knowing him, nor the voices of the prophets, which are read every sabbath, judging him, have fulfilled them.*

27. "For they that inhabited Jerusalem," &c. The object of the Apostle here would seem to be to explain more fully how this salvation was brought about, and the humiliations and sufferings, in the first instance, of the Saviour, and His subsequent glory and exaltation in fulfilment of "voices" or oracles of "the Prophets" who had minutely predicted them beforehand. "For" is regarded here by Commentators not as *causal* but *expletive*, as if the Apostle was about to explain how "the word of salvation" was effected, viz., through the crimes and ingratitude of the Jews of Jerusalem.

Others (among them Patrizzi) say "for" conveys a reason not for what is *expressed* but what is understood, as if he revolved in his mind reproachfully and sorrowfully what a sad subject of reproach, what a grievous crime is involved in this work of Redemption.

For the Jews of Jerusalem not knowing Him to be their Messiah as well "as their rulers," members of the *Sanhedrim* or Supreme Council of the Nation, blindly shutting their eyes against all evidence, utterly ignored him.

"Read every Sabbath," which rendered their rejection of Him more culpable and blameworthy.

"Judging." Condemning Him; pronouncing Him worthy of death.

28. *And finding no cause for death in him, they de-*

28. Handed Him over to Pilate, who, out of fear of the Emperor, before whom he might be charged with allowing a man, however unjustly charged with sedition to pass unpunished, regardless of justice, condemned

Commentary.

him to death. The Roman procurator alone had at this time the power to do so.

29. This proved the reality of his death. The words express the fact of His burial by whomsoever killed. They may be said to have buried Him by means of others; for, having compassed His death, they brought about His burial. Besides, some members of the *Sanhedrim*, who disapproved of the sentence, Nicodemus and Joseph, had him buried.

30. "But," implying that these expectations regarding his utter extinction in the grave were frustrated.

"God." Christ who is God, raised Himself up, as He repeatedly promised (*c.* ii. 24). St. Paul did not deem it expedient to proclaim, at this stage, the fundamental truth that Christ is God. It is not denied, however prudently passed over in silence.

31. "Seen" not only by the Apostles, but by several other disciples (1 Cor. xv., &c.).

32, 33. The witnesses referred to in the preceding verse declared this fundamental truth to the people of Palestine. The same we now declare to you, the Jews of the dispersion; "and we declare that the promise made to our fathers," Abraham, Isaac, Jacob, David, regarding the salvation and redemption of mankind is brought about by one of their seed.

"God hath fulfilled." *Completely* carried out in the Resurrection of Jesus, which perfected the accomplishment of all the promises that concerned Him. The Resurrection of our Lord with all its circumstances was the most undeniable proof, the undoubted seal of His Divinity, which embraced every other truth and promise and prediction that concerned Him.

"Raising up Jesus" from the dead.

"As in second Psalm." In some versions it is "in *first* Psalm. But in this it is supposed that *first* Psalm is merely an introduction to the whole Psalter. The first and second Psalms were by some regarded as one. However, the Vulgate reading is better sustained by the chief MSS.

"*Thou art My Son*," &c. These words are regarded by many Expositors as having reference to the Eternal generation of the Son "*before all ages*." These explain its connection with our Lord's Resurrection, thus: In our Lord's Resurrection, His human nature which was

Text.

sired of Pilate, that they might kill him.

29. And when they had fulfilled all things that were written of him, taking him down from the tree, they laid him in a sepulchre.

30. But God raised him up from the dead the third day:

31. Who was seen for many days, by them who came up with him from Galilee to Jerusalem, who to this present are his witnesses to the people.

32. And we declare unto you, that the promise which was made to our fathers,

33. This same God hath fulfilled to our children, raising up Jesus, as in the second Psalm also is written: Thou art my Son, this day have I begotten thee.

Commentary.

always even in its separated state, during the interval between His death and Resurrection, united to the Person of the Word, received, as it were, a new existence when His sacred body now glorified was united to His soul. In reference to this state of new existence, God the Father declares Him anew to be His Eternal Son, perpetuating His generation from eternity, which was not a mere *passing*, but a *continuous, permanent* act ever abiding from eternity unto eternity. This is in accordance with the teaching of St. Paul (Rom. i. 4), where he says Christ was *pre-destinated* : (in Greek, *declared*) to be the Son of God by His Resurrection, &c.

The *vv.* 32 and 33 should be interpreted and joined together, as they convey that God had fulfilled for the children the promises made to their fathers. These promises He *completely* "*fulfilled*" by raising up His son from the dead, which followed as a necessary consequence of His being the Eternal, consubstantial, natural Son of God, begotten of Him eternally by a permanent, abiding generation.

Some interpreters say *vv.* 32, 33 should be included in a parenthesis, thus, *v.* 34 would be immediately connected with *v.* 31, following up the arguments directly in proof of Christ's Resurrection.

In the two *vv.* 32, 33 is contained the point which the Apostle wishes to establish all along, viz., that the Jews had the promises of salvation fulfilled, which was now tendered to them.

"As in the second Psalm." In some versions we have, "as in the *first* Psalm." This discrepancy arose from the different divisions of the Psalms at different times and in different versions. Moreover, some looking on the *first* Psalm, as merely an introduction to the whole Psalter, made only one of the first and second Psalms.

"*Thou art My son*," &c. Some hold that these words directly refer to Christ's Resurrection, in which He was begotten and born into a new and immortal life which God communicated to Him ; and thus became His Father, and he became a son, as earthly parents are termed such when their children are born.

Others maintain that there is question directly of the eternal generation of the Son, born of the Father "*before all ages*." In order to show its connexion with the Resurrection, these say that St. Paul adduces the Eternal generation of Christ, His identity with the Father, as His Eternal Son, to prove that having died by His Father's will, He could not but rise again; impossible, He would remain in death. Just as St. Peter proves (*c.* ii. 24) that it is impossible for Him not to rise in order to fulfil the prophecies, so here, the impossibility of His not rising is derived from His Divine sonship, which would not allow of His mouldering in the grave.

"This day have I begotten Thee." "This day." God's day, determines no particular time. With God there is no *past* or *future*. All is *present*. And the generation of His Son in eternity was not a mere *passing* act, but continuous, permanent, abiding from eternity unto eternity.

Commentary.

Some say these words convey the idea expressed by St. Paul (Rom. i. 4) that in His Resurrection God *declared* him to be Son *in* the new and glorified existence conferred on His humanity, which was always since the Incarnation inseparably united to the Divine Person of the Word.

34. Having in the preceding proved the *fact* of Christ's Resurrection, the Apostle now in this and following proceeds to point out its *chief quality,* viz., permanency, "rising from the dead He shall die no more," &c. (Rom. vi. 9). He is never again to die.

"The holy things of David," &c. These words are taken from Isaias (lv. 3) according to the Septuagint, with some slight change, which does not affect the substance or meaning of the passage. St. Jerome renders it from the Hebrew "the faithful mercies of David." The words mean the holy and merciful promises made to David, of benefits to be conferred on him, especially those having reference to the glorious and ever-enduring reign of His Son, whose throne was to be established for ever (2 Kings vii. 19 ; Psalm lxxxviii., 36-38).

"Faithful." Unfailing. Sure to be carried out. Now, these promises would not be abiding and ever enduring, unless the Resurrection of our Lord were permanent and enduring.

35. A further corroboration of the same argument (*see* c. ii. 27).

36. He shows the words of the Psalm could not apply to David himself.

"In his generation." Age or period of life. "Served according to the will of God." Obeyed God's Commandments during his lifetime among the men or generation with whom he lived. "Slept," died in consequence, a holy and happy death (ii. 29-31).

37. Here he shows the passage from the Psalm could apply to one only, viz., our Lord Jesus Christ, who alone did not see corruption, being raised to a glorious and immortal life.

38. Here commences the peroration and practical conclusion of the discourse, wherein the Apostle earnestly exhorts them to have recourse, for justification and the remission of sin, to their long-expected Messiah, who alone is the fountain of salvation. This they will obtain by embracing His faith and observing His commandments. By Him comes forgiveness of the sins they committed, and absolution "from all other things," that is, all other sins, which the Law of Moses could not of

Text.

34. And to shew that he raised him up from the dead, not to return any more to corruption, he said thus: I will give you the holy things of David faithful.

35. And therefore, in another place also, he saith: Thou shalt not suffer thy holy one to see corruption.

36. For David, when he had served in his generation, according to the will of God, slept: and was laid unto his fathers, and saw corruption.

37. But he whom God hath raised from the dead, saw no corruption.

38. Be it known therefore to you, men, brethren, that through him forgiveness of sins is preached to you: and from all the things,

Text.

from which you could not be justified by the law of Moses.

39. *In him every one that believeth, is justified.*

40. *Beware, therefore, lest that come upon you which is spoken in the prophets:*

41. *Behold, ye despisers, and wonder, and perish: for I work a work in your days, a work which you will not believe, if any man shall tell it you.*

42. *And as they went out, they desired them, that on the next sabbath, they would speak unto them these words.*

Commentary.

itself confer. Whatever sins were remitted under " the Law of Moses " were remitted owing to the *retrospective* merits of Christ.

39. This justification which comes through faith, all other conditions being supplied, a justification of which " faith is the root and foundation," is confined to no particular class or nation. It embraces " every one."

40. He finally closes the oration with a threat against the incredulous, similar to that menaced by the Prophet Habacuc (i. 5-7) on their fathers, through the instrumentality of the Chaldeans who were swift in inflicting vengeance on them. God will visit them also, if they continue to be incredulous, with the severest punishment. This He did in the destruction of Jerusalem, under Titus, which exhibited a scene of carnage and suffering unexampled in the history of human misery. " In the Prophets," that is in that division of the Books of Sacred Scripture, called " the Prophets," (*see* Luke xxiv. 44 for a description of the division of the Scriptures made by the Jews into " the Law " (Pentateuch) " the Prophets," and the " *Hagiographa* "). Here, there is question of Habacuc alone.

" Ye despisers." The Hebrew means " ye, among the nations." The Septuagint translators, who are followed here, rendered the word " despisers." The copy used by them had *Bogedim* in place of *Boggoim*. The Syriac and Arabic have " wonder and perish," become annihilated through stupor and terror, " *despisers*."

" *I work a work*," &c. Do a thing. Habacuc refers to the destruction of the temple and nation by the Chaldeans, which the Jews deemed impossible, as if a house built by God's order could be destroyed. This they " could not believe," even though a prophet—" *if any man*," —were to announce it. On their temple they reposed a blind reliance (Jeremias vii. 4). In the days of the Apostles the Jews could not believe in the possibility of the destruction of their temple. This sense of fatal security lasted even during the final siege of Jerusalem.

The Apostle only quotes the first part of the threat in Habacuc (i. 6) who says that the Chaldeans would come swift upon them. He only quotes the first part, and refrains from quoting the entire passage, as by quoting one part, the Jews knew the rest of the passage.

This threat of the Apostle was fearfully realised in the destruction of Jerusalem by Titus.

42. As Paul and Barnabas were leaving the place of meeting or synagogue. " They," that is the congregation, Jews and Proselytes, " Next sabbath "—the Greek word μεταξύ, *between*, frequently means *next*. The words, v. 44, make it likely whatever may be the Greek construction here, that by the *Sabbath between*, τὸ μεταξὺ σαββάτου, there is question of " the next Sabbath." For the Greek, the reading of this verse

Commentary. | **Text.**

runs thus : "and when the Jews were gone out of the synagogue, the Gentiles besought that these words might be preached," &c. The Vulgate reading, however, is best sustained by MSS. and more in accordance with the usual synagogue attendance. Not clear that the Gentiles attended synagogue meetings.

43. "Broken up. Dismissed or concluded in the usual way, "Many of the Jews," native Jews, "and strangers," &c. Proselytes (see v, 16) accompanied them to their lodgings.
"The grace of God." The doctrine of the Gospel and faith.

43. And when the synagogue was broken up, many of the Jews, and of the strangers who served God, followed Paul and Barnabas: who speaking to them, persuaded them to continue in the grace of God.

44. "Whole city." Most of the population, including Gentiles. "came together." Where ? Not said, possibly several audiences were given, as no one synagogue could contain all together ; or, in some open space around the synagogue.

44. But the next sabbathday, the whole city almost came together, to hear the word of God.

45. "Were filled with envy." Felt great indignation on seeing the Gentiles admitted on such easy terms.
"Contradicted." Denounced as false, the teaching "of Paul," the chief speaker. "Blaspheming." Adding some reproaches, which were so many blasphemies against our Lord.

45. And the Jews seeing the multitudes, were filled with envy, and contradicted those things which were said by Paul, blaspheming.

46. "Boldly." Spiritedly, with courageous intrepidity, disregarding their anger and jealously.
"To you it behoved," &c. According to the precept of our Lord (Luke xxiv. v. 47).
"Judge yourselves," &c. By rejecting the means of salvation offered to you. Not that they deemed themselves unworthy of salvation ; but rather the opposite. Their conduct, however, in rejecting the means of salvation was a practical judgment on the subject, though they thought the reverse.

46. Then Paul and Barnabas said boldly: To you it behoved us first to speak the word of God: but because you reject it, and judge yourselves unworthy of eternal life, behold we turn to the gentiles.

47. "So the Lord commanded," &c. He does not here refer to the express command of our Lord himself, which the Jews would undervalue ; but, to the commands contained in their own highly-prized Scriptures of the Old Testament.
"I have set Thee," &c. These words, as is universally admitted, directly refer to the Messiah. They are found in Isaias (xlix. 6). They implicitly refer to the Apostles, who were to act in His name, and by preaching

47. For so the Lord hath commanded us : I have set thee to to be the light of the gentiles; that thou mayest be for salvation unto

.he utmost part of the earth.

him to the Gentiles, were to be instrumental in carrying out in his regard, what he was appointed to be " *The Light of the Gentiles,*" whom he was to draw forth from the darkness of error and ignorance, and become the source of "salvation" to all mankind, even unto the utmost parts of the earth.

48. *And the gentiles hearing it, were glad, and glorified the word of the Lord: and as many as were ordained to life everlasting, believed.*

48. Hearing from the mouths of the Jews themselves that they were to be sharers equally with the Jews in salvation, who would fain confine salvation to themselves. "Glorified the Word of God." Speaking of it with reverence and thankfulness, as a message from God. They are contrasted with the Jews who rejected God's word (*v.* 46).

"As were ordained." Does not refer to a decree, as some understand it, on the part of God predestinating men to Eternal Life, in consequence of which decree they believed and embraced the faith. There is no question at least immediately and directly of any predestinating decree at all. The Greek word for "ordained" (τεταγμενοι) is probably allusive to military dicipline, wherein men are arranged by their officers under their proper peculiar standard. The words mean, that such as were disposed and divinely directed under the influence of God's preventing graces, inspiring and strengthening them, to aspire after life everlasting, freely embraced the faith, "believed"—as one of the most essential means of attaining the object they had in view.

49. *And the word of the Lord was published throughout the whole country.*

49. The entire district of Antioch of Pisidia embraced the faith, owing to the influence and preaching of Paul and Barnabas. There is question of the Gentile population, to whom Paul and Barnabas addressed themselves, after having been rejected and resisted by the Jews.

50. *But the Jews stirred up religious and honourable women, and the chief men of the city, and raised persecution against Paul and Barnabas: and cast them out of their coasts.*

50. Honourable women." Women of high rank, connected with high families of influence.

"Chief men," &c. The civil magistrates, who exercised civil authority.

"Cast them," &c. Had a decree enacted, banishing them. This does not imply violence. Likely, they had men employed to see them depart from their country

51. *But they, shaking off the dust of their feet against them, came to Iconium.*

51. For the meaning of this symbolical mode of acting, prescribed by our Lord, in certain circumstances, to his Apostles (see Matthew x. 14, Commentary on).

52. *And the disciples were filled with joy and with the Holy Ghost.*

52. Joy infused by the Holy Ghost in communicating His gifts.

CHAPTER XIV.

1. *And it came to pass in Iconium, that they entered together into the synagogue of the Jews, and so spoke that a very great multitude both of the Jews and of the Greeks did believe.*

2. *But the unbelieving Jews stirred up and incensed the minds of the gentiles against the brethren.*

3. *A long time therefore they abode there, dealing confidently in the Lord, who gave testimony to the word of his grace, granting signs and wonders to be done by their hands.*

4. *And the multitude of the city was divided: and some of them indeed held with the Jews, but some with the apostles.*

5. *And when there was an assault made by the gentiles and the Jews with their rulers to use them contumeliously, and to stone them:*

6. *They understanding it, fled to Lystra, and Derbe, cities of Lycaonia, and to the whole country round about, and were there preaching the gospel.*

7. *And there sat a certain man at Lystra, impotent in his feet, a cripple from his mother's womb, who never had walked.*

8. *This same heard Paul speaking. Who looking upon him, and seeing that he had faith to be healed,*

9. *Said with a loud voice: Stand upright on thy feet. And he leaped up, and walked.*

10. *And when the multitudes had seen what Paul had done, they lifted up their voice in the Lycaonian tongue, saying: The gods are come down to us in the likeness of men;*

11. *And they called Barnabas, Jupiter: but Paul, Mercury; because he was chief speaker.*

12. *The priest also of Jupiter that was before the city, bringing oxen and garlands before the gate, would have offered sacrifice with the people.*

13. *Which, when the apostles Barnabas and Paul had heard, rending their clothes, they leaped out among the people crying,*

14. *And saying: Ye men, why do ye these things? We also are mortals. men like unto you, preaching to you to be converted from these vain things, to the living God, who made the heaven, and the earth, and the sea, and all things that are in them:*

15. *Who in times past suffered all nations to walk in their own way.*

16. *Nevertheless he left not himself without testimony, doing good from heaven, giving rains and fruitful seasons, filling our hearts with food and gladness.*

17. *And speaking these things, they scarce restrained the people from sacrificing to them.*

18. *Now there came thither certain Jews from Antioch, and Iconium: and persuading the multitude, and stoning Paul, drew him out of the city, thinking him to be dead.*

19. *But as the disciples stood round about him, he rose up and entered into the city, and the next day he departed with Barnabas to Derbe.*

20. *And when they had preached the gospel to that city, and had taught many, they returned again to Lystra, and to Iconium, and to Antioch.*

21. Confirming the souls of the disciples, and exhorting them to continue in the faith: and that through many tribulations we must enter into the kingdom of God.

22. And when they had ordained to them priests in every church, and had prayed with fasting, they commended them to the Lord, in whom they believed.

23. And passing through Pisidia, they came into Pamphylia.

24. And having spoken the word of the Lord in Perge, they went down into Attalia.

25. And thence they sailed to Antioch, from whence they had been delivered to the grace of God, unto the work which they accomplished.

26. And when they were come, and had assembled the church, they related what great things God had done with them, and how he had opened the door of faith to the gentiles.

27. And they abode no small time with the disciples.

ANALYSIS.

We have an account of the opposition to the preaching of Paul and Barnabas at Iconium (1-5). Their flight to Lystra and Derbe,—the cure of a cripple (6-9). The insane conduct of the multitude who taking them for Gods prepare to offer them sacrifice (10-13). The loud denunciation by the Apostles of such impiety (13-17).

Text.	Commentary.
1. *And it came to pass in Iconium, that they entered together into the synagogue of the Jews, and so spoke that a very great multitude both of the Jews and of the Greeks did believe.*	1. "Greeks." Proselytes from Paganism. In next verse, they are contrasted with unbelieving "Gentiles."
2. *But the unbelieving Jews stirred up and incensed the minds of the gentiles against the brethren.*	2. "Brethren." The teachers and their converts. It is a general term for *believers*.
3. *A long time therefore they abode there, dealing confidently in the Lord, who gave testimony to the word of his grace, granting signs and wonders to be done by their hands.*	3. "A long time," &c., owing to the success of their mission. Not likely that the public authorities took any measures, as at Antioch, for their expulsion (xiii. 50). "Confidently." Courageously trusting in the Lord. "Testimony." Gave corroborating evidence, "word," &c, to the truth of what the Apostles preached, aided by Divine grace. "The word" was the means of having interior grace bestowed on them. "Signs and wonders." Miracles wrought through their hands.
4. *And the multitude of the city was divided; and some of them indeed held with the Jews, but some with the apostles.*	4. "Apostles." This is the first time they were called "Apostles" (*v.* 14), St. Paul being such in the strictest sense of the word, as he is immediately called and saw our Lord (1 Cor. ix., &c.), and deputed to be witness of his Resurrection. Barnabas was not strictly such, like St. Paul and the twelve others; but only in a more general and wider sense (as xvi. 7; 2 Cor. xiii. 23), because deputed by the Church on a particular message (xiii. 3., xv. 26).

Commentary.

5. "Assault." A violent attack (ὁρμή), the effects of which were averted by flight. Others understand it of an intended assault, which the word "*understanding* (*v.* 6) would seem to favour.

"Rulers." Probably of the Synagogue, to bring them into contempt, and put them to death, probably on a charge of blasphemy (Acts vii. 57-59).

6. "Understanding." Apprized of their danger.

"Lycaonia." Belonged formerly to Phrygia. Augustus erected it into a separate province.

7. "Sat." Allusive to his usual posture, "there *lived*," "impotent," &c., deprived of the use of his limbs.

"A cripple," &c. His condition being so well-known, the miracle could not, therefore, be gainsaid.

8. "Looking" earnestly "upon him." Seeing from his voice, gesture, countenance, besides being interiorly enlightened by the Holy Ghost. "Faith to be healed." The necessary faith for recovering his bodily health (Matthew ix. 28; Mark ix. 22; Luke xvii. 42). This is like the miracle of St. Peter, in most of the circumstances (iii. 6-8).

9. *Said with a loud voice: Stand upright on thy feet. And he leaped up, and walked.*

10. "Lycaonian tongue." Some say a corrupt sort of Greek ; others, an admixture of Greek and Syriac. St. Chrysostom thinks the Apostles did not understand it. Hence, their silence at the blasphemous utterances. It was only when they saw the garlands and preparations for sacrifice (13) they denounced it.

"The Gods are come," &c. The Pagans fancied the Gods visited in human form the places sacred to them. Lystra was dedicated to Jupiter, who, on descending, was said to be accompanied by Mercury, the god of eloquence.

11. "Barnabas, Jupiter." "Jupiter," the supreme God, remarkable for power and prowess, was represented as the most powerful of the Gods among the Pagans. To him all the other Gods were subject. Everything but fate yielded to his sway. Commonly termed the father of Gods and men. St. Chrysostom conjectures that Barnabas was majestic in stature, well built, of a powerful frame, advanced in years. Hence, taken for "Jupiter." Paul was the opposite. Being the "chief speaker," no doubt eloquent, he was taken for "Mercury," *the God of eloquence*, and messenger of the Gods.

Text.

5. *And when there was an assault made by the gentiles and the Jews with their rulers, to use them contumeliously, and to stone them :*

6. *They understanding it, fled to Lystra, and Derbe, cities of Lycaonia, and to the whole country round about, were there preaching the gospel.*

7. *And there sat a certain man at Lystra, impotent in his feet, a cripple from his mother's womb, who never had walked.*

8. *This same heard Paul speaking. Who looking upon him, and seeing that he had faith to be healed,*

10. *And when the multitude had seen what Paul had done, they lifted up their voice in the Lycaonian tongue, saying: The gods are come down to us in the likeness of men;*

11. *And they called Barnabas, Jupiter : but Paul, Mercury ; because he was chief speaker.*

12. *The priest also of Jupiter that was before the city, bringing oxen and garlands before the gate, would have offered sacrifice with the people.*

13. *Which, when the apostles Barnabas and Paul had heard, rending their clothes, they leaped out among the people crying,*

14. *And saying: Ye men, why do ye these things? We also are mortals, men like unto you, preaching to you to be converted from these vain things, to the living God, who made the heaven, and the earth, and the sea, and all things that are in them:*

15. *Who in times past suffered all nations to walk in their own ways.*

16. *Nevertheless he left not himself without testi-*

12. "Priest of Jupiter." Charged with worshipping by offering him sacrifices.

"That was," &c., viz., Jupiter. "Before the city," of which he was the tutelary deity. His image or temple was located before the gate of the city, in a prominent position, in accordance with Pagan usage.

"Oxen." The usual sacrifice to Jupiter. "Garlands." Ribands, adorning the victims.

13. "Had heard." At their lodgings, being probably informed by some of their converts.

"Rending their clothes." A mark of intense grief and abhorrence among the Jews (See Matthew xxvi. 65, Commentary on).

14. How different from the unselfish and noble conduct of the Apostles in rejecting the proferred honour was that of the vain Herod Agrippa (xii. 22, &c.).

"Like you." Subject to the same passions and infirmities. (This is conveyed by the Greek.) Having the common feelings and propensities of other men, equally needing food, subject to pain, sickness, and death, altogether opposed to the correct notions of the nature of God.

"Preaching to you," &c. Far from pretending or claiming to be regarded as Gods, we, on the contrary, exhort you to give up the adoration of "these vain things," these false Gods, idols, unreal beings, who have no real existence, who can neither see, nor hear, nor help us, "*oculos habent et non videbunt, aures habent et non audient,*" &c. (Psalm cxiii. ; 1 Kings xii. 21). In several parts of Scripture idols are termed *vanities* (Deut. xxxii. 21 ; 4 Kings xvii. 15, &c.).

"Living God." As distinguished from false divinities. A God "who made the heavens," &c., and is, therefore, also entitled to supreme worship from His creatures.

15. "Times past." During the ages before the Gospel dispensation. "All nations " of the earth except the Jews (Acts xvii. 30) having "winked at the times of this ignorance " (xvii. 30).

"To walk in their own ways." Wicked ways of life, so opposed to the ways that lead to God, withholding from them the lights and spiritual helps conferred on the Jews—no written revelation, no occasional visits from the Prophets—and reserved in a particular way for the children of the New Law. The most polished nations were just as unable to rescue themselves from the prison of sin and infidelity as the most barbarous and least cultivated.

16. While leaving the Gentiles to the errors of their ways, imparting no revelation, God did not leave them without the means of knowing Him, without evidence and a knowledge of His existence, of His

Commentary.

attributes and claims on their services. His wonderful benefits bore testimony to him.

"Doing good from Heaven." Continually conferring benefits on the world, especially giving "rain" (the early and better rain) in due seasons. "Rain" is specially a gift from God (2 Kings viii. 35 ; Job v. 10 ; Psalms lxvi. 9, &c., cxlvi. 8), most necessary for human existence. Without it the earth would be dried up and rendered desolate.

"Fruitful seasons." The earth rendering abundant fruit by God's ordination corresponding to the labour of the husbandman.

"Filling our hearts," viz., ourselves. "Hearts," by a Hebraism, designates the entire person.

"Food." Necessary for existence. "Gladness." Resulting from our daily wants having been supplied.

From this, the Apostle leaves it to be inferred, without expressly stating it, that if the Gentiles did not come to the knowledge of God, it was their own fault.

The discourse at Athens, rather lengthy (xvii. 23, 24) and Rom. (i. 20–23) are on the same lines with this.

17. Notwithstanding this address dissuading them ; still, on account of the miracles, they could hardly be restrained ; or, this discourse, coupled with the miracles, convinced the Pagans the more that they were Gods, and, therefore, these foolish people could hardly be restrained.

18. "Certain Jews." No doubt from among those who rebelled against the Apostle (xiii. 45 ; xiv. 5). *Contin . . .*

"Antioch," of Pisidia.

"Persuading," &c. Likely, ascribing the miracle to sorcery and the black art.

"Stoning Paul." Who was more obnoxious on account of his eloquence (2 Cor. xi. 27).

"Drew him out of the city." Left him there as unworthy of burial.

19. "Disciples." His late converts, fancying him dead, and preparing to perform the rites of sepulture.

"He rose up." Which was regarded by many as miraculous, as happened St. Sebastian under Diocletian. Some conjecture that his rapture into Paradise may have occurred then (2 Cor. xii. 2, &c.).

20, 21. "Returned again" courageously to the scene of their former persecution to exhort their converts not to deflect from the right path on account of sufferings, since, "through many tribulations," &c. It is a fixed law of God's adorable providence that the road to Heaven is the royal highway of the Cross, the only gate for entering it, the narrow gate

Text.

mony, doing good from heaven, giving rains and fruitful seasons, filling our hearts with food and gladness.

17. And speaking these things, they scarce restrained the people from sacrificing to them.

18. Now there came thither certain Jews from Antioch, and Iconium : and persuading the multitude, and stoning Paul, drew him out of the city, thinking him to be dead.

19. But as the disciples stood round about him, he rose up and entered into the city, and the next day he departed with Barnabas to Derbe.

20. And when they had preached the the gospel to that city, and had taught many, they re-

COMMENTARY ON

Text.

turned again to Lystra, and to Iconium, and to Antioch:

Commentary.

of tribulations, which are "many." It was in this way the Head entered; so must also the members. "All who wish to live piously in Christ Jesus must suffer persecution" (2 Tim. iii. 12). This life is a time for suffering here; the next, for enjoying the reward of suffering.

21. *Confirming the souls of the disciples, and exhorting them to continue in the faith: and that through many tribulations we must enter into the kingdom of God.*

22 And when they had ordained to them priests in every church, and had prayed with fasting, they commended them to the Lord, in whom they believed.

22. "Ordained to them Priests." The Greek word for "ordained" literally means, in classic authors, to *choose* or *elect, by holding out the hands* (χειροτονησαντες). It was originally applied to the voting of the people in public assemblies in favour of candidates for office. It is clear that here the election, appointment, or ordination, strictly speaking, took place irrespective of any voting on the part of the people. The whole operation, as the context shows, was performed solely by Paul and Barnabas. The threefold action was performed by the same persons, viz., ordaining, praying, with fasting, commending to the Lord.

Who else but Paul and Barnabas "commended their converts to the Lord"? Considering all the actions and circumstances, viz., praying with fasting, which accompanied this "ordaining," it clearly can refer to nothing else save the conferring of the Sacrament of Holy Orders which was given by the imposition of the hands of Paul and Barnabas.

The word, χειροτονια, is well known to have been employed by the Greek Fathers to designate the Sacrament of Holy Orders, of which it became with them the official designation, probably grounded on this passage. While χειροθεσια, *imposition of hands,* is the term they used for the Sacrament of *Confirmation.*

It is also deserving of remark that the conjunction "and" is omitted in Greek before "*had prayed.*" The passage would then read thus: "And when they ordained to them Priests, praying with fasting," &c. From this it is clear that all the operations performed together, viz., praying, fasting, imposing hands, manifestly refer to the same sacred rite, whereby the members of the Church were consecrated Priests."

The word, "Priest," comprises the clergy as well of the *first* as of the *second* order. The term, "Bishop," by ecclesiastical and Apostolic usage, is applied only to the clergy of the *first* order, whom we know, as a defined point of faith, to be superior to the Priests in order and jurisdiction (Council of Trent, SS. xxiii. c. 4 canon 7).

"Commended to the Lord." This was their valedictory farewell on leaving them.

23. And passing through Pisidia, they came into Pamphylia,

23. "Pisidia" (c. xiii. 14).

24. And having spoken the word of the Lord in Perge, they went down into Attalia:

24. "Attalia," in Pamphylia, on the sea coast.

Commentary.

25. "Antioch" of Syria (xi. 19 ; xiii. 1). "Delivered to the grace of God." Commended to the Divine protection on entering on the great missionary work, which they brought to a successful conclusion.

26. "Opened the door of faith," &c. Supplied the means and opportunity of preaching the faith to the Gentiles, which, by God's grace, they embraced.

27. How long cannot be exactly determined. The next we hear of them is at the Council of Jerusalem (c. xv.).

Text.

25. And thence they sailed to Antioch, from whence they had been delivered to the grace of God, unto the work which they accomplished.

26. And when they were come, and had assembled the church, they related what great things God had done with them, and how he had opened the door of faith to the gentiles.

27. And they abode no small time with the disciples.

CHAPTER XV

1. *And some coming down from Judea, taught the brethren: That except you be circumcised after the manner of Moses, you cannot be saved.*

ns.

2. *And when Paul and Barnabas had no small contest with them, they determined that Paul and Barnabas and certain others of the other side, should go up to the apostles and priests to Jerusalem about this question.*

Ceremonies

3. *They therefore being brought on their way by the church, passed through Phenice, and Samaria, relating the conversion of the gentiles; and they caused great joy to all the brethren.*

4. *And when they were come to Jerusalem, they were received by the church, and by the apostles and ancients, declaring how great things God had done with them.*

5. *But there arose some of the sect of the Pharisees that believed, saying: They must be circumcised, and be commanded to observe the law of Moses.*

6. *And the apostles and ancients assembled to consider of this matter.*

cil f

7. *And when there had been much disputing, Peter rising up, said to them: Men, brethren, you know, that in former days God made choice among us, that by my mouth the gentiles should hear the word of the gospel, and believe.*

us.

8. *And God, who knoweth the hearts, gave testimony, giving unto them the Holy Ghost, as well as to us;*

9. *And put no difference between us and them, purifying their hearts by faith.*

ussion)

10. *Now therefore, why tempt you God to put a yoke upon the necks of the disciples, which neither our fathers nor we have been able to bear?*

11. *But by the grace of the Lord Jesus Christ, we believe to be saved, in like manner as they also.*

12. *And all the multitude held their peace: and they heard Barnabas and Paul telling what great signs and wonders God had wrought among the gentiles by them.*

13. *And after they had held their peace, James answered, saying: Men, brethren, hear me.*

14. *Simon hath related how God first visited to take of the gentiles a people to his name.*

15. *And to this agree the words of the prophets, as it is written.*

16. *After these things I will return, and will rebuild the tabernacle of David, which is fallen down; and the ruins thereof I will rebuild, and I will set it up:*

17. *That the residue of men may seek after the Lord, and all nations upon whom my name is invoked, saith the Lord who doth these things.*

18. *To the Lord was his own work known from the beginning of the world.*

19. *For which cause I judge that they, who from among the gentiles are converted to God, are not to be disquieted.*

20. *But that we write unto them, that they refrain themselves from the pollutions of idols, and from fornication, and from things strangled, and from blood.*

21. *For Moses of old time hath in every city them that preach him in the synagogues, where he is read every sabbath.*

22. *Then it pleased the apostles and ancients, with the whole church, to choose men of their own company, and to send to Antioch, with Paul and Barnabas, namely, Judas, who was surnamed Barsabas, and Silas, chief men among the brethren.*

23. *Writing by their hands : The apostles and ancients, brethren, to the brethren of the gentiles that are at Antioch, and in Syria and Cilicia, greeting.*

24. *Forasmuch as we have heard, that some going out from us have troubled you with words, subverting your souls ; to whom we gave no commandment :*

25. *It hath seemed good to us, being assembled together, to choose out men, and to send them unto you, with our well beloved Barnabas and Paul :*

26. *Men that have given their lives for the name of our Lord Jesus Christ.*

27. *We have sent therefore Judas and Silas, who themselves also will, by word of mouth, tell you the same things.*

28. *For it hath seemed good to the Holy Ghost and to us, to lay no farther burden upon you than these necessary things :*

29. *That you abstain from things sacrificed to idols, and from blood, and from things strangled, and from fornication ; from which things keeping yourselves, you shall do well. Fare ye well.*

30. *They therefore being dismissed, went down to Antioch ; and gathering together the multitude, delivered the epistle.*

31. *Which when they had read, they rejoiced for the consolation.*

32. *But Judas and Silas, being prophets also themselves, with many words comforted the brethren, and confirmed them.*

33. *And after they had spent some time there, they were let go with peace by the brethren, unto them that had sent them.*

34. *But it seemed good unto Silas to remain there ; and Judas alone departed to Jerusalem.*

35. *And Paul and Barnabas continued at Antioch, teaching and preaching, with many others, the word of the Lord.*

36. *And after some days, Paul said to Barnabas : Let us return and visit our brethren in all the cities wherein we have preached the word of the Lord, to see how they do.*

37. *And Barnabas would have taken with them John also, that was surnamed Mark ;*

38. *But Paul desired that he (as having departed from them out of Pamphylia, and not gone with them to the work) might not be received.*

39. *And there arose a dissension, so that they departed one from another ; and Barnabas indeed taking Mark, sailed to Cyprus.*

40. *But Paul choosing Silas, departed, being delivered by the brethren to the grace of God.*

41. *And he went through Syria and Cilicia, confirming the churches, commanding them to keep the precepts of the apostles and the ancients.*

ANALYSIS.

In this Chapter we have an account of the mission of Paul and Barnabas to Jerusalem to consult the Apostles about grave questions mooted relative to the necessity of Jewish Ceremonies (1-3). The Council of Jerusalem—the discussion therein (6-21). Their decree on the subject in question (23-28) forwarded by St. Paul and Barnabas, Judas and Silas (v. 29). The arrival of the Delegates at Antioch, with the Council's Decree (31-34). A dispute between Paul and Barnabas, as to their taking with them John Mark in their visitation of the cities wherein they had already preached. This ended in their separation each going in a different direction, Barnabas and John Mark proceeding to Cyprus, Paul and Silas to Syria and Cililcia, promulgating the Decrees of the Apostles.

L

Text.

1. *And some coming down from Judæa, taught the brethren: That except you be circumcised after the manner of Moses, you cannot be saved.*

Commentary.

1. " And some coming down," &c.   While Paul and Barnabas were at Antioch some Jews converted to Christianity, as is clear from their consenting or wishing to have the matter in dispute referred to the Apostles (v. 2).   "Coming down."   Judæa was in a higher position than the maritime districts.   "Taught the brethren."   Went about teaching on their own private authority, the necessity, on the part of the converts from heathenism, of submitting to the rite of circumcision—the chief distinguishing profession of Judaism—in order to be saved.   This was a grand subject of discussion among the early Christians as is clear from the Epistles of St. Paul, especially that to the Galatians.

"After the manner of Moses," in accordance with the Mosaic Ritual. Circumcision was anterior to Moses.   It existed in the days of Abraham. It was sanctioned by Moses, and was a profession of Judaism, as Baptism is of Christianity.

Text.

2. *And when Paul and Barnabas had no small contest with them, they determined that Paul and Barnabas, and certain others of the other side, should go up to the apostles and priests to Jerusalem about this question.*

2. " No small contest " (in Greek, "*no small dissension and disputation*"), signifying that Paul and Barnabas exerted all their powers to put down the false teaching of these men.   They did not, however, succeed in establishing peace.   Hence, "they," "the brethren" at Antioch (v. 1) determined on referring the matter in dispute to the supreme authority of the Apostles at Jerusalem.   Hence, they depute Paul and Barnabas on one side, with some others on the other.

This is not opposed to what St. Paul says of his visit (Gal. ii. 2) to which the visit here spoken of refers, that "he went up according to revelation," as the revelation and deputation from Antioch both coincided.

"And Priests" of the *first order*, viz., bishops, and of the *second* order also.   The bishops decided.   The priests attended as advisers and counsellors (A. Lapide quoting *Bellarmine*).   The "Apostles" present in Jerusalem were Peter, James and John (Gal. ii. 9).

Text.

3. *They therefore being brought on their way by the church, passed through Phenice, and Samaria, relating the conversion of the gentiles; and they caused great joy to all the brethren.*

4. *And when they were come to Jerusalem, they were received by the church, and by the apostles and ancients, declaring how great things God had done with them.*

3. " Brought on their way," escorted by way of honour and respect as was usual in those days.

"Phenice and Samaria" lay directly on the route to Jerusalem. The bulk of the converts in these districts were principally from paganism.   Hence, the universal joy.

"Received " hospitably and kindly " by the church," the faithful at large, and especially the chief men among them, who acknowledged them as brethren in Christ (Gal. ii. 9).

"Ancients." Bishops and priests.   "Declaring," &c.   Paul and Barnabas gave a full account in presence of the assembled brethren, people and rulers of the success of their labours through God's grace, and most likely of the cause of the present controversy which gave rise to this deputation.

Commentary.

5. From St. Luke's narrative it would seem this took place at Jerusalem after Paul and Barnabas returned.

"There arose up." Those referred to (*v.* 1) as having gone down to Antioch.

These converted Pharisees, "who believed," persisted in the necessity of uniting the Mosaic rites with the Christian profession.

6. "Assembled." Came specially together to consider the subject debated with reference to uniting Mosaic rites to Christianity.

This meeting or assembly constituted what was termed the first General Council of Jerusalem, the model of all future general councils of the church, convened, no doubt, and presided over by the Prince of the Apostles, who after due discussion spoke first as supreme judge of controversy. Some of the simple faithful, and those especially who raised the controversy were present, but only as consultors and witnesses: whereas, it was only the Apostles and ancients that, as judges, examined the matter "to consider of this matter."

7. "Much disputing" and warm debating on both sides previous to the judgment.

"Peter," as head of the church and supreme judge of controversy, "rising up" to define this grave subject of faith.

"In former days" has special reference to the conversion of Cornelius, the centurion (x. 20).

"God made choice," &c. Hath chosen us and selected me, among all the Apostles, to bring about the conversion of the Gentiles. He specially alludes to Cornelius and his conversion.

8. God, who alone searches the hearts, and cannot be deceived as to men's sincerity and dispositions, testified to their sincerity and the reality of their conversion, by pouring out His Spirit on them as well as on us.

9. Made no difference between them who did not conform to the Mosaic Law and "us," thus showing they were equally as we, acceptable to Him.

"Purifying their hearts," hitherto wallowing in the mire of infidelity, idolatry and sin. "By faith," contradistinguished from Mosaic observances—"faith"—the foundation of the system of justification established by Him; "by faith" and not by Mosaic observances; "by faith," accompanied with the other conditions, especially good works, required as essential.

Text.

5. But there arose some of the sect of the Pharisees that believed, saying: They must be circumcised, and be commanded to observe the law of Moses.

6. And the apostles and ancients assembled to consider of this matter.

7. And when there had been much disputing, Peter rising up, said to them: Men, brethren, you know, that in former days God made choice among us, that by my mouth the gentiles should hear the word of the gospel, and believe.

8. And God, who knoweth the hearts, gave testimony, giving unto them the Holy Ghost, as well as to us;

9. And put no difference between us and them, purifying their hearts by faith.

Text.	Commentary.

10. *Now therefore, why tempt you God to put a yoke upon the neck of the disciples, which neither our fathers nor we have been able to bear?*

10. "Tempt God," in SS. Scriptures signifies to put unnecessarily to the test any of the Divine attributes. Here it means to provoke Him to wrath or anger (" *tentaverunt me patris vestri,* Psalm lxxvii.") by perversely opposing His manifest will, by imposing on men, as necessary, what He exonerated them from and showed to be unmeaning—the "yoke"—the ceremonial precepts of the Mosaic Law, an oppressive burden unjustly interfering with their just liberty, requiring more than God required. This "yoke" cannot apply to the *moral* or natural law, binding in men at all times.

"Have been able to bear," means *great difficulty*, not *absolute impossibility*, as God would not sanction anything impossible. But the precepts of the Mosaic Law were burthensome, especially as they did not carry with them the grace necessary for self-fulfilment. These precepts had for object to withdraw the people from idolatry. That they were not, strictly speaking, impossible is clear from the examples of Zachary and Elizabeth commended for having observed them in every point without blame (Luke i.), also Josue (Josue xi. 15), David, (Acts xiii. 22), &c.

11. *But by the grace of the Lord Jesus Christ, we believe to be saved, in like manner as they also.*

11. "But." This adversative particle has reference to the negative idea, or negation contained in the foregoing interrogation. Do you expect salvation through the observance of the multiplied precepts forming an intolerable yoke of the Mosaic Law? No, it is not by the Law of Moses or circumcision we are to be saved, "but by the grace of the Lord Jesus Christ, we," converted Jews, "believe we shall be saved" in the same manner as they too shall be saved who never were subjected to the rites of the Mosaic. "In the same manner." Through the same uniform means, the grace and faith of Christ, we Jews and Gentiles shall be saved.

Some, among whom St. Augustine (Lib. 2 contra Pelagium, c. xxi.) say, the comparison instituted here is not between the converted Jews and Gentiles of the present day among themselves; but, between the converts of the day and their Fathers who went before them, so that "in like manner as they also" refers to the ancient Fathers, who were saved only through the grace and merits of Christ, since it is undoubted, that no one was ever saved, even of old, save through the retrospective merits of Christ, "the Lamb that was slain from the beginning of the world" (Apoc. iii. 8). The salvation, however, of their Jewish ancestors, clearly referrible to the merits of Christ, seems to have but little connexion with the subject now under consideration, viz.: the conversion of the Pagans to Christianity and their exemption from legal ceremonies having one uniform system of justification in common with the converted Jews. Whereas, it will certainly be in point, if we understand the Apostle to refer to one uniform system of justification for all, Jews and Gentiles, viz.: the grace and faith of our Lord Jesus Christ, without regard to Jewish ceremonies.

Commentary.

12. "The multitude," the entire assembly present, convened for the purpose of considering the question in dispute, "held their peace," as a mark of respect and reverence for the chief Pastor. Neither party could gainsay. Peter's words calmed their troubled spirits, and put an end to the controversy. No further disputing. *"Petrus locutus est, causa finita est"*—as is said of Rome, to which were communicated Peter's privileges, *" Roma locuta est, causa finita est."*

They listened to Barnabas and Paul narrating the wonderful miracles God had wrought in the admittance of the Gentiles into the Church without submitting to Jewish rites, thus setting on such admission and the doctrine regarding it, the seal of his approbation.

13. "James," the lesser, son of Alpheus, as Bishop of Jerusalem, spoke next, after Peter. "Answering" in Scripture language does not imply a question. It signifies, to *begin to speak*. His personal character sustained by Prophetical oracles, corroborative of Peter's opinion, carried with it great weight. He did not dispute with Peter; but, only spoke in corroboration of Peter's decision, quoting the ancient Scriptures, which had the greatest weight with the Jews.

14. "Simon" in Greek "*Simeon*" speaking to Hebrews, he calls him by his Hebrew name.

15. The statement of Peter was in accordance with the predictions of the Prophets.

"As it is written." Take, for instance, the prophecy of Amos, among the other prophecies on the subject. "Prophets" in the plural, shows there were several other Prophecies bearing on the point, which he might quote. He refers, however, only to one (Amos ix. 11, 12), or it may refer to the division of the Bible, called "*Prophets.*"

16, 17. The quotation in these *vv.* from Amos is not literally from either the Hebrew or the Septuagint. While *v.* 17 is literally from the Septuagint, which in the literal rendering differs from the Hebrew; *v.* 16 only conveys the general meaning of the Prophet, whom St. James quotes, to show that the Gentiles would be admitted to the privilege of Divine Sonship without submitting to circumcision and the Jewish ceremonial Law.

"*After these things.*" In Hebrew, *on that day.* Both, however, substantially refer to the same thing. Both phrases signify, in the Books of the Old Testament, the times of the New Testament.

"*I will return,*" signifying reconciliation with God, who in His anger deserted them, and now, in His mercy, revisits them. These words are found neither in the Hebrew nor the Septuagint. They contain an allusion to the destruction of the house of Israel (Amos ix. 7-10), when

12. *And all the multitude held their peace: and they heard Barnabas and Paul telling what great signs and wonders God had wrought among the gentiles by them.*

13. *And after they had held their peace, James answered, saying: Men, brethren, hear me.*

14. *Simon hath related how God first visited to take of the gentiles a people to his name.*

15. *And to this agree the words of the prophets, as it is written:*

16. *After these things I will return, and will rebuild the tabernacle of David, which is fallen down: and the ruins thereof I will rebuild, and I will set it up:*

17. *That the residue of men may seek after the Lord, and all nations upon whom my name is invoked, saith the*

Text.	Commentary.

Text.
Lord who doth these things.

God handed them over to their enemies, and to His return now to repair all their losses.

"*Rebuild the Tabernacle of David,*" viz., his palace, deserted and given over to a state of ruin and neglect during the Chaldean captivity; this he shall now restore to its former splendour and magnificence, and rebuild its ruins.

"*The ruins* (Hebrew, the *breaches thereof*)." Thus rebuilt, it shall be an emblem of the vast spiritual blessings in store for the Jewish people.

"*That the residue,*" &c., "*and all nations* may seek after Him." In the Hebrew it is: *that they* (the Israelites) *may possess the residue of Edom and all nations*, &c. Edom is specified as an example of all the other nations and peoples foreign to Israel, who are admitted to a participation of the spiritual blessings bestowed on Israel, that is to say, on that house and restored kingdom of David, through the glorious descendant, on whom his Father promised to bestow the Gentiles as an inheritance, and the ends of the earth, as his possessions.

"*May seek,*" put contingently (ὅπως ἄν) in the Greek, should they themselves possibly desire it or co-operate, aided by God's assistance in securing it.

"*Upon whom my name,*" who, after embracing the faith, shall be called, by my name, Sons of God, Christians.

"Saith the Lord," &c., who will accomplish, without fail, His own prophecy. This cannot refer to the time of Ezechias, or return from captivity, or Machabees, or any other period prior to our Lord, since the Jews did not possess all nations. It can only refer to the restoration of David's kingdom, in a spiritual and more exalted sense, through that blessed Seed, to whom "the Lord God will give the throne of his Father David . . . . and of his kingdom no end" (Luke i. 32, 33).

18. *To the Lord was his own work known from the beginning of the world.*

18. "To the Lord," &c. These are the words of St. James, not of Amos. This vocation of the Gentiles, without conforming to Jewish ceremonies, formed a part of God's eternal design and plan in bestowing on them all the privileges He thought fit. We should not, therefore, attach conditions to God's unspeakable boon, which He never required, nor meant to require, in His eternal designs "from the beginning of the world." These eternal designs we should not oppose.

19. *For which cause I judge that they, who from among the gentiles are converted to God, are not to be disquieted.*

19. St. James now gives his judgment. "For which cause," on account of the Prophecies declaring that the Gentiles were to be admitted into the Church regardless of Jewish ceremonies, and on account of his experience quoted by Peter. "I judge." "Not disquieted" by imposing on them Jewish ceremonies.

20. *But that we write unto*

20. "But," in order to consult the feelings of my Jewish fellow-citizens and avoid all offence, and that thus all may unite, Jews and

Commentary.

Gentiles, in the same common Christian profession, they should be written to, to refrain from pollution of Idols or Idolothytes (1 Cor. viii. x.), *v.* 29. These things were strictly prohibited by the Mosaic Law, and abhorred by the Jews, as savouring of Idolatry (Exod. xxxiv. 13).

"From fornication." This, though prohibited by the natural law itself, was regarded as a matter of indifference with the Pagans. The general state of Pagan licentiousness rendered this prohibition necessary, lest the converts should regard "fornication" as a matter of indifference.

"Things strangled and blood." Prohibited by the Mosaic Law (Levit. iii. 17 ; xii. 26 ; xvii. 13, 14).

These instructions, so far as the ceremonial Law was concerned, were only local and temporary, to last only for a time, as long as the motives for enacting them and the circumstances which rendered them necessary lasted—viz., the avoidance of offence to the converted Jews. But, after a time, they ceased and fell into desuetude. St. Augustine (Lib. contra Fanstum, xxxii. 18) explains the object of this Law of the Council, and informs us, that it was not observed at Hippo, and fell into desuetude in the Latin Church.

21. "For Moses"—referring to the Law of Moses—"of old time," from a very long past period, from the time of Esdras. The meaning is that the Law of Moses was constantly read and preached every Sabbath, in every city where there was a sufficient number of Jews to have synagogues. Hence, as the Jews would be always, at that age of the Church, reminded of the Law of Moses, they could not easily forget it. It was, therefore, expedient that no offence would be given them ; and that the Gentile converts would refrain from partaking of "things strangled, blood," &c., to avoid giving them offence who always had the enactments of the Law of Moses before their minds.

It is not easy to see the connexion of this verse with the context, or the subject for which a reason is assigned, as indicated by the causal particle, "for." Beelen professes his utter inability to see it, nor does he know of any other that has seen it. The whole context clearly shows that the words of this verse must have some connexion with St. James' argument that, to avoid giving offence, it is expedient for the Gentile converts to abstain from the things specified. Hence "For" refers, as often happens, to something understood, and gives a reason why the foregoing "necessary things" (*v.* 28) are required, as the disregarding of them would cause not only private, but public scandal. For the Law of Moses has, from the remotest antiquity, its followers in every city, and its Scriptures publicly read in the synagogues every Sabbath (*Bloomfield*).

22. "The Apostles and the ancients," to whom the case in dispute was referred (*v.* 2), "with the whole Church," who fully approved of

Text.

them, that they refrain themselves from the pollutions of idols, and from fornication, and from things strangled, and from blood.

21. For Moses of old time hath in every city them that preach him in the synagogues, where he is read every sabbath.

22. Then it pleased the

Text.	**Commentary.**

apostles and ancients, with the whole church, to choose men of their own company, and to send to Antioch, with Paul and Barnabas, namely Judas, who was surnamed Barsabas, and Silas, chief men among the brethren.

the decree of "the Apostles and ancients," in whose name it was forwarded (*v.* 23).

"To choose" (*having chosen*) "men of their own company" from among themselves, "leading" prominent men of authority among them, and send them with Paul and Barnabas to Antioch to prove the authenticity of the Decree, and draw more closely together the bonds of union.

"Judas Barsabas," said to be the brother of Joseph Barsabas, mentioned for the Apostleship (*c.* 1), "and Silas" Sylvanus, who accompanied St. Paul on his journeys (xv. 10 ; 1 Cor. 7-19).

23. *Writing by their hands: The apostles and ancients, to the brethren of the gentiles that are at Antioch, and in Syria and Cilicia, greeting.*

23. "Writing by their hands." Handing the document to them as its bearers. They were to explain it by word of mouth (*v.* 27).

The Greek of this verse is considered by some not to be in accordance with the ordinary rules of grammatical construction. By others, the contrary is asserted—Beelen, &c., who adduce several passages of similar grammatical construction from ancient classical writers.

"The Apostles and ancients brethren." From them the Decree emanates "to the brethren of the Gentiles." Both are thus regarded as equals. "Antioch," the capital of Syria ; "and in Syria," the rest of Syria, where, likely, the dispute was carried on. "Cilicia," close to Syria. Likely the dispute reached there also. In these three places it would seem the dispute had arisen. "Greeting," wishing them the abundance of all happiness.

24. *Forasmuch as we have heard, that some going out from us have troubled you with words, subverting your souls; to whom we gave no commandment:*

24. "Forasmuch," whereas, "words," doctrines, "subverting your souls," creating disturbance and anxiety by their teachings, touching the Law of Moses. The Greek word means, *unsettling,* "no commandment," self-sent, having no commission whatever to teach thus.

25. *It hath seemed good to us, being assembled together, to choose out men, and to send them unto you, with our well beloved Barnabas and Paul:*

25. "Assembled together." Acting in concert, and coming unanimously to this conclusion.

26. *Men that have given their lives for the name of our Lord Jesus Christ.*

26. "Given their lives," which they have not hesitated to expose; "the name," the cause (see *c.* xiv.). This testimony was calculated to increase their influence with the churches. It showed they were identified with the body of the Apostles.

Commentary.

27. The bearers of the letters were hereby authorized to explain, by word of mouth if necessary, more explicitly the contents of the written message, and clear up any obscure points.

28. "To the Holy Ghost and to us," who are enlightened and directed by him in this Decree. The Holy Ghost is the *principal cause ;* the Apostles and bishops, heads of the Church, who act under his impulse, guidance, and superintendence, the *Ministerial cause.* Both are here united. *Holy Ghost and us.* This is *the unchangeable Dogmatic Decree* which is of Divine authority. That regarding Idolothytes, &c., an *Ecclesiastical* Decree, could be, and really was, abrogated.

"No farther burden," no further restrictions, "than these necessary things," *necessary* not of themselves. Fornication was always to be necessarily avoided as a breach of the moral law, but "necessary" for a time, in the cause of charity, union, and the avoidance of scandal. "Necessary" to conciliate the Jews, "necessary" as long as the circumstances that called for them existed. It was but *a temporary* prohibition, and long since done away with, especially in the Western Church.

"Do well," will please God, and advance the cause of peace and religion and secure your own happiness.

30. *They therefore being dismissed, went down to Antioch ; and gathering together the multitude, delivered the epistle.*

31. "Rejoiced," &c. These heathen converts at Antioch were filled with consolation at the cheering message that they were not to be subjected to the Mosaic Law, nor disturbed in the possession of their Christian liberty.

32. "Prophets." This word does not simply designate men endowed with the faculty of predicting future events, though some were (xi. 27). It also designates *teachers sent by God,* to instruct the people in the duties of religion. It also designates those endowed with the gift of explaining the truths of faith in an extraordinary manner, as the result of sudden inspiration (see 1 Cor. xi. 5, Commentary on).

Judas and Silas had been manifestly preachers of the Gospel before going to Antioch.

"Confirmed." Strengthened them in the faith by their teachings.

33. "With peace." With affectionate good wishes "to them that sent them." The Apostles at Jerusalem. Hence, in the common Greek reading it is "*unto the Apostles.*" The Vulgate is the reading of the chief MSS.—αποστειλαντες αυτους.

Text.

27. *We have sent therefore Judas and Silas, who themselves also will, by word of mouth, tell you the same things.*

28. *For it hath seemed good to the Holy Ghost and to us, to lay no farther burden upon you than these necessary things :*

29. *That you abstain from things sacrificed to idols, and from blood, and from things strangled, and from fornication ; from which things keeping yourselves, you shall do well. Fare ye well.*

31. *Which when they had read, they rejoiced for the consolation.*

32. *But Judas and Silas, being prophets also themselves, with many words comforted the brethren, and confirmed them.*

33. *And after they had spent some time there, they were let go with peace by the brethren, unto them that had sent them.*

Text.	Commentary.
34. *But it seemed good unto Silas to remain there; and Judas alone departed to Jerusalem.*	34. This verse is wanting in many MSS., and rejected by some able critics, who maintain it was introduced and inserted to complete the sense.
35. *And Paul and Barnabas continued at Antioch, teaching and preaching, with many others, the word of the Lord.*	35. It is thought, it was during this time Paul rebuked Peter at Antioch (Gal. ii. &c.).
36. *And after some days Paul said to Barnabas: Let us return and visit our brethren in all the cities wherein we have preached the word of the Lord, to see how they do.*	36. " To see how they do." Both in regard to faith and purity of morals. This visitation was a work of great zeal.
37. *And Barnabas would have taken with them John also, that was surnamed Mark;*	37. John Mark was a kinsman of Barnabas, cousin-german (Col. iv. 10). He wished to accompany them on their mission.
38. *But Paul desired that he (as having departed from them out of Pamphylia, and not gone with them to the work) might not be received.*	38. Paul, it seems, having no confidence in John Marks' persever-ance in the work of the ministry and bearing its attendant privations, labours and dangers, which may have been his reason for leaving them, while in Pamphylia (xiii. 13), thought it fit not to receive him. Whatever the cause of his leaving was, Paul did not think the explanation satisfactory ; and hence, he regarded him as unfit to be associated with them.
39. *And there arose a dissen-sion, so that they departed one from ano-ther; and Bar-nabas indeed taking Mark, sailed to Cy-prus.*	39. " Dissension." The Greek word "*Paroxysm,*" denotes any mental excitement, great bitterness of mind, sometimes, taken in a good sense (Heb. x. 24). The result was a separation for a time. They were afterwards reconciled (1 Cor. ix. 6). St. Paul speaks of John Mark in terms of commendation (2 Tim. iv. 11 ; Col. iv. 10). "Sailed to Cyprus," his native place. This separation served the propagation of the Gospel. This is the last time Barnabas is spoken of in the history of the Acts.
40. *But Paul choosing Silas, departed, being delivered by the*	40. " Delivered by the brethren." By the assembled Church, commended to the Divine favor with prayer and hearty good wishes for their success, in their new field of labour. This being omitted in the

Commentary.

the case of Barnabas and John Mark, would show the Church of Antioch sided, in the controversy, with Paul.

41. "Through Syria and Cilicia," which lay close to each other. They were already visited by Paul and Barnabas.

"Commanding them to keep," &c. These words are wanting in several MSS. and versions. No doubt, Paul and Silas did what is here recorded of them—viz., impressing upon all the obligation of attending to and observing the precepts lately enacted in the council of Jerusalem.

Text.

brethren to the grace of God.

41. And he went through Syria and Cilicia, confirming the churches, commanding them to keep the precepts of the apostles and the ancients.

Paul + Silas + Luke + Timothy.

CHAPTER XVI.

1. *And he came to Derbe and Lystra. And behold there was a certain disciple there named Timothy, the son of a Jewish woman that believed, but his father was a gentile.*

2. *To this man the brethren that were in Lystra and Iconium, gave a good testimony*

3. *Him Paul would have to go along with him: and taking him he circumcised him, because of the Jews who were in those places. For they all knew that his father was a gentile.*

4. *And as they passed through the cities, they delivered unto them the decrees for to keep, that were decreed by the apostles and ancients who were at Jerusalem.*

5. *And the churches were confirmed in faith, and increased in number daily.*

6. *And when they had passed through Phrygia and the country of Galatia, they were forbidden by the Holy Ghost to preach the word in Asia.*

7. *And when they were come into Mysia, they attempted to go into Bithynia, and the Spirit of Jesus suffered them not.*

8. *And when they had passed through Mysia, they went down to Troas.*

9. *And a vision was showed to Paul in the night, which was a man of Macedonia standing and beseeching him, and saying: Pass over into Macedonia, and help us.*

10. *And as soon as he had seen the vision, immediately we sought to go into Macedonia, being assured that God had called us to preach the gospel to them.*

11. *And sailing from Troas we came with a straight course to Samothracia, and the day following to Neapolis:*

12. *And from thence to Philippi, which is the chief city of part of Macedonia, a colony. And we were in this city some days conferring together.*

13. *And upon the sabbath-day, we went forth without the gate by a river side, where it seemed that there was prayer: and sitting down we spoke to the women that were assembled.*

14. *And a certain woman named Lydia, a seller of purple of the city of Thyatira, one that worshipped God, did hear: whose heart the Lord opened to attend to those things which were said by Paul.*

15. *And when she was baptized, and her household, she besought us, saying: If you have judged me to be faithful to the Lord, come into my house and abide there. And she constrained us.*

16. *And it came to pass as we went to prayer, a certain girl, having a pythonical spirit, met us, who brought to her masters much gain by divining.*

17. *This same following Paul and us, cried out, saying: These men are the servants of the most high God, who preach unto you the way of salvation.*

18. *And this she did many days. But Paul being grieved, turned and said to the spirit: I command thee, in the name of Jesus Christ, to go out from her. And he went out the same hour.*

19. *But her masters seeing that the hope of their gain was gone, apprehending Paul and Silas, brought them into the market-place to the rulers.*

20. *And presenting them to the magistrates, they said: These men disturb our city, being Jews:*

21. *And preach a fashion which it is not lawful for us to receive, nor observe, being Romans.*

22. *And the people ran together against them : and the magistrates rending off their clothes commanded them to be beaten with rods.*

23. *And when they had laid many stripes upon them, they cast them into prison, charging the gaoler to keep them diligently.*

24. *Who having received such a charge, trust them into the inner prison, and made their feet fast in the stocks.*

25. *And at midnight, Paul and Silas praying, praised God.   And they that were in prison heard them.*

26. *And suddenly there was a great earthquake, so that the foundations of the prison were shaken.   And immediately all the doors were opened : and the bands of all were loosed.*

27. *And the keeper of the prison awaking out of his sleep, and seeing the doors of the prison open, drawing his sword, would have killed himself, supposing that the prisoners had been fled.*

28. *But Paul cried with a loud voice, saying : Do thyself no harm, for we all are here.*

29. *Then calling for a light, he went in, and trembling fell down at the feet of Paul and Silas.*

30. *And bringing them out, he said : Masters, what must I do, that I may be saved?*

31. *But they said : Believe in the Lord Jesus : and thou shalt be saved, and thy house.*

32. *And they preached of the word of the Lord to him and to all that were in his house.*

33. *And he taking them the same hour of the night, washed their stripes : and himself was baptized, and all his house immediately.*

34. *And when he had brought them into his own house, he laid the table for them, and rejoiced with all his house, believing God.*

35. *And when the day was come, the magistrates sent the sergeants, saying : Let those men go.*

36. *And the keeper of the prison told these words to Paul : The magistrates have sent to let you go : now therefore depart, and go in peace.*

37. *But Paul said to them : They have beaten us publicly, uncondemned, men that are Romans, and have cast us into prison : and now do they thrust us out privately? Not so, but let them come,*

38. *And let us out themselves.   And the sergeants told these words to the magistrates. And they were afraid, hearing that they were Romans.*

39. *And coming they besought them ; and bringing them out they desired them to depart out of the city.*

40. *And they went out of the prison, and entered into the house of Lydia : and having seen the brethren, they comforted them, and departed.*

ANALYSIS.

Passing through Lystra and Derbe, the Apostle fell in with Timothy whose father was a Gentile ; his mother a Jewess. He was highly recommended ; and Paul wishing to have him for companion, had him circumcised (1-3).   They visited several cities, promulgating the decrees of the Apostles (4-7).   They afterwards went to Troas, where a man of Macedonia stood before Paul in a vision, inviting him to pass over and help them (8, 9).   At Philippi, a woman named Lydia entertained them hospitably (12-15). They were cast into prison at the instigation of certain men, whose gain they interfered with in the cure of a pythoness, who was their slave (15-26).   The earthquake which caused the prison doors to be flung open.   The conversion of the affrighted gaoler (26-32).   Their liberation (35-40).

Text.

1. *And he came to Derbe and Lystra. And behold there was a certain disciple there named Timothy, the son of a Jewish woman that believed, but his father was a gentile.*

2. *To this man the brethren that were in Lystra and Iconium, gave a good testimony.*

3. *Him Paul would have to go along with him: and taking him he circumcised him, because of the Jews who were in those places. For they all knew that his father was a gentile.*

4. *And as they passed through the cities, they delivered unto them the decrees for to keep, that were decreed by the apostles and ancients who were at Jerusalem*

5. *And the churches were confirmed in faith, and increased in number daily.*

6. *And when they had passed through Phrygia and the country of Gal-*

Commentary.

1. "He," Paul, accompanied by Barnabas, came to Derbe &c. Their order in travelling here is the opposite of what is recorded (xiv. 6). They now proceed from east to west.

"Timothy," whether he was a native of Lystra or Derbe cannot be determined. To him St. Paul addressed two of his epistles. "Jewish woman," Eunice, by name (2 Tim. i. 5) that had "believed," a Christian woman distinguished for piety. "His father, a gentile," clearly uncircumcised, and, probably, an Idolater. If he were circumcised, Timothy too would have been circumcised. The Jewish law prohibiting intermarriages between Jews and Gentiles (Nehemiah xiii. 3; Esdras ix. 12) probably was not strictly enforced in countries where Jews lived among Pagans.

2. He was then young. For, later on, after the lapse of some years, St. Paul when giving him in charge the Church of Ephesus, addresses him, as a young man (1 Tim. iv. 12).

3. Though a mere youth, St. Paul wished to take him as an associate. His birth of Jewish and Pagan parents would make him acceptable to both Jews and Gentiles, to whom the Gospel was to be preached. Before taking him, however, St. Paul as a matter of prudent accommodation to the feelings of the Jews, but, not as a matter of necessity, subjected him to circumcision, then allowable; but not necessary, as had been decreed in the Council of Jerusalem. Thus he became all to all, to gain all to Christ (1 Cor. ix. 20). He thus removed the grounds for the insuperable objection on the part of the Jews to receive the Gospel at the hands of an uncircumcised Israelite. This he did not do as a matter of necessity; and hence he did not act against the Council of Jerusalem. He showed his firmness in maintaining the Decree of the Council by his persistent refusal to circumcise Titus born of Gentile parents, though strongly urged to do so (Gal. ii. 3).

"They knew that his father," &c., and they, therefore, knew that the rite of circumcision was neglected in his case.

4. "Cities" of Syria and Cilicia where Paul and Barnabas had lately founded Churches (xv. 36).

"They," Paul and Silas delivered to the faithful of these cities.

"The decrees," &c., "to keep," to be obeyed and observed. Hence obedience is due to the laws of the Church.

6. "Forbidden," either by an express revelation or some interior inspiration of the "Holy Ghost."

"Asia." Pro Consular Asia, that district of Asia Minor bordering on the Ægean sea, called Ionia, having Ephesus for capital. Here were

Commentary.

situated the seven churches mentioned (Apoc. i. 11).   The object of this prohibition probably was to have the preaching of the Gospel carried into Greece which would not have been done had they remained in Asia.   This prohibition was the occasion of introducing the Gospel, for the first time, into Europe.

7. "Into Mysia," to the confines of Mysia.   Being prohibited to preach in Asia, to which Mysia belonged, they proceeded northward to "Bithynia," a province of Asia Minor to the east of Mysia.

"Spirit of Jesus."   Hence the Holy Ghost proceeds from the Son as well as from the Father.

"Troas," on the Hellespont.   It designates sometimes a city; sometimes a whole district.   Within the district of Troas was situated ancient Troy, so celebrated in Grecian history.

9. "A vision," &c., whether in a dream while asleep—a mode of communicating the Divine Will not unfrequently employed by God—or while awake, cannot be ascertained.

"A man of Macedonia."   Paul, who may have seen Macedonians in his youth at Tharsus, knew him to be such from his dress, language, &c.

"And help us," by dispelling through the light of the Gospel their spiritual darkness and helping them to abandon their sinful Pagan lives.

10. "We sought," &c.   For the first time St. Luke makes any reference to himself.   It is clear he joined Paul and Silas at Troas.   As to how he came there St. Luke is silent.

11. "Neapolis," on the coast bordering on Thrace, some say it was in Thrace.   The Apostle made no stay there as he was commanded to go to Macedonia.

12. "Philippi."   It was Philip, Father of Alexander the Great, that enlarged and beautified it.   Hence, called after his name.

"Chief city," &c.   The Greek would also convey that it was the first or nearest city of Macedonia they came to.   It was in one of the four parts into which Paulus Emilius, after having conquered it, divided Macedonia.   Philippi was detached by King Philip from Thrace, to which

Text.

atia, they were forbidden by the Holy Ghost to preach the word in Asia.

7. And when they were come into Mysia, they attempted to go into Bithynia, and the Spirit of Jesus suffered them not.

8. And when they had passed through Mysia, they went down to Troas:

9. And a vision was shewed to Paul in the night, which was a man of Macedonia standing and beseeching him, and saying: Pass over into Macedonia, and help us.

10. And as soon as he had seen the vision, immediately we sought to go into Macedonia, being assured that God had called us to preach the gospel to them.

11. And sailing from Troas we came with a straight course to Samothracia, and the day following to Neapolis:

12. And from thence to Philippi, which is the chief city of part of Macedonia, a colony. And we were in this

Text.	Commentary.

city some days conferring together.

Commentary.

it formerly belonged. Being made a Roman colony, it became the capital in course of time.

"A colony" inhabited by Roman citizens with advantages secured by the laws of Rome. Augustus confirmed its privileges of being a Roman colony, first conferred on it by Julius Cæsar.

"Some days." The interval between his arrival and the next Sabbath. That he spent "*many days*" there is clear from *v.* 18. No doubt, he remained there for a sufficient period to discharge the duty for which he was sent there by God's Spirit.

---

13. *And upon the sabbath-day, we went forth without the gate by a river side, where it seemed that there was prayer: and sitting down we spoke to the women that were assembled.*

13. "Sabbath-day" immediately succeeding Paul's advent to Philippi.

"By a river's side." The Jews were dispersed everywhere. No doubt, there were some in this city. They usually built their synagogues or oratories near water, in view of the numerous ablutions practised in their religious worship.

"Where it seemed that there was prayer." The Greek would signify *where prayer is usually offered*, or " Prayer," *Proseuche*, may also denote the *place* for prayer. The Jews, whenever they could not erect synagogues erected *oratories* for prayer meetings and other religious rites on the Sabbath.

"Spoke to the women," probably before the congregation had assembled. He mentions the address to the women especially in order to introduce the case of Lydia next verse.

---

14. *And a certain woman named Lydia, a seller of purple of the city a Thyatira, one that worshipped God, did hear: whose heart the Lord opened to attend to those things which were said by Paul.*

14. "Of the city of Thyatira," born there, she resided at Philippi.

"A seller of purple." Probably the trade of this woman, a native of Thyatira, where the art of dying purple was cultivated, was very profitable. "Worshipped God." A Jewish Proselyte "did hear" points to the operation of the human will. "Whose heart the Lord opened," &c., points to the operation of Divine grace. She, aided by God's grace, corresponded with the strong impulse of Divine grace, the chief or principal cause in the assent of faith, without which no faith, no embracing the Gospel.

---

15. *And when she was baptized, and her household, she besought us, saying: If you have judged me to be faithful to the Lord, come into my house and abide there. And she constrained us.*

15. "If ye have judged," &c. *Since, whereas*, ye have judged me to be "faithful," &c., she says, "if," out of a feeling of modest humility.

"Constrained us," by repeated and modest entreaties she prevailed on them to accept her proffered hospitality, which, very likely, they declined at first, as the Apostle did not want to be a burden to anyone (2 Cor. xi. 9).

---

16. *And it came to pass as we went to prayer, a certain girl, hav-*

16. "Went to prayer" may mean to offer up prayers, or it may refer to the place of prayer, *Proseuche*.

"A certain girl." The Greek word means, a *slave*. In her, several masters had a common interest.

Commentary.

"Having a Pythonical spirit." The word *Python* is allusive to the Serpent, said in Pagan Mythology, to have been slain by Apollo, who himself afterwards went by that name. Without dwelling on Pagan Mythology, it may be said briefly that the word here refers to an evil spirit, real Demoniac possession, like unto that recorded (Mark i. 23, &c.), and St. Paul treated it as such *v.* 18.

"Brought to her masters much gain" by exercising the art of divination, foretelling future events, and disclosing hidden mysterious matters. Those who had recourse to her for such knowledge paid her liberally; and hence she was a source of great gain to her masters who had in common a share in the profits. She acted under the influence of the wicked spirit, expelled by St. Paul (*v.* 18). Demons possess natural powers beyond those of man, being of a superior order of intelligence. They therefore knew things far beyond human reach or foresight, and it was the Demon that spoke through this girl whom he possessed.

17. Under the influence of the wicked spirit, she bore testimony to the Divine Mission of St. Paul, &c. Why she did so, we cannot exactly ascertain, as St. Luke says nothing of it. Likely, she was influenced by the same reasons that made the wicked spirit bear testimony to our Lord (Mark i. 24).

18. "Grieved." The Greek means *excessively grieved.* Like our Lord Himself (Mark i. 25) he would not have testimony borne to the truth by the Father of lies, or seem to have any communication or enter into any league with him. He would not have this wicked spirit to put forward pretensions to respect equal to his own.

"In the name"—by the authority—"of Jesus Christ, to go out." He was, therefore, interiorly in possession, "and he went out the same hour," shows *real possession* by an evil spirit. There must have been some visible sign that he left her at that moment, in obedience to the mandate, otherwise, how could her masters know that their hope of gain was gone, without waiting for some time to test the matter, and see if the spirit of Divination—the loss of much gain—had left her? The whole passage shows there was real personal possession.

19. "Her masters" seeing all hope of gain was gone, out of a spirit of vengeance, seizing Paul and Silas, who were more prominent than Luke or Timothy, dragged them into the public square before the city magistrates, who, in the Roman colonies were generally two in number, *Duumvirs*, with the rank, or at least the assumed power of Prætors.

Text.

ing a pythonical spirit, met us, who brought to her masters much gain by divining.

17. *This same following Paul and us, cried out, saying: These men are the servants of the most high God, who preach unto you the way of salvation.*

18. *And this she did many days. But Paul being grieved, turned and said to the spirit: I command thee, in the name of Jesus Christ, to go out from her. And he went out the same hour.*

19. *But her masters seeing that the hope of their gain was gone, apprehending Paul and Silas, brought them into the market place to the rulers.*

M

Text.

20. *And presenting them to the magistrates, they said: These men disturb our city, being Jews:*

21. *And preach a fashion which it is not lawful for us to receive, nor observe, being Romans.*

22. *And the people ran together against them: and the magistrates rending off their clothes commanded them to be beaten with rods.*

23. *And when they had laid many stripes upon them, they cast them into prison, charging the gaoler to keep them diligently.*

24. *Who having received such a charge, thrust them into the inner prison, and made their feet fast in the stocks.*

25. *And at midnight, Paul and Silas praying, praised God. And they that were in prison heard them.*

26. *And suddenly there was a great earthquake, so that the founda-*

Commentary.

20. Artfully concealing their real motives, they affect zeal for the public tranquility which these men were disturbing. They cunningly appeal to the prejudices of the people by calling them "Jews," who practised a religious worship different from that of the Pagans, and were therefore, odious to the Roman colony at Philippi. Jews and Christians were regarded as all the same by the Pagans.

21. "And preach a fashion," religious tenets, a new religious system. "Which it is not lawful," &c. The Romans forbade the worship of any new God without the sanction of the Senate (Tertullian), and the teaching regarding Jesus as Lord and King was particularly objectionable. The twofold charge of disturbing the public tranquility and preaching up a new religion, without due sanction, called for punishment from the magistrates in vindication of the laws of Rome; Philippi, being a Roman colony, enforced the laws and institutions of Rome.

22. "Rending off," violently tearing off, by the hands of lictors, their clothes, as far as the waist, to expose their persons to the lash, "beaten with rods." St. Paul being a Roman citizen, this was a flagrant violation of the laws of Rome. It was, moreover, a gross violation of natural justice to punish men without hearing them in their own defence.

23. "Many stripes," very likely in number exceeding that allowed by the Jewish law, "forty." The Romans were not bound by this law. It may be to this St. Paul refers (2 Cor. xi. 23).

24. "Stocks," pieces of wood with holes to confine the feet of the prisoners.

25. Their acute suffering caused by having their feet pressed into stocks, probably without a resting place, for their bodies, covered with gore from the scourging (v. 23) did not prevent them from singing the praises of God.

26. "Suddenly," as if in response to their prayers. "Earthquake," always regarded as indicating the power, the presence and anger of God. "Hands of all were loosed." This looks like miraculous, as the shaking of the earth while it had naturally the effect of throwing all the doors

Commentary.

"open," would not of itself loose the bonds without further intervention.

27. "Would have killed himself" to escape by self-destruction the severe punishment in store for the prisoners (c. xii. 19, xxvii. 42).

28. "All here." Likely all the prisoners fled from the outer prison into that where St. Paul was confined.

29. "Light," in Greek, "*lights*," borne by his servants who accompanied him ; or, it may have a singular meaning, according to the Greek idiom.

"Trembling," from a feeling that all was supernatural. "Fell down," in token of great reverence.

30. "Masters," a term of respect. This man's conscience was evidently touched. He concluded from all he saw—the Earthquake—his own prevention from self-destruction—possibly, from the testimony of the Pythoness, that these "men were servants of the most high God," (v. 17).

He now, enlightened by God's grace, asks what was the best means of securing eternal salvation.

31. "And thy house," who after your example, believe and embrace the Christian religion. "Believe in the Lord Jesus Christ." These words have the same meaning substantially as those addressed by our Lord to His Apostles, "*Euntes docete*," &c.

Faith is the foundation of justification ; but, not the only ingredient ; other dispositions and acts are also indispensably necessary.

32. "The Word of God." They more fully developed the words, "believe in the Lord," &c., v. 31. Giving them a succinct summary explanation of the chief doctrines of the Christian religion, including the necessity of Baptism (v. 33).

"And to all that were in his house," his entire family and domestics.

Text.

tions of the prison were shaken. And immediately all the doors were opened: and the bands of all were loosed.

27. And the keeper of the prison, awaking out of his sleep, and seeing the doors of the prison open, drawing his sword, would have killed himself, supposing that the prisoners had been fled.

28. But Paul cried with a loud voice, saying: Do thyself no harm, for we all are here.

29. Then calling for a light, he went in, and trembling fell down at the feet of Paul and Silas.

30. And bringing them out, he said: Masters, what must I do, that I may be saved?

31. But they said: Believe in the Lord Jesus: and thou shalt be saved, and thy house.

32. And they preached the word of the Lord to him and to all that were in his house.

Text.	Commentary.

Some say this occurred in the vestibule of the prison, whither the gaoler brought his entire household to hear the words of salvation; others, in the house of the gaoler. The former opinion derives great probability from the words, *v.* 34, " brought them into his house," as if this did not occur before.

33. *And he taking them the same hour* — 33. "Same hour," &c. No doubt, an unreasonable time. The rite of Baptism was administered immediately, all at once.

of the night, washed their stripes: and himself was baptized and all his house immediately.

34. *And when he had brought them into his own house, he laid the table for them, and rejoiced with all his house, believing God.*

35. *And when the day was come, the magistrates sent the sergeants, saying: Let those men go.* — 35. Evidently, the Earthquake terrified the magistrates or Prætors, and made them reflect on the injustice of scourging strangers in order to please the multitude, without hearing their defence. Hence, at the earliest hour, they endeavour to undo their act by having them released, " Sergeants," lictors, who carried rods or staves, as the Greek conveys.

36. *And the keeper of the prison told these words to Paul: The magistrates have sent to let you go: now therefore depart, and go in peace.*

37. *But Paul said to them: They have beaten us publicly, uncondemned, men that are Romans, and have cast us into prison: and now do they thrust us out privately? Not so, but let them come,* — 37. St. Paul, with Silas, having patiently submitted to the outrage offered them as Roman citizens, deems it right now, as on other occasions, to assert his rights and clear his character. He, therefore, calls for public reparation, as the interests of religion demanded, that they should be publicly declared innocent of the charges publicly made against them, and should receive publicly reparation for the injuries inflicted on them being condemned unheard, contrary to the Laws of Justice and the Laws of the Roman Empire. He calls on the same judges, who publicly condemned them, publicly to declare them innocent and make reparation by coming themselves personally to release them. By thus asserting his rights, he strengthened the faith of his converts at Philippi, who might otherwise be depressed and disheartened. It might also have the effect of deterring the magistrates from hereafter interfering with the faithful.

38. *And let us out themselves. And the sergeants told these words to the magistrates, and they were afraid, hearing that they were Romans.*

39. *And coming they besought them; and bringing them out they desired them to depart out of the city.* — 39. The magistrates, fearing the consequences of their unjust and illegal treatment of Roman citizens, came themselves and "besought them" to pardon their illegal and unjust conduct. The violation of the rights of Roman citizenship was punished by Roman Law with the utmost rigour.

40. *And they went out of the prison, and entered into the house of Lydia: and having seen the brethren, they comforted them, and departed.* — 40. "Comforted them" by exhortations to perseverance, and by holding out the hopes and prospects of future rewards, in store for them.

CHAPTER XVII.

1. *And when they had passed through Amphipolis and Apollonia, they came to Thessalonica, where there was a synagogue of the Jews.*

2. *And Paul according to his custom went in unto them; and for three sabbath-days he reasoned with them out of the scriptures,*

3. *Declaring and insinuating that the Christ was to suffer, and to rise again from the dead: and that this is Jesus Christ, whom I preach to you.*

4. *And some of them believed, and were associated to Paul and Silas, and of those that served God and of the gentiles a great multitude, and of noble women not a few.*

5. *But the Jews moved with envy, and taking unto them some wicked men of the vulgar sort, and making a tumult, set the city in an uproar: and besetting Jason's house, sought to bring them out unto the people.*

6. *And not finding them, they drew Jason and certain brethren to the rulers of the city, crying: They that set the city in an uproar are come hither also,*

7. *Whom Jason hath received, and these all do contrary to the decrees of Cesar, saying that there is another king, Jesus.*

8. *And they stirred up the people, and the rulers of the city hearing these things.*

9. *And having taken satisfaction of Jason, and of the rest, they let them go.*

10. *But the brethren immediately sent away Paul and Silas by night unto Berea. Who when they were come thither went into the synagogue of the Jews.*

11. *Now these were more noble than those in Thessalonica, who received the word with all eagerness, daily searching the scriptures, whether these things were so.*

12. *And many indeed of them believed, and of honourable women that were gentiles, and of men not a few.*

13. *But when the Jews of Thessalonica had knowledge that the word of God, was also preached by Paul at Berea, they came thither also, stirring up and troubling the multitude.*

14. *And then immediately the brethren sent away Paul, to go unto the sea: but Silas and Timothy remained there.*

15. *And they that conducted Paul, brought him as far as Athens, and receiving a commandment from him to Silas and Timothy, that they should come to him with all speed, they departed.*

16. *Now whilst Paul waited for them at Athens, his spirit was stirred within him, seeing the city wholly given to idolatry.*

17. *He disputed therefore in the synagogue with the Jews, and with them that served God, and in the market-place, every day with them that were there.*

18. *And certain philosophers of the Epicureans and of the Stoics disputed with him, and some said: What is it that this word sower would say? But others: He seemeth to be a setter forth of new gods: because he preached to them Jesus and the resurrection.*

19. *And taking him they brought him to Areopagus, saying: May we know what this new doctrine is which thou speakest of?*

20. *For thou bringest in certain new things to our ears. We would know therefore what these things mean,*

21. *(Now all the Athenians, and strangers that were there, employed themselves in nothing else but either in telling or in hearing some new thing.)*

22. *But Paul standing in the midst of Areopagus, said: Ye men of Athens, I perceive that in all things you are too superstitious.*

23. *For passing by and seeing your idols, I found an altar also on which was written: To the unknown God. What therefore you worship, without knowing it, that I preach to you.*

24. *God, who made the world and all things therein, seeing he is Lord of heaven and earth, dwelleth not in temples made with hands,*

25. *Neither is he served with men's hands as though he needed anything, seeing it is he, who giveth to all life, and breath, and all things:*

26. *And hath made of one, all mankind, to dwell upon the whole face of the earth, determining appointed times, and the limits of their habitation.*

27. *That they should seek God, if happily they may feel after him or find him: although he be not far from every one of us:*

28. *For in him we live and move and are: as some also of your own poets said, For we are also his offspring.*

29. *Being therefore the offspring of God, we must not suppose the divinity to be like unto gold or silver, or stone, the graving of art and advice of man.*

30. *And God indeed having winked at the times of this ignorance now declareth unto men, that all should every where do penance,*

31. *Because he hath appointed a day wherein he will judge the world in equity, by the man whom he hath appointed, giving faith to all, by raising him up from the dead.*

32. *And when they had heard of the resurrection of the dead, some indeed mocked; but others said: We will hear thee again concerning this matter.*

33. *So Paul went out from among them.*

34. *But certain men adhering to him, did believe: among whom was also Dionysius the Areopagite, and a woman named Damaris, and others with them.*

ANALYSIS.

Paul and his companions having preached at Philippi, are forced to fly, owing to a popular commotion raised by the Jews (1-10).

They reach Berea, whence, owing to another popular commotion, Paul departs, leaving Timothy and Silas after him, and reaches Athens (11-15).

Paul's affliction on witnessing the sad benighted condition of Athens (16). His eloquent discourse in the Areopagus (22-33).

Text.	Commentary.
1. *And when they had passed through Amphipolis, and Apollonia, they came to Thessalonica, where there was a synagogue of the Jews.*	1. "Amphipolis," originally an Athenian Colony, was made by the Romans, the capital of the first of the four districts into which after becoming masters of it, they divided Macedonia. They made it a free city. "Apollonia," situated between Amphipolis and Thessalonica. "Thessalonica." On dividing the country into four districts, Paulus Emilius made this the chief city of the second part of Macedonia. "A Synagogue," in Greek, "*the* Synagogue," which would imply there was no Synagogue in the other cities in question.

Commentary.

2. Paul usually went into the Synagogues of the Jews. "Reasoned," meant to prove by disputation.

3. "Declaring," unfolding their meaning. "Insinuating," inculcating, as a truth contained in the same Scriptures, especially the prophecies regarding Jesus.

"Whom I preach to you." St. Luke uses the words as they were uttered by St. Paul in the first person, thus passing from the *indirect* to the *direct* narrative.

4. "Associated," in Greek, "*cast in their lots*," becoming their disciples, and followers.

"And of those that served God," the Proselytes to Judaism, "and of the Gentiles." In the Greek, both clauses are reduced to one "*of the devout Greeks*," "and," is omitted.

5. "Of the vulgar sort," in Greek, "*of the market place*," loiterers, idle, good for nothing characters, usually found in every city, prepared for all kinds of mischief. "Jason's house," where the Apostles were (*v.* 7).

"Out unto the people" to be maltreated.

6. "Not finding them." They may have been out on some business; or, foreseeing the storm, may have left: "drew," dragged Jason and some Christian believers, who chanced to be there.

"To the rulers," &c. To the public place where the magistrates held their court.

"Set the city." The Greek for "city" may mean "*the world*" as if to say, they set the whole world in an uproar, causing confusion wherever they went.

7. "Received." Hospitably entertained. "Contrary to the decrees of Cæsar," which prevented men from giving anyone the name of "King" in any of the conquered provinces, without leave.

Text.

2. And Paul according to his custom went in unto them; and for three sabbath - days he reasoned with them out of the Scriptures,

3. Declaring and insinuating that the Christ was to suffer, and to rise again from the dead: and that this is Jesus Christ, whom I preach to you.

4. And some of them believed, and were associated to Paul and Silas, and of those that served God and of the gentiles a great multitude, and of noble women not a few.

5. But the Jews moved with envy, and taking unto them some wicked men of the vulgar sort, and making a tumult, set the city in an uproar: and besetting Jason's house, sought to bring them out unto the people.

6. And not finding them, they drew Jason and certain brethren to the rulers of the city, crying: They that set the city in an uproar are come hither also,

7. Whom Jason hath received, and these all do con-

Text.	Commentary.

Text.

trary to the decrees of Cæsar, saying that there is another king, Jesus.

8. And they stirred up the people, and the rulers of the city hearing these things.

Commentary.

"Saying," &c.   It may be, these men well understood the sense, in which the first preachers of the Gospel proclaimed our Lord, as King. But, maliciously affecting to understand it, in a different sense, they made it a political charge against them.   The Jews affected great zeal for the honour of Cæsar (Luke xxiii. 2 ; John xix. 12-15).

Text.

9. And having taken satisfaction of Jason, and of the rest, they let them go.

Commentary.

9. "Satisfaction," by his becoming answerable to the magistrates for Paul and *the others*.   It may be, they deposited a sum of money, or gave bail.

Text.

10. But the brethren immediately sent away Paul and Silas by night unto Berea. Who when they were come thither went into the synagogue of the Jews.

Commentary.

10. "Sent away" for greater security sake.   "Berea," a city of Macedonia, some distance to the west of Thessalonica.

Text.

11. Now these were more noble than those in Thessalonica, who received the word with all eagerness, daily searching the scriptures, whether these things were so.

Commentary.

11. "More noble," more generous, ingenuous, disposed candidly to hear the truth.   The word denotes nobility of character.

"Daily searching the Scriptures," *before* embracing the Faith, for many of them afterwards believed (*v.* 12).

Likely, Paul and Silas recommended them, at this stage of doubt, *before* they believed, to inquire into the grounds for believing the Gospel.   Different would it be *after* embracing the Gospel.   Such doubts would be incompatible with the certainty of faith.

12. And many indeed of them believed, and of honourable women that were gentiles, and of men not a few.

13. But when the Jews of Thessalonica had knowledge that the word of God was also preached by Paul at Berea, they came thither also, stirring up and troubling the multitude.

Text.

14. And then immediately the brethren sent away Paul, to go unto the sea: but Silas and Timothy remained there.

Commentary.

14. They *took* him to the coast, and thence, he probably went by sea to Athens.

Text.

15. And they that conducted Paul, brought him as far as Athens, and receiving a commandment

Commentary.

15. "Athens."   No other city of ancient times was so celebrated for philosophy, learning, and the arts.

"Commandment," a message to Silas and Timothy to come to him to Athens with all possible despatch.

Probably he expected a great harvest of souls there.

from him to Silas and Timothy, that they should come to him with all speed, they departed.

Commentarp.

16. "Waited." How long cannot be known. However, it was long enough for him to witness the spiritual destitution of the city.

"Stirred within him," Moved with grief and strong feelings of indignation.

"Wholly given to Idolatry." The Greek means "*filled with Idols.*" We learn from Pagan sources—Pausanias (1, xxiv. 3) and others—that there were more temples, shrines and statues of false gods in Athens than in the rest of Greece besides.

17. "Disputed," discoursed, argued "with the Jews," who were such by birth, "and them that served God," Proselytes to Judaism. With those he discoursed regularly "in the Synagogue."

"And in the market place," the Forum where the people assembled, and the philosophers often carried on public discourses. The zeal and indignation against the worship of false Gods, which fired the Apostle were such, that he omitted no opportunity of preaching Jesus crucified, as the eternal Son of God, the promised Messiah, who was to redeem the world.

18. "Certain Philosophers of the Epicureans," &c. There were four schools of philosophy in Greece.

1. The *Academicians* founded by Plato. His tenets were not so very much opposed to Christianity.

2. The *Peripatetics,* founded by Aristotle, so called because he taught while walking about. Their tenets also were not so opposed to Christianity. The treasure of natural truths derived from Aristotle became, in the hands of St. Bonaventure, St. Thomas of Aquin, &c., the rational foundation of the scholastic system, in the middle ages. The two other systems referred to here, "Epicureans and Stoics," were in direct opposition to Christianity. The followers of Epicurus became in course of time rabid opponents. The Epicurean philosophy made all happiness consist in natural pleasures. Practising voluptuousness, without restraint, they rejected the belief in a superintending Providence. They also denied the immortality of the soul. They referred the origin of all things to a fortuitous combination of atoms.

Stoicism was so called from the portico or porch (stoa), in which its founder, Zeno, delivered his lectures at Athens. These held that everything, even God, was subject to fatal necessity; that God was the soul of the universe. They had doubts regarding the existence of a future state. The leading tenets of these sects, St. Paul had now to encounter and refer to.

"Word sowers," in Greek, *collectors of grain*, denotes such as picked up scattered seeds; or, poor men who collected in the market place the seeds that fell from the merchants. It is used to designate those who collected scraps of knowledge, which they gave out without order or method. Hence, it designates a *vain babbler* or parasite, as the Athenians termed such.

Text.

16. *Now whilst Paul waited for them at Athens, his spirit was stirred within him, seeing the city wholly given to idolatry.*

17. *He disputed therefore in the synagogue with the Jews, and with them that served God, and in the market place, every day with them that were there.*

18. *And certain philosophers of the Epicureans and of the Stoics disputed with him, and some said: What is it that this word-sower would say? But others: He seemeth to be a setter forth of new Gods: because he preached to them Jesus and the resurrection.*

Text.

Commentary.

"Because he preached Jesus," &c.   These are the words of St. Luke, explaining why Paul was regarded as proclaiming new Gods. "Jesus," as the promised Messiah.

"The Resurrection," or *anastasis* was regarded by them, as one of the Divinities, as a Goddess proclaimed by St. Paul (St. Chrysostom).

19. *And taking him they brought him to Areopagus, saying: May we know what this new doctrine is which thou speakest of?*

20. *For thou bringest in certain new things to our ears. We would know therefore what these things mean.*

19. "Taking him" in a friendly way, gently urging him. "Areopagus" —the hill of Mars, situated in the centre of Athens.   Here was held the highest law court in all Greece, one of the most celebrated, if not, the most celebrated of law courts in the world.   It was not for the purpose of accusing him—St. Paul did not address the Judges at all—they brought him there; but, in order that his doctrine would be uttered in presence of the most celebrated judges in their court whither the Athenians usually flocked in crowds.   This was a fine theatre for Paul to proclaim Jesus crucified.

"May we know?" &c.   They question him, in a respectful way, free from sarcasm, reproach or cavilling.

21. *(Now all the Athenians, and strangers that were there, employed themselves in nothing else but either in telling or in hearing some new thing.)*

21. The sacred writer adds this parenthetically to show that it was not the desire of ascertaining truth, but rather curiosity, that influenced them.   Curiosity and a desire for news was one of the leading characteristics of the Athenians at all times.   This is the account Demosthenes gives of them.

22. *But Paul standing in the midst of Areopagus, said: Ye men of Athens, I perceive that in all things you are too superstitious.*

22. "In all things," by all means, "too superstitious," more religious than men in general; or than the other Greeks.   Considering the tact for which St. Paul was always distinguished, the place he spoke on, the polished audience he addressed, with all the other circumstances, it is likely the word is meant in a good sense, to denote more than ordinarily religious in their own way, as they viewed them very attentive to religious observances.   It is not likely, he would apply to them any epithet, calculated to alienate their minds or create a prejudice against his teaching.   Some, however, are of opinion that the Apostle designedly employs the ambiguous term "superstitious," tempered by "ὡς," "*as if*" found in the Greek, that they were more than ordinarily religious, although their religion was false, directed to false divinities.

It is not, however, likely St. Paul would commence his address to the Athenians in any other than a conciliatory spirit—Patrizzi is of a contrary opinion—so as not to create a prejudice against his teaching. Not likely, he would give unnecessary offence.

23. *For passing by and see-*

23. "Seeing." Closely observing and examining. "Your idols." Your objects of religious worship.

Commentary.

"I found an altar." This would imply, it was not in any prominent place, but only in some obscure corner.

"*To the unknown God.*" Ancient writers (among them, St. Jerome) tell us there were several altars at Athens, "*to the unknown and strange gods.*" They seem to think it was one of these St. Paul saw, and in *accommodation* to his subject uses the singular, *unknown God.* But the authority of St. Paul makes it almost certain that he saw an altar of which there was no vestige left in the days of those ancient authors, with the inscription in the singular number, as he describes it, especially as he spoke in presence of those who could easily refute him if no such altar with this inscription existed in Athens.

He quotes the fact of their having such an altar among them in proof of their being more religious than the others, who had no such altar. Hence, the word "superstitious" is, in some measure, meant in a good sense.

They worshipped this unknown God "without knowing it." Worshipped him for having averted evil, plagues, pestilence, and as the source of the blessings conferred on them, for which they did not give credit to the Gods known to Paganism, Jupiter, Juno, Minerva, &c. Whatever might be said of the principle, their *mode* of worship was to be reprobated. [When worshipping and returning thanks, in their own way, to the source from which they derived benefits, it was implicitly the true God they were worshipping, since He alone is the source of good.]

St. Chrysostom thinks the Athenians erected an altar to *an unknown God*, to escape the punishment of not worshipping some god whom they might not have known or heard of. This is the very God, the source of every blessing, whom they were worshipping without knowing it. It was He whom St. Paul was preaching to them, proclaiming His infinite perfections, especially His boundless goodness and beneficence, the fountain of all good. The Apostle adroitly turns to account the goodness of God, the source of every blessing, to preach to them, Him, to whom they were indebted for everything, though hitherto unknown to them. "*The unknown God.*" The Greek has not the definite article. It is "*an* unknown god." "What therefore you worship." The Greek has ὅ, *what*, to convey generic and *indefinite* worship, its *mode* not particularized.

24. "Made the world," &c. The idea of creation was novel to the Greeks.

"Dwelleth not," &c. Whilst temples are erected in His honour, He needs them not to dwell in them; since, to Him belongs the earth and its fulness. He is not confined to them, like the idols of the Pagans with whom He is here implicitly contrasted. This is by no means opposed to the external worship of God, to the erection of temples, the offering of sacrifices in His honour; since there is question here only of the false worship and absurd notions of the Pagans.

Text.

25. *Neither is he served with men's hands as though he needed anything, seeing it is he who giveth to all life, and breath, and all things:*

26. *And hath made of one, all mankind, to dwell upon the whole face of the earth, determining appointed times, and the limits of their habitation.*

27. *That they should seek God, if haply they may feel after him or find him: although he be not far from every one of us:*

Commentary.

25. This is clearly allusive to the worship of idols, served with the hands of men, as if needing food, raiment, help to move, from place to place. This the Apostle ridicules here as the excess of folly. It is not so with the true God. Far from depending on creatures for anything; on the contrary, it is on Him every creature depends for whatever is necessary for supporting human life. It is He and He alone that bestows on creatures all the blessings they enjoy, all that is necessary to support life and continue in existence, which He upholds by His conservative Providence. It is *we* not *He* that needs structures raised by hands.

26. "And hath made of one." The Greek has *one blood*, one parent stock, "all mankind."

The Athenians derided the idea of the unity of the human origin. They fancied their own origin to be different from that of other peoples. For "all mankind" the Greek has "*every nation of men.*" In this, the Apostle conveys that all nations, Jew and Gentile, were members of the same family, and should respect each other as children of the same common parent.

"Determining appointed times." The Greek is, *before appointed*, the meaning is: He allotted to the different nations of the earth several epochs for existence and distributed among them the boundaries of the places wherein they might dwell. The Apostle thus refutes the false notions of the philosophers, especially the Epicureans and Stoics, regarding the free Providence of God and the necessitating action of the Fates.

27. God's object in the exercise of His Adorable Providence, in thus ordering and arranging the human race is "that they should seek God" and be brought to Him. "If haply, they may feel after Him" by examining and inquiring into His wonderful works and the order established by Him.

This is done in an obscure way, just as by the sense of touch—conveyed in the words "feel after him"—allusive to the groping of a blind man—we may discover the existence and qualities of an object. The imperfection of their knowledge is aptly conveyed in the groping of a blind man, relying on the sense of touch. God gives men an opportunity, wherever located on the face of the earth, of knowing Him from His wonderful works. If they neither find nor worship Him, nor give Him thanks, they are inexcusable. In this, the Apostle may have in view to reprove the stupid idolatry of the Athenians. "Haply" may imply that while they may "find him," it is doubtful, whether generally speaking, they would do so, owing to their own fault.

"Although He is not far," &c., meaning, He is *quite near*, as indicated in His creative and Preserving Power. Hence, we can easily find Him by the light of reason, prescinding from the still clearer light of revelation.

Commentary.

28. "For in Him we live," &c. The particle "*in*," as Beelen observes after St. Chrysostom, clearly refers not to mere instrumentality (*by*), but to locality or place. For, it is given as a reason, why God is so intimately present that we may "feel Him.". "In Him we live." To Him we owe our coming into existence; to Him we are indebted for every operation intimately connected with existence. "Move." To Him we owe our *continuance* in existence. "We are." Let Him but withdraw His protecting hand conserving us in existence, and we fall into our original nothingness.

"In Him" also indicates, though not directly intended to prove it, God's immensity. Some distinguished commentators—among them St. Chrysostom—illustrate God's omnipresence in us and our living in Him, by the example of the air which we inhale, and, as it were, touch and sensibly feel in the act of respiration. Without Him we could neither have life nor *motion*, such as may be seen in inanimate creatures, the clouds, &c., nor continuance in existence. These three pregnant words are neither a climax nor an anti-climax. They only more emphatically convey the same thing—our entire dependence on God, for our coming into existence, for the functions appertaining to existence, for our continuance in existence.

The words can also be accommodated to the supernatural state. By sanctifying grace, even more than in our natural state, "we *live, move,* and *are* in God." St. Ambrose says: (*de bono mortis*) "in Deo *movemur*, quasi in *via. Sumus,* quasi in *veritate. Vivimus,* quasi in vita eterna." The word "move" in the middle voice, in Greek, is use in an *active* sense.

Speaking of God St. Gregory (lib. 2 *mor.* c. 8) says : " Deus manet *intra* omnia ; *extra* omnia ; *supra* omnia ; *infra* omnia ; *superior,* per potentiam ; *inferior,* per sustentationem ; *exterior,* per magnitudinem ; *interior,* per subtilitatem, nec alia exparte, superior—inferior—exterior—interior. Sed unus idemque totus ubique præsidendo, sustinens, sustinendo, præsidens, circumdando, penetrans, penetrando, circumdans."

"As some also of your own Poets said : *For we are also His offspring.*" These words are half an Hexameter, taken from the Poet Aratus, a Cilician, in his famous book, the *Phænomena,* so much prized. The statement is substantially found in Cleanthes, in a hymn to Jupiter, and several other Greek poets, on which account St. Paul uses the plural number, "*Some of your own Poets.*"

When addressing the Jews St. Paul quotes their own Inspired Scriptures. Addressing the Gentiles, he quotes an authority highly esteemed by them, their own celebrated Poets. This quotation from Pagan authors occurs in some passages of the New Testament (1 Cor. xv.; Titus i. 12). What the Pagans wrote concerning their false Gods, St. Paul applies in a higher and more exalted sense, knowing it to be true, in his own understanding of the words, to the true God and His relations to creatures, who were created and educed out of nothing by Him, and who, in a supernatural sense, became, by sanctifying grace, partakers of

Text.

Commentary.

the Divine nature (1 Peter i. 4), receiving through it a new spiritual existence, thus becoming new creatures.

source higher.

29. *Being therefore the offspring of God, we must not suppose the divinity to be like unto gold or silver, or stone, the graving of art and device of man.*

29. "Being therefore," &c. Ourselves gifted with life and intelligence, which we received from Him, as the bountiful giver—the great source of life and intelligence as rational creatures, who are by nature far superior to senseless idols, we must know that He is Himself gifted with life and intelligence in a still Infinitely higher order and degree. We cannot suppose Him to be like the senseless dumb idols, made by the hands of man, formed out of earthly materials, devoid of life and understanding, having ears and hear not, eyes and see not.

In this St. Paul, with a great amount of tact, identifies himself with them. "*We* must not," &c., insinuates the utter folly of worshipping or adoring idols.

30. *And God indeed having winked at the times of this ignorance now declareth unto men, that all should every where do penance.*

30. "Having winked at " The Greek means "*overlooked,*" as if not seeing them ; refraining from punishing them ; showing patient forbearance.

"The times of this ignorance." Allowing the nations to walk their own ways (xiv. 10).

"Ignorance." Out of prudence, he uses a mild phrase while referring to the great crimes of the Pagans in past times ; though to the haughty Athenians, who boasted of enlightenment of all sorts, "ignorance" was a bold, strong term.

"Of this ignorance." In regard to their ideas of dumb idols and their worship of them.

"Now declareth." *Commands, enjoins.* He will no longer exhibit the same patience. Now, His judgment is near. He enjoins on all men, without exception or distinction of Jew or Gentile, "to do penance," which is the only means of reparation for grievous sins.

31. *Because he hath appointed a day wherein he will judge the world in equity, by the man whom he hath appointed giving faith to all, by raising him up from the dead.*

31. God's great mercy and long suffering will not last for ever. He has fixed the term for stern justice in judging mankind, Jew and Gentile.

"By the man whom He hath appointed." Constituted Sovereign Judge of all.

"Giving faith to all." " Faith " means a guarantee or assurance of His having been Divinely accredited to act the part of Sovereign Judge, in the splendid miracle of raising Him from the dead—the clearest proof of his Divinity, as also of His veracity when claiming to act the part of Judge. From this it appears that it is as *man*, Christ is to be Judge. It is congruous that man should be the judge of men. The Council of Ephesus, c. 31, says :—"*In eo qui forinsecus apparebit, et ab omnibus qui judicandi sunt palam cernetur, divina natura occulte latitans judicium exercebit.*" (Quoted by Beelen.)

Commentary.

32. Very likely, after having referred to the Resurrection of Jesus, the Apostle introduced the doctrine of the General Resurrection of all men, as is inferred from the words, " Resurrection of the dead."

"Some mocked." The Epicureans principally. Whatever ideas the Pagans may have had of the duration or immortality of the soul, they all spurned the idea of the resurrection of the body, rejecting it as absurd.

" Hear thee again." A polite way of dismissing him, and of intimating their unwillingness to hear him now or hereafter, as their curiosity seemed to be fully satisfied. St. Paul saw they had no idea of hearing him again. Hence, his stay at Athens was so brief.

Text.

32. *And when they had heard of the resurrection of the dead, some indeed mocked ; but others said: We will hear thee again concerning this matter.*

33. *So Paul went out from among them.*

34. *But certain men adhering to him, did believe : among whom was also Dionysius the Areopagite, and a woman named Damaris, and others with them.*

CHAPTER XVIII.

1. *After these things, departing from Athens, he came to Corinth.*

2. *And finding a certain Jew, named Aquila, born in Pontus, lately come from Italy, with Priscilla, his wife (because that Claudius had commanded all Jews to depart from Rome), he came to them.*

3. *And because he was of the same trade, he remained with them and wrought: (now they were tent-makers by trade.)*

4. *And he reasoned in the synagogue every sabbath, bringing in the name of the Lord Jesus, and he persuaded the Jews and the Greeks.*

5. *And when Silas and Timothy were come from Macedonia, Paul was earnest in preaching, testifying to the Jews that Jesus is the Christ.*

6. *But they gainsaying and blaspheming, he shook his garments, and said to them: Your blood be upon your own heads: I am clean; from henceforth I will go unto the gentiles.*

7. *And departing thence, he entered into the house of a certain man, named Titus Justus, one that worshipped God, whose house was adjoining to the synagogue.*

8. *And Crispus the ruler of the synagogue believed in the Lord with all his house: and many of the Corinthians hearing believed, and were baptized.*

9. *And the Lord said to Paul in the night by a vision: Do not fear, but speak, and hold not thy peace.*

10. *Because I am with thee: and no man shall set upon thee to hurt thee: for I have much people in this city.*

11. *And he stayed there a year and six months, teaching among them the word of God.*

12. *But when Gallio was proconsul of Achaia, the Jews with one accord rose up against Paul, and brought him to the judgment-seat,*

13. *Saying: This man persuadeth men to worship God contrary to the law.*

14. *And when Paul was beginning to open his mouth, Gallio said to the Jews: If it were some matter of injustice, or an heinous deed, O you Jews, I should with reason bear with you.*

15. *But if they be questions of word and names, and of your law, look you to it: I will not be judge of such things.*

16. *And he drove them from the judgment-seat.*

17. *And all laying hold on Sosthenes the ruler of the synagogue, beat him before the judgment-seat: and Gallio cared for none of those things.*

18. *But Paul when he had stayed yet many days, taking his leave of the brethren, sailed thence into Syria (and with him Priscilla and Aquila), having shorn his head in Cenchra. For he had a vow.*

19. *And he came to Ephesus, and left them there. But he himself entering into the synagogue, disputed with the Jews.*

20. *And when they desired him, that he would tarry a longer time, he consented not.*

21. *But taking his leave and saying: I will return to you again, God willing, he departed from Ephesus.*

22. *And going down to Cesarea, he went up to Jerusalem, and saluted the church, and so came down to Antioch.*

23. *And after he had spent some time there, he departed, and went through the country of Galatia and Phrygia, in order, confirming all the disciples.*

24. *Now a certain Jew, named Apollo, born at Alexandria, an eloquent man, came to Ephesus, one mighty in the scriptures.*

25. *This man was instructed in the way of the Lord : and being fervent in spirit spoke, and taught diligently the things that are of Jesus, knowing only the baptism of John.*

26. *This man therefore began to speak boldly in the synagogue.   Whom when Priscilla and Aquila had heard, they took him to them, and expounded to him the way of the Lord more diligently.*

27. *And whereas he was desirous to go to Achaia, the brethren exhorting, wrote to the disciples to receive him.   Who, when he was come, helped them much who had believed,*

28. *For with much vigour he convinced the Jews openly, shewing by the scriptures, that Jesus is the Christ.*

ANALYSIS.

He founds the church of Corinth, preaching and labouring there in the midst of contradiction and opposition for six months, during which time he received a vision strengthening him (1-11). He was arraigned before Gallio the Proconsul, who unceremoniously dismissed the Jews from his court (12-16). He preached in Ephesus (17-19). Apollo comes to Corinth and preaches there. He is more fully instructed in the faith by Priscilla and Aquila (26).

Commentary.

1. Corinth, the capital of Achaia. For description of (see Preface 1 Ep. to Corinthians).

2. "Aquila." There was no distinction made in the public acts of the Empire, between Jews and Christians. Christians, therefore, were comprised in the Edict of Claudius. Whether Aquila was converted at Rome, and professing the Christian religion when St. Paul came to Corinth, or was converted by St. Paul, is disputed (Vide Beelen).

3. "Same trade." Tent-making, manufacturing tents from skins or cloth. The Apostle gloried in labouring for his livelihood (Acts xx. 34 ; 2 Thess. iii. 9, 10). He was brought up at the feet of Gamaliel, and originally destined for the legal profession. The Jews made it a custom to have their children taught some useful trade, as a part of their education. This was inculcated by the Rabbins.

"Tent-making." Making portable tents out of cloth or skins was a pretty remunerative trade in the East.

Text.

1. *After these things, departing from Athens, he came to Corinth.*

2. *And finding a certain Jew, named Aquila, born in Pontus, lately come from Italy, with Priscilla, his wife (because that Claudius had commanded all Jews to depart from Rome) he came to them.*

3. *And because he was of the same trade, he remained with them and wrought:(now they were tentmakers by trade.)*

N

Text.	Commentary.

Text.

4. *And he reasoned in the synagogue every sabbath, bringing in the name of the Lord Jesus, and he persuaded the Jews and the Greeks.*

Commentary.

4. "Reasoned," discoursed, incidentally "bringing in the name of Jesus." It was only after the arrival of Silas and Timothy, he entered boldly into discussion regarding our Lord (*v.* 5).

"Persuaded." Strove to persuade. "Greeks," Proselytes of the gate, who frequented the synagogue.

Text.

5. *And when Silas and Timothy were come from Macedonia, Paul was earnest in preaching, testifying to the Jews that Jesus is the Christ.*

Commentary.

5. "Silas," &c. (xvii. 15), "earnest;" was animated by their presence to preach to the Jews, "that Jesus is the Christ" their long-expected Messiah.

Very likely, Silas and Timothy brought him from Macedonia some pecuniary aid (2 Cor. xi. 8, 9) so that now he needed not to labour for his support and could devote his undivided attention and all his time to preaching and the work of the ministry.

Text.

6. *But they gainsaying and blaspheming, he shook his garments, and said to them: Your blood be upon your own heads: I am clean; from henceforth I will go unto the gentiles.*

Commentary.

6. "Blaspheming," Uttering opprobrious language against our Lord, vilifying him, speaking of him scornfully and contemptuously.

"Shook his garments." A symbolical action, conveying that he gave up all commuication with them; had nothing in common with them.

"Blood." Destruction and ruin "on your own heads." "I am clear." I have done my part.

"Henceforth." This was peculiar and exceptional treatment of the Corinthian Jews. For, we find that he afterwards laboured for the conversion of his Jewish brethren elesewhere.

Text.

7. *And departing thence, he entered into the house of a certain man, named Titus*

Commentary.

7. Thence," the synagogue, "entered into the house," &c., which served for the purpose of instruction, which he gave before in the synagogue. He lodged with Aquila.

"Worshipped God." This Titus Justus was a proselyte.

Justus, one that worshipped God, whose house was adjoining to the synagogue.

8. *And Crispus the ruler of the synagogue believed in the Lord with all his house: and many of the Corinthians hearing believed, and were baptized.*

Text.

9. *And the Lord said to Paul in the night by a vision: Do not fear, but speak, and hold not thy peace.*

Commentary.

9. Possibly disheartened by opposition, he may have contemplated leaving Corinth. Hence, the vision to strengthen him.

Text.

10. *Because I am with thee: and no man shall set upon thee to hurt thee: for I have much people in this city.*

Commentary.

10. "In this city." The theatre of voluptuousness and sin. "Much people." Not Christians as yet, but well disposed to embrace the faith, which they did, at the preaching of the Apostle.

11. *And he stayed there a year and six months, teaching among them the word of God.*

Text.

12. *But when Gallio was proconsul of Achaia, the*

Commentary.

12. "Gallio." He assumed this name on being adopted by Gallio, the famous rhetorician, His real name was Marcus Annœus Novatus. He was brother of Seneca, and bore the character of great amiability.

Commentary.

"Proconsul of Achaia." This was one of the provinces into which the Romans, after conquering Greece, divided the country. Macedon formed the chief part of the other province. Gallio on becoming Proconsul was deputed by the Senate, to whom it was now transferred for Pro-consular appointment by the Emperor, who had the appointment before.

"One accord," in a body, "brought him to judgment," arraigned him as a disturber of the peace.

13. "The law" of Moses. The free exercise of the Jewish religion being permitted to the Jews in Greece. It may embrace the Roman law also, which forbade any new Gods to be proclaimed without the sanction of the Senate. Most likely, it refers to the Jewish laws, as appears from Gallio's answer.

14. Clearly Gallio anticipates St. Paul's defence.—If there were question of justice or crime he would hear them, and impartially investigate the matter.

Gallio said to the Jews: If it were some matter of injustice, or an heinous deed, O you Jews, I should with reason bear with you.

15. "Words," doctrines—"names." Such as, whether Jesus should be called their Messiah or not. These and other such disputes they should settle among themselves, as best they could.

16. He ordered their removal out of court.

17. "Sosthenes, the ruler of the synagogue." He afterwards became converted (1 Cor. i. 1.) was very prominent in the riots, the chief accuser of the Christians. Seeing his conduct in promoting disturbances on account of the Jews, the Gentiles who were present in court when Gallio ignominously drove them away, avenged it on Sosthenes, the leader and promoter of these discreditable disturbances. "Beating him." Buffeting him with their fists in the very presence of the judge. Gallio probably, glad that Sosthenes and the whole of the Jews, whose unmeaning, unseemly conduct disgusted him, should pay the penalty of exciting popular fury and disquiet, paid no heed to this conduct. Rather strange, however, on the part of a judge.

18. "Having shorn his head,"&c. This, according to a certain punctuation, may be understood of Aquila. According to the Vulgate punctuation, it refers to St. Paul. It was so understood by St. Jerome, St. Augustine, Ven. Bede, and others. It seems to be a small matter for recording whether Aquila made a vow or not. Moreover, Paul is the

Text.

Jews with one accord rose up against Paul, and brought him to the judgment-seat,

13. *Saying: This man persuadeth men to worship God contrary to the law.*

14. *And when Paul was beginning to open his mouth,*

15. *But if they be questions of a word and names, and of your law, look you to it: I will not be judge of such things.*

16. *And he drove them from the judgment-seat.*

17. *And all laying hold on Sosthenes the ruler of the synagogue, beat him before the judgment-seat: and Gallio cared for none of those things.*

18. *But Paul when he had stayed yet many days, taking his leave of the brethren, sailed thence*

Text.	Commentary.

into Syria, (and with him Priscilla and Aquila,) having shorn his head in Cenchra. For he had a vow.

more prominent figure in the narrative, and if referred to Aquila, he should repair to Jerusalem, instead of remaining at Ephesus.

"For he had a vow." What this vow was is disputed. The greater number of commentators understood it of the vow of the Nazarites referred to (Numbers vi. 1-21). During the time fixed for the vow, before its final accomplishment in the Temple of Jerusalem, with all the prescribed ceremonies, those who were under it were obliged to abstain from all intoxicating drinks, and not allow their heads to be *shaved*. Here St. Paul did not *shave* his head. He only had it *shorn* or *cropped*, reserving the final ceremony of *shaving* it, for its accomplishment at Jerusalem.

Very likely, his chief motive in thus undertaking the vow of Nazarite was to conform in all things lawful to the usages of the Jews becoming "all to all." He would thus disarm the prejudices sought to be created against him on the plea that he was an enemy to the Law of Moses (xxi. 23, 24).

"Cenchra," one of the ports of Corinth to the East, on the Saronic Gulf.

"Yet many days," during which he, likely, performed many miracles (2 Cor. xii. 12).

19. *And he came to Ephesus, and left them there. But he himself entering into the synagogue, disputed with the Jews.*

19. "Left them there," Aquila and Priscilla.

20. *And when they desired him, that he should tarry a longer time, he consented not.*

21. *But taking his leave and saying: I will return to you again, God willing, he departed from Ephesus.*

21. "Saying, I will return," &c. After the word "saying," we have in several Greek MSS. the words, "*I must by all means keep the approaching Feast in Jerusalem.*" The necessity of his going to Jerusalem for the approaching Feast (Pasch or Pentecost) was, it is conjectured, owing to his vow, which he should accomplish in the Temple with the usual ceremonies.

"I will return to you again." So he did, and remained three years (xx. 31).

22. *And going down to Cæsarea, he went up to Jerusalem, and saluted the church, and so came down to Antioch.*

22. "Went up to Jerusalem." Jerusalem is not in the Text. But it is generally understood to be meant; and if the words above referred to, "*I must by all means,*" &c., be genuine, there can be no doubt that he speaks of going up to Jerusalem, where he accomplished his vow, and went through the usual concluding ceremonies, in the temple (Numbers vi., &c.). Others understand gone up from the ship to the city of Cæsarea, and "saluted the Church" at Cæsarea. It more likely means going up to Jerusalem.

23. *And after he had spent some time there, he departed, and went through the country of Galatia and Phrygia, in order, confirming all the disciples.*

24. *Now a certain Jew,*

24. "Apollo." It should be written Apollos, as appears, from the Greek. Likely an abbreviation of Apollonius, "born in Alexandria,"

Commentary.

so famous for its schools. Likely Apollo had his natural abilities, which were of the highest order, cultivated in their schools.

"An eloquent man." "Eloquent" might also mean, *learned ;* it means gifted with great and ready powers of speech. "Mighty in the Scriptures," well versed in the Scriptures of the Old Testament.

25. "Instructed." *Catechized,* according to the Greek, received elementary instruction in the Christian doctrine by word of mouth. "Fervent in spirit," zealous and earnest. "Spoke," discoursed in *private* and "taught" publicly in the synagogues. "Diligently," with zeal and fervour.

"The things that are of Jesus." The doctrines relating to Jesus, as far as he himself had been acquainted with them.

"Knowing only the Baptism of John." Likely, this Apollos, who was afterwards baptized and became a distinguished preacher of the Gospel (1 Cor. i. 12; iii. 4,5), had many years previously attended the instructions of the Baptist, and may have received his Baptism, which contained the faith in a future Messiah, and pointed out Jesus as that Messiah. This, then, was the extent of Apollo's Christian knowledge. He defended earnestly the teaching that our Lord was the promised Messiah of the Jews.

26. With earnestness and zeal he fearlessly proclaimed the Messiah-ship of our Lord.

"Whom when Aquila," &c. Seeing his knowledge of the faith to be imperfect, they therefore, with Christian zeal and piety, "took him" to their own house and instructed him more accurately in the doctrine of faith. From this may be seen the admirable humility of Apollo. This distinguished orator, who submitted to be more fully taught in private by Aquila and Priscilla. This was in *private,* so it does not conflict with the Apostle's injunctions regarding women (1 Cor. xiv. ; 1 Tim. ii. 12).

27. "Exhorting" may mean exhorting him to go to Achaia, or, "exhorting" the brethren in Achaia to receive him with hospitality. "Who had believed." To this is added in the Greek, "*through grace.*"

28. He bore down all opposition, proving openly from the Scriptures, that "Jesus was the Christ," that in him were fulfilled all the marks as to time, place, and other circumstances given of him in the sacred Scriptures.

Text.

named Apollo, born at Alexandria, an eloquent man, came to Ephesus, one mighty in the scriptures.

25. This man was instructed in the way of the Lord: and being fervent in spirit spoke, and taught diligently the things that are of Jesus, knowing only the baptism of John.

26. This man therefore began to speak boldly in the synagogue. Whom when Priscilla and Aquila had heard, they took him to them, and expounded to him the way of the Lord more diligently.

27. And whereas he was desirous to go to Achaia, the brethren exhorting, wrote to the disciples to receive him. Who, when he was come, helped them much who had believed,

28. For with much vigour he convinced the Jews openly, shewing by the scriptures, that Jesus is the Christ.

CHAPTER XIX.

1. *And it came to pass, when Apollo was at Corinth, that Paul having passed through the upper parts, came to Ephesus, and found certain disciples :*

2. *And he said to them : Have you received the Holy Ghost since ye believed? But they said to him : We have not so much as heard whether there be a Holy Ghost.*

3. *And he said : In what then were you baptized? Who said : In John's baptism.*

4. *Then Paul said : John baptized the people with the baptism of penance, saying : That they should believe in him who was to come after him, that is to say, in Jesus.*

5. *Having heard these things, they were baptized in the name of the Lord Jesus.*

6. *And when Paul had imposed his hands on them, the Holy Ghost came upon them, and they spoke tongues and prophesied.*

7. *And all the men were about twelve.*

8. *And entering into the synagogue, he spoke boldly for the space of three months, disputing and persuading concerning the kingdom of God.*

9. *But when some were hardened and believed not, but spoke ill of the way of the Lord before the multitude, departing from them, he separated the disciples, disputing daily in the school of one Tyrannus.*

10. *And this continued for two years, so that all that dwelt in Asia, heard the word of the Lord, Jews and gentiles.*

11. *And God wrought special miracles by the hand of Paul :*

12. *So that even there were brought from his body to the sick handkerchiefs and aprons, and the diseases departed from them, and the wicked spirits went out of them.*

13. *Now some of the Jewish exorcists, who went about, attempted to invoke over them, that had evil spirits, the name of the Lord Jesus, saying : I conjure you by Jesus, whom Paul preacheth.*

14. *And there were certain men, seven sons of Sceva, a Jew, a chief priest, who did this.*

15. *But an evil spirit answering, said to them : Jesus I know, and Paul I know : but who are you ?*

16. *And the man in whom the evil spirit was, leaping upon them, and mastering them both, prevailed against them, so that they fled out of that house naked and wounded.*

17. *And this was known to all the Jews and the gentiles who dwelt at Ephesus : and fear fell on them all, and the name of the Lord Jesus was magnified.*

18. *And many of those who believed, came confessing and declaring their deeds.*

19. *And many of those who had followed curious things, brought their books together, and burnt them before them all : and the price of them being computed, they found the money to be fifty thousand pieces of silver.*

20. *So mightily increased the word of God, and was confirmed.*

21. *Now these things being ended, Paul purposed in the spirit, as soon as he had passed through Macedonia and Achaia, to go to Jerusalem, saying : After I have been there, I must also see Rome.*

22. *And sending into Macedonia two of those that ministered to him, Timothy and Erastus, he himself remained for a time in Asia.*

23. *Now at that time there arose no small disturbance about the way of the Lord.*

24. *For a certain man, named Demetrius, a silversmith, who made silver temples for Diana, brought no small gain to the craftsmen:*

25. *Whom having called together, with workmen of like occupation, he said: You men, you know that our gain is by this trade:*

26. *Now you see, and hear, that this Paul, by persuasion hath drawn away a great multitude, not only at Ephesus, but almost throughout all Asia, saying: That they are no gods which are made with hands.*

27. *So that not only this our craft is in danger to be vilified, but also the temple of great Diana shall be thought nothing of, yea, and her majesty shall begin to be destroyed, whom all Asia and the world worshippeth.*

28. *Having heard these things, they were full of anger, and cried out, saying ; Great is Diana of the Ephesians.*

29. *And the whole city was filled with confusion, and they rushed with one accord into the theatre, having caught Gaius and Aristarchus, men of Macedonia, companions of Paul.*

30. *And when Paul would have entered in unto the people, the disciples suffered him not.*

31. *And some also of the rulers of Asia, who were his friends, sent unto him, desiring that he would not venture himself into the theatre.*

32. *Now some cried out one thing, some another. For the assembly was confused, and the greater part knew not for what cause they were come together.*

33. *And they drew forth Alexander out of the multitude, the Jews thrusting him forward. And Alexander, beckoning with his hand for silence, would have given the people satisfaction.*

34. *But as soon as they perceived him to be a Jew, all with one voice, for the space of about two hours, cried out: Great is Diana of the Ephesians.*

35. *And when the town-clerk had appeased the multitude, he said: Ye men of Ephesus, what man is there that knoweth not that the city of the Ephesians is a worshipper of the great Diana, and of Jupiter's offspring ?*

36. *Seeing, therefore, these things cannot be contradicted, you ought to be quiet, and do nothing rashly.*

37. *For you have brought hither these men, neither guilty of sacrilege, nor of blasphemy against your goddess.*

38. *But if Demetrius, and the craftsmen who are with him, have a cause against any man, the courts of justice are open, and there are proconsuls: let them accuse one another.*

39. *And if you inquire after any other matter, it may be decided in a lawful assembly.*

40. *For we are in danger of being charged with this day's uproar: there being no man guilty (of whom we can give an account) of this concourse. And when he had said these things, he dismissed the assembly.*

ANALYSIS.

Coming to Ephesus, the Apostle finding some converts imperfectly instructed in some points of faith, he more fully instructs them, baptizes them, and imposing hands on them, imparts the Holy Ghost (1-7). He continues instructing them for two years, working miracles, casting out devils, which some unauthorized men attempting were overpowered by the demon (8-17). The violent tumult caused by Demetrius the silversmith and his fellow craftsmen (23-34). The intervention of the City Magistrate, warning them of the possible consequences of their disorderly conduct, restored order (35-40).

Text.

1. *And it came to pass, when Apollo was at Corinth, that Paul having passed through the upper parts, came to Ephesus, and found certain disciples:*

2. *And he said to them: Have you received the Holy Ghost since ye believed? But they said to him: We have not so much as heard whether there be a Holy Ghost.*

3. *And he said: In what then were you baptized? Who said: In John's baptism.*

4. *Then Paul said: John baptized the people with the baptism of penance, saying: That they should believe in him who was to come after him, that is to say, in Jesus.*

Commentary.

1. "Upper coasts," or regions of Asia. Phrygia and Galatia, situated in a high country, a distance from the Ægean sea.

"Came to Ephesus," according to promise (xviii. 21). It was situated in the lower maritime district.

"Certain disciples," who were baptized into John's Baptism, and received John's teaching regarding the near Advent of the Messiah. They like Apollos, had not heard that the Messiah had come, nor anything regarding the Holy Ghost.

2. Assuming these disciples to be baptized members of the Church, but doubting if they were confirmed, he now asks them after having believed and consequently having received Baptism, if they had received the Sacrament of Confirmation which was veribly accompanied by the external gifts of the Holy Ghost, such as the gift of tongues, miracles, &c. These twelve men may have been natives of Palestine, at a time when the Faith of Christ was not preached, but only the teaching of John and his Baptism was known. "We have not so much as heard," &c.

3. St. Paul then asks, as from their answer it would seem they could not have received the Baptism of Christ in the very form of which the Holy Ghost is expressly mentioned. (The word "then" or *therefore* implies that there was mention of the Holy Ghost in Christ's Baptism), what other Baptism did they receive, "in what then," &c. ? The Greek is, *into what*, into whose name, what Faith or doctrine. What Faith did you profess at Baptism?

"In John's Baptism." A necessary condition of which was faith *in* the Messiah now come, John's preaching had reference, in a special way, to the Messiah and not to the Holy Ghost. Hence the disciples of John not having been instructed in Christian doctrine, knew nothing of the Holy Ghost.

4. "With the baptism of penance, which was a symbol of and an incentive to penance for their sins. The Greek construction is different. The word "people" is connected with "saying" thus ; John baptized, saying to the people. However, there is but little difference of signification in both constructions.

"Saying they should believe in Him," &c. From this St. Jerome, St. Thomas, Bonaventure and others infer, that the *form* used in John's baptism—if *form* and not rather their protestation or profession of faith it could be called—was in the words "I baptize thee that thou mayest believe in Him who is to come, that is in Jesus Christ." These words are hortatory and convey an exhortation and admonition to do penance and have faith in Christ.

The words "who was to come after him," are a paraphrase for the Messiah or Christ.

Commentary.

5. Having heard Paul concerning John's baptism and its effects to which he most likely, added instructions on the principal points of Christian doctrine, including the necessity of Christian baptism and its effects. "Baptized in the name," &c. Received Christian baptism, as instituted by our Lord Jesus, incorporated with Him, members of His Mystical Body, bearing His Name, and embracing His religion. No doubt, St. Paul in conferring the baptism of Christ, employed the *form* with the distinct mention of the Trinity presented by our Lord. Indeed, this is implied in the words "in what then were you baptized?"

6. "Imposed his hands on them." By administering confirmation. "The Holy Ghost came," &c., in the visible appearance of fire and tongues. "And they spoke with tongues and prophesied," either by foretelling future events, or sounding forth the praises of God with great fervour of spirit, making known the hidden things of God (viii. 15-17).

8. "Concerning the Kingdom of God." Pointing out the economy of Redemption, the means and necessary course to be pursued in order to secure Eternal life.

9. "Speaking evil." Reproachfully and insultingly of our Lord, of His Gospel and doctrines.

"He separated the disciples." Such as believed or were well disposed to believe, these he removed from the wicked gainsayers, lest their contagious example might corrupt them.

"Disputing daily." Reasoning, teaching of the Gospel truths "in the school," the office or hall occupied by this Tyrannus in teaching his scholars. "Tyrannus," likely a Jew, not hostile to the faithful.

10. "Who dwelt in Asia." A great number of those who dwelt in Asia, Jews and Gentiles, who had commercial relations with Ephesus, "heard the word of the Lord." By Asia is meant the Proconsular province of Asia Minor, of which Ephesus was the capital, a sense in which the term "Asia" is sometimes used (ii. 9).

11. "More than common." Unusual, remarkable, "miracles."

Text.

5. *Having heard these things, they were baptized in the name of the Lord Jesus.*

6. *And when Paul had imposed his hands on them, the Holy Ghost came upon them, and they spoke tongues and prophesied.*

7. *And all the men were about twelve.*

8. *And entering into the synagogue, he spoke boldly for the space of three months, disputing and persuading concerning the kingdom of God.*

9. *But when some were hardened and believed not, but spoke ill of the way of the Lord before the multitude, departing from them he separated the disciples, disputing daily in the school of one Tyrannus.*

10. *And this continued for two years, so that all that dwelt in Asia, heard the word of the Lord, Jews and gentiles.*

11. *And God wrought special miracles by the hand of Paul*

Text.

12. *So that even there were brought from his body to the sick handkerchiefs and aprons, and the diseases departed from them, and the wicked spirits went out of them.*

13. *Now some of the Jewish exorcists, who went about, attempted to invoke over them, that had evil spirits, the name of the Lord Jesus, saying: I conjure you by Jesus, whom Paul preacheth.*

14. *And there were certain men, seven sons of Sceva, a Jew, a chief priest, who did this.*

15. *But an evil spirit answering, said to them: Jesus I know, and Paul I know: but who are you?*

16. *And the man in whom the evil spirit was, leaping upon them, and mastering them both, prevailed against them, so that they fled out of that house naked and wounded.*

17. *And this was known to all the Jews and the gentiles who dwelt at Ephesus: and fear fell on them all, and the name of the Lord Jesus was magnified.*

Commentary.

12. "Brought from His body." May mean, that he used them, or, that the faithful applied them to His person or brought them in contact with Him, with a view of applying them to the sick for miraculous cures.

"Diseases departed." Of "wicked spirits" it is said, *they went* out of them. This passage furnishes a very strong argument in favour of the religious worship of relics as approved of by the Church (C. Trent, ss. xxv.).

13. Certain Jews, "who went about" from place to place, having no fixed abode, practising exorcisms.

"Exorcists." These probably refer to a class of men among the Jews, who by the invocation of the name of God, cast out devils (Matthew xii. 27, Mark ix. 27). We are informed by Josephus (Antiq. lib. viii. c. 2), that Solomon instructed this class of men, by Divine authority, in the art of expelling demons. These, probably, regarded Paul as belonging to some such class, seeing he expelled demons by invoking the name of Jesus, they fancied there was some latent spell or virtue in this name and so they invoked him.

14. "A chief priest." Likely he was never high priest; but may be called such, because he was a distinguished priest, who held the office of ruler; or, he may have been the head of one of the twenty-four (24) sacredotal ranks or orders into which David divided the entire posterity of Aaron (1 Par. xxiv. 1-19).

15. On hearing them utter the adjuration, then the wicked spirit said, I know the power of Jesus in expelling devils (Matthew viii. 29), and of Paul (v. 62). "But who are ye," what right or power have you in this matter, as you belong neither to Jesus nor to Paul?

16. "Leaping on them" (Luke ix. 49; Mark v. 3, &c.) "Mastering them both." It would seem, that only two of the sons of Sceva were engaged in the operation.

17. The failure of these pretenders showed the real power of Paul and the truth of his doctrines.

Commentary.

18. " Many of them that believed," and were converted to the faith, on seeing what befel the exorcists, came to the assembly of the faithful, in the fulness of their fervour, publicly proclaiming and confessing their past misdeeds. This may refer to their sins committed in the exercise of the black acts of the exorcists or to their iniquities in general. This does not refer to sacramental confession ; it was public, similar to that made by the Jews who came to John's Baptism (Math. iii. 6). It was an exterior profession of sincere repentance, of their real conversion to God and detestation of their sins. Among the penitents were those who followed " curious arts " (*v.* 19).

19. " Curious arts." Magic and all sorts of incantations calculated to delude the people. Ephesus was specially addicted to the practice of magic, which originally had reference to the worship of Diana. Magical formulas, written on parchment, designated by the name of EPHESIAN LETTERS, carried about as amulets, were celebrated all over the East.

To prove the sincerity of their conversion and detestation of the black arts which they publicly practised, these men now make public reparation by publicly committing to the flames their magical books of great value.

" Counting the price of them." Probably the multitude, who were astonished at this great act of sacrifice, computed their value at " fifty thousand pieces of silver."

What the value of these " pieces of *silver* " was, is not mentioned in the Text. They were probably *Attic Drachmæ*, all amounting to about *fifteen thousand pounds* (£15,000) of our money. At all events, they amounted to a very large sum, which shows the sincerity of the possessors in sacrificing so much in attestation of their sincere conversion.

20. This great sacrifice of valuables and resolve in future to give up all such illicit gains would prove the strength of the faith of the believers at Ephesus.

21. " Things ended." No further necessity for remaining, the faith being so firmly established. " Purposed in the spirit," resolved in his mind, " passed through Macedonia and Achaia," visiting the churches he already established there.

22. " Timothy " who had been with Paul (*c.* xvi. 3) in founding the church of Corinth, " and Erastus," treasurer of the city of Corinth. He

18. *And many of those who believed, came confessing and declaring their deeds.*

19. *And many of those who had followed curious things, brought their books together, and burnt them before them all: and the price of them being computed, they found the money to be fifty thousand pieces of silver.*

20. *So mightily increased the word of God, and was confirmed.*

21. *Now these things being ended, Paul purposed in the spirit, as soon as he had passed through Macedonia and Achaia, to go to Jerusalem, saying: After I have been there, I must also see Rome.*

22. *And sending into Mace-*

Text.	Commentary.

donia two of those that ministered to him, Timothy and Erastus, he himself remained for a time in Asia.

confined himself to Asia (Ephesus) for some time. How long is not known.

23. Now at that time there arose no small disturbance about the way of the Lord.

23. "Disturbance." Popular excitement. "About." On account of. "The way of the Lord," or the doctrines which Paul enunciated. The Greek has only "the way," but it clearly means "the way of the Lord," or the doctrines of Christianity as the Vulgate supplements it.

24. For a certain man, named Demetrius, a silversmith, who made silver temples for Diana, brought no small gain to the craftsmen:

24. "Silversmith." Chiefly occupied in making small shrines modelled after the celebrated temple of Diana. Not unlikely in these shrines were contained or enclosed small silver statues of the Goddess so celebrated all over Asia. With the pagans it was customary to carry about their persons images of their Gods as amulets or charms. Some kept them in their houses. Hence, the Romans called them their *penates* or household gods.

"Craftsmen." The tradesmen and labourers employed in the manufacture of these statues or shrines.

25. Whom having called together, with workmen of like occupation, he said: You men, you know that our gain is by this trade:

25. "Gain." Property, means of livelihood.

26. Now you see, and hear, that this Paul, by persuasion hath drawn away a great multitude, not only at Ephesus, but almost throughout all Asia, saying: That they are no Gods which are made with hands.

26. "All Asia" Minor, of which Ephesus was the capital.

27. So that not only this our craft is in danger to be vilified, but also the temple of great Diana shall be thought nothing of, yea, and her majesty shall begin to be destroyed, whom all Asia and the world worshippeth.

27. "This our craft." In Greek, *this our part*, our business, our occupation. "To be set at nought." To be undervalued, discredited. "Temple." One of the wonders of the world.

"Of the Great Diana." "*Great*" was one of her distinguishing epithets.

"Whom all Asia," &c. She attracted the whole world to pay her divine honours in her favourite city of Ephesus. Demetrius and his followers, in order to gain public sympathy and support, like the artful, dishonest Philippians (xvi. 20-22), affect great zeal for the public welfare.

28. Having heard these things, they were full of anger, and cried out, saying: Great is Diana of the Ephesians.

29. And the whole city was filled with confusion, and they rushed with one accord into the theatre, having caught Gaius and

29. "Having caught Gaius," &c. They rushed impetuously into the theatre, bringing in with them "Gaius," &c., to have them and any other Christians there present severely punished and maltreated. Likely the Apostle was not, at this moment, in his usual dwelling.

The "theatres" among the Greeks were used for all sorts of public meetings, elections, &c.

Aristarchus, men of Macedonia, companions of Paul.

Commentary.

30. St. Chrysostom (Hom. 7, de laudibus Pauli) extols the magnanimity and apostolic courage displayed here by the Apostle in exposing his life in defence of the cause of Christ.

31. "Some also of the rulers," &c. "*Rulers*," called *Asiarchs*. These discharged certain functions in the Proconsular Province of Asia, the same as the *Bithynarchs, Cappadociarchs, Phœniciarchs*, &c., discharged in their several districts, viz., they had charge of or presided over the public rites of religion and the public games. These duties they discharged at their own expense. On this account men of wealth were elected. Ten were elected annually in the several cities of Proconsular Asia. Their presence in Ephesus now was probably owing to the great games celebrated in honour of Diana. At other times, they were present in other cities, such as Smyrna, Colophon, &c. Among them some were kindly disposed towards the Apostle. They, therefore, dissuaded him from exposing his life and increasing the tumult. It is observed by commentators, Beelin among the rest, that *vv.* 30, 31 are to be read parenthetically. At *v.* 32 the account of the tumult omitted in *v.* 29 is again resumed.

33. Who this "Alexander" was and why put forward by the Jews is not known for certain. Some say that having been converted from Judaism to Christianity, the Jews wished to draw the whole ire of the assembled crowd down on him. It would, however, seem more probable that he was urged on by the Jews to make a defence of the Jews, and to show that in their doctrines they held nothing in common with Paul or his teachings; that the Jews were altogether different from the Christians; that they had nothing to say to this tumult. This seems the natural inference from the words "would have given the people satisfaction," and would have defended the Jews from any charge of sympathy with Paul or his.

34. From his whole appearance they saw he was a Jew. The Jews were universally disliked. The people also knew that the Jews were quite opposed to idol worship. Hence, they refused to give him a hearing, thinking he might speak against Diana, and continued crying out vociferously, for the space of about two hours, "Great is Diana," &c.

35. "Town Clerk." In Greek, "*a Scribe*," who was after arriving. Here the word is used to signify, the keeper of the city archives, an officer of great authority among the Ephesian magistrates. He "appeased (quieted) the multitude," so as to get a hearing.

"Worshipper," in Greek, *a temple keeper*. A term of honour among the Pagans, who regarded it as a great and honourable distinction to take charge of the temples of their Gods, to sweep, clean, and keep them in order. It denotes a fervent, zealous worshipper of the God to whom the

30. And when Paul would have entered in unto the people, the disciples suffered him not.

31. And some also of the rulers of Asia, who were his friends, sent unto him, desiring that he would not venture himself into the theatre.

32. Now some cried out one thing, some another. For the assembly was confused, and the greater part knew not for what cause they were come together.

33. And they drew forth Alexander out of the multitude, the Jews thrusting him forward. And Alexander, beckoning with his hand for silence, would have given the people satisfaction.

34. But as soon as they perceived him to be a Jew, all with one voice, for the space of about two hours, cried out: Great is Diana of the Ephesians.

35. And when the town-clerk had appeased the multitude, he said: Ye men of Ephesus, what man is there that knoweth not that the city of the Ephesians is a worshipper

Text.

of the great Diana, and of Jupiter's offspring?

Commentary.

temple was dedicated. The speaker displays great tact in his address to the people, by first showing zeal for their worship and the Goddess they adored.

"Jupiter's offspring." The Greek means "*fallen down from Jupiter*," the word "*image*" being understood. Hence, it means the image of Diana, which the Ephesians venerated so much, firmly maintaining that it fell down from heaven. (It may have been a meteoric stone).

This image, the manufacture of which traceable to the most remote antiquity, of which there is no record, was an object of the greatest veneration with the Ephesians. It may have been a meteoric stone. The Trojans too had their *Palladium*, which they fancied to be sent down from heaven. Among the Romans, Numa pretended that his *ancilia* or *sacred shields* were sent down from heaven.

---

36. *Seeing, therefore, these things cannot be contradicted, you ought to be quiet, and do nothing rashly.*

36. These things being indisputable. This on his part was a sort of official lie. For Paul had confuted them.

They should not persist unceasingly in their tumultuous conduct. No cause for it.

---

37. *For you have brought hither these men, neither guilty of sacrilege, nor of blasphemy against your Goddess.*

37. In this is implied that they acted rashly, by bringing forward men who gave no grounds for accusation, not "guilty of sacrilege" in rifling their shrines or temples, "nor of blasphemy" in speaking contemptuously "against your Goddess."

"For you"—Demetrius and the craftsmen—who were the real cause of the tumult.

---

38. *But if Demetrius, and the craftsmen, who are with him, have a cause against any man, the courts of justice are open, and there are proconsuls: let them accuse one another.*

38. "Courts of justice." The Greek might better be rendered, *the days for holding the courts and trials.*

"Are open." "And Proconsuls." Judges regularly appointed for the impartial administration of justice.

"Proconsuls." There was only *one*, who occasionally employed deputies, who may have been popularly looked upon as Proconsuls, or the *plural* may have been used for the *singular* in a *popular* and *generic* sense.

"Accuse one another." Plead their own cause and speak in self-defence, or accuse the opposite party. The laws will secure justice for both sides.

---

39. *And if you inquire after any other matter, it may be decided in a lawful assembly.*

39. "Any other matter" of public interest, "in a lawful assembly," convened by the public authorities, whom it concerns, at a proper time and place, according to law, but not in a tumultuous, excited gathering like this.

---

40. *For we are in danger of being charged with this day's uproar: there being no man*

40. "Called in question" by the Roman authorities. The Roman law was very severe on the promoters of riot. It made it as a capital crime for any one to be engaged in a riotous assembly. *Qui cætum et concursum fecerit, capite prematur* (Seneca. Controvs. iii. 8).

"Assembly." The riotous gathering.

guilty (of whom we can give an account) of this concourse. And when he had said these things, he dismissed the assembly.

CHAPTER XX.

1. *And after the tumult was ceased, Paul calling to him the disciples, and exhorting them, took his leave, and set forward to go into Macedonia.*

2. *And when he had gone over those parts, and had exhorted them with many words, he came into Greece:*

3. *Where when he had spent three months, the Jews laid wait for him, as he was about to sail into Syria: so he took a resolution to return through Macedonia.*

4. *And there accompanied him Sopater the son of Pyrrhus, of Berea: and of the Thessalonians, Aristarchus, and Secundus, and Gaius of Derbe, and Timothy: and of Asia, Tychicus and Trophimus,*

5. *These going before, stayed for us at Troas.*

6. *But we sailed from Philippi after the days of the azymes, and came to them to Troas in five days, where we abode seven days.*

7. *And on the first day of the week, when we were assembled to break bread, Paul discoursed with them, being to depart on the morrow: and he continued his speech until midnight.*

8. *And there were a great number of lamps in the upper chamber where we were assembled.*

9. *And a certain young man named Eutychus, sitting on the window, being oppressed with a deep sleep (as Paul was long preaching), by occasion of his sleep fell from the third loft down, and was taken up dead.*

10. *To whom when Paul had gone down, he laid himself upon him; and embracing him, said: Be not troubled, for his soul is in him.*

11. *Then going up, and breaking bread and tasting, and having talked a long time to them until daylight, so he departed.*

12. *And they brought the youth alive, and were not a little comforted.*

13. *But we going aboard the ship, sailed to Assos, being there to take in Paul; for so he had appointed, himself purposing to travel by land.*

14. *And when he had met with us at Assos, we took him in and came to Mitylene.*

15. *And sailing thence, the day following we came over against Chios: and the next day we arrived at Samos: and the day following we came to Miletus.*

16. *For Paul had determined to sail by Ephesus, lest he should be stayed any time in Asia. For he hasted, if it were possible for him, to keep the day of pentecost at Jerusalem.*

17. *And sending from Miletus to Ephesus, he called the ancients of the church.*

18. *And when they were come to him, and were together, he said to them: You know from the first day that I came into Asia, in what manner I have been with you for all the time,*

19. *Serving the Lord with all humility, and with tears, and temptations which befel me by the conspiracies of the Jews:*

20. *How I have kept back nothing that was profitable to you, but have preached it to you, and taught you publicly, and from house to house,*

21. *Testifying both to Jews and gentiles penance towards God, and faith in our Lord Jesus Christ.*

22. *And now behold, being bound in the Spirit, I go to Jerusalem: not knowing the things which shall befal me there:*

23. *Save that the Holy Ghost in every city witnesseth to me, saying : That bands and afflictions wait for me at Jerusalem,*

24. *But I fear none of these things, neither do I count my life more precious than myself, so that I may consummate my course and the ministry of the word which I received from the Lord Jesus, to testify the gospel of the grace of God.*

25. *And now behold I know that all you, among whom I have gone preaching the kingdom of God, shall see my face no more.*

26. *Wherefore I take you to witness this day, that I am clear from the blood of all men.*

27. *For I have not spared to declare unto you all the counsel of God.*

28. *Take heed to yourselves, and to the whole flock, wherein the Holy Ghost hath placed you bishops, to rule the church of God, which he had purchased with his own blood.*

29. *I know that after my departure ravening wolves will enter in among you, not sparing the flock.*

30. *And of your own selves, shall arise men speaking perverse things, to draw away disciples after them.*

31. *Therefore watch, keeping in memory, that for three years I ceased not with tears to admonish every one of you night and day.*

32. *And now I commend you to God and to the word of his grace, who is able to build up, and to give an inheritance among all the sanctified.*

33. *I have not coveted any man's silver, gold or apparel, as*

34. *You yourselves know : for such things as were needful for me and them that are with me, these hands have furnished.*

35. *I have shewed you all things, how that so labouring you ought to support the weak, and to remember the word of the Lord Jesus, how he said : It is a more blessed things to give, rather than to receive.*

36. *And when he had said these things, kneeling down he prayed with them all.*

37. *And there was much weeping among them all ; and falling on the neck of Paul, they kissed him,*

38. *Being grieved most of all for the word which he had said, that they should see his face no more.   And they brought him on his way to the ship.*

ANALYSIS.

He sets out for Macedonia and Greece, zealously preaching as he went along (1-4). He goes to Troas, where he raises a dead man to life (7-12).   At Miletus he addresses an affecting, valedictory address to the Clergy of Ephesus (18-38).

Text.	Commentary.
1. *And after the tumult was ceased, Paul calling to him the disciples, and exhorting them, took his leave, and set forward to go into Macedonia.*	1. "Took his leave," in Greek, "*having embraced them,*" giving manifestations of holy friendship. "Macedonia," on his way to Jerusalem, whither he intended going (*c.* xix. 21).

Commentary.

2. "These parts." The countries of Macedon. Likely he made for Troas, where he expected to meet Titus (2 Cor. ii. 12, 13).

His way. Not finding him, he returned to Greece, sometimes called, in official language, *Achaia.*

3. "Where," Corinth chiefly, "three months" during which he wrote to the Romans.

"Jews laid wait," &c. Probably, intending to assassinate him at Cenchrea, the port of departure.

The discovery of the plot caused him to travel by land—a more circuitous and slower route.

solution to return through Macedonia.

4. *And there accompanied him Sopater the son of Pyrrhus, of Berea : and of the Thessalonians, Aristarchus, and Secundus, and Gaius of Derbe, and Timothy : and of Asia, Tychicus and Trophimus,*

5. "Going before," To get all things ready for his journey— "stayed for us," viz., Paul, and Luke who now joined Paul, having been left at Philippi, at the house of Lydia. Why he did not accompany the Apostle to Athens, Corinth, Ephesus, &c., cannot be ascertained. He joined him on this occasion.

6. "Days of Azymes." They celebrated the Pasch at Philippi. Likely, Luke mentions this to note the time. It took "five days" to come to Troas, across the Ægean. It is said (*c.* xvi. 11) that he crossed it before in two days. The winds may have not been so favourable now.

7. "First day of the week." Sunday, termed the *Lord's* Day.

"Assembled to break bread." The phrase, "to break bread" is in some measure, a consecrated phrase, referring to the celebration of the Holy Eucharist. Its happening on the Lord's Day, together with other circumstances would, probably, indicate this. Nothing to show, it was a profane banquet, no one would "sit on the window" (*v.* 9) at such a banquet. On the Lord's Day, they assembled to celebrate the Holy Eucharist ; and Paul, as he was about leaving them, delivered a discourse which continued up to midnight.

8. The lamps were intended for light, and, probably, also for greater solemnity. This circumstance may have been mentioned in answer to the slanders against the early Christians, that they carried on their sacred rites in darkness, thus perpetrating all kinds of iniquity ; and also to show it was a place of public worship. Jews and Gentiles were wont to have lamps lighted in such places.

Text.

2. *And when he had gone over those parts, and had exhorted them with many words, he came into Greece :*

3. *Where when he had spent three months, the Jews laid wait for him, as he was about to sail into Syria : so he took a resolution to return through Macedonia.*

5. *These going before, stayed for us at Troas.*

6. *But we sailed for Philippi after the days of the azymes, and came to them to Troas in five days, where we abode seven days.*

7. *And on the first day of the week, when we were assembled to break bread, Paul discoursed with them, being to depart on the morrow : and he continued his speech until midnight.*

8. *And there were a great number of lamps in the room where we were assembled.*

O

Text.	Commentary.
9. *And a certain young man named Eutychus, sitting on the window, being oppressed with a deep sleep (as Paul was long preaching), by occasion of his sleep fell from the third loft down, and was taken up dead.*	9. " And was taken up dead." The common opinion is that he was not merely stunned ; but really dead, miraculously resuscitated by St. Paul.
10. *To whom when Paul had gone down, he laid himself upon him; and embracing him, said: Be not troubled, for his soul is in him.*	10. " Laid himself on him." Elias acted similarly (3 Kings xvii. 24), and so did Elizeus (4 Kings iv. 34). " Soul is in him." Through modesty he refrains from saying he himself resuscitated him.
11. *Then going up, and breaking bread and tasting, and having talked a long*	11. Continuing the rite of celebrating the Eucharist, he discoursed until daylight. "Tasting," may refer to the Agape celebrated in the early Church, in connection with the Eucharist ; or; it may designate a repast which strengthened the Apostle to continue his lengthened discourse.

time to them until daylight, so he departed.

12. *And they brought the youth alive, and were not a little comforted.*

13. *But we going aboard the ship, sailed to Assos, being there to take in Paul; for so he had appointed, himself purposing to travel by land.*

14. *And when he had met with us at Assos, we took him in and came to Mitylene.*

15. *And sailing thence, the day following we came over against Chios: and the next day we arrived at Samos: and the day following we came to Miletus.*	15. "Arrived at Samos." To which is added in the Greek, "*and tarried at Trogyllum,* which is a promontory opposite Samos, having near it a small island called *Trogyllum* (Strabo, lib. 14). These words, however, are wanting in the best MSS., and omitted in the most recent critical editions.
16. *For Paul had determined to sail by Ephesus, lest he should be stayed any time in Asia. For he hasted, if it were possible for him, to keep the day of pentecost at Jerusalem.*	16. "Sail by." Sail past Ephesus, without calling there for fear of being delayed on his forward journey, which he wished to expedite. It would seem he had particular reasons to reach Jerusalem for the Feast of Pentecost.
17. *And sending from Mile-*	17. Miletus was not far from Ephesus. about a day's journey, *forty* miles or so.

Commentary.

"Ancients of the Church." It is a subject of discussion among commentators whether this term refers to the clergy of the *First* order only, whom the Apostle calls, v. 28. *Episcopi* or bishops. Some Commentators say the Apostle summoned the several bishops from the surrounding districts of the Province of Ephesus, each having its own bishop; or, whether it refers to priests of the *Second* order only, as is maintained by some, who, however, admit the superiority of bishops over priests, defined as a point of faith (C. of Trent, *ss.* xxiii., *c.* 4, *can.* 7), some hold that it includes priests as well of the *first* as of the *second* order. The opinion which understands the term as common to bishops and priests, seems to be the one more generally adopted by Commentators and Ecclesiastical writers as more probable.

The term, *Presbyter*, according to Etymology, means, one *advanced in age*. *Episcopus* or *Bishop*, an *overseer*, or superintendent. But, according Ecclesiastical and Scriptural usage, *Presbyter* designates, a sacred minister or priest; *Episcopus* or *Bishop*, one who holds the first place in a church, *oversees* things and exercises jurisdiction over others. The term, *Episcopus*, while strictly denoting bishops, priests of the *first* order, to whom it is confined, and the high office they exercise, may also, to a certain extent, designate priests of the *second* order, who participate in the sacred office which the bishops exercise in its *plenitude*, in virtue of which they delegate a portion of their power, as also care and duty of superintendence to the clergy of the *second* order (see Ep. ad Philip 1; Titus i. 5; 1 Tim. iii. 8, Commentary on).

18. This valedictory address contains much in praise of the Apostle. It proceeded, however, not from vain glory, but from a sincere desire to point out to the pastors the line of conduct they should pursue, and the great zeal they should display, after his example.

He speaks only of what they knew already regarding his life, labours, and sufferings.

19. "Serving the Lord" by the faithful discharge of the duties of his high Apostolic office.

"With all humility," not puffed up; humbly referring all his success to God.

"With tears" caused by the perverse conduct of his persecutors. "And temptations," trials, arising from the snares and murderous designs of the Jews, and their plots against his life (*v.* 3).

20. "Nothing profitable." Whether palatable or otherwise, provided he saw it would ultimately prove of service to them.

tus to Ephesus, he called the ancients of the church.

18. *And when they were come to him, and were together, he said to them: You know from the first day that I came into Asia, in what manner I have been with you for all the time,*

19. *Serving the Lord with all humility, and with tears, and temptations which befel me by the conspiracies of the Jews:*

20. *How I have kept back nothing that was profitable to you, but have preached it to you, and taught you publicly, and from house to house,*

Text.	Commentary.

Text.

21. *Testifying both to Jews and gentiles penance towards God, and faith in our Lord Jesus Christ.*

22. *And now behold, being bound in the Spirit, I go to Jerusalem: not knowing the things which shall befal me there:*

23. *Save that the Holy Ghost in every city witnesseth to me, saying: That bands and afflictions wait for me at Jerusalem.*

24. *But I fear none of these things, neither do I count my life more precious than myself, so that I may consummate my course and the ministry of the word which I received from the Lord Jesus, to testify the gospel of the grace of God.*

25. *And now behold I know that all you, among whom I have gone preaching the kingdom of God, shall see my face no more.*

26. *Wherefore I take you to witness this day, that I am*

Commentary.

21. " Testifying," inculcating and urging, by all means, on all, " Jews and Gentiles," the necessity of doing penance for their sins against God, and of " faith in our Lord," &c., by whose blood they were redeemed.

22. " Bound in the spirit." Some understand " spirit " of the Holy Ghost, impelling, constraining him by his influences, to go forward, heedless of personal risks. In the next verse, however, he speaks of the "*Holy Ghost.*" Hence, others understand it of his *own will*, which, under a sense strong of duty, not, however, without the superintending guidance of God's spirit, urges him forward.

" Not knowing," having no clear or distinct knowledge in detail, as to their issue, or what particular kinds of persecutions await me, or if the issue of them be death.

23. " Save that." Excepting that "in every city" through which I passed, "the Holy Ghost," either by direct revelation or through the Prophets, whom he inspired in each of these places—of this we have an example (xxi. 4-11) " witnesseth," testifies, " that at Jerusalem, bands," &c. " Jerusalem," is wanting in almost all Greek copies.

24. " More precious," &c. I don't value life more than my eternal salvation ; so that no risks or perils can turn me aside from "consummating my course" as a faithful Apostle, and from discharging the duties of the ministry confided to me by no other than " the Lord Jesus " himself (Acts ix. 15-17).

" To testify the Gospel," &c. To bear witness to the joyous message of the grace which God, as a merciful Father, is prepared to confer on mankind. This is the direct design of the ministry confided on me—

The reading in the Greek is somewhat different, but substantially the same, "neither do I count my life dear *unto myself*, that I may consummate my course," &c. I look upon it, as a fixed idea, that my life is to be accounted by me for nothing, and all dangers regarded as nought, in attaining the object of my ministry, &c.

25. " I know," I have the firmest conviction, &c. This he adds to fix their attention on the admonitions he was about giving them, for the last time.

" All of you," &c. None of you shall see me again. " Among whom," &c. Very likely, there came together the priests and bishops from the districts round Ephesus. Possibly, on hearing of Paul's transit, they may have come of their own accord.

26. He appeals to themselves as witnesses of his fidelity, so that if any of them die the second death in mortal sin, "their blood," be they Jew or Gentile, their eternal loss will be chargeable to themselves and

Commentarg.

not to him.   Hence, it is inferred, that the pastor, who neglects his duty is guilty of the " blood," the eternal loss of his people.

27. " For "—a reason why he is not answerable—"not spared," shrunk from any motives or influences, whether of fear or selfishness, from fully "declaring" and making known to them "all the counsel of God," the entire will of God in regard to the salvation of men.   He fearlessly threw open to them, the full economy of God, in the work of redemption, the Faith to be believed and professed, the morals and deeds of virtue to be practised to gain eternal life ; and the vices and crimes to be shuned, to escape eternal torments.

28. " Take heed to yourselves."   The first and chief thing for pastors if they wish to have their labours successful and abiding, is to attend first to the work of their own sanctification.   This St. Paul inculcates (Tim. iv. 16), *attende Tibi and doctrinæ*.   See Commentary on.

" And the whole flock."   Our Lord himself is fond of using a pastoral image or metaphor, when speaking of his people, whom he often represents under the image of a flock, cared by shepherds, of whom he is himself the chief and head.

" Wherein."   That portion of the universal church over which "the Holy Ghost has placed you bishops."   The word "bishop" means *overseer, superintendent*, with power communicated by the spirit of fortitude and strength, to oversee all, priests and people.   No doubt, several bishops were present, as also some priests.   The designation "bishops" marks their office of superintending and ruling priests and people, and of conducting them in the way of salvation.

" To *rule*."   The Greek word—ποιμαίνειν—a pastoral term— means to rule, guide, govern and direct.   This is specially addressed to such of the audience as were bishops or priests of the *first* order, of whom some, no doubt, came together from the outlying districts, bordering on Ephesus.

" The Church of God."   There is a diversity of reading here, some MSS. have the *Church of the Lord*, others, the "*Church of the Lord and God*."   The Vulgate reading is best sustained by the testimony of the Fathers.   The Vulgate reading is more in accordance with the language of St. Paul, who, frequently in his writings, speaks of the "*Church of God;*" never, "*of our Lord*."   These words furnish an unanswerable proof of our Lord's Divinity.   He who purchased the Church is called " God."   It was our Lord Jesus Christ that, with the blood of His humanity hypostatically united to His Divinity, purchased the Church.   It is said here, it was " God" that purchased the Church.   Hence, our Lord is " God." It was through His humanity he purchased it, by the effusion of His blood.   It was His Divine Person that imparted an infinite value to all the works performed through His human nature.

Text.

clear from the blood of all men.

27. *For I have not spared to declare unto you all the counsel of God.*

28. *Take heed to yourselves, and to the whole flock, wherein the Holy Ghost hath placed you bishops, to rule the church of God, which he hath purchased with his own blood.*

Text.	Commentary.

Text.

29. *I know that after my departure ravening wolves will enter in among you, not sparing the flock.*

30. *And of your own selves shall arise men speaking perverse things, to draw away disciples after them.*

31. *Therefore watch, keeping in memory, that for three years I ceased not with tears to admonish every one of you night and day.*

32. *And now I commend you to God and to the word of his grace, who is able to build up, and to give an inheritance among all the sanctified.*

33. *I have not coveted any man's silver, gold or apparel, as*

34. *You yourselves know: for such things as were needful for me and them that are with me, these hands have furnished.*

35. *I have shewed you all things, how that so labouring you ought*

Commentary.

29. They should attend to their flock now more diligently, on account of the dangers they were exposed to from *without*, from the Judaizers after his departure.

"Ravening wolves." In Greek *heavy*, destructive *wolves*, false teachers, hypocrites.

30. Also from *within*. Heretics who sprung forth from the bosom of the Church, in which Gnosticism soon appeared. In his Epistles to Timothy, whom the Apostle appointed bishop of Ephesus, he refers to several false teachers (1 Tim. i. 20; 2 Tim. i. 45; ii. 17).

31. Surrounded with such dangers, they should "watch," be ever on the alert to meet these heretics. They should also gratefully remember the zeal and burning charity he himself displayed in admonishing all, both by night and by day. The fruit of such zeal among the people should not be allowed to be lost through their fault.

"For three years" or *thereabouts*. He was only two years teaching in the school of Tyrannus (xix. 8-10), and about three months more in the synagogue, " three years " more or less.

32. " Now" about to leave them for ever, he commends them to God.

"The word of His grace," viz., the word of the Gospel to which, provided it be faithfully believed and its precepts carried out in practice, is attached the grace of salvation, and all the particular graces that conduct thereto.

"Build up." Make them advance in Christian life and the work of sanctification.

"And to give you an inheritance," make you His heirs and partakers with all God's saints in the inheritance in store for them.

33, 34. He concludes this magnificent, valedictory address by inculcating disinterestedness, of which he gave so noble an example. They all knew his disinterestedness, free from not alone the stain, but the very suspicion of sordid avarice, or any desire to become possessed of any of their worldly goods. All he sought for was, not their worldly substance; but, their *immortal souls*. By labouring hard and with the work of his hands, he supported himself and those who were with him.

35. "Showed" by word and example, "all things," in regard to all things appertaining to the apostolic and pastoral mode of life. " How you ought," by labouring, after my example, "to support the weak," by administering to the corporal wants of the needy too weak to labour

Commentary.

for themselves; or, it more likely means the infirm in faith. By thus labouring to procure a livelihood, we would accommodate ourselves to the weakness of our infirm brethren, who might be scandalized by seeing us receive temporal remuneration and support for having laboured spiritually in the cause of the Gospel. By thus labouring for our own sustenance, we would support and stretch to them *a helping hand*, so that they would not be scandalized at our seeming selfishness, and be saved from the temptation of abandoning the faith.

"And to remember . . . it is a more blessed thing," &c. This saying of our Lord is found no where in the Gospels, which, however, do not claim to record all his sayings (John xvi. 15). St. Paul supposes it to be well known to those whom he addresses. He learned it from some of our Lord's disciples. It has reference to temporal matters. By renouncing their just claim to temporal support, the Apostles would have fulfilled in themselves and realized this adage. In preaching the Gospel gratuitously, they give of their own to others.

Text.

to support the weak, and to remember the word of the Lord Jesus, how he said: It is a more blessed thing to give, rather than to receive.

36. And when he had said these things, kneeling down he prayed with them all.

37. And there was much weeping among them all; and falling on the neck of Paul, they kissed him,

38. *Being grieved most of all for the word which he had said, that they should see his face no more. And they brought him on his way to the ship.*

CHAPTER XXI.

1. *And when it came to pass that, being departed from them, we set sail, we came with a direct course to Coos, and the day following to Rhodes, and from thence to Patara:*

2. *And having found a ship bound for Phenice, we went aboard, and set sail.*

3. *And when we had discovered Cyprus, leaving it on the left hand, we sailed into Syria, and came to Tyre: for there the ship was to unlade her burden.*

4. *And finding disciples, we stayed there seven days: who said to Paul through the Spirit that he should not go up to Jerusalem.*

5. *And the days being expired, departing, we went forward, they all bringing us on our way, with their wives and children, till we were out of the city: and kneeling down on the shore, we prayed.*

6. *And when we had taken leave of one another we took ship; and they returned home.*

7. *But we having finished the voyage by sea, from Tyre came down to Ptolemais; and saluting the brethren, we stayed one day with them.*

8. *And the next day, departing, we came to Cæsarea; and entering into the house of Philip the evangelist, who was one of the seven, we stayed with him.*

9. *And he had four daughters, virgins, who did prophesy.*

10. *And as we stayed there for some days, there came from Judea a certain prophet, named Agabus.*

11. *And when he was come to us, he took Paul's girdle, and binding his own feet and hands, he said: These things saith the Holy Ghost: The man whose girdle this is, thus shall the Jews bind in Jerusalem, and shall deliver him into the hands of the gentiles.*

12. *And when we had heard this, both we, and they who were of that place, besought him not to go up to Jerusalem.*

13. *Then Paul answered and said: What do you mean weeping and afflicting my heart? for I am ready not only to be bound, but also to die in Jerusalem, for the name of the Lord Jesus.*

14. *And when we could not persuade him, we ceased, saying: The will of the Lord be done.*

15. *And after those days, being prepared, we went up to Jerusalem:*

16. *And there went also with us some of the disciples from Cæsarea, bringing with them one Mnason, a Cyprian, an old disciple, with whom we should lodge.*

17. *And when we were come to Jerusalem, the brethren received us gladly.*

18. *And the day following Paul went in with us to James, and all the ancients were assembled.*

19. *And when he had saluted them, he related particularly what things God had wrought among the gentiles by his ministry.*

20. *But they, hearing it, glorified God, and said to him: Thou seest, brother, how many thousands there are among the Jews who have believed; and they are all zealous for the law.*

21. *Now, they have heard of thee, that thou teachest those Jews who are among the gentiles to forsake Moses, saying that they ought not to circumcise their children, nor to walk according to the custom.*

22. *What is it, therefore? the multitude must indeed come together: for they will hear that thou art come.*

23. *Do, therefore, this that we say to thee: We have four men who have a vow upon them.*

24. *Having taken these with thee, purify thyself with them: and bestow on them, that they may shave their heads: and all will know that the things which they have heard of thee are false; but that thou thyself also walkest, keeping the law.*

25. *As for those of the gentiles who have believed, we have written, decreeing that they should refrain themselves from that which has been offered to idols, and from blood, and from things strangled, and from fornication.*

26. *Then Paul having taken to him the men, the next day been purified with them, entered into the temple, giving notice of the accomplishment of the days of purification, until an oblation should be offered for every one of them.*

27. *But while the seven days were drawing to an end, those Jews who were of Asia, when they saw him in the temple, stirred up all the people, and laid hands upon him, crying out:*

28. *Men of Israel, help: This is the man that teacheth all men every where against the people, and the law, and this place: and moreover hath brought in gentiles into the temple, and has violated this holy place.*

29. *For they had seen Trophimus the Ephesian in the city with him, whom they supposed that Paul had brought into the temple.*

30. *And the whole city was in an uproar; and there was a concourse of people. And having seized on Paul, they drew him out of the temple: and immediately the doors were shut.*

31. *And as they were seeking to kill him, it was told the tribune of the band, that all Jerusalem was in confusion:*

32. *Who forthwith, taking with him soldiers and centurions, ran down to them: and when they saw the tribune and the soldiers, they left off beating Paul.*

33. *Then the tribune, coming near, took him, and commanded him to be bound with two chains; and demanded who he was, and what he had done.*

34. *And some cried out one thing, some another, among the multitude: and when he could not know the certainty because of the tumult, he commanded him to be brought into the castle.*

35. *And when he was come to the stairs, it happened that he was borne up by the soldiers, because of the violence of the people.*

36. *For the multitude of the people followed after, crying out: Away with him.*

37. *And as Paul was about to be brought into the castle, he said to the tribune: May I speak something to thee? Who said: Canst thou speak Greek?*

38. *Art not thou that Egyptian, who before these days didst raise a tumult, and didst lead forth into the desert four thousand men that were murderers?*

39. *But Paul said to him: I am indeed a Jew, a man of Tarsus in Cilicia, a citizen of no mean city: and I beseech thee, permit me to speak to the people.*

40. *And when he had given him leave, Paul, standing on the stairs, beckoned with his hand to the people. And a great silence being made, he spoke to them in the Hebrew tongue, saying:*

ANALYSIS.

On his way to Jerusalem, the Apostles and his companions made a short stay in several places, Tyre, Ptolemais, Cæsarea (1-7). At Cæsarea he stopped at the house of Philip the Deacon. While there, Agabus predicted and illustrated by a symbolical action, the sufferings that awaited Paul at Jerusalem (8-11). Paul goes up to Jerusalem prepared for any event, bringing with him one Mnason, an old disciple, with whom they were to lodge (12-16). Having called on James the Bishop of Jerusalem, and related the success of their mission among the Gentiles, he is persuaded, in order to disarm Jewish prejudices, to go through a course of purification in the temple (17-26). While thus engaged, the Jews finding him in the temple, create an uproar and tumult, and were on the point of killing him when the Tribune interposed to save his life (27-32).

Text.

1. *And when it came to pass that, being parted from them, we set sail, we came with a direct course to Coos, and the day following to Rhodes, and from thence to Patara:*

2. *And having found a ship bound for Phenice, we went aboard, and set sail.*

3. *And when we had discovered Cyprus, leaving it on the left hand, we sailed into Syria, and came to Tyre: for there the ship was to unlade her burden.*

4. *And finding disciples, we stayed there seven days: who said to Paul through the Spirit, that he should not go up to Jerusalem.*

5. *And the days being expired, departing, we went forward, they all bringing us on our way, with their wives and children, till we were out of the city: and kneeling down on the shore, we prayed.*

6. *And when we had taken leave of one another we took ship; and they returned home.*

7. *But we having finished the voyage by sea, from Tyre came down to Ptolemais; and saluting the brethren, we stayed one day with them.*

8. *And the next day, departing, we came to Cæsarea; and entering into the house of Philip the evangelist, who was one of the seven, we stayed with him.*

9. *And he had four daughters, virgins, who did prophesy.*

Commentary.

1. " Being parted from them." The Greek would imply a great interior struggle, as if he said; *having torn ourselves away from them.*

2, 3. The course they took is here described. It can be easily traced on the map of Asia Minor.

4. The Faith had been preached in Phenice (xv. 3)—the number of believers here was small. Hence, they were obliged to look for them, "*finding* disciples."

" Through the Spirit." The Holy Ghost, who inspired the believers thus to counsel Paul about whose welfare they were solicitous. This was not a command ; but an inspired *warning*, that by going up to Jerusalem, he ran a risk. He was free to accept this warning or take the consequences. His mind was made up to choose the latter.

5. " And," in Greek " *but* " as if to say, notwithstanding this *warning*, when the seven days had expired we set out on our journey, the faithful of both sexes escorting us outside the city.

8. The end of their sea voyage was Ptolemais, the rest of the journey was by land.

" Philip, the Evangelist," one of the seven deacons appointed at Jerusalem. " Evangelist," one who preaches the Gospel. Philip, likely, held a prominent place among the deacons, who were appointed not to preach, but to superintend the distribution of alms (vi. 1-6). Philip may have received a special commission from the Apostles to preach He laboured hard in Samaria in the cause of the Gospel (viii. 5).

9. The gift of prophecy was sometimes conferred on females, so as to foretell future events or explain the mysterious truths of God in *private*, not, however, in public, or in the congregation (1 Cor. xv. 24). The word generally means to be under Divine influence or inspiration whether in foretelling future events or instructing others, or speaking foreign tongues under Divine influence. Very likely, these virgins exercised the gift of prophecy in foretelling to St. Paul the dangers that

Commentary.

Text.

awaited him, on which account St. Luke, probably, makes mention of them here, in connection with the Prophecy of Agabus, *v.* 10.

10. "Came down." Judea was an elevated country higher than the maritime districts. "Agabus," see xi. 28.

10. *And as we stayed there for some days, there came from Judæa a certain prophet named Agabus.*

11. "Paul's girdle," which was a portion of the dress of the Orientals.

"Binding," &c. A striking mode of prediction, *emblematical* of what was to happen Paul. This was a symbolical and exterior prediction by act—a thing by no means uncommon among the Jews. Jeremiah acted in this way; (Jeremiah xiii. 4, xxvii. 2-4). So did Isaias (xx. 3, 4), so did Ezechiel (iv. 4-6; 3 Kings xxii. 11).

"Into the hands of the Gentiles." The Romans—then masters of Judea.

11. *And when he was come to us, he took Paul's girdle, and binding his own feet and hands, he said: These things saith the Holy Ghost: The man whose girdle this is, thus*

shall the Jews bind in Jerusalem, and shall deliver him into the hands of the gentiles.

12. *And when we had heard this, both we, and they who were of that place, besought him not to go up to Jerusalem.*

13. "Afflicting my heart," by such alarms and expressions of tenderness, when I am determined on suffering every evil for the sake of Christ.

13. *Then Paul answered and said: What do you mean weeping and afflicting my heart? for I am ready not only to be bound, but also to die in Jerusalem, for the name of the Lord Jesus.*

14. "The Will of the Lord," &c. Considering Paul's unalterable resolve, they considered it to be clearly the will of God that he was to go up to Jerusalem.

14. *And when we could not persuade him, we ceased, saying: The will of the Lord be done.*

15. "Being prepared." Baggage and everything required for journeying by land got together.

15. *And after those days, being prepared, we went up to Jerusalem.*

16. "Mnason." An early convert, probably, from the time of our Lord himself. He dwelt in Jerusalem. The Greek text might be so rendered as to convey that this man accompanied them from Cæsarea; or, that the disciples brought Paul and his companions to Mnason, in whose house they lodged, enjoying his hospitality.

16. *And there went also with us some of the disciples from Cæsarea, bringing with them one Mna-*

son, a Cyprian, an old disciple, with whom we should lodge.

17. *And when we were come to Jerusalem, the brethren received us gladly.*

Text.	Commentary.
18. *And the day following Paul went in with us to James, and all the ancients were assembled.*	**18.** "James," the *less*, Bishop of Jerusalem, our Lord's cousin; likely, the only Apostle in Jerusalem at the time. "Ancients." The clergy of the *first* and *second* order.
19. *And when he had saluted them, he related particularly what things God had wrought among the gentiles by his ministry.*	**19.** "Saluted." With respect and affection.
20. *But they, hearing, glorified God, and said to him: Thou seest, brother, how many thousands there are among the Jews who have believed, and that are all zealous for the law.*	**20.** "The Jews that have believed. Zealots for the law." For the observance of the Mosaic Ritual, and observe it themselves with great care and accuracy.
21. *Now, they have heard of thee, that thou teachest those Jews who are among the gentiles to forsake Moses, saying that they ought not to circumcise their children, nor to walk according to the custom.*	**21.** Likely some Jews from the countries where the Apostle preached the Gospel, calumniously charged him with teaching the Jews, who dwelt amongst the Gentiles, to give up the Law of Moses and desert his Ritual. Among other things, not to circumcise their children nor observe the other precepts of the Law of Moses. This they maliciously circulated. At this time, the Law of Moses, though not obligatory on the converted Jews, nor necessary for Salvation, was not, however, *forbidden* to them, *mortua*; but, not *mortifera*. Nor did St. Paul teach the contrary. Hence, the rumour regarding him was a malicious calumny, which James and those with him knew well. The observance of Mosaic ceremonies was *prohibited*, however, in regard to *converted Gentiles*.
22. *What is it, therefore? the multitude must indeed come together: for they will hear that thou art come.*	**22.** "What is it, therefore?" What is to be done to meet this calumny and avert its consequences, chiefly, riotous conduct and violence? "The multitude" of the Jews are sure to come together and create a riot. Something, therefore, must be done to prevent such excitement. It is to be done in the following manner: We have here in this Christian church of Jerusalem, "four men," converts from Judaism, "who have a vow on them." From their "shaving their heads" (*v.* 24), it clearly denotes the vow of the *Nazarites*.—For how long a time they bound themselves is not mentioned.—The time for which they took the vow being now accomplished, they were to be shaven, according to the usage in such cases.
23. *Do, therefore, this that we say to thee: We have four men who have a vow upon them.*	

Commentary.

24. In order to show that the ceremonial Law of Moses is neither despised nor underrated by thee, "take these," join thyself with them in observing the rite of purification or sanctification usually observed in regard to such vows, "and bestow on them." Share in the expenses for offerings and sacrifices presented at the completion of the vow ; or, rather defray for them the necessary expenses (which was looked upon as a meritorious act of religion), "that they may shave their heads," and cut off the hair which they permitted to grow during the time of the vow. This shaving of the head would show that the vow, in all its parts, had been previously faithfully observed, the shaving of the head being the last act performed.

"And all will know that the charges made against thee touching the observance of the Mosaic Law are false," utterly groundless ; and that thou thyself dost fully comply with the requirements of the Mosaic Law. What was directly meant by this advice was, that Paul would show by submitting to a rite still lawful and permitted to him, though not necessary, that he was not an enemy of the Jewish Law. He would thus conciliate the Jews.

25. St. James wishes to remind St. Paul of the Decree of the Council of Jerusalem (c. xv. 20, &c.) regarding the Gentile converts, who were not to be subjected to any Jewish observances in general, such as the Jewish converts might *lawfully* practise for a time.

"We have written, decreeing that they should only refrain," &c. After the word, "decreeing," are inserted in the Greek reading the words—"*that they observe no such thing,* but only refrain," &c. This reading is adopted by many critics as the most probable. The words are certainly implied in the decree of the Apostles (xv. 20), &c.

26. This prudent advice of St. James is at *once* complied with by St. Paul. "Paul took the men," &c. Joined with them in the ceremonies relating to their vows, carrying out what he declared (1 Cor. ix. 20) becoming "a Jew unto the Jews," &c.—in all things not prohibited by the moral law.

"Being purified with them." Joining them in the process or ceremonies of purification prescribed in such cases.

"Giving notice" to the priests of the temple of his intention to observe the vow, as the law regulating Nazarites required.

"Of the accomplishment of the days of purification." Of the period when the days would be accomplished by *himself.* Others say by his four companions. But the former is the more probable, as it was to clear himself of the charge of hostility to the Jewish Law and Ritual, James gave him this counsel.

It may refer to himself and them also, who could give no notice for

Text.

24. *Having taken these with thee, purify thyself with them: and bestow on them, that they may shave their heads: and all will know that the things which they have heard of thee are false; but that thou thyself also walkest, keeping the law.*

25. *As for those of the gentiles who have believed, we have written, decreeing that they should refrain themselves from that which has been offered to idols, and from blood, and from things strangled and from fornication.*

26. *Then Paul having taken to him the men, the next day being purified with them, entered into the temple, giving notice of the accomplishment of the days of purification, until an oblation should be offered for every one of them.*

Text.

Commentary.

themselves, not having the means wherewith to pay the expenses which Paul paid for them.

"Until an oblation," &c.   These days were to last "until an oblation," &c.   " Until " might be rendered *at which* purification or its accomplishment, "an oblation (or victim) should be offered," &c.

Paul charged himself with the expenses in this case, as the men were poor ; and it was regarded as a meritorious act of religion among the Jews to pay the expenses of purification for poor Nazarites.

27. *But while the seven days were drawing to an end those Jews who were of Asia, when they saw him in the temple, stirred up all the people, and laid hands upon him, crying out:*

27. " The seven days."   The definite article, *the,* in the Greek would imply that there was question of seven fixed definite days, "were drawing to an end."   In Greek *" were about to be accomplished."*

Some understand these of the days that remained *for* the four men, after Paul joined them, participated in their vow and announced to the priests that he would pay their expenses.

Likely, it was usual to have such declaration made seven days before the expiration of the vow.   It may also be understood of the temporary and voluntary vow of *seven days* made by Paul, when, by the advice of James, he joined them.

It is, however, a matter of controversy, *how* or *from what time* these " seven days " were to be computed.

"That were of Asia," who came up to worship in Jerusalem, enemies of the Apostle, whom they at once recognized, owing to his long sojourn in their districts.

28. *Men of Israel, help: This is the man that teacheth all men every where against the people, and the law, and this place: and moreover hath brought in gentiles into the temple, and hath violated this holy place.*

28. " Men of Israel."   Lovers of the Law of Moses.

"This place," the temple.   Possibly, Paul may have said on some occasion, as did our Lord before him, that the temple would one day be destroyed.

"Brought in Gentiles into the temple."   The outer of the many courts of the temple was set apart for the Gentiles.   Hence, called the court of the Gentiles.   But the inner courts were appropriated for the Jews exclusively, into which it was unlawful for the Gentiles to enter. To this reference is made here.

"Violated the holy place " by the introduction of Gentiles into it.

29. *For they had seen Trophimus the Ephesian in the city with him, whom they supposed that Paul had brought into the temple.*

29. "Trophimus," who accompanied him on his way from Ephesus (*c.* xx. 4).

" In the city " of Jerusalem, and, therefore, inferred most erroneously that he accompanied him into the temple.

30. *And the whole city was in an uproar; and there was*

30. " Drew him out of the temple," on pretence that he violated it ; but, in reality, with a view of killing him (*v.* 31).   They would not shed his blood within the precincts of the temple, which would thus be

Commentary.

polluted. " Doors were shut," evidently by the Levite door keepers, to save the temple from profanation.

31. "Tribune." Claudius Lysias (xxiii. 26).

32. "Ran down," in a hurry from the castle, Antonia, where he dwelt.

diers and centurions, ran down to them: and when they saw the tribune and the soldiers, they left off beating Paul.

33. "Two chains," for his hands and feet, as foretold by Agabus (v. 11) not in such a way, however, as to prevent him from walking (v. 34). By thus binding him, the Tribune meant to convey to the people that he reserved him for just punishment, if the charges alleged against him were proved. "And demanded." Asked the multitude who he was, and what his crime.

34. "Into the castle." The tower, Antonia, the citadel of Jerusalem, where the soldiers kept guard. It was situated at the angle of the western and northern porticos of the temple (Josephus de Bello, Lib. 5 ; c. 5).

35. "Stairs." The flight of stairs leading from the temple to the tower, Antonia, which was built on an eminence overlooking the temple. On these stairs, when the soldiers were returning with Paul, the violence was so great and the crowd so pressing, that the soldiers were obliged to carry Paul on their shoulders to rescue him.

36. "Away," &c., that is to say, death to him.

Text.

a concourse of people. And having seized on Paul, they drew him out of the temple: and immediately the doors were shut.

31. *And as they were seeking to kill him, it was told the tribune of the band, that all Jerusalem was in confusion.*

32. *Who forthwith taking with him sol-*

33. *Then the tribune, coming near, took him and commanded him to be bound with two chains; and demanded who he was, and what he had done.*

34. *And some cried out one thing, some another, among the multitude: and when he could not know the certainty because of the tumult, he commanded him to be brought into the castle.*

35. *And when he was come to the stairs, it happened that he was borne up by the soldiers, because of the violence of the people.*

36. *For the multitude of the people followed after, crying out : Away with him.*

Text.

37. *And as Paul was about to be brought into the castle, he said to the tribune: May I speak something to thee? Who said: Canst thou speak Greek?*

38. *Art not thou that Egyptian, who before these days didst raise a tumult, and didst lead forth into the desert four thousand men that were murderers?*

39. *But Paul said to him: I am indeed a Jew, a man of Tarsus in Cilicia, a citizen of no mean city: and I beseech thee, permit me to speak to the people.*

Commentary.

37. "Something to thee." In my own defence, and in explanation of all this uproar. This was spoken in Greek, as appears from the following question of the Tribune, who was surprised at hearing Paul speak in Greek, supposing him to be a native of Egypt, where Greek was not commonly spoken.

"Canst thou speak Greek?" an expression of surprise that Paul would have addressed him in the Greek language. Likely, Greek was the native language of the Tribune, who, it would seem, was not a native of Rome, having purchased Roman citizenship at a great price (xxii. 28).

38. "That Egyptian." Likely a Jew who resided in Egypt. Josephus (Antiq., xx. 6 ; De Bello, ii. 13, 5) gives us an account of him. He states that this man, whose name is not given, came from Egypt to Jerusalem ; gave out, or pretended, that he was a Prophet, and induced the people to follow him to Mount Olivet, where he promised them they would see the walls of Jerusalem fall down at his command, thus securing to them a safe entrance through the breach. Josephus informs us that he conducted from the wilderness *thirty thousand* (30,000) men whom he got together and led them round Mount Olivet. Felix, the governor, on being apprised of it, led out the Roman soldiers, and having slaughtered a large number, captured a great many, the rest betaking themselves to flight. Among those who thus escaped was the false prophet himself. The Tribune fancied it was the same who caused this great uproar.

"The desert." The mountainous tract to the east of Jerusalem, between it and the Jordan (Matthew iii. 1).

"Four thousand cut-throats." Josephus states the number to be *thirty thousand* (30,000). Between him and the Tribune there is the greatest discrepancy as to numbers. Possibly, the Tribune may have referred to the number who survived the slaughter by Felix. But the narrative of Josephus seems strange ; for while he states (Antiq.) there were *thirty thousand*, of whom very many were slain (De Bello, &c.), he says four hundred (400) were slain, and two hundred (200) taken prisoners. This would be comparatively a small amount out of *thirty thousand*. Most likely the number given by the Tribune, as recorded by St. Luke, is the accurate account, as it would be most difficult to collect so large a number as *thirty thousand* (30,000). However, it matters but little, which is the true account. St. Luke is not answerable for the number ; he only *records* the words of the Tribune, giving no statement at all of his own.

39. "No mean city." Well known and distinguished. Once the rival of Athens and Alexandria for learning. Josephus (Antiq. Lib. i. *c.* 6) speaks of it in terms of great praise.

Commentary.

40. "Hebrew tongue," or rather the Syro-Chaldaic, the vernacular of Judea at this time.

The use of the old Hebrew ceased during the seventy years of the Babylonish captivity. On their return, the Jews brought back the Chaldaic or Aramaic language with which they mixed up some Hebrew words. This was the language composed chiefly of the Chaldaic, but partly of the Hebrew that was commonly in use in Judea after the captivity until the destruction of Jerusalem. St. Paul employed this language, in order to conciliate the good will of the Jews.

Text.

40. *And when he had given Paul, standing on the stairs, him leave, beckoned with his hand to the people. And a great silence being made, he spoke to them in the Hebrew tongue, saying:*

CHAPTER XXII

1. *Men, brethren, and fathers, hear ye the account which I now give unto you.*

2. *(And when they heard that he spoke to them in the Hebrew tongue, they kept the more silence).*

3. *And he saith: I am a Jew, born at Tarsus in Cilicia, but brought up in this city, at the feet of Gamaliel, taught according to the truth of the law of the fathers, zealous for the law, as also all you are this day:*

4. *Who persecuted this way unto death, binding and delivering into prisons both men and women.*

5. *As the high priest doth bear me witness, and all the ancients: from whom also receiving letters to the brethren, I went to Damascus, that I might bring them bound from thence to Jerusalem to be punished.*

6. *And it came to pass, as I was going, and drawing nigh to Damascus at mid-day, that suddenly from heaven there shone round about me a great light:*

7. *And falling on the ground, I heard a voice saying to me: Saul, Saul, why persecutest thou me?*

8. *And I answered: Who art thou, Lord: And he said to me: I am Jesus of Nazareth, whom thou persecutest.*

9. *And they that were with me, saw indeed the light, but they heard not the voice of him that spoke with me.*

10. *And I said: What shall I do, Lord? And the Lord said to me: Arise, and go to Damascus; and there it shall be told thee of all things that thou must do.*

11. *And whereas I did not see for the brightness of that light, being led by the hand by my companions, I came to Damascus.*

12. *And one Ananias, a man according to the law, having testimony of all the Jews who dwelt there,*

13. *Coming to me, and standing by me, said to me: Brother Saul, look. And I the same hour looked upon him.*

14. *But he said: The God of our fathers hath pre-ordained thee that thou shouldst know his will, and see the Just One, and shouldst hear the voice from his mouth.*

15. *For thou shalt be his witness to all men, of those things which thou hast seen and heard.*

16. *And now why tarriest thou? Rise up, and be baptized, and wash away thy sins, invoking his name.*

17. *And it came to pass when I was come again to Jerusalem, and was praying in the temple, that I was in a trance.*

18. *And saw him saying unto me: Make haste, and get thee quickly out of Jerusalem: because they will not receive thy testimony concerning me.*

19. *And I said: Lord, they know that I cast into prison, and beat in every synagogue, them that believed in thee.*

20. *And when the blood of Stephen thy witness was shed, I stood by and consented, and kept the garments of them that killed him.*

21. *And he said to me: Go, for unto the gentiles afar off will I send thee.*

22. *And they heard him until this word, and then lifted up their voice, saying: Away with such an one from the earth: for it is not fit that he should live.*

23. *And as they cried out and threw off their garments, and cast dust into the air,*

24. *The tribune commanded him to be brought into the castle, and that he should be scourged and tortured: to know for what cause they did so cry out against him.*

25. *And when they had bound him with thongs, Paul saith to the centurion that stood by him: Is it lawful for you to scourge a man that is a Roman, and uncondemned?*

26. *Which the centurion hearing, went to the <u>tribune</u>, and told him, saying: What art thou about to do? For this man is a Roman citizen.*

27. *And the tribune coming, said to him: Tell me, art thou a Roman? But he said: Yea.*

28. *And the tribune answered: I obtained the being free of this city with a great sum. And Paul said: But I was born so.*

29. *Immediately therefore they departed from him that were about to torture him. The tribune also was afraid after he understood that he was a Roman citizen, and because he had bound him.*

30. *But on the next day meaning to know more diligently, for what cause he was accused by the Jews, he loosed him, and commanded the priests to come together and all the council: and bringing forth Paul, he set him before them.*

ANALYSIS.

Addressing the people from the stairs of the Castle, in presence of the Tribune, the Apostle gives them an account, in the Hebrew tongue, of his conversion (1-12). His Divine Commission to preach the Gospel (12-20). The fury of the Jews at his speaking of being sent to the Gentiles (21-23). The Tribune's anxiety on account of having ordered him to be scourged, when he discovered that he was a Roman citizen (25-29). The Tribune has him set before the Council of the Chief men among the Jews.

Commentary.

1. "Brethren," the Jewish people generally. "Fathers." Among his audience were some Priests, Levites, Magistrates, whom he addresses in the language of respect, as well as of affection. St. Stephen acted similarly (vii. 2).

"My account," my defence in reply to the accusations brought against me.

2, 3. "Hebrew tongue." (See xxi. 40). A Jew by extraction, although a Hellenist. He was brought up in the city of Jerusalem, having been sent there to learn the Law fully in the school of Gamaliel, a famous Doctor of the Law. He was taught the Law, in all its exactitude, written and traditional, under that distinguished doctor.

To sit "at the feet" of anyone, conveys the idea of a disciple or listener (Deuteronomy xxxiii. 3). The Jewish teachers occupied an elevated chair, the disciples or scholars sitting on benches beneath them.

"Zealous for the Law." The Pharisees, to whose sect he belonged, professed great zeal for the strict observance of the Law. The Greek has, "zealous *towards God*," which is well sustained by MSS. authority, and versions.

Text.

1. *Men, brethren, and fathers, hear ye the account which I now give unto you.*

2. *(And when they heard that he spoke to them in the Hebrew tongue, they kept the more silence.)*

3. *And he saith: I am a Jew, born at Tarsus in Cilicia, but brought up in this city, at the feet of Gamaliel, taught according to the*

Text.	Commentary.

Text.

truth of the law of the fathers, zealous for the law, as also all you are this day:

4. Who persecuted this way unto death, binding and delivering into prisons both men and women.

5. As the high priest doth bear me witness,

and all the ancients : from whom also receiving letters to the brethren, I went to Damascus, that I might bring them bound from thence to Jerusalem to be punished.

6. And it came to pass, as I was going

and drawing nigh to Damascus at midday, that suddenly from heaven there shone round about me a great light:

7. And fall- ing on the ground, I heard a voice saying to me: Saul, Saul, why persecutest thou me?

8. And I answered: Who art thou, Lord? And he said to me : I am Jesus of Nazareth, whom thou persecutest.

9. And they that were with me, saw indeed the light, but they heard not the voice of him that spoke with me.

10. And I said: What shall I do, Lord? And the Lord said to me: Arise, and go to Damascus ; and there it shall be told thee of all things that thou must do.

11. And whereas I did not see for the brightness of that light, being led by the hand by my companions, I came to Damascus.

12. And one Ananias, a man according to the law, having testimony of all the Jews who dwelt there,

13. Coming to me, and standing by me, said to me : Brother Saul, look. And I the same hour looked upon him.

14. But he said: The God of our fathers hath pre-ordained thee that thou shouldst know his will, and see the Just One, and shouldst hear the voice from his mouth.

15. For thou shalt be his witness to all men, of those things which thou hast seen and heard.

Commentary.

"As all you," &c., zealous, no doubt, but "not according to knowledge," or properly applied and directed (Romans x.).

4. "This way," those of the Christian profession, intending to put them to death.

5. "All the ancients," the entire body of the *Sanhedrim* or Supreme Council of the nation.

6. "Midday," omitted (c. ix. 3, 4). He mentions it here to show there was no delusion caused by nightly appearances.

7-13. (See ix. 4-17).

14. "Pre-ordained thee," by an Eternal and Immutable Decree which left man's will quite free.

"That thou shouldst know His will," in relation to your future destination and His designs regarding you.

"See the just one," the Messiah, and be qualified to become an Apostle.

15. "Shalt be His witness," &c. Similar is the commission given the twelve (c. i. 8). These words would seem to constitute Paul an Apostle. Thou shalt testify "to all men," concerning the Messiah, His advent, His death for the salvation of mankind. In c. ix. 15 it is said he was to carry the name of Christ before the Gentiles, the Kings and Children of Israel. Here, addressing the jealous Jews, he only uses general terms, "all men," and cautiously abstains from speaking of the

Commentary.

Gentiles. The storm which the mention of the Gentiles created afterwards (*v.* 22) fully justified this cautious mode of proceeding.

16. "Why tarriest thou?" This shows Paul was not unduly hurried or precipitate.

"Be baptized and wash away thy sins." The cleansing from sin was the effect and consequence of the process or rite of Baptism. Although before this, Paul had given himself entirely to God, and, by an act of contrition, had his sins remitted, still, this act of contrition included the purpose of receiving Baptism (Council of Trent c. ss. xiv. c. 4). This Baptism should be preceded by the invocation of the name of Jesus, that is, by a profession of faith in Him.

17. "Was come again to Jerusalem," three years after his conversion (Galatians i. 17, 18). He remained, during the interval, in Damascus and Arabia.

"And was praying in the Temple." Like other Jewish converts, he practised the Jewish devotions after the manner of the Jews—a thing not prohibited *then*. This he states, as a proof that he had not given up the Jewish worship at the time ; that he was no enemy of the Jewish religion, as had been laid to his charge.

"In a trance." In Greek, "*ecstasy*," transported out of himself. The Apostle refers to the vision here for the purpose of showing that the same God, who gave him the grace of conversion, had commissioned him in their own Temple, while engaged at his devotions, to preach the Gospel to the far-off Gentiles. The Jews heard patiently, or without murmur, the history of his conversion. It was only when he spoke of his commission to preach to the Gentiles, the storm arose (*v.* 22).

18. "Saw him" clearly refers to the Lord Jesus (*v.* 14). "Saying to me." The verbs for *seeing* and *hearing* are frequently interchanged in Sacred Scripture. St. Paul certainly saw Him, and bore testimony to His Resurrection.

"Because they will not receive," &c. The Jews abhorred him as an Apostate. The Christians feared him (ix. 26).

19, 20. Paul reverently remonstrates, and means to show, that he would be listened to more readily than anyone else, considering his former hostility to the Christians, exhibited in the occurrences recorded in these two verses. They would, he fancied, respect the sincerity of his conversion, and hear his reasons for this wonderful event in his life, *that believed in thee.*

20. *And when the blood of Stephen thy witness was shed, I stood by and consented, and kept the garments of them that killed him.*

21. Our Lord pays no heed to his reasoning or remonstrance. He had His own fixed purpose in regard to his destination to preach to

Text.

16. *And now why tarriest thou? Rise up and be baptized, and wash away thy sins, invoking his name.*

17. *And it came to pass when I was come again to Jerusalem, and was praying in the temple, that I was in a trance.*

18. *And saw him saying unto me: Make haste, and get thee quickly out of Jerusalem: because they will not receive thy testimony concerning me.*

19. *And I said: Lord, they know that I cast into prison, and beat in every synagogue, them*

21. *And he said to me: Go, for unto the*

Text.

gentiles afar off
will I send
thee.

Commentary.

" the Gentiles afar off."   His duty was at once to obey the Divine Will. " Unto the Gentiles," &c.   This he adds to show, that the Jews should not blame him, as he had no choice, but to conform to the Divine Will, and obey, by preaching to the Gentiles.

Text.

22. And they
heard him un-
til this word,
and then lifted
up their voice,
saying: Away
with such an
one from the
earth; for it is
not fit that he
should live.

Commentary.

22. " Until this word."   They heard him patiently up to this.   But, then fanatical jealousy was roused to the utmost pitch of fury, when they saw a preference given to the Idolatrous Gentiles, whom they held in such contempt.

" Away with such a man." He is not fit to live. He should be put to death.

Text.

23. And as
they cried out
and threw off
their garments,
and cast dust
into the air,

Commentary.

23. " Their garments," the outward garments, as if they meant to inflict summary punishment on him on the spot, and perhaps stone him (vii. 57).   This shows their excited feelings.

" Cast dust," &c., to express their rage and furious indignation, and impotent resolve to inflict summary punishment on him, if he were not in the hands of the Roman soldiers.

Text.

24. The trib-
une command-
ed him to be
brought into
the castle, and
that he should
be scourged and
tortured: to
know for what
cause they did
so cry out a-
gainst him.

Commentary.

24. " Castle," Tower Antonia, to be beyond the reach of his murderous assailants.

" Scourged and tortured."   The Tribune, seeing the fury of the Jews, and not understanding their language, nor perhaps, the *defence* of himself by Paul, thinking that Paul must have been some great male-factor and desperate character, thought fit to subject him to the lash. This, however unjust and barbarous, and against the provisions of Roman Law (Digest, 1-48, Lib. 48), was by no means uncommon at the time, as a means of eliciting the truth from those charged with grievous crimes.

Text.

25. And when
they had bound
h i m w i t h
thongs, Paul
saith to the
centurion that
stood by him:
Is it lawful
for you to
scourge a man
that is a Ro-
man, and un-
condemned?

Commentary.

25. " Bound with thongs " to the whipping post, preparatory to the scourging.

A " Centurion " among the Romans usually superintended such a kind of punishment.

Text.

26. Which
the centurion
hearing, went
to the tribune,
and told him,
saying: What
art thou about
to do? For
this man is a
Roman citizen.

Commentary.

26-27. The Porcian and Sempronian Laws secured Roman citizens against the injustice and indignity to which Paul was about to be subjected. At Philippi, Paul did not claim the rights of Roman citizenship, because as he suffered then for the name of Christ, he endured it silently. Here he was charged with a grievous crime, and was about to be punished, as a common criminal, he would not silently submit to it.

---

27. And the tribune coming, said to him: Tell me, art thou a Roman? But he said: Yea.

Commentary.

28. "The being free," &c., the freedom of Roman citizenship.

"With a great sum." Under the earlier Cæsars, it was difficult to secure the rights of Roman citizenship. But, under Claudius and his wife, Messalina, it became a matter of mere traffic. The name of the Tribune, *Claudius* Lysias, would make it probable he was one of those who purchased it in this way.

"I was born so," as a native of Tharsus, a free city of the Roman Empire (Pliny 5.27). Appian tells us, Tharsis was endowed by Augustus with the privileges of a free city. As the fact of its being a free city did not confer on all its inhabitants the rights of Roman citizenship. Some conjecture that one of Paul's ancestors may have obtained this privilege for some military services, or by purchase.

29. "Because he had bound him." It was against the Roman Law to bind a Roman citizen with the view of scourging him, untried and uncondemned. Cicero against Verres tells us, "*it was a grievous crime to bind a Roman citizen*"—"*facinus est vincire civem Romanum.*" However, in case of doubt as to Roman citizenship, or when the accused was to be guarded until he was brought before a legitimate Tribunal to try his case, he might be bound. Thus Paul was kept bound till, on the following day, "he loosed him."

30. "And all the Council"—the *Sanhedrim*. "Commanded the Priests," &c. This convening of a Council by a Roman Military Tribunal shows what little liberty, even in religious matters, the Jews enjoyed under the Roman dominion.

"Bringing forth Paul" from the Castle to the place where the meeting was held, usually, in the house of the High Priest.

"Set him before them," to plead his cause, and let all see the true state of the case and the nature of the accusations brought against him.

Text.

28. And the tribune answered: I obtained the being free of this city with a great sum. And Paul said: But I was born so.

29. Immediately therefore they departed from him that were about to torture him. The tribune also was afraid after he understood that he was a Roman citizen, and because he had bound him.

30. But on the next day meaning to know more diligently, for what cause he was accused by the Jews, he loosed him, and commanded the priests to come together and all the council: and bringing forth Paul, he set him before them.

CHAPTER XXIII.

1. *And Paul looking upon the council, said: Men brethren, I have conversed with all good conscience before God, until this present day.*

2. *And the high-priest Ananias commanded them that stood by him to strike him on the mouth.*

3. *Then Paul said to him: God shall strike thee, thou whited wall. For sittest thou to judge me according to the law, and contrary to the law commandest me to be struck?*

4. *And they that stood by said: Dost thou revile the high-priest of God?*

5. *And Paul said: I knew not, brethren, that he is the high-priest. For it is written : Thou shalt not speak evil of the prince of thy people.*

6. *And Paul knowing that the one part were Sadducees, and the other Pharisees, cried out in the council: Men brethren, I am a Pharisee, the son of Pharisees: concerning the hope and resurrection of the dead I am called in question.*

7. *And when he had so said, there arose a dissension between the Pharisees and the Sadducees ; and the multitude was divided.*

8. *For the Sadducees say that there is no resurrection, neither angel, nor spirit: but the Pharisees confess both.*

9. *And there arose a great cry. And some of the Pharisees rising up, strove, saying : We find no evil in this man. What if a spirit hath spoken to him, or an angel?*

10. *And when there arose a great dissension, the tribune fearing lest Paul should be pulled to pieces by them, commanded the soldiers to go down, and to take him by force from among them, and to bring him into the castle.*

11. *And the night following the Lord standing by him, said: Be constant ; for as thou hast testified of me in Jerusalem, so must thou bear witness also at Rome.*

12. *And when day was come, some of the Jews gathered together, and bound themselves under a curse, saying, that they would neither eat nor drink, till they killed Paul.*

13. *And they were more than forty men that had made this conspiracy.*

14. *Who came to the chief priests and the ancients, and said: We have bound ourselves under a great curse that we will eat nothing till we have slain Paul.*

15. *Now therefore do you with the council signify to the tribune, that he bring him forth to you, as if you meant to know something more certain touching him. And we, before he come near, are ready to kill him.*

16. *Which when Paul's sister's son had heard, of their lying in wait, he came, and entered into the castle and told Paul.*

17. *And Paul calling to him one of the centurions, said: Bring this young man to the tribune, for he hath something to tell him.*

18. *And he taking him, brought him to the tribune, and said: Paul the prisoner desired me to bring this young man unto thee, who hath something to say to thee.*

19. *And the tribune taking him by the hand, went aside with him privately and asked him: What is it that thou hast to tell me?*

20. *And he said: The Jews have agreed to desire thee, that thou wouldst bring forth Paul to-morrow into the council, as if they meant to inquire something more certain touching him,*

21. *But do not thou give credit to them ; for there lie in wait for him more than forty men of them, who have bound themselves by oath, neither to eat nor to drink till they have killed him: and they are now ready, looking for a promise from thee.*

22. *The tribune therefore dismissed the young man, charging him that he should tell no man that he had made known these things unto him.*

23. *Then having called two centurions, he said to them : Make ready two hundred soldiers to go as far as Cesarea, and seventy horsemen, and two hundred spearmen for the third hour of the night.*

24. *And provide beasts, that they may set Paul on, and bring him safe to Felix the governor.*

25. *(For he feared lest perhaps the Jews might take him away by force and kill him, and he should afterwards be slandered as if he was to take money). And he wrote a letter after this manner :*

26. *Claudius Lysias to the most excellent governor Felix, greeting.*

27. *This man being taken by the Jews and ready to be killed by them, I rescued coming in with an army, understanding that he is a Roman :*

28. *And meaning to know the cause which they objected unto him, I brought him forth into their council.*

29. *Whom I found to be accused concerning questions of their law ; but having nothing laid to his charge worthy of death or of bands.*

30. *And when I was told of ambushes that they had prepared for him, I sent him to thee, signifying also to his accusers to plead before thee. Farewell.*

31. *Then the soldiers, according as it was commanded them, taking Paul, brought him by night to Antipatris.*

32. *And the next day leaving the horsemen to go with him, they returned to the castle.*

33. *Who when they were come to Cesarea, and had delivered the letter to the governor, did also present Paul before him.*

34. *And when he had read it, and had asked of what province he was : and understood that he was of Cilicia :*

35. *I will hear thee, said he, when thy accusers come. And he commanded him to be kept in Herod's judgment-hall.*

ANALYSIS.

Placed before the Council, Paul is treated contumeliously by the High Priest (1-2). The Apostle reproaches him and then apologizes for having addressed him so as he was ignorant of the character and office of his assailant (3-6). The great dissension between the two leading sects, the Pharisees and Sadducees, that composed the Council. Owing to the great clamour, the Tribune has Paul brought into the Castle (10). A conspiracy entered into by the Jews to murder him, the timely disclosure of it to the Tribune by the son of Paul's sister (12-22). Energetic means adopted by the Tribune to defeat these wicked designs, and save Paul from assassination who is dispatched at once to Cæsarea under a strong escort, with a letter explaining all to the Governor (23-35).

Commentary.

1. Paul looks steadfastly on the council, in order to scan the character of the judges, of whom some were, no doubt, known to him. It was by this council, he was commissioned to go to Damascus to persecute the Christians (ix. 1, 2). He might have wished to see the relative number of Pharisees and Sadducees.

"Council." Greek *Sanhedrim.* "Have conversed," &c. I so conducted myself during life, believing what I did to be right, as to maintain a good conscience ; and this even when persecuting the Christians

Text.

1. *And Paul looking upon the council, said : Men brethren, I have conversed with all good conscience before God, until this present day.*

Text.	Commentary.

(xxvi. 9). This showed a strong conviction of self-innocence, even after the tumults and furious uproar, that lately took place on his account.

"Before God." In God's sight, who searches the heart, "until this present day," both before and after my conversion Even in persecuting, he acted up to the convictions of his mind.

2. *And the high - priest Ananias commanded them that stood by him to strike him on the mouth.*

2. "To strike him," &c. A glaring violation of every form of law and justice.

"Ananias the high priest." He had been formerly high priest; but, not so now. The office of high priest was now vacant, after the last high priest, Jonathan, was murdered at the instigation of Felix (Josephus, Antiq., lib. xx. c. 10). Ananias having formerly filled the office of high priest is now termed such; and probably, by the consent of its members, was called on by the *Sanhedrim* to preside at their deliberations. Paul's confident assertion of his innocence, as they wished to find him guilty, roused them to fury.

3. *Then Paul said to him: God shall strike thee, thou whited wall. For sittest thou to judge me according to the law, and contrary to the law commandest me to be struck?*

3. "God shall strike." This was a *prediction* founded on God's justice, who would not allow such an outrage to go unpunished. It was verified. Ananias was slain on the occasion of the robbers under Manahen taking possession of the city. He was dragged forth from the aqueduct and slain. (Josephus de Bello, lib. ii., c. xvii. 8).

"Thou whited wall," conveys the idea of hypocrisy. Pretending to act as a just judge, he glaringly violated the commonest forms of justice. Our Lord applies a similar epithet to the Pharisees (Matthew xxiii. 27).

"According to the Law" of Moses, which gave every man the right to defend himself. With this right the high priest unjustly interfered.

4. *And they that stood by said: Dost thou revile the high-priest of God?*

4. "Dost thou revile?" &c. Speak disrespectfully. Though not the high priest, he on this occasion, occupied the place of high priest.

5. *And Paul said: I knew not, brethren, that he is the high - priest. For it is written: Thou shalt not speak evil of the prince of thy people.*

5. "I knew not," &c. Probably Paul knew who he was, being deposed at this time from the office of high priest. Now he presided at the invitation of others. Thus the words would mean, that he did not address Ananias, as being really high priest. Had he been really high priest, even though guilty of manifest injustice, Paul, out of respect for his office, would not have addressed him as he did. But not being high priest, and having perpetrated an act of gross injustice, the fact of his occupying a place, which was not his own, gave him no claim to the respect due to one who was in reality a ruler of the people. The Greek according to some (Beelen, &c.) should be rendered; "I did not know that *there is a high priest.*" This he would say from his knowledge of the state of things, the corrupt sale and purchase of the high priesthood, and the vacancy, which occurred, and, as far as Paul could know, not yet filled up. Nor could he recognise as high priest, a man guilty of

Commentary.

such gross injustice. "For it is written" (Exod. xxii 28). Paul quotes it, to show he would not knowingly violate the law.

"*The prince of the people*." This is a general precept inculcating respect to all men in authority, having no particular reference to the high priest. But, as the office of high priest was one of great moment, Paul says he would observe the general precept in regard to him, had he known him to be such.

6. Knowing from his former acquaintance with the members and their character.

"Pharisees" and "Sadducees," (see Matthew iii. 7, Commentary on).

He wishes to enlist in his favour a great number of the members, by a kind of side issue, in introducing the much controverted question, especially among the Pharisees and Sadducees, regarding the Resurrection of the dead.

"A Pharisee," formerly when professing Judaism.

7. "The multitude," composing the *Sanhedrim.*

he had so said, there arose a dissension between the Pharisees and the Sadducees; and the multitude was divided.

8. For the Sadducees say that there is no resurrection, neither angel, nor spirit: but the Pharisees confess both.

9. "If a spirit or an angel." The chief distinctive doctrine of the Pharisees was, the Resurrection of the dead. The opposite was the case with the Sadducees, which Paul well knew. He turns to account on this occasion, his knowledge of their discordant feelings and opinions.

10. It was on account of his knowing, that Paul was a Roman citizen, that the Tribune felt much interest in his safety.

sion, the tribune, fearing lest Paul should be pulled in pieces by them, commanded the soldiers to go down, and to take him by force from among them, and to bring him into the castle.

11. "Night following." How this consoling and encouraging apparition took place is not mentioned. It conveyed an assurance that Paul's mode of acting before the *Sanhedrim* was pleasing to our Lord. There is no allusion to a dream or ecstasy. Hence, many hold it occurred while Paul was awake. He ardently desired to visit Rome (xix. 21). He now receives an assurance that his wishes will be gratified. "*Constant,*" in Greek "take courage," "be without fear."

Text.

6. And Paul knowing that the one part were Sadducees, and the other Pharisees, cried out in the council: Men brethren, I am a Pharisee, the son of Pharisees: concerning the hope and resurrection of the dead I am called in question.

7. And when

9. And there arose a great cry. And some of the Pharisees rising up, strove, saying: We find no evil in this man. What if a spirit hath spoken to him, or an angel?

10. And when there arose a great dissen-

11. And the night following the Lord standing by him, said: Be constant; for as thou hast testified of me in Jerusalem, so must thou bear witness also at Rome.

Text.	Commentary.

12. *And when day was come, some of the Jews gathered*

12. Some of the Jews, over forty in number (*v.* 13) entered into a wicked conspiracy to "kill Paul," binding themselves "under a curse," an *anathema*, under penalty of divine vengeance, not to eat, &c.

together, and bound themselves under a curse, saying, that they would neither eat nor drink, till they had killed Paul.

13. *And they were more than forty men that had made this conspiracy.*

14. *Who came to the chief priests and the ancients, and said: We have bound ourselves under a great curse that we will eat nothing till we have slain Paul.*

14. This appeal of a band of murderous assassins to the supreme Tribunal of the nation to become sharers in their guilt, shows the low moral condition of the Jewish nation, at the time.

15. *Now therefore do you with the council signify to*

15. "Before he come near." So that the *Sanhedrim* might be exonerated from all suspicion of being privy to the murderous design and not be accountable to the Roman authorities.

the tribune, that he bring him forth to you, as if you meant to know something more certain touching him. And we, before he come near, are ready to kill him.

16. *Which when Paul's sister's son had heard, of their lying in wait, he came, and entered into the castle and told Paul.*

16. How this young man knew of it, cannot be ascertained. The forty conspirators themselves did not seem to be very reticent, as they disclosed it to the *Sanhedrim.* "Entered the castle." Likely, as a Roman citizen, still untried and unconvicted the Apostle was not closely guarded, and might see his friends.

17. *And Paul calling to him one of the centurions, said:*

17-21. 21. "Expecting a promise from thee." Hoping he would send Paul to the council, and then murder him in the passage from the castle to the council room.

Bring this young man to the tribune, for he hath something to tell him.

18. *And he taking him, brought him to the tribune, and said: Paul the prisoner desired me to bring this young man unto thee, who hath something to say to thee.*

19. *And the tribune taking him by the hand, went aside with him privately and asked him: What is it that thou hast to tell me?*

20. *And he said: The Jews have agreed to desire thee, that thou wouldst bring forth Paul to-morrow into the council, as if they meant to inquire something more certain touching him,*

21. *But do not thou give credit to them ; for there lie in wait for him more than forty men of them, who have bound themselves by oath, neither to eat nor to drink till they have killed him: and they are now ready, looking for a promise from thee.*

22. *The tribune therefore dismissed the young man, charging him that he should tell no man that he had made known these things unto him.*

23. *Then having called two centurions, he said to them: Make ready two hundred soldiers to go as far as Cæsarea, and seventy*

23. "Two centurions," each in command of one hundred men. "Cæsarea," where the Roman governor ordinarily resided, about sixty (60) miles from Jerusalem. "Two hundred soldiers," heavy-armed foot soldiers, who were to guard him and conduct him safely out of Jerusalem. It was not meant they would proceed to Cæsarea. The horsemen only did this (32). "Seventy horsemen." "Horsemen "

Commentary.

were usually attached to foot soldiers and accompanied them. " Two hundred spearmen." The Greek δεξιολαβους is found only here in the New Testament, and never in any classical writers. In strict Etymology, it means *right hand holders*, such as *take* or *apprehend the right hand*. The Vulgate understands it of those who hold javelins or *spears*. Likely, they were armed with *darts*, and attended on the Tribune personally, as a body guard. He instructed the centurions to have this imposing body of soldiers in readiness for setting out, as he knew the enemies of Paul to be reckless desperadoes, banditti, ready for any crime, however enormous or shocking.

"From the third hour of the night," which according to Roman computation of time, then adopted in Judea, corresponded with our 9 o'clock. The Tribune wished them to leave Jerusalem by night ; for, if such an array of soldiers were seen to accompany Paul, it is hard to say what resistance might be organised.

24. "Provide beasts to set Paul on," so that, as the journey was long, about seventy miles, there might be an exchange of horses or asses, the more easily and expeditiously to compass their journey.

25. This verse is wanting in all Greek copies and most Latin MSS. of the Vulgate, as far as "and he wrote a letter," &c., which is acknowledged to be genuine.

26. "Most excellent," a title of office. "Governor Felix." He got this title, although he was only deputy. He was a freedman of Antonia, mother of Claudius. His vices are depicted by Tacitus. He governed with all the authority of a king and the insolence of a slave.

"*Per omnem sævitiam ac libidinem jus regium servili ingenio in Judeæ Provincia exercuit.*

A copy of this letter may have been given to Paul or Luke on their arrival, as the letter given him, purports to be a verbal copy of the original.

27. "I rescued coming in with an army," the band of soldiers under my command, "understanding," &c., Lysias claims credit for having rescued a Roman citizen, though, in reality, he did not know him to be such, till he was about scourging him, untried (xxii. 26).

Text.

horsemen, and two hundred spearmen for the third hour of the night.

24. And provide beasts, that they may set Paul on, and bring him safe to Felix the governor.

25. (For he feared lest perhaps the Jews might take him away by force and kill him, and he should afterwards be slandered as if he was to take money.) And he wrote a letter after this manner :

26. Claudius Lysias to the most excellent governor Felix, greeting.

27. This man being taken by the Jews, and ready to be killed by them, I rescued coming in with an army, understanding that he is a Roman :

Text.	Commentary.

28. *And mean-*
ing to know the cause which they objected unto him, I brought him forth into their council.

29. *Whom I found to be accused concerning question of their law; but having nothing laid to his charge worthy of death or of bands.*

30. *And when I was told of ambushes that they had prepared for him, I sent him to thee, signifying also to his accusers to plead before thee. Farewell.*

28. " Nothing worthy of death," acording to Roman law.

31. *Then the soldiers, according as it was commanded them, taking Paul, brought him by night to Antipatris.*

32. *And the next day, leaving the horse-men to go with him, they returned to the castle.*

31, 32. "Antipatris." Twenty-six (26) miles from Cæsarea, and about forty-two (42) from Jerusalem.

Their journey continued during the night. They left at 9 o'clock, and reached early the following morning, probably, about 6 or 7 o'clock a.m. As they were now out of the reach of pursuit, these two hundred (200) foot or heavy-armed soldiers, and two hundred (200) spearsmen returned to their barracks, leaving the horsemen to conduct Paul to Cæsarea.

33. *Who when they were come to Cæsarea, and had delivered the letter to the governor, did also present Paul before him.*

34. *And when he had read it, and had asked of what province he was: and understood that he was of Cilicia:*

34. Knowing him to be a Roman citizen, he wished to know from what province, as it might involve a question of jurisdiction.   Tharsus, the capital of Cilicia; was in the Province of Syria, of which Felix was governor, as well as of Palestine.

35. *I will hear thee, said he, when thy accusers come. And he commanded him to be kept in Herod's judgment-hall.*

35. " Herod's judgment hall." This was formerly Herod's palace, built and magnificently adorned by him. It afterwards became the residence of the Roman Governors. In it, or attached to it, was a place of confinement for special prisoners.

Paul before

Felix —

CHAPTER XXIV.

1. And after five days, the high-priest, Ananias, came down, with some of the ancients, and one Tertullus, an orator, who went to the governor, against Paul.

2. And Paul being cited, Tertullus began to accuse him, saying: Whereas through thee we live in much peace, and many things are rectified by thy foresight,

3. We accept it always, and in all places, most excellent Felix, with all thankfulness.

4. But that I be no further tedious to thee, I beseech thee, of thy clemency, to hear us in a few words.

5. We have found this a pestilent man, and raising seditions among all the Jews throughout the whole world, and author of the sedition of the sect of the Nazarens:

6. Who also attempted to profane the temple: whom we apprehended, and would have judged according to our law.

7. But Lysias, the tribune, coming upon us, took him away with great violence out of our hands.

8. Commanding his accusers to come to thee: from whom, thou being judge, mayest know all these things, of which we accuse him.

9. And the Jews also assented, and said that these things were so.

10. Then Paul answered, (the governor making a sign to him to speak) Knowing that for many years thou hast been judge over this nation, I will with good courage answer for myself.

11. For thou mayest understand, that there are yet but twelve days, since I went up to adore in Jerusalem:

12. And neither in the temple did they find me disputing with any man, or causing any concourse of the people, neither in the synagogues,

13. Nor in the city: neither can they prove to thee the things of which they now accuse me.

14. But this I confess to thee, that according to the way, which they call a heresy, so do I serve the Father, and my God, believing all things which are written in the law and the prophets:

15. Having hope in God, which these also themselves look for, that there shall be a resurrection of the just and unjust.

16. In this I myself also study to have always a conscience without offence towards God, and towards men.

17. Now, after many years, I came to bring alms to my nation, and offerings, and vows.

18. In which they found me purified in the temple: not with a crowd, nor with a tumult.

19. But certain Jews of Asia, who ought to be present before thee, and to accuse, if they had anything against me.

20. Or let these men themselves say, if they found in me any iniquity, when standing before the council,

21. *Except it be for this one voice only, that I cried out, standing among them : That concerning the resurrection of the dead am I judged this day by you.*

22. *And Felix put them off, knowing most certainly of this way, saying : When Lysias, the tribune, shall come down, I will hear you.*

23. *And he commanded a centurion to keep him, and to let him be easy, and that he should not hinder any of his friends to minister to him.*

24. *And after some days, Felix coming with Drusilla, his wife, who was a Jewess, called for Paul, and heard from him the faith, which is in Christ Jesus.*

25. *And as he treated of justice, and chastity, and of the judgment to come, Felix being terrified, answered : For this time, go thy way : but at a convenient time, I will send for thee.*

26. *Hoping also withal, that money would be given him by Paul : for which account he also frequently sent for him, and spoke with him.*

27. *But when two years were ended, Felix had for successor Portius Festus. And being willing to gratify the Jews, he left Paul a prisoner.*

ANALYSIS.

Grave charges against Paul before the Governors by the Jews who came down to Cæsarea to accuse him, employing, at the same time, an advocate to plead their cause (1-9). Paul's defence and reply, challenging proof and proclaiming his faith in the Resurrection (10-21). Felix puts off the discussion, and with his wife, Drusilla, a Jewess, heard from Paul the chief points of the Christian faith (22-24). Terrified at the teaching of Paul regarding judgment to come, he at once dismisses him with the declaration, he would hear him at a future day, and often conversed with him in hope of receiving money from him. On giving up the office of Governor, he leaves Paul in chains to gratify the Jews (25-27).

Text.

1. *And after five days, the high-priest, Ananias, came down, with some of the ancients, and one Tertullus, an orator, who went to the governor, against Paul.*

Commentary.

1. "And after five days." How these days are to be computed, or when they commenced, whether from the arrival of Paul at Cæsarea or his departure from Jerusalem, is not agreed upon by commentators, nor does it matter much one way or the other. Likely it means five days after Paul reached Cæsarea. A deputation from the *Sanhedrim* naturally headed by Ananias, the acting high-priest, came down from Jerusalem bringing with them one Tertullus, a Roman lawyer, to urge their accusations against Paul before Felix, as they themselves were not well acquainted with the forms of Roman pleadings.

2. *And Paul being cited, Tertullus began to accuse him, saying: Whereas through thee we live in much peace, and many things are rectified by thy foresight,*

2. "Called for" from his prison in Herod's Hall. "We live in much peace." He commences in a complimentary style, almost amounting to flattery, in order to gain the good will of the judge. Although Felix was by no means a good man, still some good acts were done under his administration, calculated to establish order in Judea. Among the rest he apprehended a band of robbers, headed by Eleazar, and sent them to Rome for punishment (Josephus, Antiq., lib. xii. c. vii.) and arrested the Egyptian false prophet (c. xxi. 38 ; De Bello, c. xiii. 2).

"Thy Providence." Foresight, prudence.

Commentary.

3. "Accept it." Admit that these blessings are owing to thy fore-sight. "Always." Whether in your presence or absence. "Most *excellent* Felix." A title of place or position.

4. *But that I be no further tedious to thee, I beseech thee, of thy clemency, to hear us in a few words.*

5. "Pestilent man." Turbulent, a very plague itself.
"And raising seditions." Exciting tumults by his preaching against the Law of Moses, &c.
"And author." In Greek, *ringleader*. The words "of the sedition" are not in the Greek, which runs thus: "*ringleader of the sect of the Nazarenes.*" The Greek for "sect" is *heresy*, a term taken sometimes in a good and sometimes in a bad sense.
"Nazarenes." A term of contempt applied to the Christians, our Blessed Lord being from Nazareth.

6. "Gone about." Exerted himself "to profane the temple." An unfounded charge refuted by the Apostle (*v.* 18).
"Have judged." Condemned and punished "according to our law," which strictly interdicts the introduction of strangers into the temple.

7. Far from proceeding according to law or justice, they would have assassinated him on the spot only for the timely interference of Lysias.

8, 9. Whether they examined individually or spoke in a body, is not stated. They unanimously confirmed the false statements of Tertullus.
of whom, thou being judge, mayest know all these things, of which we accuse him.
9. *And the Jews also assented, and said that these things were so.*

10. "Governor." Procurator over Judea. *Felix* .
"Many years." About seven (7) years, which might be termed "*many*," compared with the short reign of others who preceded him. It was a time sufficiently long to enable him to become acquainted with Jewish usages. In his exordium, Paul, unlike Tertullus, refrains from flattering him, relying solely on the justice of his cause, which Felix had experience enough to be able to discern.

11. "Understand." Ascertain from duly examining witnesses. "Twelve days." A period too short for creating a tumult. He commences by absolutely denying the *charges* made against him.
"To adore." His sole object, and not to excite tumult or sedition.

Text.

3. *We accept it always, and in all places, most excellent Felix, with all thankfulness.*

5. *We have found this a pestilent man, and raising seditions among all the Jews throughout the whole world, and author of the sedition of the sect of the Nazarenes:*

6. *Who also attempted to profane the temple: whom we apprehended, and would have judged according to our law.*

7. *But Lysias, the tribune, coming upon us, took him away with great violence out of our hands,*

8. *Commanding his accusers to come to thee*

10. *Then Paul answered, (the governor making a sign to him to speak) Knowing that for many years thou hast been judge over this nation, I will with good courage answer for myself.*

11. *For thou mayest understand that there are yet but twelve days, since I went up to adore in Jerusalem.*

Q

12. *And neither in the temple did they find me disputing with any man, or causing any concourse of the people, neither in the synagogues,*

13. *Nor in the city: neither can they prove to thee the things of which they now accuse me.*

14. *But this I confess to thee, that according to the way, which they call a heresy, so do I serve the Father, and my God, believing all things which are written in the law and the prophets.*

15. *Having hope in God, which these also themselves look for, that there shall be a resurrection of the just and unjust.*

16. *I this I myself also study to have a conscience without offence towards God, and towards men.*

12. He denies the charges made by Tertullus (*v.* 5). His conduct everywhere was remarkably pacific.

13. He challenges enquiry and investigation.

14. In this and the following verse he addresses himself to the charge of being a "ringleader of the Nazarene sect" (*v.* 5), openly professing his Christian faith. He admits his Christian belief. But, in such a way, as to carefully observe the law of his Fathers, carrying out all that was propounded in the law and the Prophets, having the same hopes his adversaries themselves entertained and cherished.

"According to the sect." In Greek, the "*way,*" the Christian religion (xix. 23; ix. 2), the religious *way* in which they walked—"which they call heresy" (*v.* 5). I do adhere to it, without abandoning the worship of "the Father and my God." The word "heresy" here does not imply "*error of doctrine;*" but a certain profession of faith, distinctive ideas on religious matters.

"So I serve." Continue, as heretofore, "to serve the Father and my God." The fact of my having been found in the temple *worshipping,* is a proof that in my new religious profession I have not abandoned the religion of my Fathers as propounded in the law and the Prophets.

15. "Having hope," a firm hope, founded in the Divine promises, what some of those men themselves, members of the *Sanhedrim,* my accusers here present look to and expect to be realized, "that there shall be a Resurrection," &c. He refers to such of the deputation as were Pharisees. Josephus (Bello, xviii. 13; II. viii. 14) tells us that the Pharisees maintained the resurrection of the just only. This is denied by others who assert that the body of the Pharisees held the general resurrection of all, though a few of them may have only believed in the resurrection of the just only.

16. "Herein." With this view to future resurrection.

"Do I endeavour." Exert myself to act up to the dictates of conscience, and lead a life such as will enable me to avoid giving offence to God or man in the discharge of my duty whether of a *public* or *private* nature.

Commentary.

17. "Many years'" absence from Jerusalem, far from having any intention of desecrating the temple, I came for quite a different object, to be the bearer of "alms," charities collected from several churches, "to my nation," to the distressed poor among the saints; "and offerings" to be presented to God in the temple, "and vows." These latter words are not found in the Greek.

In this verse, he refutes the charge of Tertullus (*v.* 6), that he intended profaning the temple.

18. "In which." In the midst of which occupations. "Found purified." Going through the process of finishing my vow (xxi. 24) and this, in a quiet way.

"Certain Jews of Asia" Minor who, if they saw him guilty of any improper act or of any crime, should be present and come forward to prove it before the judge.

20. "Or," else, in default to prove, on their part, that I desecrated the temple, let these very men here present testify as to my conduct anywhere else. "Standing before their council" (xxiii. 1). He challenges those present, in regard to his conduct when standing before their council.

21. Their only one subject of complaint against me, when standing before their council (xxiii. 6) was the declaration or utterance made by me, in a loud voice, "concerning the Resurrection of the Dead," &c. If of this they complain, let them say so. This is more or less ironical. They impute to him as a crime, what many of themselves maintained.

22. "Put them off." Adjourned further enquiry—"of this way" the tenets of the Christian religion, which he knew were not prejudicial to the public safety, nor could he with the knowledge he had, feel warranted in looking on Paul, the chief promulgator of Christianity, as a dangerous character.

As Governor or Procurator of Judea, he must have become acquainted with the teachings of a religion propagated and professed far and near. He could not, therefore, condemn Paul. On the other hand, it might not be prudent to release Paul and declare him blameless, as this would displease the Jews whose good will, on grounds of public policy, and personal safety, lest they might denounce him at Rome, he was anxious to gain. So, he adopts a middle course, viz., to await the

Text.

17. *Now, after many years, I came to bring alms to my nation, and offerings, and vows.*

18. *In which they found me purified in the temple: not with a crowd, nor with a tumult.*

19. *But certain Jews of Asia, who ought to be present before thee, and to accuse, if they had anything against me.*

20. *Or et these men themselves say, if they found in me any iniquity, when standing before the council,*

21. *Except it be for this one voice only, that I cried out, standing among them: That concerning the resurrection of the dead am I judged this day by you.*

22. *And Felix put them off, knowing most certainly of this way, saying: When Lysias, the tribune, shall come down, I will hear you.*

Text.

Commentary.

arrival of Lysias, a most important witness, fully cognizant of the whole case, from its very inception.

23. *And he commanded a centurion to keep him, and to let him be easy, and that he should not hinder any of his friends to minister to him.*

23. Clearly, Felix, convinced of Paul's innocence, wished to treat him most leniently, allowing his friends free access, who might furnish him with money to bribe Felix, and procure his release.

"Easy." Freed from his chains, in free custody, in charge of the centurion.

24. *And after some days, Felix coming with Drusilla, his wife, who was a Jewess, called for Paul, and heard from him the faith, which is in Christ Jesus.*

24. "Drusilla, his wife." She was daughter of Herod Agrippa, the elder, who put James the Greater to death, and imprisoned Peter (c. xii). She was sister of Agrippa the younger, spoken of in the next chapter. She married Azizus, King of Emesa, and left him to marry Governor Felix, who fell in love with her, thus living in adultery (Josephus, Antiq., lib. xx., c. vii.). She bore a very bad reputation.

"Sent for Paul." Likely to gratify his adulterous wife, who, being a Jewess, was curious to know the teachings and principles of Christianity, as contradistinguished from those of Judaism, the religion she herself professed.

"The faith," &c. The whole Christian teaching and principles of the Christian religion.

25. *And as he treated of justice, and chastity, and the judgment to come, Felix being terrified, answered: For this time, go thy way: but at a convenient time I will send for thee.*

25. "Treated of justice," &c. Among other points of Christian teaching, he, with Apostolic courage and intrepidity, discoursed fully on these unwelcome truths, the very points which came directly home to the souls of his hearers. Unlike pleaders who treat of topics calculated to please and conciliate the favor of their judges, Paul, fearing not the countenance of the mighty, standing a bound criminal, before a judge, who had power to release him, courageously sets before him the grave moral duties, which Felix signally outraged, and those leading virtues, in which he was notoriously wanting.

"Justice," which involves not only interior rectitude and sanctification in regard to God ; but also the relations of fair dealings with our fellow-men. In this, Felix was notoriously wanting. He was an unjust, partial judge, open to bribes in his official capacity (*v.* 26). Tacitus says of him, "*cuncta malefacta sibi impune ratus*" (Annal. xii. 54). "*Per omnem sævitiam et libidinem jus regium servili ingenio exercuit.*" (Hist. v. 9).

"And chastity." The Greek word εγκρατειας, will mean this, in a special way. In general, it denotes self-control, mastery over the passions that subserve sensuality. It had special significance when addressed to this adulterous, sensual judge.

"Judgment to come," treated heretofore in the Areopagus, at Athens (xvii. 31). In order to stimulate them not to resist the warnings of conscience in regard to their sinful state, he proposes the dread judg-

Felix, a grafter.

Commentary.

ment of God, who will hereafter sit in judgment on them and punish their crimes. The Greek has "*the* judgment" a topic well-known to Drusilla, a Jewess.

"Felix being terrified." Considering his grievous sins and the punishment in store for him.   Wonderful effect of God's Word, which made a haughty judge, wielding supreme power, tremble in presence of his bound captive.   It is not said, Drusilla, who trampled on the laws of God and of her Fathers, was affected.   Having heard of this before, she became hardened and obdurate.

"A convenient time." Felix was alarmed for the moment.   Sunk in the mire of sensuality and sin, he became insensible to everything else, *save* present sensual gratification.

26. He knew the friends of Paul would make any sacrifice to obtain his release.   It was solely with the view of getting a bribe, he sent for him and spoke with him so often.

The stern prohibition of the Julian Law, in regard to governors accepting bribes, and discrediting their government at home, thus turning their administration into mean traffic, was disregarded by the Roman governors, in distant provinces.   Paul was proof against his base insinuations and hints, in regard to offering a bribe.   Being innocent, he had a right to be set free.   This was not to be purchased with money.

27. Paul was unjustly detained a prisoner for two years, the governor hoping to tire out his patience and have his own avarice gratified.

"Willing to show the Jews a pleasure." Wishing to save himself from further accusations.   In this, he did not succeed.   They accused him at Rome, which caused his removal.   Josephus tells us (Antiq. xx. 8), that some of the chief men of Cæsarea, accused him at Rome, before Nero, of wicked deeds and unjust administration.   This caused his removal.   But, the influence of his brother Pallas—himself too a manumised slave—Nero's favourite, saved him from further and condign punishment.

Text.

26. Hoping also withal, that money would be given him by Paul: for which account he also frequently sent for him, and spoke with him.

27. But when two years were ended, Felix had for successor Portius Festus. And being willing to gratify the Jews, he left Paul a prisoner.

CHAPTER XXV

1. *Now when Festus was come into the province, after three days he went up to Jerusalem from Cæsarea.*

2. *And the chief priests, and principal men of the Jews went unto him against Paul: and they besought him,*

3. *Requesting favour against him, that he would command him to be brought to Jerusalem, laying wait to kill him in the way.*

4. *But Festus answered: That Paul was kept in Cæsarea: and that he himself would very shortly depart thither.*

5. *Let them therefore, saith he, among you that are able, go down with me, and accuse him, if there be any crime in the man.*

6. *And having tarried among them no more than eight or ten days, he went down to Cæsarea, and the next day he sat in the judgment-seat: and commanded Paul to be brought.*

7. *Who being brought, the Jews stood about him, who were come down from Jerusalem, objecting many and grievous causes which they could not prove;*

8. *Paul making answer for himself: Neither against the law of the Jews, nor against the temple, nor against Cæsar, have I offended in anything.*

9. *But Festus willing to do the Jews a favour, answering Paul, said: Wilt thou go up to Jerusalem, and there be judged of these things before me?*

10. *Then Paul said: I stand at Cæsar's judgment-seat where I ought to be judged. To the Jews I have done no injury, as thou very well knowest.*

11. *For if I have injured them, or have committed anything worthy of death, I refuse not to die. But if there be none of these things whereof they accuse me, no man may deliver me to them: I appeal to Cæsar.*

12. *Then Festus having conferred with the council, answered: Hast thou appealed to Cæsar? To Cæsar shalt thou go.*

13. *And after some days King Agrippa and Bernice came down to Cæsarea to salute Festus.*

14. *And as they tarried there many days, Festus told the king of Paul, saying: A certain man was left prisoner by Felix.*

15. *About whom, when I was at Jerusalem, the chief priests and the ancients of the Jews came unto me, desiring condemnation against him.*

16. *To whom I answered: It is not the custom of the Romans to condemn any man, before that he who is accused have his accusers present, and have liberty to make his answer, to clear himself of the things laid to his charge.*

17. *When therefore they were come hither, without any delay, on the day following, sitting in the judgment-seat, I commanded the man to be brought.*

18. *Against whom, when the accusers stood up, they brought no accusation of things which I thought ill of:*

19. *But had certain questions of their own superstition against him, and of one Jesus deceased, whom Paul affirmed to be alive.*

20. *I therefore being in a doubt of this manner of question, asked him whether he would go to Jerusalem, and there be judged of these things.*

21. *But Paul appealing to be reserved unto the hearing of Augustus, I commanded him to be kept, till I might send him to Cæsar.*

22. *And Agrippa said to Festus: I would also hear the man myself. To-morrow, said he, thou shalt hear him.*

23. *And on the next day when Agrippa and Bernice were come with great pomp, and had entered into the hall of audience, with the tribunes and principal men of the city, at Festus's commandment, Paul was brought forth.*

24. *And Festus saith: King Agrippa, and all ye men who are here present with us, you see this man, about whom all the multitude of the Jews dealt with me at Jerusalem, requesting and crying out that he ought not to live any longer.*

25. *Yet have I found nothing that he hath committed worthy of death. But forasmuch as he himself hath appealed to Augustus, I have determined to send him.*

26. *Of whom I have nothing certain to write to my lord. For which cause I have brought him forth before you, and especially before thee, O King Agrippa, that examination being made, I may have what to write.*

27. *For it seemeth to me unreasonable, to send a prisoner and not to signify the things laid to his charge.*

ANALYSIS.

In this Chapter, we have an account of the grievous charges made by the Jewish authorities against Paul to Festus, the new Governor, when he went up to Jerusalem. Their request to have Paul sent up to Jerusalem intending to assassinate him on the way. Paul's defence and appeal to Cæsar (1-11). Festus mentions the case of Paul to Agrippa and Bernice who came to visit him. He utters certain maxims of Roman and natural justice in connexion with the case (12-20). Agrippa desires himself to hear Paul's defence (22). Festus describes the state of the case to Agrippa (23-27).

Commentary.

1. "Province." Judea was made a Roman province.

"Jerusalem," the former capital, the seat of learning and religion, where the rich and learned resided. There he could obtain an accurate knowledge of the province. It was in search of such knowledge, so necessary on entering on the duties of his office, that Festus went up from Cæsarea—the usual residence of the governors—and the capital of the province, so far as the Romans were concerned. Though Jerusalem held its pre-eminence in the eyes of the Jews.

2. "Chief Priests." In some editions it is in the singular, "chief priest."

"Went unto him." Seeking to prejudice him against Paul.

3. They meant to kill him. But God, mindful of His promise to Paul, of being witness at Rome (xxiii. 12) set all their wicked designs at nought.

Text.

1. Now when Festus was come into the province, after three days he went up to Jerusalem from Cæsarea.

2. And the chief priests, and principal men of the Jews, went unto him against Paul: and they besought him,

3. Requesting favour against him, that he would command him to be brought to Jerusalem, laying wait to kill him in the way.

Text.	Commentary.

Text.

4. *But Festus answered: That Paul was kept in Cæsarea: and that he himself would very shortly depart thither.*

5. *Let them therefore, saith he, among you that are able, go down with me, and accuse him, if there be any crime in the man.*

6. *And having tarried among them no more than eight or ten days, he went down to Cæsarea, and the next day he sat in the judgment-seat: and commanded Paul to be brought.*

7. *Who being brought, the Jews stood about him, who were come down from Jerusalem, objecting many and grievous causes, which they could not prove;*

8. *Paul making answer for himself: Neither against the law of the Jews, nor against the temple, nor against Cæsar, have I offended in anything.*

9. *But Festus willing to do the Jews a favour, answering Paul, said: Wilt thou go up to Jerusalem, and there be judged of these things before me?*

10. *Then Paul said: I stand at Cæsar's judgment-seat where I ought to be judged. To the Jews I have done no injury, as thou very well knowest.*

Commentary.

4. Festus, possibly informed by Lysias or some one else of the former conspiracy, refused, as Paul a Roman citizen was now at Cæsarea, the seat of empire. Let them go there (*v.* 5).

6. "Eight or ten days." Some difference of reading in the Greek: but not of any importance.

7. These charges which they failed to prove, were probably the same as those alleged already before Felix (xxiv. 13-19).

8. Paul denied that he violated any law, or transgressed in any way against religion or civil society.

9. Festus at the commencement of his administration wished to conciliate the good will of the Jews.

"Before me." He would not let out of his own hands the cause of a Roman citizen.

10. Paul, who knew the persistent malice of his countrymen, and probably fearing violence, prudently declining the proposal of the governor, who left him free to accede to it or not, at once appeals to the Roman emperor for a fair trial.

"Cæsar." The Roman emperors at the time took the name of "Cæsar," as the kings of Egypt went by the name of *Pharaoh*, each, however, retaining his own proper name also. Nero was, at the time, the reigning emperor. Under him Paul was beheaded.

"Where I ought to be judged." Entitled to a fair trial, which I cannot expect from my countrymen.

"No injury," either in person, property or religion. "As thou knowest." Festus knew that Paul was tried by Felix, and that he was perfectly innocent.

11. Here is shown the magnanimity of Paul. His rights should be respected. If he committed crimes worthy of death, he is prepared to die.

"No man may deliver me," &c. No one had a right to deliver over for punishment an innocent man. The laws of justice and of Rome forbade it, and Festus dare not act against the laws. Festus seemed to be pursuing the same iniquitous, vacillating course adopted by Felix, who kept him two years in unjust detention though conscious of his innocence. Paul appeals, as he had a right to do, to the Roman emperor—the highest tribunal in the empire.

12. "Council." The judges associated with him, composed of military and civil magistrates, in the administration of the province.

13. "After some days." While awaiting some favourable opportunity of sending Paul to Rome on appeal.

"King Agrippa." Son of Agrippa, whose shocking death is recorded (c. xii.). "And Bernice," his sister, who lived with him. (Josephus, Antiq., xx. c. vii. charges her with scandalous incest with her brother.) She bore the repute of being a shocking character. Her relations with Titus, son of the Emperor Vespasian, who took her to Rome as his mistress, are recorded by Suetonius (Titus, c. 7). Titus resolved on marrying her. But public opinion was too strong against it, so he reluctantly dismissed her. "*Dimisit invitus invitam*" (Tacitus, Hist. xi. 81).

"To salute Festus." To pay him a visit of respect as new governor of the province.

14. "Told the king of Paul." Informed him of the cause of Paul, whose trial was probably a matter generally spoken of. Agrippa, being a Jew, might be naturally supposed to feel some interest in his case.

"Left prisoner." Probably, in care of a soldier (xxiv. 23-27).

15. "Sentence of condemnation," &c. Wishing me to pass sentence of condemnation against him.

11. *For if I have injured them, or have committed anything worthy of death, I refuse not to die. But if there be none of these things whereof they accuse me, no man may deliver me to them: I appeal to Cæsar.*

12. *Then Festus having conferred with the council, answered: Hast thou appealed to Cæsar? To Cæsar shalt thou go.*

13. *And after some days King Agrippa and Bernice came down to Cæsarea to salute Festus.*

14. *And as they tarried there many days, Festus told the king of Paul, saying: A certain man was left prisoner by Felix.*

15. *About whom, when I was at Jerusalem, the chief priests and the ancients of the Jews came unto me, desiring condemnation against him.*

Text.

16. *To whom I answered: It is not the custom of the Romans to condemn any man before that he* who is accused have his accusers present, and have liberty to make his answer, to clear himself of the things laid to his charge.

17. When therefore they were come hither, without any delay, on the day following, sitting in the judgment-seat, I commanded the man to be brought.

18. *Against whom, when the accusers stood up, they brought no accusation of things which I thought ill of:*

19. *But had certain questions of their own superstition against him, and of one Jesus deceased, whom Paul affirmed to be alive.*

20. *I therefore being in doubt of this manner of question, asked him whether he would go to Jerusalem, and there be judged of these things.*

21. *But Paul appealing to be reserved unto the hearing of Augustus, I commanded him to be kept, till I might send him to Cæsar.*

22. *And Agrippa said to Festus: I would also hear the man myself.*

Commentary.

16. This just principle of Roman jurisprudence, thoroughly in accordance with natural equity is, unhappily, in many instances departed from in practice. There is no proof, however, that Festus was guilty of violating it. "To condemn anyone." The Greek would mean *to hand over for destruction* (capital punishment) *any one as a favour to another.*

18. No grievous violation of the laws of Rome was proved against him.

19. "Certain questions." Certain disputed points, controverted among them.

"Of their own superstition"—δεισιδαιμονιας—literally, *fear of demons.* Among the Greeks and Romans the term was used to designate the worship of their Gods, as xvii. 22, where it is taken in a good sense, as it was a term he would employ in speaking of his own worship of the Gods. Moreover, on addressing Agrippa, his guest, whom he knew to be a Jew, he certainly would not use the word in an offensive sense any more than would Paul when commencing his address to the Athenians (xvii. 22) whom it was his interest and the interest of his ministry to conciliate and render favourable.

"One Jesus deceased." In Greek, *one deceased Jesus.* It would seem Festus paid no heed to the teaching of Paul regarding the Resurrection of our Lord.

20. I doubted how to give judgment regarding questions of this sort, being wholly ignorant of their nature and import. *Perplexed*, as to the whole matter.

21. Making an appeal. Claiming to be reserved, &c. "Augustus," which signifies *venerable*, worthy of *honour.* This was the surname given to all the Roman emperors from Cæsar Octavianus, to whom it was first given, usually called Augustus Cæsar The name, "Cæsar," which belonged to the Julian family, was also given from the time of Julius Cæsar, the first Roman emperor, to all his successors in the empire. Nero was the reigning emperor at this time.

22. "Agrippa," himself a Jew, doubtless, heard much about our Lord and the Christian following, and was curious to hear the defence of Christianity from its chief champion.
To-morrow, said he, thou shalt hear him.

Commentary.

23. "Great pomp," regal splendour and state; and this in a city, where their father, thirteen (13) years before, died a horrible death.

"Hall of audience," where the judges usually sat to hear and decide cases of litigation.

Text.

23. *And on the next day when Agrippa and Bernice were come with great pomp, and had entered into the hall of audi- ence, with the tribunes and principal men of the city, at Festus's com- mandment, Paul was brought forth.*

24. "All ye men," Jews of Cæsarea, "here present." These also joined in the clamour.

"Dealt with me," appealed to me.

24. *And Fes- tus saith: King Agrippa, and all ye men who*

are here present with us, you see this man, about whom all the multitude of the Jews dealt with me at Jerusalem, requesting and crying out that he ought not to live any longer.

25. *Yet have I found nothing that he hath committed worthy of death. But forasmuch as he himself hath appealed to Augustus, I have determined to send him.*

26. "Of whom" concerning whom. "Nothing certain," definite or precise, nothing against the Laws of the State, the whole accusation having reference to Jewish Laws and Customs, to which I am stranger. "My lord," the Emperor, Nero. The title "lord," though rejected by Augustus and Tiberius, was accepted by Caligula, Claudius and subsequent Emperors. Nero exacted it.

"Brought him before you." As Agrippa was a Jew, acquainted with Jewish laws and usages, Festus hoped to receive some light and information from him on this subject, so as to be able to present a satisfactory statement to the Emperor Nero.

26. *Of whom I have nothing certain to write to my lord. For which cause I have brought him forth before you, and es- pecially before thee, O King Agrippa, that examination being made, I may have what to write.*

27. Festus felt perplexed. Having tried the case, he could not under- stand the nature of the accusations or charges brought against the prisoner who appealed from his jurisdiction. It would be only reasonable, that the judge of appeal should be informed by the inferior judge, who tried the case, of the nature of the charge—the defence, and the reasons adduced on both sides. Of these things Festus was ignorant, and was glad to get some assistance from King Agrippa, a Jew, acquainted with Jewish customs and laws.

"Signify," specify with precision and accuracy, "the things laid to his charge."

"Unreasonable," against reason and law, as well.

27. *For it seemeth to me unreasonable, to send a pri- soner, and not to signify the things laid to his charge.*

CHAPTER XXVI

1. *Then Agrippa said to Paul: Thou art permitted to speak for thyself. Then Paul stretching forth his hand, began to make his answer.*

2. *I think myself happy, O king Agrippa, that I am to answer for myself this day before thee, touching all the things whereof I am accused by the Jews,*

3. *Especially as thou knowest all, both customs and questions that are among the Jews: Wherefore I beseech thee to hear me patiently.*

4. *And my life indeed from my youth, which was from the beginning among my own nation in Jerusalem, all the Jews do know:*

5. *Having known me from the beginning (if they will give testimony) that according to the most sure sect of our religion I lived a Pharisee.*

6. *And now for the hope of the promise that was made by God to the fathers, do I stand subject to judgment:*

7. *Unto which, our twelve tribes, serving night and day, hope to come. For which hope, O king, I am accused by the Jews.*

8. *Why should it be thought a thing incredible, that God should raise the dead?*

9. *And I indeed did formerly think that I ought to do many things contrary to the name of Jesus of Nazareth.*

10. *Which also I did at Jerusalem, and many of the saints did I shut up in prison, having received authority of the chief priests; and when they were put to death, I brought the sentence.*

11. *And oftentimes punishing them, in every synagogue, I compelled them to blaspheme: and being yet more mad against them, I persecuted them even unto foreign cities.*

12. *Whereupon when I was going to Damascus with authority and permission of the chief priests,*

13. *At mid-day, O king, I saw in the way a light from heaven above the brightness of the sun, shining round about me, and them that were in company with me.*

14. *And when we were all fallen down on the ground, I heard a voice speaking to me in the Hebrew tongue: Saul, Saul, why persecutest thou me? It is hard for thee to kick against the goad.*

15. *And I said: Who art thou, Lord? And the Lord answered: I am Jesus whom thou persecutest.*

16. *But rise up and stand upon thy feet: for to this end have I appeared to thee, that I may make thee a minister and a witness of those things which thou hast seen, and of those things wherein I will appear to thee,*

17. *Delivering thee from the people, and from the nations, unto which now I send thee:*

18. *To open their eyes, that they may be converted from darkness to light, and from the power of Satan to God, that they may receive forgiveness of sins, and a lot among the saints by the faith that is in me.*

19. *Whereupon, O king Agrippa, I was not incredulous to the heavenly vision:*

20. *But to them first that are Damascus, and at Jerusalem, and unto all the country of Judea, and to the gentiles did I preach, that they should do penance, and turn to God, doing works worthy of penance.*

21. *For this cause the Jews, when I was in the temple, having apprehended me, went about to kill me.*

22. *But being aided by the help of God, I stand unto this day, witnessing both to small and great, saying no other thing than those which the prophets and Moses did say should come to pass:*

23. *That Christ should suffer, and that he should be the first that should rise from the dead, and should shew light to the people and to the gentiles.*

24. *As he spoke these things, and made his answer, Festus said with a loud voice: Paul, thou art beside thyself: much learning doth make thee mad.*

25. *And Paul said: I am not mad, most excellent Festus, but I speak words of truth and soberness.*

26. *For the king knoweth of these things, to whom also I speak with confidence. For I am persuaded that none of these things are hidden from him. For neither was any of these things done in a corner.*

27. *Believest thou the prophets, O king Agrippa? I know that thou believest.*

28. *And Agrippa said to Paul: In a little thou persuadest me to become a Christian.*

29. *And Paul said: I would to God, that both in a little and in much, not only thou, but also all that hear me this day, should become such as I also am, except these bands.*

30. *And the king rose up, and the governor, and Bernice, and they that sat with them.*

31. *And when they were gone aside, they spoke among themselves, saying: This man hath done nothing worthy of death, or of bands.*

32. *And Agrippa said to Festus: This man might have been set at liberty, if he had not appealed to Cæsar.*

ANALYSIS.

Paul's defence of himself before Agrippa. His early religious Profession (1-7). His zeal in the cause of Judaism (8-11). His conversion to Christainity owing to the vision he saw (13-21). His zeal in preaching the gospel (22). Festus regards him as mad (27).

Commentary.

1. " Permitted." He uses this form, and not, *I permit thee,* on account of the presence of Festus.

"Stretching forth his hand,"—the gesture usually employed by pleaders and orators.

2. The language of courtesy, but not of adulation.

3. "Agrippa," himself a Jew, knew all the Laws, customs, and institutions of the Jews.

"Questions," matters disputed among them.

"Wherefore," because, unlike the Roman Tribunals, by whom all matters connected with the Jewish religion were treated with contempt, he knew and respected everything connected with the Jewish religion.

"I beseech thee to hear me patiently." This I could not expect from the Roman Tribunals, in regard to Jewish customs and Laws.

Text.

1. *Then Agrippa said to Paul: Thou art permitted to speak for thyself. Then Paul stretching forth his hand, began to make his answer.*

2. *I think myself happy, O king Agrippa, that I am to answer for myself this day before thee, touching all the things whereof I am accused by the Jews.*

3. *Especially as thou knowest all, both customs and questions that are among the Jews: Wherefore I beseech thee to hear me patiently.*

Text.	Commentary.
	Paul's object was not to obtain his release, as he knew he was destined for Rome, which he eagerly desired; but to defend his character and furnish Festus with the desired information for Nero's Tribunal.
4. And my life indeed from my youth, which was from the beginning among my own nation in Jerusalem, all the Jews do know:	4. Born at Tharsus, he spent his youth at Jerusalem, whither he was sent for his education. He was brought up at the feet of Gamaliel (xxvi. 3), " all the Jews do know." Likely he was distinguished in the school of Gamaliel for his zeal in the cause of religion. He was known for this, as the commission given him shows (*c.* ix.).
5. Having known me from the beginning (if they will give testimony) that according to the most sure sect of our religion, I lived a Pharisee.	5. " Having known me " (Greek, *foreknown*) "from the beginning," my earliest days (" if they will give testimony ") which they won't do, Paul's conversion being a deadly blow to the Jewish religion. "Most sure." Most strictly observant of the law. "Sect of our religion," that is the sect among the Jews most strictly observant of the laws and traditions of the Jewish religion. "I lived a Pharisee," embraced the doctrines, and practically observed the rules of that strict religious sect.
6. And now for the hope of the promise that was made by God to the fathers, do I stand subject to judgment:	6. " I stand subject," &c., am arraigned and stand subject to trial, " for the hope," &c., on account of the hope which I entertain in common with all the Jewish people. "Of the promise," which I believe to be now fulfilled in regard to the coming of the Messiah, who is to redeem Israel, and what is closely and intimately connected with him—the Resurrection of the Dead, which must naturally follow from His own Resurrection whereby He proved that He was God. The promise *primarily* regards the coming of the Messiah, and secondarily the general Resurrection of all.
7. Unto which, our twelve tribes, serving night and day, hope to come. For which hope, O king, I am accused by the Jews.	7. " Unto which," promise, whereof they are awaiting the fulfilment in their Messiah, and the benefits accruing therefrom. "They hope to come" and see fully realized, and thus enjoy, in due time, all the blessings its realization is sure to carry with it. "Our twelve Tribes." The designation of the Jewish Nation even after *ten* Tribes (10) were carried off into captivity, two only, Juda and Benjamin remaining. They expected the Messiah, "the hope of Israel" (xxviii. 20). In Him, they hoped, and in the attainment of the blessings He was to bestow, especially the Resurrection of the Body, in which, with the exception of a small fragment of the people (the Sadducees) they believed and hoped. "Serving"—(to which is added in the Greek, intently, with zeal)—worshipping, at least externally, in their attendance at His worship in the Temple. They did so as a Nation, while many did not worship in their hearts, " honouring Him with their lips, their hearts far away from Him."

Commentary.

"Day and night," constantly, with untiring zeal and devotion (Luke ii. 37).

The time ordinarily marked out for Sacrifice among the Jews was morning and evening. Hence, it might be said they worshipped "day and night."

"For which hope" entertained by the great mass of my countrymen as well, regarding the promised Messiah, his Resurrection from the dead, the forerunner and cause of the General Resurrection of all, just and unjust.

"I am accused by the Jews." Brought to trial for what they hold in common with me.

8. "Why should it be thought," &c. The meaning will be better seen if we place an interrogation or exclamation after "why," which in Greek will mean, "What!" should it be thought a thing incredible with you," &c. " _You_ " is in the plural, addressed to all present, the Jews, who ought to know something about God's omnipotent power, and Agrippa, who might have been tinged with the scepticism of the Sadducees, some of whom he promoted to the highest offices. He may also have meant to address Festus and his Pagan followers, who rejected as an _absurdity_ the _possibility_ of the Resurrection of Christ and the dead in general, and the teaching regarding it. The Sadducees denied it, as a _fact_. This doctrine being the foundation of all faith, as preached by St. Paul, on this account he puts the question. Likely, he may have intended it for his accusers among the Sadducees there present, and specially addressed to them.

9. The Apostle now gives an account of his conversion to the Christian faith, to which he had been so violently opposed, and showing it in his conduct. "Contrary to the name of Jesus," &c., to eliminate from the earth, the religion, of which he was the head and founder.

10. (See viii. 3.). "Saints," the Christians.

"When they were put to death," or, _when tried_, with a view to their death. "I brought the sentence." The Greek would signify, _I threw in my vote_ against them, as if he was one of those who took a part in the sentence. It means, he was fully an abetting or consenting party (xxii. 20). Although in the Acts we have only an account of the death of Stephen, most likely, many others also, who were not so prominent, and whose death is not, therefore, recorded, were put to death in the general slaughter (c. viii.). The Vulgate reading, "_detuli sententiam_." "I brought the sentence." I was the bearer of the condemnatory sentence, passed on them by the judges, to those on whom devolved the duty of carrying it out. This would favour the opinion of those who do not confine it to St. Stephen, as it was not by a judicial sentence, but by the violence of the rabble Stephen was put to death.

8. _Why should it be thought a thing incredible, that God should raise the dead?_

9. _And I indeed did formerly think that I ought to do many things contrary to the name of Jesus of Nazareth._

10. _Which also I did at Jerusalem, and many of the saints did I shut up in prison, having received authority of the chief priests; and when they were put to death, I brought the sentence._

Text.

11. *And often-times punishing them, in every synagogue, I compelled them to blaspheme: and being yet more mad against them, I persecuted them even unto foreign cities.*

12. *Whereupon when I was going to Damascus with authority and permission of the chief priests,*

13. *At mid-day, O king, I saw in the way a light from heaven above the brightness of the sun, shining round about me, and them that were in company with me.*

14. *And when we were all fallen down on the ground, I heard I voice speaking to me in the Hebrew tongue: Saul, Saul, why persecutest thou me? It is hard for thee to kick against the goad.*

15. *And I said: Who art thou, Lord? And the Lord answered: I am Jesus whom thou persecutest.*

16. *But rise up and stand upon thy feet: for to this end have I appeared to thee, that I may make thee a minister, and a witness of those things which thou hast seen, and of those things wherein I will appear to thee,*

17. *Delivering thee from the people and from the nations, unto which now I send thee:*

18. *To open their eyes, that they may be converted from darkness to light, and from the power of Satan to God, that they may receive forgiveness of sins, and a lot among the saints, by the faith that is in me.*

Commentary.

11. "Compelled." Strove to force them to "blaspheme," deny Jesus, and regard Him as an impostor. In this, he generally failed, the majority of the Christian converts being so staunch and firm. Possibly some few from time to time may have weakly yielded and apostatized.

"Punishing them" (xxii. 19).

"Yet more mad," raging with all the fury of a maniac.

"Foreign cities," outside the confines of Judea. Damascus is specially known as one of them. He may have visited other foreign cities, as well, though not recorded.

16. In this and following verses, Paul dwells on certain circumstances and events not recorded in the history of his conversion (c. ix.) to show, he did not proceed to preach among the Gentiles without being duly commissioned by God. "A minister," preacher of the Gospel . . . and witness (c. xxii. 15).

"Which thou hast seen," when struck down on thy way to persecute the Saints at Damascus.

"And of those things," &c. These words refer to further declarations of God's will (as in c. xxii. 17-18).

17. "From the people," his own countrymen, the Jews. "The nations," the Gentiles, who repaid his sacrifices for them with such ingratitude.

"Unto which I now send thee." Hence his commission to preach to the Gentiles. To this, he calls the attention of Agrippa.

18. "Open their eyes," by holding forth the saving light and truths of the Gospel.

"From darkness," in which they were enveloped and grovelling. "To light," the light of the Gospel, wherein they can discern the truths of faith and the world to come.

"From the power of Satan," who reigns over the children of unbelief, and tyrannizes over them.

"To God," the Eternal ruler and Creator of the universe, the Sovereign benefactor, to whom they are indebted for all they possess, or hope for, either in this world or the next.

"That they may receive forgiveness," &c., through His infinite merits and His blood of the cross.

"A lot," the inheritance in store for the sons of God.

"By the faith," &c., *Faith* is the first condition for obtaining the grace

Commentary.	Text.

Commentary.

of justification. To this other qualities, as necessary conditions, hope, charity, good works, &c., must be added, to obtain justification.

19. "Whereupon." In consequence of the clear, convincing proof, that Jesus, risen from the dead who appeared to me, was the promised Messiah, that he had commissioned me to preach the Gospel.

"I was not incredulous," I at once obeyed "the heavenly vision," obeyed him, who, from heaven, appeared to me. "Vision" is taken for the object of vision. I gave myself over to him, to do his will and obey his commands.

20. He acted as God commanded him, which is described in this verse.

cus, and at Jerusalem, and unto all the country of Judea, and to the gentiles did I preach, that they should do penance, and turn to God, doing works worthy of penance.

21. Because I obeyed God's will, the Jews meant "to kill me."

22. "Help of God," to whom I owe my deliverance from imminent dangers.

"Witnessing," testifying, to what he had seen. "Small," the humble and ignorant, "great," those in exalted station, kings, nobles, learned.

"Saying no other things," &c., advancing nothing strange or novel, but only what was declared in the Old Testament, what "Moses and the Prophets," beforehand announced would take place in due time.

23. "Christ," the Messiah, should lead a hard life, and be put to death—a point which the Jews could not bear, the cross being to them a scandal (1 Cor. i., &c.).

"The first that should rise," &c. "*First*," not in point of time. The Sunamite having been formerly raised by Elias; Lazarus and the son of the Widow of Naim, by our Lord Himself—but, the *head*, the principal of those who rose, the first born, entitled to all the rights and pre-eminence of primogeniture. He raised himself by his own power (John x. 18).

He rose to die no more. He conquered death (1 Cor. xv.).

"To the people," the Jews, to whom he preached in the first place.

"And to the Gentiles," to whom he turned, as was predicted everywhere in the Old Testament, after having been rejected by his own people, the Jews.

Text.

19. *Whereupon, O king Agrippa, I was not incredulous to the heavenly vision:*

20. *But to them first that are at Damas-*

21. *For this cause the Jews, when I was in the temple, having apprehended me, went about to kill me.*

22. *But being aided by the help of God, I stand unto this day, witnessing both to small and great, saying no other thing than those which the prophets, and Moses did say should come to pass:*

23. *That Christ should suffer, and that he should be the first that should rise from the dead, and should show light to the people and to the gentiles.*

Text.

24. *As he spoke these things, and made his answer, Festus said with a loud voice: Paul, thou art beside thyself: much learning doth make thee mad.*

25. *And Paul said: I am not mad, most excellent Festus, but I speak words of truth and soberness.*

26. *For the king knoweth of these things, to whom also I speak with confidence. For I am persuaded that none of these things are hidden from him. For neither was any of these things done in a corner.*

27. *Believest thou the prophets, O king Agrippa? I know that thou believest.*

Commentary.

24. **Festus**, who despised everything connected with the Christian religion, fancied that Paul must be out of his mind to show such earnestness about so absurd a matter, as if it were of any importance whatever. Likely, he regarded the vision spoken of by Paul as a pure imagination, a proof of delirium and insanity. However, on the last day will be found many *who*, like Festus, jeered at religion, and will, when too late, find out their sad mistake. "*Hi sunt quos habuimus in derisum et in similitudinem improperii, nos insensati vitam illorum estimabamus, insaniam,*" &c.

"**Much learning.**" Festus, likely, knew Paul to be a man of letters and educated at Jerusalem, and seeing him defending with such earnestness, what Festus despised, he thought him "mad." This he attributed to excessive application to study, as if learning turned his brain.

25. In his calm reply, respectfully denying the imputation of Festus, Paul exhibits consummate tact and prudence by appealing to Agrippa, who being a Jew, understood these things to which Festus was a stranger, and would thus enlist him on his own side, to bear testimony in his favour with Festus.

"**Most noble Festus,**" the usual title of honour bestowed on Roman Governors.

"**Truth,**" long ago asserted by Moses and the Prophets, and founded on events which certainly took place in connexion with our Redeemer's death and Resurrection. "Truth," opposed to delusion and fraud.

"**Soberness,**" wisdom, indicating a mind free from all derangement, worthy of one, who was commanded to preach the words of an Infinitely veracious God to the nations.

26. "**For the King.**" Agrippa could not be a stranger to the events connected with the Jews, having lived so long in the district, where they occurred. He knew about the Prophecies that regarded the expected Messiah, his death in Jerusalem.

"**I am persuaded,**" thoroughly convinced, "none of these things are hidden," &c., he is well acquainted with them.

"**Any of these things.**" His own conversion to the Christian religion, from being a mad persecutor, was public, calculated to attract public attention. With so remarkable an event and the causes leading thereto, Agrippa must have been acquainted.

27. "**King Agrippa,**" &c. This was addressed to Agrippa to convince him, that from his knowledge of the Prophets and the several predictions regarding our Lord, Paul was only uttering the language of "truth"; that, far from being deranged or "mad," he used words of wisdom and "soberness." Paul anticipates Agrippa's answer, giving him credit for being a religious observer of the Jewish ordinances and for believing the Prophecies.

Commentary.

28. Far from saying he disbelieved the Prophets, or that Paul's defence and arguments were weak, or that all the Prophecies were not fulfilled in Jesus ; far from doubting the miracles that led to Paul's conversion, Agrippa, on the contrary, declares that all he said deeply impressed him ("in a little"). Almost convinced him of the truth of Christianity, and almost persuaded him to embrace it. Some obstacles, however, impeded the operation of grace. Among them were possibly, his unwillingness to give up his sinful life, or to be ranked with the despised followers of the Galilean. Whatever they were, it seems he did not embrace it, and resisted the grace of God.

29. "All that hear me."   Including Festus and his officials.
"Except these bands."   The chains that bound him.

Text.

28. And Agrippa said to Paul : In a little thou persuadest me to become a Christian.

29. And Paul said: I would to God,

that both in a little, and in much, not only thou, but also all that hear me, this day, should become such as I also am, except these bands.

30. And the king rose up, and the governor, and Bernice, and they that sat with them.

31. And when they were gone aside, they spoke among themselves, saying: This man hath done nothing worthy of death, or of bands.

32. And Agrippa said to Festus: This man might have been set at liberty, if he had not appealed to Cæsar.

CHAPTER XXVII

1. And when it was determined that he should sail into Italy, and that Paul, with the other prisoners, should be delivered to a centurion, named Julius, of the band Augusta.

2. Going on board a ship of Adrumetum, we launched, meaning to sail by the coasts of Asia, Aristarchus, the Macedonian of Thessalonica, continuing with us.

3. And the day following we came to Sidon. And Julius treating Paul courteously, permitted him to go to his friend, and to take care of himself.

4. And when we had launched from thence, we sailed under Cyprus, because the winds were contrary.

5. And sailing over the sea of Cilicia, and Pamphilia, we came to Lystra, which is in Lycia.

6. And there the centurion finding a ship of Alexandria sailing into Italy, removed us into it.

7. And when for many days we had sailed slowly, and were scarce come over against Gnidus, the wind not suffering us, we sailed near Crete by Salmone:

8. And with much a-do sailing by it, we came into a certain place, which is called Good-havens, nigh to which was the city of Thalassa.

9. And when much time was spent, and when sailing now was dangerous, because the fast was now passed, Paul conforted them,

10. Saying to them: Ye men, I see that the voyage beginneth to be with injury and much damage, not only of the lading and ship, but also of our lives.

11. But the centurion believed the pilot and the master of the ship, more than those things, which were said by Paul.

12. And whereas it was not a commodious haven to winter in, the greatest part gave counsel to sail thence, if by any means they might reach Phenice to winter there, which is a haven of Crete, looking towards the south-west and north-west.

13. And the south wind gently blowing, thinking that they had obtained their purpose, when they had loosed from Asson, they sailed close by Crete.

14. But not long after, there arose against it a tempestuous wind, called Euro-aquilo.

15. And when the ship was caught, and could not bear up against the wind, giving up the ship to the winds, we were driven.

16. And running under a certain island, that is called Cauda, we had much work to come by the boat.

17. Which being taken up, they used helps, under-girding the ship, and fearing lest they should fall into the quicksands, they let down the sail-yard, and so were driven.

18. And we being mightily tossed with the tempest, the next day they lightened the ship.

19. And the third day they cast out with their own hands the tackling of the ship.

20. And when neither sun nor stars appeared for many days, and no small storm lay on us, all hope of our being saved was now taken away.

21. *And after they had fasted a long time, Paul standing forth in the midst of them, said: You should indeed, O ye men, have hearkened unto me, and not have loosed from Crete, and have gained this harm and loss.*

22. *And now I exhort you to be of good cheer. For there shall be no loss of any man's life among you, but only of the ship.*

23. *For an angel of God, whose I am, and whom I serve, stood by me this night,*

24. *Saying: Fear not, Paul, thou must be brought before Cæsar; and behold, God hath given thee all them that sail with thee.*

25. *Wherefore, sirs, be of good cheer; for I believe God, that it shall so be, as it hath been told me.*

26. *And we must come unto a certain island.*

27. *But after the fourteenth night was come, as we were sailing in Adria, about midnight, the ship-men deemed that they discovered some country.*

28. *Who also sounding, found twenty fathoms; and going on a little further, they found fifteen fathoms.*

29. *Then fearing lest we should fall upon rough places, they cast four anchors out of the stern, and wished for the day.*

30. *But as the ship-men sought to fly out of the ship, having let down the boat into the sea, under colour, as though they would have cast anchors out of the fore-part of the ship.*

31. *Paul said to the centurion, and to the soldiers: Except these stay in the ship, you cannot be saved.*

32. *Then the soldiers cut off the ropes of the boat, and let her fall off.*

33. *And when it began to be light: Paul besought them all to take meat, saying: This day is the fourteenth day that you expect and remain fasting, taking nothing.*

34. *Wherefore I pray you to take some meat for your health's sake; for there shall not an hair of the head of any of you perish.*

35. *And when he had said these things, taking bread, he gave thanks to God in the sight of them all; and when he had broken it, he began to eat.*

36. *Then were they all of better cheer, and they also took some meat.*

37. *And we were in all in the ship, two hundred threescore and sixteen souls.*

38. *And when they had eaten enough, they lightened the ship, casting the wheat into the sea.*

39. *And when it was day, they knew not the land; but they discovered a certain creek that had a shore, into which they minded, if they could, to thrust in the ship.*

40. *And when they had taken up the anchors, they committed themselves to the sea, loosing withal the rudder-bands; and hoisting up the mainsail to the wind, they made towards shore.*

41. *And when we were fallen into a place where two seas met, they run the ship aground; and the fore part indeed, sticking fast, remained unmoveable; but the hinder part was broken with the violence of the sea.*

42. *And the soldiers' counsel was, that they should kill the prisoners, lest any of them swimming out, should escape.*

43. *But the centurion, willing to save Paul, forbade it to be done; and he commanded that they who could swim, should cast themselves first into the sea, and save themselves, and get to land.*

44. *And the rest, some they carried on boards, and some on those things that belonged to the ship. And so it came to pass, that every soul got safe to land.*

ANALYSIS.

In this Chapter we have an account of St. Paul's voyage to Rome whither he was sent by Festus to stand his trial, as he himself desired, before the Emperor Nero. Sailing slowly and cautiously along the coast, they reached "Good-havens," near the city of Thalassa (1-8). Paul warned them of their danger in case they sailed farther at this season. Unheeding his warning, they made for Crete (9-13). Overtaken by a tempest, Paul comforts them in a state of despair, by telling them on the assurance of an Angel, that no lives would be lost among the number on board, 276 souls. Paul warned the centurion not to allow the sailors to leave the ship (23-36). Nearing an island, the passengers all got safe to shore (40-45).

Text.

1. *And when it was determined that he should sail into Italy, and that Paul, with the other prisoners, should be delivered to a centurion, named Julius, of the band Augusta,*

Commentary.

1. "Determined" by Festus and his council, and the convenient time fixed for sailing having arrived—"he," Luke, was with St. Paul, though not accused, and accompanied him. Hence, the Greek has "we."

"With the other prisoners." These, possibly, may have also appealed to Cæsar, and their case was likely to be tried before the Emperor himself.

"Of the band Augusta." "Band," comprised about four or six hundred men (400-600). Very likely, "band" was the same as *cohort*, sixth part of a legion. The division of the army to which these men belonged was called "Augusta," in honour of the Emperor Augustus; likely, they were treated with some distinction. The Greek has "band of *Sebaste*." It may have been levied or raised in Sebaste.

2. *Going on board a ship at Adrumetum, we launched, meaning to sail by the coasts of Asia, Aristarchus, the Macedonian of Thessalonica, continuing with us.*

2. "Adrumetum," in Mysia, Asia Minor, opposite Lesbos. This ship, built at Adrumetum, was then in the port of Cæsarea. There was but very little direct communication at this time, between Italy and Palestine. The centurion calculated that by availing himself of this trading vessel, he would fall in with some vessel bound for Italy, and so he did at Lystra, or rather *Myra* (v. 6).

"Launched," hoisted our sails. "Coasts of Asia" Minor. The owners of the ship, likely, meant to call at the different ports for the purposes of traffic.

"Aristarchus" (c. xix. 29), is referred to as Paul's travelling companion. He now voluntarily attended him, prepared to share his dangers. He went with him to Rome, and was there his fellow prisoner (Col. v. 10; Philemon, v. 24).

3. *And the day following we came to Sidon. And Julius treating Paul courteously permitted him to go to his friends, and to take care of himself.*

3. "Sidon," over sixty miles north of Cæsarea. "Courteously," humanely allowing him to visit his friends at Sidon, where he was well known, having called there on his travels to and from Jerusalem.

"Take care of himself," to receive their attentions, and likely some supplies to lighten the hardships of his voyage.

4. *And when*

4. "Under Cyprus," along the coast, instead of launching into the

Commentary.

open sea, they sailed between Cyprus and the main land of Asia Minor, leaving Cyprus to the left.

"Winds." West and north-west winds prevalent at that season. To escape their violence, they sailed to the left of Cyprus. They were thus saved from the fury of these winds on the open sea.

5. "Cilicia," &c. The sea off the coasts of these countries. "We came to Lystra." The Greek and best sustained readings have " *Myra*." Lystra being in *Lycaonia*, and inland (xiv. 6). "Lycia;" in the south-west part of Asia Minor.

6. "Of Alexandria," bound for Italy. Probably, driven into Myra from stress of weather and the contrary winds referred to. She was a large transport ship, carrying corn or wheat from Egypt to Rome. Two hundred and seventy-six (276) passengers and crew (*v.* 37) were accommodated in her, not to speak of her cargo (*vv.* 10, 38).

7. "Slowly." In consequence of the prevailing west winds. "Gnidus," a city of Asia Minor, situated on a promontory of the same name. North-west of the Island of Rhodes.

"The wind," &c. The wind did not allow them to pursue a direct course. They, therefore, sailed close by Crete, to break the violence of the wind.

"Salmone." A promontory on the eastern extremity of Crete.

8. With much difficulty and danger of shipwreck. "Sailing by it," &c.

"Good Havens," on the south-eastern part of the island of Crete.

9. "Much time," in sailing, owing to the contrary winds, along the coasts of Asia Minor or at "Good Havens" in hopes of good weather and favourable winds. Likely, he expected to reach Italy, before the dangerous period of navigation in the Mediterranean had set in, as happened now when the most tempestuous season of the year had come upon them.

"Because the fast," &c. It is generally agreed upon, that there is question of the Jewish fast, on the great day of atonement, which took place on the 10th of the month, *Tisri*, the seventh month of the Jewish ecclesiastical year, corresponding with the end of our September and beginning of October, towards the autumnal Equinoxes. Then, the Etesian winds which partake of the Equinoctial gales, are very violent, and render navigation most dangerous. It was usual with the Jews to

Text.

we had launched from thence, we sailed under Cyprus, because the winds were contrary.

5. And sailing over the sea of Cilicia, and Pamphilia, we came to Lystra, which is in Lycia.

6. And there the centurion finding a ship of Alexandria sailing into Italy, removed us into it.

7. And when for many days we had sailed slowly, and were scarce come over against Gnidus, the wind not suffering us, we sailed near Crete by Salmone:

8. And with much a-do sailing by it, we came into a certain place, which is called Good - havens, nigh to which was the city of Thalassa.

9. And when much time was spent, and when sailing now was dangerous, because the fast was now past, Paul comforted them.

fix certain periods of the year, and compute them from great Festivals.
The same is usual among Christians also. Hence, we speak of Christmas,
Michaelmas, &c.

Some Commentators, among them, A. Lapide, say the fast in question
occurred in December, and that St. Luke speaks of the Christian fast
of *quatuor tense,* then celebrated.

"Paul comforted them." Admonished, warned them of their impending danger. Should they attempt to sail.

10. *Saying to them: Ye men, I see that the voyage be-ginneth to be with injury and much dam-age, not only of the lading and ship, but also of our lives.*

10: "Injury," &c.   Should they commence to sail.   Not only to
the ship, the property and cargo of wheat on board (*v.* 38) but also imminent danger to the lives of all the passengers, 'also of our lives."

Independently of his impressions of the dangers of navigation at this
season, and the condition of the ship, he may also have some lights from
inspiration, or revelation (22-25).

11. *But the centurion be-lieved the pilot and the master of the ship, more than those things, which were said by Paul.*

11. "Pilot," steersman.   "Master of the ship," who may have been
a different person from the pilot, employed by the owner to steer the
vessel.

12. *And where-as it was not a commodious haven to winter in, the greatest part gave coun-sel to sail thence, if by any means they might reach Phenice to win-ter there, which is a haven of Crete, looking towards the south-west and north-west.*

12. "The greatest part" of the crew. "Phenice," a harbour in the
south of Crete, to the west of "Good Havens."

"Looking towards the south-west." In Greek, looking towards
Lybia or Africa, the country situated south-west of the mouth of the
harbour, the entrance to which had a south-westerly aspect.

"North-west." The Greek, κατα χωρον, means a wind blowing from
the north-west. The harbour was curved, with one shore towards the
north-west; the other, towards south-west. It was entered in a
south-west direction, then curved in a north-west direction, thus affording
a secure harbour for wintering.

13. *And the south wind gently blowing, thinking that they had ob-tained their purpose, when they had loosed from Asson, they sailed close by Crete.*

13. "South wind gently blowing." Thus inspiring them with hope
to be able to sail along the coasts of Crete. Likely, it blew from another
direction before; and now veered round to the south. "Their purpose"
to sail quietly along the coasts of Crete to Phenice.

"Asson," is supposed by many not be a proper name; but a Greek
adverb signifying *nearer,* and then the words would mean, that they
sailed nearer the coasts of Crete, not venturing on the open sea. It was
while sailing thus, that the violent storm (next verse) burst upon them.

14. *But not long after, there arose a-gainst it a tem-*

14. "Against it." In the Greek "it" is in the feminine gender
αυτης. It cannot apply to "ship," which is in the neuter—πλοιον. It is
commonly understood of the Island of Crete.

Commentary.

"Tempestuous wind." In Greek a _Typhonic wind_, like the _Typhon_, a tempestuous wind, then prevalent in these seas, blowing a _hurricane_, coming not from any one quarter, but from every quarter. "Euro-Aquilo," the Vulgate reading preferred by the best critics and editors, the north-east wind. It is a Latin term which St. Luke likely learned from the Romans on board the ship. The ordinary Greek reading, _Euroclydon_.

15. "Caught" by the storm, "and could not bear up," &c. The Greek is _look up_, "were driven," drifted before the storm, unable to guide our course or manage the vessel.

16. "Running under," quite close to, "_Cauda_," a small island south-west of Crete.
"Come by the boat." Get it on deck and save it from being broken by the violence of the waves.

17. "Helps." Means of protection against the tempest, viz., ropes, chains, cables _to keep_ her planks and timber together.
"Undergirding" with the helps at hand just referred to, thus preventing her planks from starting under the force of the storm. Likely, these helps were stowed on board against time of danger.
"Quicksands." There were two great syrtes or sandbanks on the opposite coast of Africa. They were far away. But the violence of the storm might waft the ship thither. They were the more dangerous, as the sandbanks shifting their position moved from one place to another. "Quicksands." The Greek article prefixed to syrtis, την Συρτιν, _the syrtis_, shows there was question of a particular syrtis, the great syrtis on the north of Africa to the south-west of Crete, towards which the wind was impelling them.
"Sail-yard." The sails with the great yard and rigging supporting them were let down to retard the impetuous course of the ship. Some understand it of taking away the mast, which sometimes among the ancients was set in _sockets_. So, no necessity for cutting it away.
"And so." In this plight, without sails, "driven," tossed about at the mercy of the waves.

18. "Lightened." By throwing out everything on board not necessary; probably also a part of the cargo. They waited, however, for things to become worse before throwing it all out (38).

Text.

19. *And the third day they cast out with their own hands the tackling of the ship.*

20. *And when neither sun nor stars appeared for many days, and no small storm lay on us, all hope of our being saved was now taken away.*

21. *And after they had fasted a long time, Paul standing forth in the midst of them, said: You should indeed, O ye men, have hearkened unto me, and not have loosed from Crete, and have gained this harm and loss.*

22. *And now I exhort you to be of good cheer. For there shall be no loss of any man's life among you, but only of the ship.*

23. *For an angel of God, whose I am, and whom I serve, stood by me this night,*

24. *Saying: Fear not, Paul, thou must be brought before Cæsar; and behold, God hath given thee all them that sail with thee.*

25. *Wherefore, sirs, be of good cheer; for I believe God, that it shall so be, as it hath been told me.*

26. *And we must come unto a certain island.*

27. *But after the fourteenth night was come, as we were sailing in Adria, about midnight, the ship-men deemed that they discovered some country.*

Commentary.

19. "Tackling." Sails, cables, &c., and everything that could be dispensed with. Probably, some of the anchors. Some they retained.

20. "Sun," &c. They could take no observations, and so gave up all for lost. Having no compass, which was unknown at that time, they could not know where they were, or whither they were drifting. So they gave up all for lost.

21. "Fasted." The fear of impending death took away all relish for food.

"Paul standing forth." In their extreme dejection, Paul strives to console and inspirit them.

"Gained this loss," &c. Not have subjected yourselves to this harm, &c. You might have escaped it. The Greek word literally means to "avoid gaining this loss," a strange form of expression. However, we might be said to gain, what we avoid losing (Kenrick).

22, 23. He predicts the safety of the crew; it having been revealed to him by God. "Stood by me." Appeared to me. "This night." Whether in dream or while he was awake cannot be ascertained. Likely the latter, as he hardly slept in the storm.

24, 25. "Brought before Cæsar," and thy life therefore spared, "given thee," &c., and the lives of all the others on your account, in response to your prayers. In the sweet dispensation of God's adorable Providence, he often spares sinners on account of the just.

26. "Come." In Greek *be cast upon* a "certain island." There by Divine appointment we shall be saved from shipwreck.

27. "Fourteenth night." After leaving Good Havens, "in Adria." This, according to the usage of speaking among the ancients, does not refer to what is now called the Adriatic Gulf; but to the sea between Italy, Greece and Africa.

"The ship-men," or sailors, "that they discovered some country," were approaching some land.

Commentary.

28. "Sounding." As is usually done, in such circumstances.

29. "Four anchors." The better to secure the ship. "Wished for the day," in order the more accurately to see their position and danger.

30. "Under colour." That it was necessary to be in the boat in order to cast the anchors more securely, whereas they meant to escape.

31. "Centurion," who had the direction of the ship, carrying Government prisoners. "Except these "seamen, who alone knew how to manage a ship—the centurion and soldiers knew nothing of such things.

"Stay in the ship, you cannot be saved." The ship will go to pieces and be wrecked. The assurance from Paul that the passengers would be all saved, supposed that proper means would be employed for that purpose, and no tempting of God to perform a miracle; whereas, here these means being neglected, God did not mean to work an unnecessary miracle for the purpose, when ordinary human exertions would suffice.

32. "Fall off." Go adrift.

33. "Taking nothing." They may have hurriedly taken some scanty, but no regular meals.

34. "Not an hair," &c. A common or proverbial form of expression frequently to be met with in SS. Scripture, denoting that no harm

Text.

28. Who also sounding, found twenty fathoms; and going on a little further, they found fifteen fathoms.

29. Then fearing lest we should fall upon rough places, they cast four anchors out of the stern, and wished for the day.

30. But as the ship-men sought to fly out of the ship, having let down the boat into the sea, under colour, as though they would have cast anchors out of the fore-part of the ship.

31. Paul said to the centurion, and to the soldiers: Except these stay in the ship, you cannot be saved.

32. Then the soldiers cut off the ropes of the boat, and let her fall off.

33. And when it began to be light: Paul besought them all to take meat, saying: This day is the fourteenth day that you expect, and remain fasting, taking nothing.

34. Wherefore I pray you to take some

Text.

meat for your health's sake; for there shall not an hair of the head of any of you perish.

Commentary.

whatever even the slightest, would befall them; that they would be perfectly safe.

---

35. And when he had said these things, taking bread,

35. "Gave thanks." In accordance with the Jewish custom and the example of our Lord Himself (Matthew xiv. 19 ; John vi. 44), in giving thanks before meals.

he gave thanks to God in the sight of them all; and when he had broken it, he began to eat.

36. Then were they all of better cheer, and they also took some meat.

37. And we were in all in the ship, two hundred threescore and sixteen souls.

---

38. And when they had eaten enough, they lightened the ship, casting the wheat into the sea.

38. No hope of saving the cargo. They, therefore, lightened the ship, by throwing it overboard, so that as they were preparing to run the ship on the beach, a light draft of water would make matters easier in nearing the shore.

---

39. And when it was day, they knew not the land; but they discovered a certain creek that had a shore, into which they minded, if they could thrust in the ship.

39. "They knew not," &c. Likely the Alexandrian sailors, although not strangers to Malta, never saw this side of the island now before them. It was distant from the great and frequented harbour, which alone they may have known.

"They minded." Resolved.

---

40. And when they had taken up the anchors, they committed themselves to the sea, loosing withal the rudder-bands; and hoisting up the mainsail to the wind, they made towards shore.

40. "Taken up." The Greek clearly means *letting go* the anchors, cutting the ropes and leaving them in the sea, thus lightening the ship, the more easily to reach land.

"Rudder bands." The Greek has "rudder" in the plural, conveying that there were more than one rudder. In the large vessels of the ancients they had a rudder at the prow; and another, at the stern. Sometimes, one, at the sides. "The bands" were fastenings binding the rudder to the side of the ship for taking them out of the water in case of storm to prevent them from being carried away. They were useless in the tempest (v. 15-17). Now that the storm was over, they are let loose in order to get the vessel more easily into port.

"Mainsail." As the mainmast had been flung away, some are of opinion that there is question here of a foremast or bowsprit, having some small sail towards the prow.

---

41. And when we were fallen into a place where two seas met, they run the ship aground; and the fore-part indeed, sticking fast, remained

41. "A place where two seas met." In Greek, it literally is "*a place of double sea*," meaning a kind of isthmus or tongue of land, extending from the mainland and washed on both sides by the sea. It seems to be a sunken sandbank which they did not perceive. On making their way towards land, they fell in with this hidden sandbank.

"They run the ship aground," not intentionally. "The forepart" caught in the sand, remained immovable, while the hinder part, being

Commentary.

still in deep water, was broken to pieces by the violence of the waves. It was owing to this circumstance they got boards on which they strove to make land (*v.* 44).

42. "The soldiers" fearing if the prisoners under their charge escaped, they might be chargeable with neglect of duty, which according to Roman law would entail the heaviest punishment—the punishment the prisoners would themselves undergo—gave the barbarous counsel here spoken of. It was, besides, considered disgraceful for Roman soldiers to allow prisoners to escape.

43. "The centurion" who from the outset was favourably disposed towards Paul forbade the execution of this cruel project. No doubt Paul's conduct on board, his courage, prudence and foresight increased the respect of the centurion for him. To him they were indebted for their lives. He seemed to be specially under the protection of heaven. Frequently to one just man in the designs of God may be due the salvation of thousands. See the case of the Sodomites who would be spared had they even *ten* just men among them (Genesis xvii. 32).

"All who could swim." Likely, all were freed from their chains.

44. "Boards." Probably, planks which may have been on board the ship.

Others, "on those things that belonged to the ship," the broken pieces detached from the stern of the ship, when broken to pieces by the violence of the waves (*v.* 41).

"Every soul," &c. In accordance with the promise of God to Paul they all providentially were saved after incredible perils and heavy disasters (*v.* 24).

Text.

unmoveable, but the hinder part was broken with the violence of the sea.

42. *And the soldiers' counsel was, that they should kill the prisoners, lest any of them, swimming out, should escape.*

43. *But the centurion, willing to save Paul, forbade it to be done; and he commanded that they who could swim, should cast themselves first into the sea, and save themselves, and get to land:*

44. *And the rest, some they carried on boards, and some on those things that belonged to the ship. And so it came to pass, that every soul got safe to land*

CHAPTER XXVIII.

1. *And when we had escaped, then we knew that the island was called Melita. But the barbarians shewed us no small courtesy.*

2. *For, kindling a fire they refreshed us all, because of the present rain and of the cold.*

3. *And when Paul had gathered together a bundle of sticks, and had laid them on the fire, a viper coming out of the heat, fastened on his hand.*

4. *And when the barbarians saw the beast hanging on his hand, they said one to another: Undoubtedly this man is a murderer, who though he hath escaped the sea, yet vengeance doth not suffer him to live.*

5. *And he indeed shaking off the beast into the fire, suffered no harm.*

6. *But they supposed that he would begin to swell up, and that he would suddenly fall down and die. But expecting long, and seeing that there came no harm to him, changing their minds they said, that he was a god.*

7. *Now in these places were possessions of the chief man of the island named Publius, who receiving us, for three days entertained us courteously.*

8. *And it happened that the father of Publius lay sick of a fever, and of a bloody flux. To whom Paul entered in: and when he had prayed, and laid his hands on him, he healed him.*

9. *Which being done, all that had diseases in the island came, and were healed.*

10. *Who also honoured us with many honours, and when we were to set sail, they laded us with such things as were necessary.*

11. *And after three months, we sailed in a ship of Alexandria, that had wintered in the island, whose sign was the Castors.*

12. *And when we were come to Syracuse, we tarried there three days.*

13. *From thence compassing by the shore, we came to Rhegium: and after one day the south wind blowing, we came the second day to Puteoli;*

14. *Where finding brethren, we were desired to tarry with them seven days: and so we went to Rome.*

15. *And from thence when the brethren had heard of us, they came to meet us as far as Appii Forum and the Three Taverns, whom when Paul saw, he gave thanks to God, and took courage.*

16. *And when we were come to Rome, Paul was suffered to dwell by himself with a soldier that kept him.*

17. *And after the third day he called together the chief of the Jews. And when they were assembled, he said to them: Men brethren, I have done nothing against the people, or the custom of our fathers, was delivered prisoner from Jerusalem into the hands of the Romans,*

18. *Who when they had examined me, would have released me, for that there was no cause of death in me:*

19. *But the Jews contradicting it, I was constrained to appeal unto Cæsar, not that I had anything to accuse my nation of.*

20. *For this cause therefore I desired to see you and to speak to you. Because that for the hope of Israel, I am bound with this chain.*

21. *But they said to him: We neither received letters concerning thee from Judea, neither did any of the brethren that came hither, relate or speak any evil of thee.*

22. *But we desire to hear of thee what thou thinkest: for as concerning this sect, we know that it is gainsayed every where.*

23. *And when they had appointed him a day, there came very many to him unto his lodgings; to whom he expounded, testifying the kingdom of God, and persuading them concerning Jesus, out of the law of Moses and the prophets, from morning until evening.*

24. *And some believed the things that were said: but some believed not.*

25. *And when they agreed not among themselves, they departed, Paul speaking this one word: Well did the Holy Ghost speak to our fathers by Isaias the prophet,*

26. *Saying: Go to this people, and say to them: With the ear you shall hear, and shall not understand: and seeing you shall see, and shall not perceive.*

27. *For the heart of this people is grown gross, and with their ears have they heard heavily, and their eyes they have shut, lest perhaps they should see with their eyes, and hear with their ears, and understand with their heart, and should be converted, and I should heal them.*

28. *Be it known therefore to you that this salvation of God is sent to the gentiles, and they will hear it.*

29. *And when he had said these things, the Jews went out from him, having much reasoning among themselves.*

30. *And he remained two whole years in his own hired lodging: and he received all that came in to him,*

31. *Preaching the kingdom of God, and teaching the things which concern the Lord Jesus Christ with all confidence, without prohibition.*

ANALYSIS.

Landing on the island which they knew to be Melita, St. Paul and his companions were treated with the greatest humanity. The inhabitants were in no small degree astonished at seeing that Paul was by no means injured by a viper that fastened on his hand. Publius, the chief man of the island, treated them very generously (1-11). They tarried there three months and made for Syracuse; thence, for Rhegium and Puteoli (11-14). The fame of the Apostles being near Rome, attracted several of the Christians to go out to meet him at Appii Forum and the Three Taverns (15). Arriving at Rome, where he was placed in custody in charge of a soldier, the Apostle summoned the chief men among the Jews to come to him. He then explained his position (17-22). On an appointed day, he expounded the Christain Faith. Some believing and others rejecting his doctrine, which elicited from him a reference to the Prophecy of Isaias on the subject (24-28). He remained there two years.

Commentary.

1. "Escaped." Safely landed on the beach. "We knew" from the inhabitants. "Melita." The well-known island of "Malta."

"Barbarians." The inhabitants of the island. The Greeks and Romans regarded all the nations that did not speak their own language as barbarians. "No small courtesy" treated them with more than ordinary humanity.

2. "Fire," &c. Literally, having set fire to a piece of wood, "refreshed," by protecting and caring us. "Because of the present rain" succeeding the storm, "and of the cold." It was the month of October. Besides, they were drenched in the water in scrambling to get on shore.

Text.

1. *And when we had escaped, then we knew that the island was called Melita. But the barbarians shewed us no small courtesy.*

2. *For, kindling a fire, they refreshed us all, because of the present rain and of the cold.*

Text.	Commentary.

Text:

3. *And when Paul had gathered together a bundle of sticks, and had laid them on the fire, a viper coming out of the heat, fastened on his hand.*

4. *And when the barbarians saw the beast hanging on his hand, they said one to another:*

Commentary:

3. "A viper," a most venemous animal that lay torpid in the cold brushwood, and now owing to the heat revived, and "fastened on his hand" evidently with his teeth, in which it is tacitly conveyed that he had *bitten* him.

4. "Beast." A word applied by Greek writers to serpents. "A murderer." Murder was regarded as the greatest of crimes. "Doth not suffer him," &c. They regarded him already as a dead man, the serpent's bite being sure to cause death.

Undoubtedly this man is a murderer, who though he hath escaped the sea, yet vengeance doth not suffer him to live.

5. *And he indeed shaking off the beast into the fire, suffered no harm.*

6. *But they supposed that he would begin to swell up, and*

6. "To swell up," also means *inflammation.* "A God," as none but a God could thus be preserved. The Maltese were, no doubt, at this time idolaters and worshippers of the Gods.

that he would suddenly fall down and die. But expecting long, and seeing that there came no harm to him, changing their minds they said, that he was a God.

7. *Now in these places were possessions of the chief man of the island named Publius, who receiving us, for three days entertained us courteously.*

7. "In these places," this part of the island. "Possessions," residence and property. "Chief-man." He may have been governor of the island; or, as Malta was subject to the Prætor of Sicily, this Publius may have been his deputy. He treated Paul and his companions with great hospitality.

8. *And it happened that the father of Publius lay*

8. "Bloody flux." In Greek, *dysentery.* "Prayed," &c. St. Peter acted similarly (ix. 40). Thus was fulfilled the Divine promise (Mark xvi. 18).

sick of a fever, and of a bloody flux. To whom Paul entered in: and when he had prayed, and laid his hands upon him, he healed him.

9. *Which being done, all that had diseases on the island came, and were healed:*

10. *Who also honoured us with many honours, and when we were to sail, they laded us with such things as were necessary.*

10. Bestowed many gifts in gratitude for the blessings received at the hands of the Apostle, and "laded us," &c. Supplied what was necessary for the coming journey.

11. *And after three months, we sailed in a ship of Alexandria, that had wintered in the island, whose sign was the Castors.*

11. "Three months" from the time of the shipwreck. The time for safely embarking had not come earlier; most likely, they had no means or opportunity for leaving sooner.

"Of Alexandria," belonging to Alexandria, they had wintered at Malta.

"Whose sign," an ornamental image either painted, or, in *bas relief*

Commentary.

on the prow. "The Castors," Castor and Pollux, twin Deities, were supposed to be tutelary Deities of seafaring men.

12. "Syracuse," the ancient capital of Sicily, on the South Eastern coast, about eighty (80) miles from Malta. "Three days," possibly, to land some cargoes or in hopes of a favourable breeze.

13. "Compassing," &c. Coasting along the eastern shore of Sicily. "Rhegium" on the south-west extremity of Italy, nearly opposite Messina in Sicily.
"South wind," so favourable for wafting them on their journey. "Puteoli," the favourite port of ships from Alexandria (Strabo 1-17 ; Seneca Ep. 77).

14. Christian believers. How the Gospel was preached then cannot be ascertained.

15. "From thence." Puteoli, whence, during over seven days sojourn, accounts either by letter or by verbal message, reached the brethren at Rome, owing to the frequent communications between both places.
"Appii Forum," over fifty miles distant from Rome, so-called from Appius Claudius, the builder of this city, as well as of the Appian way. It was a *forum* or *market* place, where travellers stopped for refreshment. Horace (Sat. 6) is not over complimentary to it.
It was an extraordinary mark of respect for them to come so far, over fifty miles, to meet him.
"The Three Taverns," ten miles from Rome, so-called from three retail shops, resorted to for refreshment by travellers to and from Rome.
"Gave thanks to God," that His desire of seeing the Christians of Rome was now on the eve of fulfilment (Rom. i. 10; xv. 23-32), "and took courage," inspired with fresh vigour. Probably, he may have been in a state of depression up to this.

16. "Come to Rome "—to which is added in the Greek, " The centurion delivered the prisoners to the *Captain of the Guard.*" (Roman Law required that all prisoners sent to Rome should be handed over to the custody of the Captain of the Guard.)   "Paul was suffered," &c. Most likely it was owing to the influence of the Centurion, on whom he made so favourable an impression during the voyage (xxvii. 43) who also witnessed the welcome shown him on nearing Rome by the Christians, that he was allowed to live in private lodgings " with a soldier who kept him." This is what was termed *custodia libera*.   In such cases, the

Text.

12. *And when we were come to Syracuse, we tarried there three days.*

13. *From thence compassing by the shore, we came to Rhegium: and after one day the south wind blowing, we came the second day to Puteoli;*

14. *Where finding brethren, we were desired to tarry with them seven days: and so we went to Rome.*

15. *And from thence when the brethren had heard of us, they came to meet us as far as Appii Forum and the Three Taverns, whom when Paul saw, he gave thanks to God, and took courage.*

16. *And when we were come to Rome, Paul was suffered to dwell by himself with a soldier that kept him.*

s

Text.

17. *And after the third day he called together the chief of the Jews. And when they were assembled, he said to them: Men brethren, I having done nothing against the people, or the custom of our fathers, was delivered prisoner from Jerusalem into the hands of the Romans,*

18. *Who when they had examined me, would have released me, for that there was no cause of death in me:*

19. *But the Jews contradicting it, I was constrained to appeal unto Cæsar, not that I had anything to accuse my nation of.*

20. *For this cause therefore I desired to see you and to speak to you. Because that for the hope of Israel, I am bound with this chain.*

21. *But they said to him: We neither received letters concerning thee from Judæa, neither did any of the brethren that came hither, relate or speak any evil of thee.*

Commentary.

prisoner was bound to the soldier. Hence, he says (v. 20) "with this chain." The necessity of changing the guard gave the Apostle an opportunity of having the Gospel made known throughout the entire Prætorian camp, from which the soldiers in their turn, came to guard him.

17. "Called together," &c. Chiefly with the view of preaching the Gospel as he did, "in season and out of season," especially to his Jewish brethren, in the first instance. Moreover, he likely wished to remove any false or unfavourable impressions they might have entertained regarding him, especially, as he supposed it to be very likely that some unfavourable reports may have been forwarded against him to the Jews of Rome, by the Jews of Judea, "the chief of the Jews," the principal persons amongst them.

"Against the people." The Jewish people, "or the custom," &c., their religious usages.

"Delivered . . . hands of the Romans." The hands of Roman governor or Procurator at Cesarea.

18. (xxvi. 32).

19. "Contradicting it." Opposing his being set at liberty.

"Not that I had," &c. He had no idea of recriminating, though he had good grounds for doing so. It was for his own safety solely he appealed.

20. "For this cause," viz. To make known that I appealed solely in my own defence, and not for the purpose of making counter-charges.

"Hope of Israel." In preaching the Advent of the Messiah, whose coming the Jewish people longed for to redeem them. In him they hoped, as their deliverer.

"I am bound with this chain." Whereby I am attached to the soldier on guard.

21. Having failed before all the Tribunals, it would seem the Jews of Palestine did not care to prosecute the case farther. Moreover, they may not have had sufficient time; and the communication with Rome was so uncertain.

Commentary.

22. "What thou thinkest." In defence of this universally despised sect of Nazarenes (xxiv. 5). Likely, in thus speaking scornfully and disparagingly of Christianity, they had in view to dissuade Paul from preaching up its odious tenets. Whether in referring to the universal opposition to Christianity there is allusion to the vile calumnies afterwards circulated regarding the lives of the Christians, it is hard to say. Tacitus speaking of them, scornfully describes them, as the abettors of an *exitialis superstitio*, as *"guilty of atrocious and abominable crimes, convicted by the hatred of mankind."* (Annal. xv. 44.) Suetonius describes them as *"a race of men, maintaining a new and criminal superstition.* (Nero, *c.* xvi.)

23. "Testifying," &c. Announcing the doctrines and principles, regarding the reign of the Messiah and the establishment of His church. "Concerning Jesus," as the expected Messiah, liberator of the Jewish race ; showing all that was said of the Messiah in the Law of Moses and predicted by the Prophets, to be fully realized in Jesus of Nazareth. In him was fully realized all that was said and predicted of the Messiah.

"From morning," &c. Shows the indefatigable zeal of the Apostle.

dom of God, and persuading them concerning Jesus, out of the law of Moses and the prophets, from morning until evening.

24. *And some believed the things that were said : but some believed not.*

25. This division among his unbelieving countrymen caused the Apostle to utter " one word," one parting solemn warning and denunciation of their stiff-necked incredulity, the peculiar characteristic of their race, long before denounced by the Prophet Isaias.

"Well," truly, did the Holy Ghost, in describing the character of the Jews of old say, what applied, no less to the Jews, he was then addressing, as it was meant for them, than it did to their fathers in the days of Isaias, with whom they but formed one body morally.

26, 27. " *With ears,*" &c. This is put imperatively in Isaias (*c.* vi. 9, 10). See this fully explained (Matthew xiii. 14; John xii. 39, Commentary on).

the ear you shall hear, and shall not understand: and seeing you shall see, and shall not perceive.

27. *For the heart of this people is grown gross, and with their ears have they heard heavily, and their eyes they have shut: lest perhaps they should see with their eyes, and hear with their ears, and understand with their heart, and should be converted, and I should heal them.*

28. "This Salvation." The full knowledge, as contained in the Gospel, of how this Salvation may be secured, the whole economy and Divine dispensation of God in imparting it.

"Is sent to the Gentiles " (*c.* xiii. 46), after being first preached to the Jews. The Gentile world "will hear it," obey and embrace it, so that the Divine seed is not scattered through the world in vain.

22. But we desire to hear of thee what thou thinkest : for as concerning this sect, we know that it is gainsayed every where.

23. And when they had appointed him a day, there came very many to him unto his lodgings ; to whom he expounded, testifying the king-

25. And when they agreed not among themselves, they departed, Paul speaking this one word: Well did the Holy Ghost speak to our fathers by Isaias the prophet,

26. Saying: Go to this people, and say to them : With

28. Be it known therefore to you that this salvation of God is sent to the gentiles, and they will hear it.

Text.	Commentary.

29. *And when he had said these things, the Jews went out from him, having much reasoning among themselves.*

30. *And he remained two whole years in his own hired lodging: and he received all that came in to him,*

31. *Preaching the kingdom of God, and teaching the things which concern the Lord Jesus Christ with all confidence, without prohibition.*

29. "Much reasoning." Discussion regarding what Paul uttered among the believing and unbelieving Jews.

This verse is omitted in some MSS., and rejected by some eminent critics.

30. "Two whole years." No doubt, guarded by soldiers, as up to this, it would seem he was not finally tried before the Emperor, though, no doubt, he was questioned on some one occasion (2 Tim. iv. 16). Why he was not yet brought before the Emperor, cannot be known for certain.

"Received all." Jew and Gentile, imparting the knowledge of Salvation.

"In his own hired lodging." Though a prisoner, he enjoyed more liberty than was ordinarily given to prisoners, being something like what was termed, *libera custodia.*

31. "Kingdom of God." In reference to these words, Beelen observes, that, although having different significations in the SS. Scriptures, such as the Advent of the Messiah and the Messiah Himself as King; Life Eternal; the society instituted by our Lord, His church and all appertaining to it; in a word, the economy of the New Law; it is only in the latter sense, it can be understood throughout this Book of the Acts. Only in one place (*c.* xiv. 21), does it designate Life Eternal.

"And teaching the things," &c. All the truths relating to our Lord's Divinity and Humanity, taken in the most general sense, as propounded in the Holy Gospels.

"With all confidence." Intrepidly, and the greatest freedom of speech.

"Without prohibition." This shows how the Roman authorities were affected in regard to the Gospel at this time, when a prominent propagator of the doctrines of this "sect every where contradicted," was permitted to announce them freely, without let or hindrance.

All hitherto recorded of St. Paul occurred before and during his *first* imprisonment. The Acts of the Apostles go no further. The history of the several occurrences connected with his preaching and writings, after his release from his *first* imprisonment, his martyrdom in the year 65, under Nero, in the 12th year of his reign, are all derived from other authentic sources.

www.ingramcontent.com/pod-product-compliance
Lightning Source LLC
Chambersburg PA
CBHW030627030726
47497CB00006B/1671